BASIC READING INVENTORY

I believe Johns' **Basic Reading Inventory** *is the most user-friendly IRI on the market. Its layout is exceptional, with comprehensive directions for teacher use. Having multiple passages to choose from also makes it easier to evaluate various reading strategies in oral, silent, and listening reading modes. Directions for miscue analysis and an excellent mix of comprehension questions, including directions for retellings, give the teacher confidence in both implementation and scoring.*
Kenneth Schatmeyer, Ph.D.
Grand Strand Educational Consultants

Johns' **Basic Reading Inventory** *works well with a variety of graduate students including certified teachers and those in our MAT program. By pairing the* **Basic Reading Inventory** *with Johns'* **Improving Reading: Interventions, Strategies, and Resources**, *I feel like my students have a solid background in reading assessment and useful resources for their future careers.*
Jennifer L. Altieri, Ph.D.
The Citadel

I find the **Basic Reading Inventory** *to be a very useful assessment tool. The word lists allow for fast initial assessment. They help me gauge the approximate reading level prior to moving to the reading passages.*
Angela Marr-Sabean, School Based Literacy Lead
Princess Elizabeth School (New Brunswick, Canada)

Vacaville Christian Elementary School has used Jerry Johns' **Basic Reading Inventory** *for the past three years. We have found it very helpful in identifying students with potential learning differences. This tool also gives our teachers many ways to keep track of student progress throughout the year. Jerry Johns'* **Basic Reading Inventory** *is a tool that is easy to understand, takes very little time to administer, and provides many options to choose from depending on need.*
Ella Blair, Reading Specialist
Vacaville Christian Schools (CA)

Jerry Johns' **Basic Reading Inventory** *is an excellent resource for anyone involved in the teaching of reading: thorough, practical—a rich resource!*
Alvin Granowsky, Ed.D.

There are so many aspects to the **Basic Reading Inventory** *that it really makes getting a whole picture of a student as a reader just so easy. Together with Johns'* **Improving Reading**, *these two manuals make planning instruction as well as interventions for our struggling readers so much more efficient and thoughtful.*
Tracey Orzo, Elementary Literacy Developer
Rye City School District, New York

I love the **Basic Reading Inventory**. *It opened my eyes and thinking to not just what was "wrong." It led me to discovering the truth and the "what next" approach that my students, teachers, administrators and families need!*
Nancy Roberts, Reading Specialist—Lockport City High School,
Adjunct Professor—Canisius College

I love the **Basic Reading Inventory**! *I use it with all my students from 10 years old to 60 years old.*
Lynne Zimmer
Learning Solutions, Inc.

Jerry Johns' **Basic Reading Inventory** *has been a staple used in all sections of both our undergraduate Elementary and Master's of Science in Reading Education programs for many, many years. It offers both the pre-service and in-service teacher very explicit directions for assessing a student's strengths and areas for growth. Each edition includes suggestions for using the insights that are gained with this instrument. Learning to administer the* **BRI** *has been a significant element contributing to the outstanding quality of our programs!*
Joyce C. Fine, Ed. D.
Florida International University

I find the **Basic Reading Inventory** *to be easy to use and very versatile. I am very pleased that the reading passages address levels pre-primer through grade 12 and that many passages are available at each level, both for oral reading and silent reading.*
Gianna Tedesco, B. Ed.
Teacher/ Home School Program Facilitator

ELEVENTH EDITION

BASIC READING INVENTORY

PRE-PRIMER THROUGH GRADE TWELVE
AND EARLY LITERACY ASSESSMENTS

Multi-Media CD Enclosed
Includes Video Clips,
Performance Booklets,
Summary Sheets, History
of the Informal Reading
Inventory (IRI), and
Annotated Bibliography
on IRIs

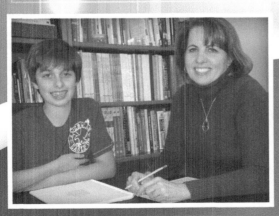

JERRY L. JOHNS
Distinguished Teaching Professor Emeritus
Northern Illinois University, DeKalb

With Contributions by

LAURIE ELISH-PIPER
Presidential Teaching Professor & Literacy Clinic Director
Northern Illinois University, DeKalb

BETH JOHNS
Writer and Editor
Seattle, Washington

Kendall Hunt
publishing company

Book Team

Chairman and Chief Executive Officer   Mark C. Falb
President and Chief Operating Officer   Chad M. Chandlee
Vice President, Higher Education   David L. Tart
Director of Publishing Partnerships   Paul B. Carty
Vice President, Operations   Timothy J. Beitzel
Senior Developmental Coordinator   Angela Willenbring
Project Coordinator   Charmayne McMurray
Permissions Editor   Tammy Hunt
Cover Designer   Mallory Blondin

Author Information for Correspondence and Workshops

Jerry L. Johns, Ph.D.
Consultant in Reading
jjohns@niu.edu
Fax: 815-899-3022

Laurie Elish-Piper, Ph.D.
Presidential Teaching Professor
Literacy Clinic Director
laurieep@niu.edu

Beth Johns
Writer and Editor
bjohns012@gmail.com

Ordering Information

Address: Kendall Hunt Publishing Company
4050 Westmark Drive, P.O. Box 1840
Dubuque, IA 52004-1840

Telephone: 800-247-3458, ext. 4

Web site: www.kendallhunt.com/readingresources

Dedication

MARY C. JOHNS
September 10, 1922—December 4, 2009
A teacher for thirty years
What a beautiful difference one single life made!

She left a legacy of an awesome family.

My Mom and Brothers and Sisters
Dan, Becky, Nancy, Yours Truly, Tom, Susan, and Mother Mary

(celebrating her 85th birthday in 2007)

Brief Contents

Contents

viii *Contents*

Figures and Tables

About the Author

Jerry L. Johns

Jerry Johns has been recognized as a distinguished professor, writer, and outstanding teacher educator. He completed his B.A. at Oakland University with special honors. He taught in the public schools in Pontiac, Michigan, while working on his M.A. at Michigan State University (MSU). After receiving his M.A., Dr. Johns was awarded a fellowship to pursue doctoral studies at MSU. He served as an instructor at Michigan State, teaching various reading courses. Then he accepted the position of special reading teacher for the Waterford, Michigan, Public Schools where he taught students with severe reading problems. Dr. Johns has had a long, distinguished career at Northern Illinois University. He was also a Visiting Professor at Western Washington University and the University of Victoria in British Columbia.

In addition to his major teaching responsibilities, Dr. Johns has been elected to leadership positions at the local, state, national, and international levels. He has been president of the Northern Illinois Reading Council, the Illinois Reading Council, and the College Reading Association. He also served on the Board of Directors of the International Reading Association and was the Association's president. In addition, Dr. Johns has served on numerous committees of the International Reading Association and other professional organizations. His more than 800 presentations, workshops, and professional development sessions for school systems and reading associations has involved travel throughout the world.

Dr. Johns has numerous publications, including his well-known *Basic Reading Inventory* (now in its 11th edition) and the fifth edition of *Improving Reading: Strategies and Resources.* Other widely used co-authored books include the revised editions of *Teaching Beginning Reading: Pre-K–Grade 3* (3rd ed.), *Reading & Learning Strategies: Middle Grades through High School* (4th ed.), and *Fluency: Interventions, Strategies, and Progress-Monitoring Assessments.* He also co-authored *Improving Writing K–8: Strategies, Assessments, and Resources*, *Visualization: Using Mental Images to Strengthen Comprehension*, and *Enhancing Writing through Visualization.* Other co-authored works include a *Spanish Reading Inventory*, a book chapter dealing with informal assessment in literacy, and *Essential Comprehension Strategies for the Intermediate Grades.* He has authored nearly 300 articles, monographs, pamphlets, books, and research studies. Dr. Johns also serves on the editorial advisory boards for *Reading Psychology* and the *Illinois Reading Council Journal.*

Dr. Johns has been the recipient of numerous awards for his contributions to various professional organizations. He received the Outstanding Service Award from the Association of Literacy Educators and Researchers and was honored by the Illinois Reading Council with induction into the Reading Hall of Fame. Other recognitions include the Alpha Delta Literacy Award for Scholarship, Leadership, and Service to Adult Learners and the A.B. Herr Award for outstanding contributions to the field of reading, and the Laureate Award for life-long contributions to the field of reading presented by the Association of Literacy Educators and Researchers. The International Reading Association renamed the Outstanding Teacher Educator in Reading Award in his honor.

Dr. Johns now serves as a consultant and speaker to schools, conferences, and professional organizations. He enjoys travel, walking, visiting his family, driving his sports car, and playing pinball.

Acknowledgments

It is with great pleasure that I acknowledge Laurie Elish-Piper and Beth Johns for their numerous contributions to this edition of the *Basic Reading Inventory*. They have both assisted behind the scenes in previous editions. Laurie has been involved in numerous videos that provided a sample administration of the Basic Reading Inventory, a tradition that continues. In addition, she has taken a more active role in this edition. Laurie is a Presidential Teaching Professor and Literacy Clinic Director at Northern Illinois University where I taught for thirty years. For nearly twenty years, Laurie and I have worked together on a variety of professional books and presentations.

Beth Johns is a writer and editor who lives in Washington State. She is also my daughter. Beth has assisted me for many years in presentations related to the Basic Reading Inventory. During my tenure at Northern Illinois University, she graciously agreed to be the student when I demonstrated the Basic Reading Inventory in many of my undergraduate and graduate classes. She also assisted me in the same capacity at the University of Victoria in British Columbia. In more recent years, she has helped to refine and sharpen my writing and assist with field testing. Our most recent collaboration is a chapter on informal reading inventories for a forthcoming volume on assessment.

Appreciation is extended to the following groups who contributed directly or indirectly to the eleventh edition:

TEACHERS AND SPECIALISTS. Thousands of teachers have used the Basic Reading Inventory over the years, and I want to express my grateful appreciation to each of you. Special thanks are given to teachers and specialists who assisted by sharing ideas, raising questions, fieldtesting, and/or providing support and encouragement. My workshops with the Basic Reading Inventory in schools and school districts throughout the United States and in Canada have been stimulating events resulting in the rich sharing of ideas. E-mails, conference calls, and numerous telephone conversations have given me an opportunity to respond personally to individual questions. Thanks for your partnership.

COLLEAGUES. Countless professors and instructors in the United States and Canada have directly or indirectly influenced the Basic Reading Inventory. Teaching the inventory to preservice and inservice teachers at both the undergraduate and graduate levels has provided an important basis for informal feedback when we meet at conferences or professional meetings. Your writing and research about the reading process, assessment, instructional practices, progress monitoring, and response to intervention continues to inform my work. Your contributions have made a difference in my efforts to make instruction more responsive to the needs of individual students.

STUDENTS. A fundamental purpose of the Basic Reading Inventory is to use the results to develop individual literacy plans and interventions for students to enhance reading achievement. Thousands and thousands of students have been given the reading inventory. It is my hope that the results have been used to help them become better readers. Based on many conversations with teachers, specialists, and interventionists, it is clear to me that the Basic Reading Inventory is contributing to the goal of helping students reach their potential as readers.

Preface

The eleventh edition of the *Basic Reading Inventory* continues with the well-received "two book" approach. Initially, these two books resulted from the suggestions of teachers, reading specialists, and coaches who desired to have the student word lists, passages, and student materials from the Early Literacy Assessments in a separate booklet so it would be easier to manage and use during the administration of the Basic Reading Inventory. This change has made the inventory even more useful for you.

The larger of the two books contains all you need to know to administer, score, and interpret the Basic Reading Inventory. I have devoted my efforts to refining those components that warranted revision, clarification, expansion, and updating. Special thanks to all teachers, colleagues, reading specialists, interventionists, and reading coaches who have offered help, ideas, constructive criticism, and encouragement. Here are some of the new features of the eleventh edition:

- I welcome two contributors to this edition: Laurie Elish-Piper and Beth Johns. A bit of information about them can be found in the Acknowledgments page. I'm grateful for their numerous contributions.

- A new form of Early Literacy Assessments has been included to parallel the ten existing assessments. This new form will provide an option for progress monitoring and appraising student progress.

- There are new video clips included on the CD to help you see how an examiner establishes rapport and administers a graded word list, a graded passage, and the comprehension questions that accompany the passage. These videos will help bring the written administration descriptions to life. As always, any videos used with the Basic Reading Inventory are unrehearsed and intended as a sample, not model, to help you gain confidence and competence.

- A new Expert Noticing Observation Guide has been added along with a helpful description of how to use it. Also included is a video clip so you can practice your expert noticing skills as a student reads a graded passage. You can then compare your notes to those provided on the CD.

- Using retelling as a comprehension assessment has always been possible, but new provisions to this edition makes it easier to use the retelling option. Evaluation criteria on appropriate pages of the performance booklets will help you to determine whether a passage is at the student's independent, instructional, or frustration level.

- The growing emphasis of targeting instructional strategies to student needs in classrooms and intervention programs has led to an updating of the Instructional Interventions Grid. You will now be able to target a student's needs with specific and focused teaching. In addition, the number of scenarios that target specific areas for instructional interventions has been expanded.

- This manual has undergone a large number of minor and not-so-minor changes to make it easier to use and to reflect recent research and expert opinion. There have also been some deletions and movement of certain sections to the CD. One helpful new page is located inside the back cover where you will find suggested instructions for administering the graded word lists, graded passages, and comprehension questions.

● There are pages with tabs in the back of this manual and in the accompanying book to use with students. You can cut them out and fasten them to the appropriate pages. These tabs should make it easier to find helpful information and the various forms of the Basic Reading Inventory.

The Basic Reading Inventory has seven forms and ten Early Literacy Assessments. A CD contains video clips to help you learn administration procedures, the performance booklets for all seven forms of the inventory, the record booklets for the two forms of the Early Literacy Assessments, numerous summary sheets, answers to practice exercises, and a large annotated bibliography of research and resources related to informal reading inventories.

The eleventh edition makes me thankful for your partnership over the years. I hope you, whether veteran or first-time user, will find the Basic Reading Inventory helpful in your work with all students and especially with those students who find reading difficult. Together, in partnership, we continue to help students strengthen their reading.

Cordially,

Jerry

Basic Reading Inventory Manual

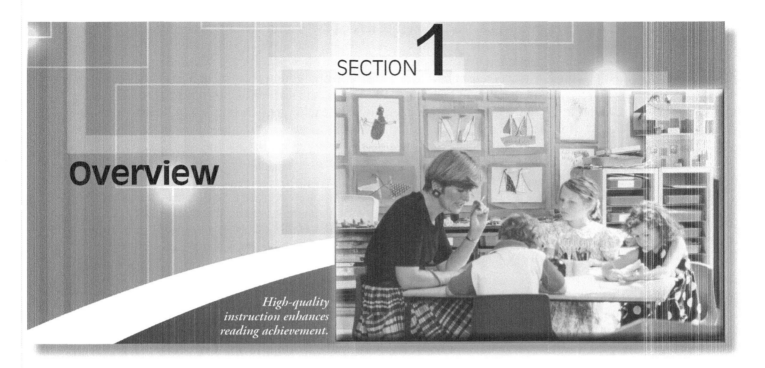

SECTION 1

Overview

High-quality instruction enhances reading achievement.

Making Instruction Responsive

"Effective reading instruction begins with assessment" (Cooter & Perkins, 2007, p. 6). For more than fifty years, the informal reading inventory has been regarded as "the comprehensive assessment instrument of choice" (Walpole & McKenna, 2006, p. 592). With the continuing impact of Reading First (part of the No Child Left Behind legislation) in establishing sound reading programs (Cummins, 2006) and the recent emphasis on Response to Intervention (RTI) (Fuchs, Fuchs, & Vaughn, 2008), informal assessments like the Basic Reading Inventory help to identify students who are struggling in reading. In addition, the Basic Reading Inventory can be used in the progress-monitoring process to assess student performance and growth and diagnose specific weaknesses in word recognition, fluency, and comprehension (Mahdavi & Haager, 2007). Furthermore, the results of the Basic Reading Inventory can serve as the basis for determining appropriate instructional interventions in classrooms, resource rooms, and special education settings. These interventions often focus on the five areas identified by the report of the National Reading Panel (2000): phonemic awareness, phonics, fluency, vocabulary, and comprehension. Table 1.3 on page 8 provides a concise overview of how the Basic Reading Inventory can help assess these five important areas. Allington (2005) and others have added to these five areas. Fink (2006, p. 131), for example, notes that informal reading inventories "can determine both the level and type of instruction likely to be most beneficial for each student." She also stresses that estimates of each student's three reading levels (independent, instructional, and frustration) are provided to make "planning instruction easier and more effective" (p. 131). If students are to reach their potential, teachers must provide responsive instruction. A fundamental principle of responsive instruction is attention to individual differences, and teachers are the critical core in making a difference in reading achievement (International Reading Association, 2007). Teachers can differentiate instructional interventions to help students make significant progress in reading. While methods come and go, teachers are the core in providing quality reading instruction that is responsive to their students. Responsive instruction has many qualities, and a fundamental principle is attention to individual differences.

Students have the right to be evaluated with appropriate reading assessments (Bass, Dasinger, Elish-Piper, Matthews, & Risko, 2008). A position statement of the International Reading Association (2000), titled *Making a Difference Means Making It Different*, notes that students "have a right to reading assessment that identifies their strengths as well as their needs . . ." (p. 7). The Basic Reading Inventory is one resource to help gather information for instructional decision making in reading. It can be used to estimate the student's instructional level—the level at which the student is challenged but not overwhelmed. It is the level where the student can profit from reading instruction (Spiegel, 1995). If students are placed in instructional materials where they are able to pronounce approximately 95 percent of the words, they tend to be successful readers who are on task (Adams, 1990). Unfortunately, many students are placed in materials that are too difficult for them (Johnston & Allington, 1995). These students fail to benefit much from lessons using grade-level texts (O'Connor, Bell, Harty, Larkin, Sacker, & Zigmond, 2002).

Responsive instructional interventions are more likely to be provided if teachers can use assessment tools to determine a student's strengths and weaknesses in reading (International Reading Association, 2007; Kibby, 1995). According to Manning (1995), valuable information can be obtained by noting the behaviors of students as they read orally in instructional materials. The Basic Reading Inventory provides one means through which teachers can systematically gain insights into a student's reading. Teachers can study and analyze a student's abilities in word identification, fluency, and comprehension. The information gained can be an important basis for responsive instruction and high-quality instructional decisions. Taylor, Pearson, Clark, and Walpole (2002) noted that systematic assessment of student progress figured prominently in their findings of effective schools. "Assessment practices should enrich teaching and learning" (Tierney, 1998, p. 388). The Basic Reading Inventory can help teachers "to become better informed and make better decisions" (Tierney, 1998, p. 388). Such decisions can be used to help develop individual literacy plans for students (Felknor, 2000). The end result should help students become more efficient and effective readers.

In an attempt to ensure that all students are effective readers who are college- and career-ready, the Common Core State Standards have been adopted by nearly all of the 50 states (Council of Chief State School Officers & National Governors Association, 2010). These standards will have a significant impact on the field of education in the coming years. The Common Core State Standards for reading are organized as a staircase of increasing difficulty for the fundamental skills of phonics, word recognition, and fluency as well as comprehension skills for both literary (narrative) and informational (expository) texts. These standards align closely with areas assessed by the Basic Reading Inventory.

Components of the Basic Reading Inventory

The Basic Reading Inventory is an individually administered informal reading test. Composed of a series of graded word lists and graded passages, the inventory helps teachers gain insights into students' reading behavior. Inventory results will help support the daily instructional decisions teachers need to make (Farr, 1992; Gillet & Temple, 2000; Gunning, 2006; Johns, 1996; McCormick, 2007; Walker, 2004). Five types of comprehension questions follow each passage: topic, fact, inference, evaluation, and vocabulary. This section explains the purposes of the Basic Reading Inventory, gives directions for administering and scoring the inventory, and provides concrete assistance for interpreting the findings of the inventory so that the results can be used to improve students' reading. The development of the Basic Reading Inventory is described in Section 6.

There are seven forms (A, B, C, D, E, LL, LI) of the Basic Reading Inventory, each denoted by one or more capital letters.

- Forms A, B, and C contain word lists ranging from pre-primer (beginning reading) through grade twelve and passages ranging from the pre-primer level through the eighth grade.

- Form D contains passages ranging from the pre-primer level through the eighth grade and is designed specifically for silent reading.

- Form E contains informational (expository) passages ranging from the pre-primer level through the eighth grade.

- Forms LL and LI each contain ten passages of approximately 250 words ranging in difficulty from third grade to twelfth grade.

Four numerals are used to code the grade level of the word lists and/or passages in the Basic Reading Inventory. Table 1.1 contains the code.

TABLE 1.1
Code of Grade Levels for the Seven Forms of the Basic Reading Inventory

Grade Level	Form of the Basic Reading Inventory						
	A	B	C	D	E	LL	LI
Pre-Primer 1	AAA	BBB	CCC	DDD	EEE	—	—
Pre-Primer 2	AA	BB	CC	DD	EE	—	—
Primer	A	B	C	D	E	—	—
1	A 7141	B 7141	C 7141	D 7141	E 7141	—	—
2	A 8224	B 8224	C 8224	D 8224	E 8224	—	—
3	A 3183	B 3183	C 3183	D 3183	E 3183	LL 3183	LI 3183
4	A 5414	B 5414	C 5414	D 5414	E 5414	LL 5414	LI 5414
5	A 8595	B 8595	C 8595	D 8595	E 8595	LL 8595	LI 8595
6	A 6867	B 6867	C 6867	D 6867	E 6867	LL 6867	LI 6867
7	A 3717	B 3717	C 3717	D 3717	E 3717	LL 3717	LI 3717
8	A 8183	B 8183	C 8183	D 8183	E 8183	LL 8183	LI 8183
9	A 4959	B 4959	C 4959	—	—	LL 4959	LI 4959
10	A 1047	B 1047	C 1047	—	—	LL 1047	LI 1047
11	A 1187	B 1187	C 1187	—	—	LL 1187	LI 1187
12	A 1296	B 1296	C 1296	—	—	LL 1296	LI 1296

Pre-Primer and Primer Levels

For the pre-primer and primer levels, capital letters designate the level.

- The pre-primer levels are designated by two or three capital letters. For example, AAA refers to pre-primer 1 in Form A.

- The primer level is designated by one capital letter. For example, B refers to the primer level in Form B.

Grade Levels 1–9

For the remaining levels through grade nine, you can determine the grade level of the word list or passage by determining which two numerals are identical.

In Table 1.1, for example, A 7141 indicates that the word list or passage in Form A is at the first-grade level because there are two 1's. The code B 8183 indicates the word list or passage in Form B is at the eighth-grade level because there are two 8's. A similar procedure is followed for the remaining word lists and passages when two numerals are the same within each grade level.

Grade Levels 10–12

For the word lists and passages at grades ten, eleven, and twelve, the first two numerals indicate the grade level.

BRI Forms

Seven forms of the Basic Reading Inventory are included so that a variety of purposes can be achieved.

- Forms A and B assess and help to monitor the student's oral reading. Teachers often use Form A as an initial assessment. Form B may be used to help monitor progress. It is especially important that students above the primary grades engage in silent reading (see Form D).

- Form C can be used as an initial assessment. It can also be used to help assess growth in reading (progress monitoring). The passages in Form C can also be used for additional oral or silent reading opportunities to better estimate the student's reading levels or to further study the student's reading behavior. This form can also be used to estimate the student's listening level.

- Form D is specifically designed for assessing silent reading. It can help assess the student's ability to read informational (expository) passsages at and above grade two.

- Form E is specifically designed for assessing informational (expository) reading.

- Forms LL and LI, because of their length (approximately 250 words), permit a more in-depth appraisal of the student's ability to read literary or narrative (LL) and informational or expository (LI) materials. The passages in these two forms may be read orally and/or silently. Each form spans grades three through twelve.

Table 1.2 contains suggestions for how the various forms of the Basic Reading Inventory may be used. This same table can also be found inside the front cover of the student booklet.

TABLE 1.2
Uses of Basic Reading Inventory Forms

Form	Primary Uses	Other Uses
A	Oral Reading Initial Assessment	Silent Reading Listening Level
B	Oral Reading Later Assessment	Silent Reading Listening Level Progress Monitoring
C	Oral Reading Initial Assessment	Silent Reading Listening Level Progress Monitoring
D	Silent Reading (Informational)*	Oral Reading Progress Monitoring
E	Oral Reading (Informational)*	Silent Reading Progress Monitoring
LL	Silent Reading (Literary)†	Oral Reading Listening Level
LI	Silent Reading (Informational)†	Oral Reading Listening Level Progress Monitoring

*beginning with grade two
† longer passages for grades three through twelve

Early Literacy Assessments

Two forms of early literacy assessments are included in Part 3. These assessments are especially useful for students who find the easiest word lists and passages difficult and who could be called emergent readers. Separate Record Booklets for each form, directions, and the following ten assessments are found in Part 3:

1. Alphabet Knowledge
2. Writing
3. Literacy Knowledge
4. Wordless Picture Reading
5. Caption Reading

6. Auditory Discrimination
7. Phoneme Awareness
8. Phoneme Segmentation
9. Basic Word Knowledge
10. Pre-Primer Passages

Elish-Piper, Johns, and Lenski (2006) have also developed a variety of early literacy assessments accompanied by complementary teaching strategies. Consult this resource for helpful assessments and suggestions for instruction.

Purposes of the Basic Reading Inventory

On the basis of the student's performance on the word lists and graded passages, you can gain insights into the student's:

- **independent reading level**—the level at which the student reads fluently with excellent comprehension.
- **instructional reading level**—the level at which the student can make maximum progress in reading with your instructional guidance.

- **frustration level**—the level at which the student is unable to pronounce many of the words and/or is unable to comprehend the material satisfactorily.
- **strategies for word identification**—you can evaluate the student's sight vocabulary and ability to use phonic analysis, context clues, and structural analysis to pronounce words.
- **fluency**—you can determine the student's rate of reading (in words per minute), assess accuracy in word identification, and make observational judgments about phrasing and expression.
- **strengths and weaknesses in comprehension**—you can evaluate the student's ability to answer various types of comprehension questions.
- **listening level**—you can determine the highest level of material that the student can comprehend when it is read to him or her.

Observations can also be made regarding the student's interests, attitudes, self-monitoring strategies, general approach to various tasks, and reading behavior (such as engagement, persistence, and predictions).

Assessing the Five Core Components of Reading with the Basic Reading Inventory

The three forms (A, B, and C) of the graded word lists and the seven forms (A, B, C, D, E, LL, and LI) of passages, coupled with two forms of the ten Early Literacy Assessments, can help assess the five core components of effective reading instruction identified by the National Reading Panel (2000): phonemic awareness, phonics, fluency, vocabulary, and comprehension. Table 1.3 lists the five core components and identifies the assessments that can be used to assess these areas so that responsive instructional interventions can be provided. A helpful grid of instructional interventions can be found on page 89.

TABLE 1.3
Core Areas from the National Reading Panel (NRP) Report Keyed to the Basic Reading Inventory (BRI)

NRP Core Area	BRI Early Literacy Assessments (Location in BRI Manual)	BRI Word Lists and Passages (Pages in Student Booklet)
Phonemic Awareness	Phoneme Segmentation, 358 Phoneme Awareness, 357	
Phonics	Auditory Discrimination, 356 Writing, 352	Word Lists: A (2–8), B (22–28), C (42–48)
Fluency	Pre-Primer Passages, 360 Caption Reading, 355 Basic Word Knowledge, 359	Word Lists: A (2–8), B (22–28), C (42–48) Passages: A (10–20), B (30–40) C (50–60), D (62–72), E (74–84), LL (86–95), LI (98–107)
Vocabulary	Wordless Picture Reading, 354 Basic Word Knowledge, 359 Pre-Primer Passages, 360	Passages: A (10–20), B (30–40). C (50–60), D (62–72), E (74–84), LL (86–95), LI (98–107)
Comprehension	Pre-Primer Passages, 360 Caption Reading, 355	Passages: A (10–20), B (30–40) C (50–60), D (62–72), E (74–84), LL (86–95), LI (98–107)

Table 1.3 reveals that the graded word lists and passages provide important information in all areas except phonemic awareness (where there are two Early Literacy Assessments for this purpose). You can observe the student's behavior while reading the word lists and passages and then analyze responses to gain insights. Below is a brief overview of some ways teachers, specialists, and interventionists have used the word lists, passages, and Early Literacy Assessments in the Basic Reading Inventory to assess phonemic awareness, phonics, fluency, vocabulary, and comprehension.

Phonemic Awareness

Refer to "Phoneme Awareness (Spelling)" and "Phoneme Segmentation" in the Early Literacy Assessments for two assessments to gain insights in this area.

Phonics

When miscues are made on the graded words lists and reading the passages, you can note the miscues and analyze them to determine areas for instruction and intervention. See "Determining Word Identification Strategies" in Section 4 of this manual for two ways to analyze the student's miscues in order to gain information about the student's phonic skills. Section 4 also contains some suggestions for instructional interventions. For three additional assessments related to phonics, refer to "Phoneme Awareness" (Spelling), "Alphabet Knowledge," and "Auditory Discrimination" in the Early Literacy Assessments.

Fluency

As a student reads word lists, you can assess the automaticity with which the words are pronounced. If a student has considerable difficulty pronouncing words on a grade-level list, it is quite possible that the student may have difficulty reading the passage at that level in a fluent manner. When the student reads graded passages, you can note phrasing, expression, and automaticity. Rate or speed of reading can also be determined by timing the student's reading and using the oral reading norms that are provided. See "Rate of Reading" in Section 2 of this manual for two ways to determine reading rate and to view norms for oral and silent reading rates. "Fluency Considerations" in Section 4 provides a concise overview of what fluency embodies and offers some instructional interventions to help with several common problems in fluency. Refer to "Pre-Primer Passages" in the Early Literacy Assessments for additional passages.

Vocabulary

There are different types of vocabulary. Sight vocabulary refers to words that the student recognizes immediately. As the student reads word lists and passages, you can note if words are mostly recognized at sight. Refer to "Basic Word Knowledge" in the Early Literacy Assessments for an additional test for sight vocabulary knowledge.

Meaning vocabulary refers to words that the student understands. You can evaluate the student's ability to answer the V (vocabulary) questions after passages are read as one assessment of meaning vocabulary. The predictions the student makes prior to reading the passages can also be used to evaluate vocabulary. Some students are much more expressive than other students, and you can informally assess the quality of the student's responses when retelling a passage or answering the comprehension questions for the passage.

For those students who are at the beginning stages of reading, refer to "Caption Reading" in the Early Literacy Assessments to help evaluate the level of language used.

Comprehension

Each time the student reads a graded passage, comprehension is assessed with questions, retelling, or a combination of the two. If you use the questions, there are five different types (topic, fact, inference, experience/evaluation, and vocabulary) and analysis by question type can be done. Another way to analyze comprehension is by lower-level comprehension and higher-level comprehension. Refer to Section 4 in this manual for explanations and examples for conducting these analyses. Appendix A contains different ways to elicit and evaluate passage retellings.

The Basic Reading Inventory contains passages that are literary (narrative/stories) and informational (expository), so you can assess the student's ability to understand these two major types of discourse.

Background Information on Reading Levels and the Listening Level

A major function of the Basic Reading Inventory is to identify a student's three reading levels: independent, instructional, and frustration. Numerous questions have been raised about standards for evaluating a student's performance on reading inventories (Johns, 1976; 1990a). Although some research (Anderson & Joels, 1986; Johns & Magliari, 1989; Powell, 1971) indicates that the original criteria suggested by Betts (1946) are too high for determining the instructional level for students in the primary grades, other studies (Hays, 1975; Homan & Klesius, 1985; Morris, 1990; Pikulski, 1974) report contradictory findings. In addition, Ekwall (1974, 1976) has presented evidence that supports retaining the traditional Betts criteria. You should remember that the numerical criteria for reading levels are not *absolute standards*; they are *guidelines* to help teachers evaluate a student's reading in conjunction with observational data. Each of the three reading levels presented here will be considered from two viewpoints: the teacher's and the student's. The listening level will also be discussed. Note that each reading level is characterized by both quantitative (numerical) and qualitative (behavioral) data.

What Is the Independent Reading Level?

Level	Characteristics	Types of Reading
Independent (Easy)	Excellent comprehension (90%+) Excellent word recognition (99%+) Few or no repetitions	All schoolwork and reading expected to be done alone Pleasure reading Very fluent Informational reading

Teacher's Viewpoint

The independent reading level is that level at which the student can read fluently without teacher assistance. In other words, the student can read the materials independently with excellent comprehension. This is the level of supplementary and recreational reading. The material should not cause the student any difficulty. If the student reads orally, the reading should be expressive with accurate attention to punctuation. At this level, the student's reading should be free from finger pointing, vocalizing, lip movement, poor phrasing, and other indications of general tension or problems with the reading material.

In order to be considered at the student's independent level, materials should be read with near-perfect accuracy in terms of word recognition. Even in a situation of oral reading at sight, the student should generally not make more than one significant miscue in each 100 running words. With respect to comprehension, the student's score, when 10 comprehension questions of various types are asked, should be no lower than 90 percent. In short, the student should be able to fully understand the material.

If a retelling strategy is used, a student "will be able to reflect most of the content of a selection and will reflect it in an organized fashion." In a narrative passage, the student will recount events in the proper order. In expository passages, the student's retelling will reflect the text structure or organization of that material. For example, a passage with the main idea followed by supporting details will usually be retold in the same manner (Johnson, Kress, & Pikulski, 1987, p. 14).

Students enjoy reading at their independent level.

It is important that the above criteria for determining a student's independent reading level be applied with careful judgment. The criteria, especially the near-perfect accuracy for word recognition, may have to be a bit more liberal when evaluating a student's reading in grades one and two. The younger reader, for example, may frequently substitute *a* for *the* and vice versa while reading. An older student may omit or substitute a number of words that do not seriously interfere with fluency and/or a good understanding of the passage. Miscues of this nature should be regarded as acceptable; they are not significant. If the teacher has correctly determined the student's independent reading level, the student will experience little difficulty with materials that are written at or below that particular level.

Caution

Student's Viewpoint

Because most students have never heard of the various reading levels, they would not refer to the percentages and related behavioral characteristics just described. A student might, however, describe the independent reading level in these terms: "I can read this book by myself, and I understand what I read. I like reading books like this; they're easy."

What Is the Instructional Reading Level?

Level	Characteristics	Types of Reading
Instructional (Just right; comfortable)	Good comprehension (75–85%) Good word recognition (95%+) Fluent A few unknown words Some repetitions	Guided reading Basal instruction Texts used for instruction

Teacher's Viewpoint

The instructional reading level is that level at which the student can, theoretically, make maximum growth in reading. It is the level at which the student is challenged but not frustrated. Many teachers are interested in finding the student's instructional level so they can provide classroom reading materials at that level (Felknor, Winterscheidt, & Benson, 1999; McTague, 1997). Allington (2005, 2012) considers matching students with materials at their instructional levels critical for students who are behind in reading. This is the level of materials used in guided reading groups. At the instructional level, the student should be free from externally observable symptoms of difficulty, such as finger pointing, produced by the reading materials. Although the student might experience some difficulties when reading classroom materials at sight, most of these difficulties should be overcome after the student has had an opportunity to read the same material silently. In other words, oral rereading should be definitely improved over oral reading at sight. If the student is to make maximum progress from instruction, he or she should encounter no more difficulty in reading materials than can be adequately dealt with through good teaching.

In order to be considered at the student's instructional level, materials should be read with no more than 5 miscues in each 100 words in terms of word recognition. According to Adams (1990, p. 113), "there is evidence that achievement in reading is improved by placement in materials that a student can read orally with a low error rate (2 percent to 5 percent), and that students placed in materials that they read with greater than 5 percent errors tend to be off-task during instruction." Additional research by Berliner (1981) and Gambrell, Wilson, and Gantt (1981) also support the 95 percent criterion. In addition, Enz (1989) found that placing students using higher standards resulted in greater engagement, higher success rates, and more positive attitudes toward reading. O'Connor, Bell, Harty, Larkin, Sackor, and Zigmond (2002) found that students who read materials at their reading (instructional) level made greater gains in fluency compared to students who read grade-level materials. Although some difficulties will probably arise in word recognition, the student should be able to use contextual cues, phonics, and other strategies to decode most unknown words. In terms of comprehension, the student should miss fewer than 3 of 10 comprehension questions.

If a retelling strategy is used, a student responding to instructional level materials will "reflect less content than at an independent level. The organization of the passage will be less complete and some minor misinterpretations and inaccuracies may begin to appear." In essence, the student is able to share the overall sense and content of the passage (Johnson, Kress, & Pikulski, 1987, p. 17).

It is at the instructional level that the student will have the best opportunity to build new reading strategies and solidify those skills and strategies already taught. This is the level at which guided reading instruction is likely to be most successful (Lenski, 1998). Teachers need to be sure that books used for reading instruction are at students' instructional levels (Burkins & Croft, 2010).

Student's Viewpoint

A student might describe the instructional level in these terms: "I can understand what I am taught from this reading book. Some of the words are hard, but after the teacher gives me some help, the story is easy to read."

What Is the Frustration Level?

Level	Characteristics	Types of Reading
Frustration (Too hard)	Weak comprehension ($\leq 50\%$) Weak word recognition ($\leq 90\%$) Word-by-word reading Many unknown words Rate is likely to be slow Lack of expression Fluency lacking Fidgeting	Materials for some diagnostic purposes Avoid instructional materials at this level Occasional self-selected material when interest and background knowledge are high

Teacher's Viewpoint

The frustration level is that level at which the student should not be given materials to read. A serious problem in many classrooms is that a large number of students are asked to read books at their frustration levels (Allington, 2012). Students at their frustration levels are unable to deal effectively with the reading material. Numerous behavioral characteristics may be observed if students are attempting to read materials that are too difficult for them. Some students may actually refuse to continue reading their books. Other students may exhibit lack of expression in oral reading, lip movement during silent reading, difficulty in pronouncing words, word-by-word reading, and/or finger pointing. A study by Jorgenson (1977) found that as reading material became more difficult, teachers judged their students as becoming more impatient, disturbing to the classroom, and reliant on persons other than themselves for directions.

The criteria for the frustration level, in addition to the behavioral characteristics just noted, are 10 or more miscues in every 100 words (90 percent or less) and comprehension scores of 50 percent or less. For example, a student who could not correctly pronounce 90 or more words in a 100-word selection and who could not answer at least half of the questions asked by the teacher is likely trying to read material that is too difficult.

If a retelling strategy is used, "materials at a frustration level are recalled incompletely or in a rather haphazard fashion. Bits of information may be recalled, but they are not related in any logical or sequential order." Questions asked by the teacher tend to go unanswered. In addition, behaviors such as finger pointing and tenseness may appear (Johnson, Kress, & Pikulski, 1987, p. 20).

Student's Viewpoint

Because reading materials at this level are too difficult for the student, it is likely that the frustration level would be described in these terms: "This book is too hard. I hate to read when books are this hard. I hardly know any of the words." Other students will say nothing when books are too difficult for them to read, but the perceptive teacher will note when books are at a student's frustration level. The teacher can then provide or suggest other materials that are at the student's independent or instructional levels.

What Is the Listening Level?

The listening level is the *highest* level at which the student can understand material that is read *to* him or her. Determining this level can help you ascertain whether a student has the potential to improve as a reader. When a substantial difference exists between the student's instructional level and listening level (generally a year or more), it usually indicates that the student should be able to make significant growth in reading achievement with appropriate instruction. The larger the difference, the more reason for you to believe that the student can profit from instruction that is responsive to the student's needs in reading. Many students who struggle with reading can improve if they are given quality instruction, placed in reading materials at their instructional levels, and have their progress monitored regularly.

The criterion for the listening level are a minimum comprehension score of at least 70 percent. In other words, the student should miss no more than 3 of 10 comprehension questions. It is also important for you to informally assess whether the student's vocabulary and language structure in conversations are as complex as that used in the reading passage.

Schell (1982), after reviewing several studies relating to the listening level, cautioned teachers not to use the procedure with students in grades one through three. He argued that reading comprehension and listening comprehension are not the same for students in the primary grades; moreover, neither grow at approximately equal rates until about sixth grade. For these reasons, you should not use the listening level procedure with students in the primary grades.

Caution

Preparation for Assessment

Understand the Procedures

To prepare for assessment, you first need to be familiar with the procedures for administering and scoring the Basic Reading Inventory. These procedures are discussed in Section 2. What is needed for assessment? There are five basic items:

1. This manual or the summary of administration and scoring procedures on page 47 or inside the front cover of this manual.
2. The separate student booklet containing the word lists and passages.
3. A piece of heavy paper to cover the passage when necessary.
4. A performance booklet in which you will record the student's responses. These performance booklets are in this manual and on the CD.
5. A desk or table and two chairs located in an area reasonably free from excessive noise and distractions. If you are right-handed, seat the student to your left. If you are left-handed, do the opposite.

Note:
The student copies of the word lists and passages in the student booklet may not be reproduced.

Selecting Word Lists and Passages

The student will read from selected pages in the separate student booklet. To aid in locating word lists and passages, consult the quick reference guide printed on the inside front cover of the student booklet. You may want to use the pre-printed tabs found in the back of the student booklet and place them at the beginning of the word lists and passages to help locate the different forms.

While the student reads, you record the student's performance and make notes on the graded word lists and the graded passages in a performance booklet.

Permission is granted to users of the Basic Reading Inventory to reproduce all, or any part, of the seven performance booklets that follow the student copies of the reading inventory. These performance booklets are also on the CD.

The validity of a student's performance on the Basic Reading Inventory is related to how completely and accurately you are able to record the student's reading performance and answers to the comprehension questions. An audio or digital recorder is recommended as a method of self-checking until your recording of the student's performance becomes automatic and swift. These recordings can also be placed in portfolios or other record-keeping devices.

Brief Overview of Administration and Scoring Procedures

To evaluate a student's reading, it is recommended that you administer the reading tests included in the Basic Reading Inventory in the following manner. More detailed directions and examples can be found in Section 2.

Word Recognition in Isolation

Select a graded word list at a reading level that will be easy for the student. Ask the student to pronounce the words at a comfortable rate. Record the student's responses in the sight column beside the corresponding word in the performance booklet. If the student miscalls a word and immediately corrects it, the recommended procedure is to put a plus (+) in the analysis column with a "sc" (self-correction) notation.

Return to mispronounced or unknown words for a second attempt and note the student's responses in the analysis column. Administer successive word lists until the student is no longer able to achieve a total of at least 14 words correct or until the student becomes frustrated. Ex-

Figure 1-1. (Left) Sample Student Copy of Graded Word Lists from Student Booklet; (Right) Sample Teacher Copy of Word Lists from Performance Booklet

ample of student and teacher copies of word lists are shown in Figure 1-1. To view the student copies of the word lists, consult the Quick Reference Guide printed on the inside front cover of the student booklet.

Scoring Word Recognition in Isolation

Total the correct responses in the sight and analysis columns. Consult the criteria in the scoring guide at the bottom of the word lists in the performance booklet to determine a rough estimate of the reading level achieved on each graded word list. Record the number-correct scores and the reading levels in the Word Recognition, Isolation column on the summary sheet of the performance booklet. See page 26 for a sample summary sheet.

Word Recognition in Context (Passages)

Ask the student to read aloud the graded passage **one level below** the highest independent level achieved on the graded word lists. As the student reads the passage from the student booklet, record miscues on the corresponding copy of the passage found in the performance booklet. A miscue occurs when the student's oral reading of a passage differs from the printed passage. For example, a miscue results if the student says *wood* when the word in the passage is *good*. Substituting *wood* for *good* is called a miscue. Other major types of miscues are omissions, insertions, and mispronunciations. A suggested method for recording a student's miscues can be found in Figure 2-3 on page 28. Examples of student and teacher passages are shown in Figure 1-2 on page 16. To view the student copies of the passages, consult the Quick Reference Guide printed on the inside front cover of the student booklet.

Scoring Word Recognition in Context (Passages)

To find the word recognition in context score, count the number of miscues (total or significant) in each graded passage in the performance booklet and record the numeral in the appropriate box

Figure 1-2. (Top) Sample Student Copy of Graded Passage from Student Booklet; (Bottom) Sample Teacher Copies of Graded Passage and Comprehension Questions from Performance Booklet

Sample Student Copy

Bill at Camp

It was the first time Bill went to camp. He was very happy to be there. Soon he went for a walk in the woods to look for many kinds of leaves. He found leaves from some maple and oak trees. As Bill walked in the woods, he saw some animal tracks. At that moment, a mouse ran into a small hole by a tree. Bill wondered if the tracks were made by the mouse. He looked around for other animals. He did not see any. The last thing Bill saw was an old bird nest in a pine tree.

Student Booklet copy is on page 14.

A 8224 (Grade 2) Activating Background: Read the title to yourself. Then tell me what you think this might be about.

Background: Low |———————| High

| MISCUES | | | | | | | |
Bill at Camp		Substitution	Insertion	Omission	Reversal	Repetition	Self-Correction of Unacceptable Miscue	Meaning Change (Significant Miscue)
It was the first time Bill went to	8							
camp. He was very happy to be there. Soon	17							
he went for a walk in the woods to look for	28							
many kinds of leaves. He found leaves	35							
from some maple and oak trees. As Bill	43							
walked in the woods, he saw some animal	51							
tracks. At that moment, a mouse ran into	59							
a small hole by a tree. Bill wondered if the	69							
tracks were made by the mouse. He looked	77							
around for other animals. He did not see	85							
any. The last thing Bill saw was an old	94							
bird nest in a pine tree.	100							
TOTAL								

Total Miscues [ ]   Significant Miscues [ ]

Word Recognition Scoring Guide

Total Miscues	Level	Significant Miscues
0–1	Independent	0–1
2–4	Ind./Inst.	2
5	Instructional	3
6–9	Inst./Frust.	4
10 +	Frustration	5 +

Oral Reading Rate

$\frac{}{6000}$ WPM

Norm Group Percentile
☐ 90 ☐ 75 ☐ 50 ☐ 25 ☐ 10

A 8224 (Grade 2)
Comprehension Questions

T 1. _____ What is this story about?
(a boy at camp; Bill's walk in the woods)

F 2. _____ Did Bill enjoy going to camp? How do you know?
(yes, the story said he was happy there)

F 3. _____ Why did Bill go walking in the woods?
(to look for leaves)

F 4. _____ What kinds of leaves did Bill find in the woods?
(maple and oak leaves)

F 5. _____ What else did Bill see besides the mouse?
(a bird nest; animal tracks)

F 6. _____ Where did the mouse go?
(into a small hole by or in a tree)

F 7. _____ What other animals did Bill see?
(none; he didn't see any)

I 8. _____ Do you think Bill went on this walk by himself? What makes you think so?
(any logical response)

E 9. _____ What other animals might Bill see if he goes for another walk?
(any logical response)

V 10. _____ What are "tracks"?
(footprints made in the dirt; something made by animals when they walk or run)

Questions Missed [ ]

Comprehension Scoring Guide

Questions Missed	Level
0–1	Independent
1½–2	Ind./Inst.
2½	Instructional
3–4½	Inst./Frust.
5 +	Frustration

Retelling Notes

Retelling Rubric for the Three Reading Levels

Independent Level/Excellent
Recalls central or key ideas
Remembers important facts
Retains the general sequence of events
Relates most of the content in an organized manner

Instructional Level/Satisfactory
Recalls most central or key ideas
Remembers some important facts
Retains the general sequence of events
Relates an overall sense of the content

Frustration Level/Unsatisfactory
Recalls bits of information in a haphazard manner
Little apparent organization

Sample Teacher Copy of Graded Passage   **Sample Teacher Copy of Comprehension Questions**

(total or significant). To determine reading levels, consult the appropriate set of criteria in the scoring guide at the bottom of the passage in the performance booklet. Then record the number of miscues and the corresponding reading levels in the Word Recognition, Context column on the summary sheet of the performance booklet.

Comprehension Questions

Ask the comprehension questions that accompany the passage in the performance booklet and record the student's responses. Continue administering graded passages until the student is unable to answer half of the comprehension questions or makes so many miscues that frustration is apparent. Also, watch for behaviors associated with frustration: lack of expression, word-by-word reading, excessive fidgeting, and so on. **Discontinue assessment when frustration is evident.**

Scoring the Comprehension Questions

To find the student's comprehension score for each passage, count the number of comprehension questions answered incorrectly. Then record the numeral in the box provided.

To convert the comprehension scores into reading levels, consult the criteria on the scoring guide at the bottom of the page in the performance booklet. Then record the number of questions missed and the corresponding reading levels for oral and silent reading in the appropriate Comprehension columns on the summary sheet of the performance booklet.

You must exercise judgment at the pre-primer levels because the limited number of questions may not permit precise measurement of achievement. At this level, a retelling of the passage by the student instead of the comprehension questions may be a better indicator of the student's reading ability.

Caution

How to Use This Manual

Those who have limited knowledge of reading inventories will profit by reading Sections 1–4 in the manual carefully. It is written to permit self-study and includes numerous practice exercises.

If you are already familiar with reading inventories, read sections of interest and use the remainder of the manual as needed. Because reading inventories differ in their orientation, Sections 3 and 4 may be especially helpful.

Guide to Understanding the Basic Reading Inventory*

Your comprehension can often be enhanced by posing questions about the Basic Reading Inventory manual *before* you actually begin reading it. With this in mind, the following tips are suggested as you read Sections 2–4 of this manual.

1. Read the questions for each section.
2. Look for the answers to the questions as you read the section.
3. Make a notation when you discover an answer for one of the questions (write notes in the margin or tag the page).

Keep in mind that the answers to *all* of these questions are explicitly stated in the text. That is, answers are "right there." Nonetheless, for some of them you might have to "think and search" because the answers may be in separate sentences or paragraphs.

Questions to Aid Understanding of the Basic Reading Inventory

Section 2
Graded Word Lists

1. What can be gained by establishing rapport?
2. What are five purposes for administering the graded word lists?
3. Why do you need to use the graded word lists with caution?
4. What do you need to administer the graded word lists?
5. What are the two scores that can be derived from the graded word lists?
6. How many word lists do you have the student read?

Graded Passages (Oral Reading)

1. What is a miscue?
2. How are miscues recorded?
3. Why might a warm-up passage be helpful?
4. With which passage should you begin?
5. Johns states that you should have the student read the title and predict what the passage might be about. What can you learn by using such a procedure?
6. What should you do after the student has predicted?
7. What is your major task while the student reads?
8. What do you do after the student finishes reading a passage?
9. How accurate do responses to comprehension questions need to be?
10. When should you have the student stop reading the passages?

*Shared by Michael F. Opitz and adapted with permission. From Jerry L. Johns, *Basic Reading Inventory* (11th ed.). Copyright © 2012 by Kendall Hunt Publishing Company (1-800-247-3458, ext. 4). May be reproduced for noncommercial educational purposes. Website: www.kendallhunt.com

Determining Reading Levels from the Word Recognition in Context Scores

1. What do you need to consider as you go about determining a student's three reading levels?
2. How is a student's word recognition score found?
3. What are *significant* miscues?
4. How should you count significant miscues on the pre-primer selections?
5. How is the percentage found?

Determining Reading Levels from the Comprehension Questions

1. What is the comprehension score?
2. How is the comprehension score derived?
3. How is the comprehension score determined for the pre-primer levels?

Determining Reading Levels from Silent Reading

1. Which passage should be used to begin silent reading?
2. What do you do as the student reads silently?
3. What do you do after the passage has been read?
4. What is the student asked to reread orally?
5. What does the oral rereading enable you to assess?
6. How many passages does the student read?

Determining Rate of Reading

1. Where would you find the formula for determining a student's rate of reading?
2. What is the other way to determine a student's rate of reading?
3. How many words per minute (WPM) would the average third grader read orally in the fall of the year?
4. What would be an estimate of a third grader's silent reading rate?

Determining Listening Level

1. What does a student's listening level convey?
2. What procedure do you use to determine a student's listening level?
3. What are some limitations for using the listening level as an indicator of reading potential?

*Shared by Michael F. Opitz and adapted with permission. From Jerry L. Johns, *Basic Reading Inventory* (11th ed.). Copyright © 2012 by Kendall Hunt Publishing Company (1-800-247-3458, ext. 4). May be reproduced for noncommercial educational purposes. Website: www.kendallhunt.com

Section 3

1. Is it possible for some students to have a range of several grades within the instructional level?
2. What should you use when making decisions about students' reading levels?
3. Are the reading levels determined by using this inventory entirely accurate?

Section 4
Determining Strengths and Weaknesses in Word Identification

1. What are some questions that can be used to guide your analysis?
2. What is Advanced Qualitative Analysis and how can it be used?

Determining Strengths and Weaknesses in Comprehension

1. What are some questions you can use to assess the student's comprehension?
2. What are five types of comprehension questions used in the BRI?
3. What is Analysis by Question Type and how can it be used?

Fluency Considerations

1. What are the four components of fluency?
2. What is probably the most important foundation for fluency?
3. What are some factors that can impact fluency?

*Shared by Michael F. Opitz and adapted with permission. From Jerry L. Johns, *Basic Reading Inventory* (11th ed.). Copyright © 2012 by Kendall Hunt Publishing Company (1-800-247-3458, ext. 4). May be reproduced for noncommercial educational purposes. Website: www.kendallhunt.com

Administration and Scoring Procedures

Working closely with students helps teachers build rapport.

Because the Basic Reading Inventory is an informal test, there is no set of procedures that must be followed rigidly. You must, nevertheless, be thoroughly familiar with the recommended procedures for administration prior to asking a student to read the graded word lists and passages. The Basic Reading Inventory will take some time to administer initially until greater familiarity with the procedures is achieved. After you are comfortable with the procedures, the inventory flows smoothly and will take less time to administer. Facility improves greatly after five or six administrations.

Before giving the Basic Reading Inventory, you need to have a general idea of the student's reading ability. You can gather this information by:

- conferring with colleagues who may have potentially helpful insights.
- consulting the student's cumulative record from the previous year to note the level at which the student was reading.
- noting the student's reading performance in the classroom.
- examining the results of other reading assessments.

Regardless of the method used to decide where to begin administration of the inventory, it is important that the student experiences success with the initial graded word lists and passages. You should begin administering the inventory at a level where the student is likely to find the material easy.

Tip!

21

The recommended procedure for administering and scoring the reading inventory is given in this section. Frequently asked questions along with answers are provided at the end of the section.

Establishing Rapport and Gaining Insights

View Laurie (teacher) establishing rapport with Jimmy (student) on the CD.

If the reading inventory is to yield valid, reliable, and useful results, it is necessary to obtain the student's cooperation. In an effort to establish rapport, you may wish to give the student some idea about how his or her reading will be evaluated. You may also want to explore the student's interests and answer questions about the assessment procedure. This brief discussion may help to reduce the anxiety that often accompanies an assessment. Remember that rapport is not always fully established before the administration of a reading inventory begins. In some cases, rapport is steadily increased throughout the assessment. In other cases, interaction between you and the student may become strained during the assessment. If this occurs, make efforts to reestablish rapport.

During the early stages of establishing rapport, as well as throughout the administration of the reading inventory, you have the opportunity to gain valuable diagnostic information in several areas. You can appraise the student's oral language facility and background knowledge through informal conversation and observe how well the student responds to specific comprehension questions that are asked after the graded passages are read. You may also gain insight into how the student attempts to decode unknown words by asking, "What do you do when you come to unknown words?" or "What did you do to finally figure out that word?" Questions such as, "What is reading?" and "What do you do when you read?" may give you insights into how the student views the reading process. When you feel that adequate rapport has been established, it is generally advisable to begin the reading inventory with the graded word lists.

Some students, especially young ones or readers who struggle, may become tired during the administration of the inventory. In such instances, "refresher" breaks can be used or the assessment can be spread over two periods. For example, the graded word lists can be given during one sitting and the graded passages can be given at another sitting. Because the graded word lists and passages increase in difficulty, it is permissible to explain this fact to the student before assessment begins. Some teachers encourage students to say "pass," "skip it," "not yet," or "I don't know" when difficult words or questions are encountered.

Graded Word Lists

There are at least five reasons for giving the graded word lists.

- First, the word lists will provide the approximate level at which the student should begin reading the graded paragraphs.

- Second, you will be able to study some of the student's word identification strategies such as structural analysis and phonics.

- Third, the word lists can be used to informally classify the student's word recognition ability as above, at, or below grade level.

- Fourth, you can assess the extent of the student's sight vocabulary and basic sight vocabulary. Many of the words on lists from pre-primer through second grade are high-frequency words.

- Fifth, you can use the easiest word list to determine if a student has some ability to pronounce words or whether the Early Literacy Assessments in Part 3 are likely to provide more helpful information.

Basic sight words (also called high-frequency words) on the graded word lists are indicated with an asterisk (*). These words are found on the Revised Dolch List (Elish-Piper, Johns & Lenski, 2006; Johns & Berglund, 2010; Johns & Lenski, 2010) and comprise over 50 percent of the running words found in all types of printed materials.

Because the word lists are not a natural reading situation, exercise extreme caution. You cannot examine all word identification strategies through the student's performance on the graded word lists. Phonics, structural analysis, and sight vocabulary are the three most common areas that can be observed. Because the words are presented in isolation, it is not possible to explore the student's overall word identification strategies and the balance between phonics and context. All aspects of a student's word identification repertoire, however, deserve careful attention, because they can provide potential insights for instruction. The best judgments about the student's word identification strategies result from a careful analysis of the student's oral reading of the graded passages coupled with insights from the graded word lists.

The graded word lists do not assess the student's ability to comprehend and are, therefore, an inappropriate measure of overall reading ability. Goodman (1965) has demonstrated that students decode much more readily when words appear in context than when they appear in lists. Also, Marzano and others (1978) have cautioned teachers about basing assessment solely on a word recognition test.

Administering Graded Word Lists

To administer the graded word lists, you will need the word lists in the student booklet and the performance booklet in which the student's responses will be recorded. The recommended procedure for administering the graded word lists is to present the student with the graded list of words and ask him or her to pronounce them at a comfortable rate. If a student reads a word correctly within one second, it is defined as a sight word (Leslie & Caldwell, 1995). As the student reads down each list of words, you would record the student's responses in a performance booklet. The word list initially selected should, if at all possible, be very easy for the student (i.e., at the student's independent level).

View Laurie (teacher) administering a fourth-grade word list to Elyse (student) on the CD.

It is important for you to note and record the student's responses promptly because any delays are likely to result in incorrect reporting. The use of an audio or digital recorder may prove quite helpful so you can review the accuracy of your notations during your first few administrations. The graded word lists are continued until the student is no longer able to achieve a total score of at least 14 correct words or when the teacher observes that the task has become frustrating for the student. Your judgment plays an important role in the administration of the entire inventory.

Scoring Graded Word Lists

Three scores are derived for each graded word list administered to the student (see Figure 2-1). One score represents the student's immediate responses to the words and is called the *sight* score. The second score represents the student's correction of any words missed during the sight presentation or words immediately self-corrected during the initial attempt. The opportunity for the student to study each word missed in an attempt to pronounce it is called the *analysis* score. If the student does not know or mispronounces any words on the first attempt without immediate self-correction (that is, at sight), you would return to each of these words after the student has finished the list and provide the student with an opportunity to analyze the word in an attempt to arrive at its correct pronunciation. The student's *immediate* responses are recorded in the sight column. The responses the student makes when given an opportunity to study the words missed are recorded in the analysis column. The third score is the total of the sight and analysis scores. The total score can be used as a rough indicator of reading levels.

✏ Scoring Jeff's Graded Word Lists

To show how the graded word lists are scored, Figure 2-1 contains Jeff's performance on the pre-primer and primer word lists. An empty space next to a word means that Jeff pronounced it correctly. You may put a plus (+) or check mark (✓) for each correct word, because it lessens students' perceptions of when they get a word wrong. Miscues in word recognition are noted as follows: "DK" indicates that he said "I don't know." Single letters or phonetic symbols represent Jeff's attempt to pronounce the word. The plus (+) indicates that he corrected a miscalled word. When Jeff said a word which was different from the stimulus word, it is noted in the appropriate column. In the sight column, the "sc" indicates that the word was self-corrected immediately. A plus is then placed in the analysis column. Other pertinent comments that might have diagnostic significance (for example, skips unknown words; uses phonic knowledge; knows basic sight words; quite persistent; gives up easily) can also be noted.

Jeff's scores are shown at the bottom of each column of words. For the pre-primer (AA) word list, the score of 15 indicates that he correctly pronounced 15 of the 20 words on the sight presentation. These 15 words were known automatically. The 5 words not correctly pronounced during the sight presentation were numbers 2, 3, 6, 17, and 20. From his score on the *analysis* column, you can note that Jeff corrected 4 of his initial miscues (numbers 2, 3, 6, and 17), thereby achieving a total score of 19 correct words. At the primer level Jeff achieved a score of 15 on the sight presentation and a total score of 18 because he corrected 3 (numbers 1, 10, and 18) of his initial miscues.

You can use the total number of words Jeff correctly pronounced on each graded word list for a very rough estimate of his reading levels. To convert total scores to a rough estimate of the various reading levels, compare the total number of correct words for each list of words to the scoring guide at the bottom of the word lists in the performance booklet. This scoring guide is also reproduced in Table 2.1.

TABLE 2.1
Scoring Guide for Graded Word Lists

Independent	Instructional	Inst./Frust.	Frustration
20 19	18 17 16	15 14	13 or less

 Determining Reading Levels—Graded Word Lists

From Jeff's responses in Figure 2-1, note that he achieved a total score of 19 correct words on the pre-primer list. According to the scoring guide below the word lists, a score of 19 would indicate an independent level. The total score of 18 for the primer word list indicates an instructional level. From the results reported thus far, it is not possible to estimate Jeff's frustration level. You would need to continue with additional word lists until Jeff mispronounced 7 words, appeared to be having considerable difficulty, or was extremely slow in pronouncing the words. When this point is reached, you would stop administering the graded word lists and proceed to the graded passages. Keep in mind that reading levels estimated with word lists represent only rough indications of reading ability. The inadequacies of graded word lists are recognized by teachers, specialists, and interventionists who know that some students can identify words in isolation that cause difficulty in reading materials. Other students who have difficulty with words in isolation can identify words in reading materials. It is important, therefore, to recognize the limitations of graded word lists and to use this knowledge when scoring and interpreting inventory results.

Figure 2-1. Jeff's Performance on Two Graded Word Lists

List AA (Pre-Primer)	Sight	Analysis	List A (Primer)	Sight	Analysis
1. me*			1. show	*she*	*+*
2. get*	*got*	*+*	2. play*		
3. home	*house*	*+*	3. be*		
4. not*			4. eat*		
5. he*			5. did*		
6. tree	*tr-*	*+*	6. brown	*OK*	*br-*
7. girl			7. is*		
8. take*			8. boat		
9. book			9. call*		
10. milk			10. run*	*ran*	*+*
11. dog			11. what*		
12. all*			12. him*	*his*	*his*
13. apple			13. wagon		
14. like*			14. over*		
15. go*			15. but*		
16. farm			16. on*		
17. went*	*want* sc	*+*	17. had*		
18. friend			18. this*	*that*	*+*
19. about*			19. around*		
20. some*	*same*	*same*	20. sleep		

*denotes basic sight word from Revised Dolch List

*denotes basic sight word from Revised Dolch List

Number Correct: _15_ _4_   Number Correct: _15_ _3_

Total: _19_   Total: _18_

Scoring Guide for Graded Word Lists			
Independent	Instructional	Inst./Frust.	Frustration
20 19	18 17 16	15 14	13 or less

🖋 Recording Jeff's Word Recognition Scores for Graded Word Lists

Figure 2-1 shows that Jeff achieved a total score of 19 on the pre-primer list and 18 on the primer list. These scores should then be entered on the summary sheet similar to that shown in Figure 2-2 and reproduced at the beginning of the performance booklets for Forms A, B, C, D, and E. To determine the reading levels corresponding to these two scores, consult Table 2.1 or the scoring guide at the bottom of the word lists. Using these criteria, Jeff achieved an independent level on the pre-primer word list and an instructional level on the primer word list. Note that the abbreviations *Ind.* and *Inst.* are written on the summary sheet to indicate the levels achieved.

You should check your understanding of this procedure by finding the reading levels that correspond to Jeff's performance on the first- through third-grade word lists as noted in Figure 2-2. This task can be accomplished by taking the total score given in Figure 2-2 for the first-grade word list (20) and finding the corresponding reading level from the scoring guide (Table 2.1 on page 25). The reading level should then be entered next to the number of words correct. This procedure can be repeated for the scores on the second-grade and third-grade word lists.

Graded Passages

Prior to actually administering the graded passages, you must develop some system for recording the student's responses. There are numerous systems and techniques for coding reading miscues (Barr, Blachowicz, Bates, Katz, & Kaufman, 2007; Block, 1997; Gillet, Temple, & Crawford, 2004; Goodman, Watson, & Burke, 1987; Gunning, 2006; Jennings, Caldwell, & Lerner, 2006; Johnson, Kress, & Pikulski, 1987; Manzo & Manzo, 1993; McCormick, 2007; McKenna & Stahl, 2003). A miscue is "an oral reading response that differs from the expected response to the written text" (Harris & Hodges, 1981, p. 199). Miscues "provide a rich source of information for analyzing language and reading development" (Harris & Hodges, 1995, p. 155). Figure 2-3 on page 28 contains examples of miscues and a suggested method for recording them during oral reading. You should carefully study and learn or adapt the suggested procedure so that it can be used and referred to later when actual examples of a student's oral reading are considered.

It is generally recommended to begin administering the graded passages at least one level below the student's highest independent level on the graded word lists. If a student, for example, achieved independent levels on the word lists for the pre-primer, primer, first-, and second-grade levels, it is recommended that you select a graded passage at the first-grade level. If the student is unable to read that passage at the independent level, go to the next lower level

FIGURE 2-2. Summary Sheet for Jeff's Performance on the Basic Reading Inventory

Grade	Word Recognition						Comprehension	
	Isolation (Word Lists)				Context (Passages)		Form A	
	Sight	Analysis	Total	Level	Miscues*	Level	Questions Missed	Level
PP2	15	4	19	*Ind.*	0	*Ind.*	0	
P	15	3	18	*Inst.*	1		½	
1	16	4	20		2		0	
2	14	2	16		5		1½	
3	9	2	11		10		5	

*Refers to *total* miscues in this example

and continue to move down until an independent level is found or the first pre-primer passage is reached. Then return to the starting point and proceed until the student reaches a frustration level. In the event that the pre-primer passage is too difficult for the student to read, selected Early Literacy Assessments in Part 3 may be used.

 ## Administering Graded Passages

Before actual reading begins, cover the passage in the student booklet with a heavy sheet of paper. Have the student read the title of the passage silently and predict or share what it might be about. The student's sharing can yield several valuable pieces of information: (1) the background experiences/knowledge the student associates with the title; (2) the student's ability to make predictions; and (3) the student's vocabulary and ability to express himself or herself. During this prereading sharing, note the student's ideas and informally evaluate the student's background on a scale of low to high. Place an x on the scale to reflect the level of background knowledge. This scale accompanies each graded passage in the performance booklet and can be found near the top of the page on the left.

View Laurie (teacher) administering a third-grade passage to Elyse (student) on the CD.

Background: Low |————|————| High

Do not describe what the passage is about, explain key concepts, or use vocabulary from the passage because the student's comprehension may be artificially enhanced. Once the student has shared or predicted, uncover the passage. The student should then be given a reason to read the passage; for example, to find out more about the title, to check predictions made about the passage, or the like. The student should also be told that comprehension questions will be asked after the passage has been read. Say something like the following, "Read the passage aloud and think about what you're reading. I'll ask you some questions when you're done reading." You may wish to audio record the student's responses to ensure accurate scoring.

Caution

✎ Recording Miscues during Oral Reading and Timing the Reading

While the student is reading from the graded passage in the student booklet, use a performance booklet to keep a careful record of the exact way in which the student reads the passage. Some students may need to be told a word if they pause for ten or fifteen seconds; however, the recommended procedure is to encourage students to read the graded passages using their strategies for word identification without any assistance. The suggested method for recording a student's oral reading, presented in Figure 2-3, should be a valuable aid for anyone who has not yet developed a system for recording. Your major task is to record the manner in which the student reads the passage by noting omissions, insertions, substitutions, and other miscues. In addition, note hesitations, word-by-word reading, finger pointing, monitoring strategies, and so on. If desired, time

A careful record is kept of the student's oral reading.

the student's reading using a stopwatch or a watch with a second hand. There is a place in the performance booklet to note the number of seconds it takes the student to read the passage. Performing division will result in the student's rate of reading in words per minute (WPM). Any timing should be done in an inconspicuous manner because some students, if they see they are being timed, do not read in their usual way. In addition, some students may focus more on pronouncing words quickly than trying to understand the passage (Johns, 2007). Further discussion of how to determine rate of reading is found under Rate of Reading on page 40.

Caution

Figure 2-3. A Suggested Method for Recording a Student's Oral Reading Miscues

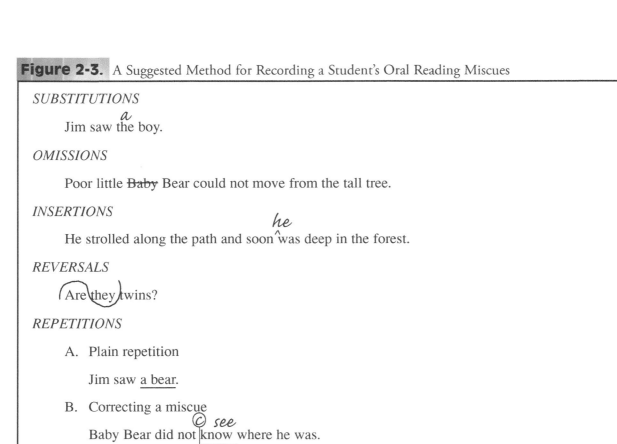

SUBSTITUTIONS

Jim saw the boy. *(a written above "the")*

OMISSIONS

Poor little ~~Baby~~ Bear could not move from the tall tree.

INSERTIONS

He strolled along the path and soon ^was deep in the forest. *(he inserted)*

REVERSALS

Are they twins? *(they circled with reversal marks)*

REPETITIONS

A. Plain repetition

Jim saw a bear. *("a bear" underlined)*

B. Correcting a miscue

Baby Bear did not know where he was. *(© see over "know")*

C. Abandoning a correct word said correctly initially

He stayed alone in the pine tree all night. *(AC along over "alone")*

D. Unsuccessfully attempting to correct an intial miscue (attempts are numbered)

He had slept hard all night. *(UC, 1. heavy, 2. ha- over "hard")*

ADDITIONAL MARKINGS

A. partial words

The hunters rescued the boys. *(res- over "rescued")*

B. Nonword substitutions

people on the frontier had shooting contests. *($ frontmer over "frontier")*

C. Punctuation ignored

. . . from some maple and oak trees/As Bill

D. Intonation

He played a record that was his favorite. *(rē´cord over "record")*

E. Word pronounced by examiner

Men on the frontier often had shooting contests. *(P over "frontier")*

F. Dialect

He went home. *(d goed over "went")*

G. Lip movement

place LM in margin

H. Finger pointing

place FP above word

I. Vocalization

place V in text

Four Ways to Assess Comprehension

After the student finishes reading the passage, assess comprehension by asking the comprehension questions, integrating the concept of engagement with the questions, using retelling, or combining retelling with the questions. Initially, you may prefer to ask the comprehension questions, at least in the first several administrations of the reading inventory.

View Laurie (teacher) asking Elyse (student) comprehension questions after she reads a third-grade passage on the CD.

ASK COMPREHENSION QUESTIONS. Each reading passage above the pre-primer levels contains 10 comprehension questions of various types: topic, fact, inference, experience/evaluation, and vocabulary. The general procedure is to remove or cover the passage and ask the student the comprehension questions. Write the student's verbatim responses to the comprehension questions or underline the "answers" given in the performance booklets. Noting the student's responses will make scoring the questions much easier. You will also be able to analyze the reasoning used by the student. **The student's answers to the comprehension questions need not conform exactly to the answers in the performance booklets**; responses similar in meaning to the printed answer should be scored as correct. In addition, some students may need to be told that the answers to some questions (vocabulary, evaluation, and inference) are not stated directly in the passage. For these questions, always give credit for responses that demonstrate understanding and/or logical thinking. **"Answers" in parentheses that are separated by semicolons mean that only one of the answers must be given for full credit (unless indicated otherwise).**

Do not help the student arrive at the correct answers to the questions (use a + for questions answered correctly). If a comprehension question is answered incorrectly (use a −), note the student's response and go on to the next question. You may, however, ask for clarification if the answer for a particular question is not clear. Neutral probes such as "Tell me more," "What else?" or "Explain that further" often help students elaborate on partial answers. Half credit (use ½) may be given for partial answers. After the student has answered the comprehension questions, you may wish to have him or her do a look-back into the text for answers to missed factual questions. Doing so may provide you with useful information about the nature of the student's lack of comprehension. Such look-backs can be noted on the appropriate record sheet in the performance booklet. You may wish to code such look-backs next to the corresponding question as LB. While look-backs are not counted as correct when calculating the comprehension score, they do offer useful information regarding the student's comprehension. Continue with subsequent passages until the student is unable to answer satisfactorily at least half of the comprehension questions or makes many miscues.

INTEGRATE THE CONCEPT OF ENGAGEMENT WITH THE QUESTIONS. Manzo and Manzo (1993) have suggested the "engagement" concept to enhance comprehension assessment by determining whether the student's responses to comprehension questions are congruent or incongruent. All correct responses are congruent. Incorrect responses "may be congruent (related but incorrect) or incongruent (unrelated as well as incorrect). An increase of congruent responses is a sound sign that the student is engaged" (Manzo & Manzo, 1993, p. 92). Unfortunately, so-called remedial students answer 55 to 80 percent of teachers' questions with totally incongruent responses (Manzo & Manzo, 1995).

If you wish to integrate the engagement concept while asking the comprehension questions, follow these guidelines:

- All comprehension questions scored as correct (+) are a sign of engagement. For correct responses that are "especially full, fresh, or elaborated in some meaningful and appropriate way," circle the numeral beside the comprehension question (Manzo & Manzo, 1993, p. 467).

- For comprehension questions scored as incorrect (−), a decision needs to be made: Is the incorrect response congruent (related to the passage in some meaningful way) or incongruent (not related to the passage in some meaningful, logical way)? For incorrect responses that are incongruent, place an X on the numeral beside the comprehension question.

General guidelines for evaluating engagement can be found in Section 4 of this manual. More extensive information can be found in an inventory developed by Manzo, Manzo, and McKenna (1995).

USE RETELLING. Retelling is sometimes referred to as free recalls plus probes (questions or imperative statements). McCormick (1995, p. 174) notes several advantages to using retellings or free recalls plus probes. They can assist the teacher in "determining whether students have noted important information, whether they can reproduce it in a manner that makes sense, and whether their background knowledge has an effect on the way they interpret the substance of the text." You can also informally assess the student's short-term retention. In retelling, the student is asked to orally recall a passage after it has been read. You could say something like the following: "After you have read the passage, you will be asked to retell it in your own words."

Other ways to initiate the retelling include the following probes:

● Tell me what the passage (story or text) is about.

● Tell me as much as you can about what you have just read.

● What is the passage (story or text) about?

Goodman, Watson, and Burke (1987) have offered suggestions to teachers who are interested in gaining proficiency in using a retelling strategy to assess a student's comprehension. A few of their suggestions for those who want to use retelling procedures include:

● familiarity with the passage,

● not giving the student information from the passage,

● asking open-ended questions, and

● retaining any nonwords or name changes given by the student.

Once you become familiar with the graded passages, it is possible to use a retelling strategy to assess comprehension. First, invite the student to tell everything about the passage that has just been read. Then ask specific questions without giving the student information that has not already been mentioned. Using Jeff's reading of the second-grade passage in Figure 2-4 for illustration, you would first ask him to describe or explain what he read. Suppose Jeff said that the passage is about a boy who went to camp for the first time. You could encourage Jeff to relate further events and also ask him the boy's name. Through experience, you will gain confidence in extracting the main ideas and important details in the passages without asking the comprehension questions.

There are some probes that teachers have found useful. Consider adapting and using the following probes (Lipson & Wixson, 1991, p. 198):

● Tell me more about what you have read.

● Tell me more about what happened.

● Tell me more about the people you just read about.

● Tell me more about where this happened.

Lipson and Wixson (2000, pp. 283–284) have suggested prompts in the form of questions asked by the teacher. Prompts vary for literary (narrative) and informational (expository) text. Some sample prompts for the two major types of text follow.

Prompts for Eliciting Literary (Narrative) Retellings

● How is the setting in the story important?

● What happens to get the story started?

- What is the main problem the characters face?
- How do the characters solve the main problem?

Prompts for Eliciting Informational (Expository) Retellings

- What is the big idea in this selection?
- Why do you think the author wrote this piece?
- How does the author organize the information to share the major ideas?
- What are the main ideas and important details?

To judge student retelling, the categories *excellent* (independent level), *satisfactory* (instructional level), and *unsatisfactory* (frustration level) may be used in conjunction with the evaluation criteria in Figure 2-4 to help assess the quality and accuracy of student retellings. There is ample space for retelling notes beside the comprehension questions in the performance booklet. The rubric in Figure 2-4 provides the specific criteria for evaluating the accuracy and quality of student retellings.

Figure 2-4. Retelling Evaluation Criteria

Level	Description
Independent Level/Excellent	Recalls central or key ideas Remembers important facts Retains the general sequence of events Relates most of the content in an organized manner
Instructional Level/Satisfactory	Recalls most central or key ideas Remembers some important facts Retrains the general sequence of events Relates an overall sense of the content
Frustration Level/Unsatisfactory	Recalls bits of information in a haphazard manner Little apparent organization

While retelling is a viable option, it "is not an easy procedure for students, no matter what their ages" (Morrow, 1988, p. 128). In addition, retelling requires considerable teacher judgment, and there is no widely used, generally accepted criteria for judging student retellings of passages. Harris and Sipay (1990) also note that retellings place a heavy demand on the student's ability to retrieve and organize information in the passage. Johnson, Kress, and Pikulski (1987) believe that it is somewhat premature to recommend retelling for widespread practical use. Those interested in pursuing this strategy in greater depth will find examples and tips in Appendix A for using retelling. Hansen (2004) also provides helpful developmentally appropriate retelling strategies.

COMBINE RETELLING WITH THE QUESTIONS. In actual practice, you may feel more comfortable combining the retelling strategy with some of the comprehension questions. This procedure gives you the necessary flexibility to gather the information needed to make an accurate assessment of the student's understanding of the passage. The recommended procedure is to invite retelling, during which time an asterisk or R (for retelling) is used to note the comprehension questions answered. The remaining questions or selected questions are asked after the retelling. This technique capitalizes on the strengths of both assessment procedures while minimizing their weaknesses.

✎ Scoring Jeff's Graded Passage

Figure 2-5 on page 33 contains Jeff's oral reading performance on a second-grade passage. The notations indicate that he substituted *Bob* for *Bill*, *so* for *soon*, *was* for *saw*, and *minute* for *moment*. These four substitutions were not corrected. He also inserted *trees*. Based on a total (quantitative) count, Jeff made 5 miscues. The numeral 5 is recorded in the "Total Miscues" box at the bottom of the page. The miscue tallies in the chart should not be done until after the assessment has been completed. Jeff's reading was also timed with a stopwatch. It was done inconspicuously, and the time in seconds was noted at the bottom of the page as the divisor (65).

On the 10 comprehension questions shown in Figure 2-6 on page 34, Jeff responded freely and demonstrated the ability to answer various types of questions (+ indicates correct responses; – indicates incorrect responses; underlining indicates his responses). Jeff didn't know why Bill went walking (so he earned no credit) and could not remember the name of the other kind of leaf Bill found in the woods so he was asked "What else?" Jeff couldn't remember (hence he received half credit). His understanding of the passage, nevertheless, was quite good. From the general criteria for the three reading levels at the bottom of Figure 2-6, it would appear that this passage is at Jeff's instructional level, because he made 5 *total* miscues, had comprehension in the *Ind./Inst.* range (see Figure 2-6), and a reading rate of 92 wpm which is average for a second grader in the spring of the school year when the assessment was done (see Table 2.5 on page 43).

 # Determining Reading Levels—Graded Passages

You can determine whether the passage is at the student's independent, instructional, or frustration level by considering: (1) the accuracy with which the student reads; and (2) the student's behavior and fluency while reading. In order to determine the accuracy with which the student reads the passage, determine the student's word recognition score. The word recognition score is found by determining the number of either *total* or *significant* miscues the student makes during the oral reading of the graded passages. Depending on your philosophy, you can count miscues in one of two ways: total miscues or significant miscues.

Word Recognition
Counting Total Miscues

Determining the word recognition in context score by counting the student's total miscues is a *quantitative* analysis of oral reading behavior. You would count all miscues, regardless of type, and use this total to help determine the student's reading level. In this procedure, all miscues are given equal weight in scoring the student's oral reading. You may find it easier to count total miscues during the actual administration of the reading passages. After the Basic Reading Inventory has been administered, further analysis, if desired, may be undertaken to determine significant miscues and to complete the miscue tally in the chart to the right of the passage.

Various guidelines have been offered for counting total miscues. After a review of five studies, Morris (1990) found that investigators counted miscues differently; nevertheless, there was consensus on certain types of miscues. Based on this information, a careful review of the literature, and input from teachers, it is recommended that you count the following for total miscues:

- substitutions (sometimes called mispronunciations)
- omissions (words and punctuation)
- insertions
- examiner aid (however, giving aid is not recommended)
- self-corrections (see comments in the following paragraph on page 35)

Figure 2-5. Jeff's Performance on a Graded Passage

Student Booklet copy is on page 14.

A 8224 (Grade 2) Activating Background: Read the title to yourself; then tell me what you think will happen.

Background: Low ├─────┼─────┤ High

Bill at Camp

									MISCUES							
		Substitution	Insertion	Omission	Reversal	Repetition	Self-Correction of Unacceptable Miscue	Meaning Change (Significant Miscue)
Bob / It was the first time Bill went to	8	1						
so / camp. He was very happy to be there. Soon	17	1						
he went for a walk in the woods to look for	28							
many kinds of leaves. He found leaves	35							
trees / from some maple and oak trees. As Bill	43		1					
was / walked in the woods, he saw some animal	51				1			
minute / tracks. At that moment, a mouse ran into	59	1						
a small hole by a tree. Bill wondered if the	69							
tracks were made by the mouse. He looked	77							
around for other animals. He did not see	85							
any. The last thing Bill saw was an old	94							
bird nest in a pine tree.	100							
TOTAL		3	1	1				

good phrasing and intonation

Total Miscues [5]   Significant Miscues [ ]

Word Recognition Scoring Guide		
Total Miscues	Level	Significant Miscues
0–1	Independent	0–1
2–4	Ind./Inst.	2
5	Instructional	3
6–9	Inst./Frust.	4
10 +	Frustration	5 +

Oral Reading Rate	Norm Group Percentile
$\frac{92}{65\overline{)6000}}$ WPM	☐ 90 ☐ 75 ☐ 50 ☐ 25 ☐ 10

Figure 2-6. Jeff's Performance on Comprehension Questions

A 8224 (Grade 2)
Comprehension Questions

T   1. _+_   What is this story about?
(a boy at camp; Bill's walk in the woods)   *Bill at camp*

F   2. _+_   Did Bill enjoy going to camp? How do you know?
(<u>yes</u>, the story said <u>he was happy there</u>)

F   3. _—_   Why did Bill go walking in the woods?
(to look for leaves)   *to find animals*

F   4. _½_   What kinds of leaves did Bill find in the woods?
(<u>maple</u> and oak leaves)   *What else? I don't know*

F   5. _+_   What else did Bill see besides the mouse?
(<u>a bird nest; animal tracks</u>)

F   6. _+_   Where did the mouse go?
(<u>into a small hole</u> by or in a tree)

F   7. _+_   What other animals did Bill see?
(none; <u>he didn't see any</u>)

I   8. _+_   Do you think Bill went on this walk by himself? What makes you think so?
(any logical response)   *Yes, he didn't talk to anyone.*

E   9. _+_   What other animals might Bill see if he goes for another walk?
(any logical response)   *deer and squirrels*

V   10. _+_   What are "tracks"?
(<u>footprints</u> made in the dirt; something made by animals when they walk or run)

| 1½ | Questions Missed |

Comprehension Scoring Guide	
Questions Missed	Level
0–1	Independent
1½–2	Ind./Inst.
2½	Instructional
3–4½	Inst./Frust.
5 +	Frustration

Retelling Notes

Retelling Rubric for the Three Reading Levels
Independent Level/Excellent
Recalls central or key ideas
Remembers important facts
Retains the general sequence of events
Relates most of the content in an organized manner
Instructional Level/Satisfactory
Recalls most central or key ideas
Remembers some important facts
Retains the general sequence of events
Relates an overall sense of the content
Frustration Level/Unsatisfactory
Recalls bits of information in a haphazard manner
Little apparent organization

In counting total miscues, a number of special considerations are warranted. They are noted below. It is important that all this information be considered carefully when analyzing the student's word identification and comprehension strategies.

- Self-corrections provide evidence that the student is monitoring his or her reading, and some teachers prefer not to count such miscues. Numerous self-corrections, however, impact fluency and rate of reading. If such miscues are not counted, they should still be considered as a qualitative source of information in the overall determination of the student's reading levels.

- Dialect variations (such as *goed* for *went*), hesitations, and repetitions should not be included in the count of total miscues although they may be recorded for later study and analysis. Hesitations and repetitions impact fluency and may offer clues to helpful instructional interventions.

- The *consistent* mispronunciation of a word more than once in a passage should only be counted once. For example, if a student reads *Bob* for *Bill* repeatedly in the passage, it should be counted as only one miscue. This same guideline also applies to situations where a particular word is used for a proper name or any other word.

- If a student omits an entire line, it should be counted as one miscue.

Counting Significant Miscues

Determining the word recognition in context score by counting only significant miscues is a *qualitative* analysis of oral reading behavior. Some evidence (for example, Goodman, 1972; Goodman & Marek, 1996; Lipton, 1972; Recht, 1976) seems to suggest that certain substitutions, insertions, omissions, and the like do not seriously damage the student's understanding of the passage; hence, such miscues should not be counted as significant. Teachers have also made similar observations.

> It must be remembered that accurate recognition is not the major objective in reading. *The goal is always meaning.* Because even proficient readers make errors on unfamiliar material, teachers must resist the temptation to meticulously correct all inconsequential mistakes. They must always ask whether a particular miscue really makes a difference (Goodman, 1971, p. 14).

Perhaps the best advice for counting significant miscues is to include those omissions, insertions, substitutions, mispronunciations, and other miscues that appear to affect comprehension. In short, significant miscues alter the meaning of the passage. To determine which miscues are significant, evaluate each miscue in the passage to judge the extent to which the meaning of the sentence or passage is altered by the miscue. For example, the miscue in this sentence (*blank* for *black*) is significant because it changes the meaning of the sentence. "Everyone turned to stare as a *blank* hooded figure whizzed by on a skateboard." See Frequently Asked Question 9 (page 50) for a detailed discussion of how to determine if miscues are significant. The following method is suggested:

1. Count the **total** number of miscues in the passage.
2. Find the total of all dialect miscues, all corrected miscues, and all miscues that do not change the meaning.
3. Subtract this number from the total miscues. The result is the number of significant miscues.

A comprehensive, chronological annotated bibliography of miscue analysis has been compiled by Brown, Goodman, and Marek (1996). In addition, Wilde (2000) has provided numerous helpful and practical suggestions for conducting a miscue analysis so the results can be used for instruction. The miscue chart provided with each graded passage makes it quite easy to determine the number, type, and significance of miscues.

✎ Scoring Jeff's Oral Reading

From Jeff's oral reading of a second-grade passage, as recorded in Figure 2-5, it is apparent that he made five total miscues. If you decided to count *total* miscues to determine Jeff's score in word recognition, you would record the numeral 5 in the "Total Miscues" box and circle the corresponding level (Instructional) in the Word Recognition Scoring Guide (see Table 2.2). Then, the numeral and the level would be written on the summary sheet of the performance booklet. The same procedure would be used to determine the word recognition score for the other graded passages.

If you decided to count *significant* miscues, each of the five miscues would be evaluated within the context of the passage to determine whether the meaning of the passage was affected. After such an analysis, three of the miscues Jeff made (*Bob*, *so*, and *was*) appear to be significant. You would record the numeral 3 in the "Significant Miscues" box and circle the corresponding level (Instructional) in the Word Recognition Scoring Guide. Then the numeral and the level would be recorded on the summary sheet of the performance booklet.

Figure 2-2 on page 26 contains various scores based on counting *total* miscues. By consulting Table 2.2 or the appropriate section of the Word Recognition Scoring Guide at the bottom of each passage, you should determine the reading levels that correspond to the various scores and place the appropriate levels in Figure 2-2. For example, at the pre-primer level, Jeff's *total* miscue count was 0. This score corresponds to a reading level of "Independent" which is written as *Ind.* in the appropriate column of Figure 2-2. For practice, write in the appropriate levels for primer, first, second, and third grade. Remember to use "Total Miscues" from the Word Recognition Scoring Guide.

TABLE 2.2
Scoring Guide for Words in Context for Forms A, B, C, D, and E

Word Recognition Scoring Guide		
Total Miscues	Level	Significant Miscues
0–1	Independent	0–1
2–4	Ind./Inst.	2
5	Instructional	3
6–9	Inst./Frust.	4
10 +	Frustration	5 +

Miscue counts of total and significant miscues may not always result in the same reading level. In such instances, reflect on the student's reading and use qualitative judgments to make the best possible appraisal. For example, a student may have a large miscue count that approaches frustration, but only a few of the uncorrected miscues result in a significant change in meaning. You may note, however, that the student appeared to be very nervous and frustrated. In addition, the student's rate of reading was quite labored and slow. Using this qualitative information will enable you to make a better judgment. In this example, it is doubtful that the passage was at the student's independent level. The passage is more likely instructional or frustration, depending on the student's comprehension.

Observation of Reading Behaviors and Other Evidence

In addition to counting miscues, pay attention to and note other evidence that may be helpful in determining the appropriateness of the passage:

- finger pointing
- expression
- phrasing (good, adequate, poor)
- rate of reading in words per minute (WPM) and/or words correct per minute (WCPM)
- flushed face or anxiety
- frustration
- refusals
- attitude
- persistence
- monitoring strategies
- background knowledge
- overall engagement

Teachers who have used the Basic Reading Inventory report that such behaviors and observations (qualitative data) are often as helpful as actual miscue counts and comprehension scores (quantitative data) in helping to determine whether a particular passage is easy, about right, or too difficult for the student. At the very least, these observations can provide additional information as tentative judgments are made regarding a student's oral reading and reading levels.

Using Expert Noticing Skills to Observe Student Reading Behaviors

You can also use a more structured approach to observe student reading behaviors. Through applying expert noticing skills (Ross & Gibson, 2010), you can use a series of questions to guide your observations of student reading behaviors. Expert noticing skills help you to cue into patterns in students' reading and metacognitive behaviors so that you can make appropriate instructional decisions. To develop expert noticing skills, you can engage in a two-step process. First, using the CD, you can practice your expert noticing skills while observing Elyse orally read a fourth-grade passage. As you watch the video clip on the CD, record your notes in Figure 2-7. Then, compare your notes to those provided on the CD.

View Elyse (student) reading a fourth-grade passage on the CD.

After completing the expert noticing process with the video on the CD, you can use the questions provided in Figure 2-7 to focus on your own students while administering the Basic Reading Inventory and during instruction. By developing and using expert noticing skills in tandem with the Basic Reading Inventory, you can enhance your understanding of your students' reading.

Figure 2-7. Expert Noticing Video Observation Guide

Question	Your Notes
What did you see the student do?	
Why is this important?	
What did you notice about the way the student responded to reading/writing/ discussion activities in terms of the knowledge, strategies, and dispositions necessary to perform the tasks?	
Why do you think the student responded this way?	
What do the student's responses tell you about how well the student understood tasks?	
What did you learn about the student that will be helpful in planning an appropriate lesson or intervention?	

 Determining Reading Levels—Comprehension Questions or Retelling

The comprehension score is determined by counting the number of questions missed. To convert this score into one of the three reading levels, consult Table 2.3 or the scoring guide at the bottom of each passage. For example, if Jeff missed five comprehension questions, that passage would be at his frustration level.

TABLE 2.3
Scoring Guide for Comprehension

Questions Missed	Level
0–1	Independent
1½–2	Ind./Inst.
2½	Instructional
3–4½	Inst./Frust.
5+	Frustration

The above procedure, however, is not directly applicable to the pre-primer passages, because they contain only five questions. You must exercise judgment in determining the student's comprehension score. If you decide that the score from the pre-primer levels does not accurately reflect the student's achievement, it would be permissible to place more emphasis on the score at the primer level when summarizing the results.

If you choose to use the retelling strategy to assess comprehension, you may (1) determine a percent score from the student's retelling or (2) identify the passage as one of the three reading levels without noting a specific percent of comprehension. When using retelling, you may circle *excellent* (independent), *satisfactory* (instructional), or *unsatisfactory* (frustration) in the retelling evaluation criteria box at the bottom of each set of comprehension questions in the performance booklet. The main issue to keep in mind is whether the student's comprehension of the passage is judged to be at the independent, instructional, or frustration level.

✑ Recording Jeff's Comprehension Scores for the Graded Passages

Figure 2-2 on page 26 contains Jeff's scores for the comprehension questions in the pre-primer through third-grade levels. Consult Table 2.3 or the scoring guide below each passage to determine the reading level that corresponds to each comprehension score and place these levels in Figure 2-2. When a student's scores fall between the reading levels, your judgment must be used. The recommended procedure is to record *Ind./Inst.* or *Inst./Frust.* on the summary sheet and circle the level closest to the actual score. If the score is exactly between two levels, circle the slash (/). The gray areas in the scoring guide indicate areas that require your judgment. The determination of reading levels that require your judgment is discussed in Section 3.

Determining Reading Levels—Silent Reading

Select a form of the Basic Reading Inventory that the student did not read orally. Form D is specifically designed for silent reading. **It is recommended that you begin the silent reading at the highest passage where the student achieved an independent level during oral reading.** If this procedure does not result in an independent level for silent reading, proceed to easier passages until an independent level is determined or the easiest pre-primer passage is read. Then, return to the original starting point and continue until the student reaches a frustration level.

As the student reads the passage silently, time the student's reading and note behavioral characteristics such as lip movement and finger pointing. Following silent reading, the passage is removed and the student's comprehension is assessed with comprehension questions, a retelling strategy, or a combination of the two.

Then the student is given the passage and asked to locate and orally reread a sentence in the passage that answers the question posed by the teacher. The question is located below the passage in Form D of the performance booklet. The correct sentence in the passage is printed in bold type. According to Johnson, Kress, and Pikulski (1987), the oral rereading permits assessment of the student's ability to (1) skim for specific information, (2) read for specific information and stop when that purpose has been achieved, and (3) demonstrate oral reading ability after the material has been read silently. Generally, oral rereading following silent reading should be better than the oral reading at sight from another passage at the same level of difficulty. For example, if a student reads one third-grade passage orally and a different third-grade passage silently, the sentence orally reread from the silent passage should generally be read more accurately and fluently than the passage read at sight.

When the student finds and rereads the sentence orally, record the reading in the same manner as was done on the passages read orally at sight. You can also note how the student located the sentence that was read (for example, skimmed to locate the information; reread the passage from the beginning; seemed confused).

The student continues to read increasingly difficult passages until a frustration level is determined. The various scores and corresponding reading levels should be entered at the appropriate place on the summary sheet. These silent reading levels can be used in conjunction with the student's oral reading performance to arrive at estimations of the three reading levels.

Rate of Reading

A formula for determining a student's rate of reading is provided on each graded-passage page in the performance booklet. The 6,000 for each graded passage above the pre-primer levels for Forms A, B, C, D, and E was determined by multiplying the number of words per selection (100) by sixty. This procedure permits the resulting division to be in words per minute (WPM). For Forms LL and LI, a similar procedure was used (multiplying the 250 words in each passage by 60). To determine a student's rate of reading, use the formula provided. Merely record as the divisor of the formula the time (in seconds) the student takes to read the passage. Perform the necessary division, and the resulting numeral will be a rough estimate of the student's rate in words per minute (WPM). For example, suppose a middle-grade student took 70 seconds to read the fourth-grade selection on Form A. You would divide 6,000 by 70. The result is a reading rate of approximately 86 words per minute (WPM) as shown in the sidebar.

Another way to determine words per minute is provided by the numerals at the end of each line of the teacher's passage (see Figure 2-8). These numerals represent the cumulative total of words to that point in the passage. Time the student's reading for one minute and draw a line or slash after the last word read by the student at the end of that minute. Then count the number of words not read on that line and subtract this numeral from the numeral at the end of the line. The

$$85.7 \text{ WPM}$$
$$70 \overline{)6000}$$
$$\underline{560}$$
$$400$$
$$\underline{350}$$
$$500$$
$$\underline{490}$$

Figure 2-8. Example of a One-Minute Timed Reading

Bill at Camp

Bob It was the first time Bill went to	8
So camp. He was very happy to be there. Soon	17
he went for a walk in the woods to look for	28
many kinds of leaves. He found leaves	35
trees from some maple and oak trees. As Bill	43
was walked in the woods, he saw some animal	51
minute tracks. At that moment, a mouse ran into	59
a small hole by a tree. Bill wondered if the	69
(end of one minute) tracks were made by the mouse. He looked	77
around for other animals. He did not see	85
any. The last thing Bill saw was an old	94
bird nest in a pine tree.	100

result will be the number of words read in one minute. The line or slash in Figure 2-8 shows that the student read to the word *by* in one minute. By subtracting the four words not read from 77, the result is 73 words per minute (WPM). Some teachers have used "one-minute reads" in their classrooms. The above procedure permits teachers to use passages from the Basic Reading Inventory in a similar manner.

Both of the above procedures determine words per minute (WPM). If you prefer to calculate words correct per minute (WCPM), the following may be done after one of the above procedures is used to determine WPM. Merely subtract the number of miscues made by the student from the WPM score. The result will be words correct per minute (WCPM). There are no universally accepted standards for which miscues to count. **It is recommended that mispronunciations, substitutions, omissions, and reversals be counted. Insertions, repetitions, and self-corrections are generally not counted in determining WCPM.** Using the example in Figure 2-8, there are five miscues: *Bob, so, trees, was,* and *minute*. Following the above recommendations, *trees* would not be counted because it is an insertion. The other four miscues, however, would be subtracted from the total number of words read (73), resulting in 69 WCPM.

You are encouraged to make general notes about a student's rate (for example, read very quickly; read slowly but accurately; seems to think that fast is best). A slow rate beyond second grade is usually an indication that the student lacks a large sight vocabulary and effective word identification strategies.

A more comprehensive estimate of a student's reading rate can be determined by averaging the rates for those passages where the student misses three or fewer comprehension questions. This procedure has the advantage of using a larger sample of behavior and taking comprehension into account. It should also be remembered that reading rate can vary according to the material being read, the student's interest and familiarity with the material, the purpose for which it is being read, and whether reading is done orally or silently. Oral and silent reading rates should be averaged separately (see Table 2.4 on page 42).

Combining Reading Rates for Shorter and Longer Passages

The passages in Forms A, B, C, D, and E each contain approximately 100 words (except for the pre-primer levels) and differ in length from the longer passages (approximately 250 words) in Forms LL and LI. If you wish to combine the results from passages in both forms (for example, Form A and Form LL), the following procedure should be used:

1. Select passages where the student missed three or fewer comprehension questions. Keep oral and silent reading separate in the calculations.

2. Add the total number of words read for all the passages where the student missed three or fewer questions and multiply by 60. The resulting numeral becomes the dividend.

3. Add the times it took the student to read each passage. This numeral is used as the divisor.

4. Complete the necessary division to determine the approximate reading rate.

For example, the data in Table 2.4 is from Terell who read seven passages orally. His resulting reading rate is approximately 80 words per minute (WPM).

TABLE 2.4
Data for Terell's Reading Rate

Level of Passage	Number of Words	Time (in Seconds)
4 (A 5414)	100	70
5 (A 8595)	100	80
6 (A 6867)	100	90
4 (LL 5414)	250	160
5 (LL 8595)	250	190
6 (LL 6867)	250	180
7 (LL 3717)	250	200
	1300	970
	× 60	
	78000	

$$970\overline{)78000} \quad 80.4\ \text{WPM}$$
$$7760$$
$$4000$$
$$3880$$

A Note about Oral and Silent Reading

"Studies have demonstrated that beginning and poor readers typically comprehend text better after reading orally rather than silently, whereas more advanced readers tend to show superior understanding after silent reading" (Prior & Welling, 2001, p. 1). In the study, however, students in grades three and four achieved significantly higher comprehension scores after oral reading; therefore, exercise caution when generalizing about which mode of reading (oral or silent) is likely to result in higher comprehension scores.

Caution

Norms for Oral and Silent Reading Rates

The norms in Table 2.5 are based on four sources of information. The first was a five-year study by Forman and Sanders (1998) who established norms for first-grade students. Over 3,500 scores were obtained from students who took part in their study. These students were from a large suburban school district whose students generally score considerably above average on state and national reading assessments. Norms were provided for three points of the school year.

The second source was a study by Hasbrouck and Tindal (1992). Their study involved over 7,000 scores from students in grades two through five who read passages at sight for one minute from their grade-level texts, regardless of the students' instructional levels. Because most classrooms have students who represent a wide range of reading levels, their procedure resulted in some students reading passages that were very easy (independent level), while other students were asked to read passages that would be too difficult (frustration level). The norms provide words correct per minute at the 75th, 50th, and 25th percentiles for students in grades two through five at three points (fall, winter, and spring) in the school year

The third source of data was reading fluency data that was gathered beginning in 1999 and ending with the 2002–2003 school year (www.edforamation.com). Over 240,000 scores for students in grades one through eight who read passages for one minute were analyzed. The passages were at grade level, which meant that they were easy for some students and difficult for other students. Separate norms were calculated for each of the four school years. The resulting norms for each year provide words correct per minute at the 90th, 75th, 50th, 25th, and 10th percentiles at three points (fall, winter, and spring) of the school year.

The fourth source of data was a follow-up study by Hasbrouck and Tindal (2006) using over 297,000 scores obtained from students in grades one through eight. Students represented all achievement levels, including those identified as gifted or reading disabled. English Language Learners (ELLs) who were receiving reading instruction in a regular classroom were also included in the data. Schools and districts from 23 states used curriculum based measures (CBMs)

TABLE 2.5
Oral Reading Norms for Students in Grades One through Eight

Grade (N)	Percentile	Fall		Winter		Spring	
		N	WCPM	N	WCPM	N	WCPM
1 (74,623)	90	2,847	32	33,366	75	38,410	105
	75		14		43		78
	50		7		22		50
	25		2		11		27
	10		1		6		14
2 (99,699)	90	29,634	102	33,683	124	36,382	141
	75		77		99		116
	50		50		72		89
	25		24		44		62
	10		12		19		34
3 (96,460)	90	29,832	128	32,371	145	34,257	161
	75		100		119		137
	50		72		91		107
	25		46		60		78
	10		24		36		47
4 (87,436)	90	29,609	144	27,373	165	30,454	180
	75		119		139		152
	50		94		111		124
	25		69		86		99
	10		42		60		72
5 (82,073)	90	28,510	165	25,229	181	28,334	194
	75		137		155		167
	50		109		126		138
	25		85		98		108
	10		60		73		81
6 (57,575)	90	18,923	177	17,668	194	20,984	204
	75		153		166		178
	50		127		140		150
	25		98		111		122
	10		67		81		93
7 (29,135)	90	10,687	176	7,313	188	11,135	200
	75		154		162		176
	50		127		134		150
	25		102		108		122
	10		79		86		97
8 (24,105)	90	8,674	183	5,986	193	9,445	198
	75		160		168		176
	50		130		142		151
	25		104		112		124
	10		79		84		97

N = number of student scores
WCPM = words correct per minute

From Jerry L. Johns and Roberta L. Berglund, *Fluency: Differentiated Interventions and Progress-Monitoring Assessments* (4th ed.). Copyright © 2010 by Kendall Hunt Publishing Company (1-800-247-3458, ext. 4). May be reproduced for noncommercial educational purposes. Website: www.kendallhunt.com

for the assessment. This procedure resulted in some students reading materials at their frustration levels. Norms were complied for students performing at the 90th, 75th, 50th, 25th, and 10th percentiles at three points throughout the school year (fall, winter, and spring) with the exception of grade one (which reported students' fluency norms for only the winter and spring).

All these data were thoughtfully studied, analyzed, and compiled into Table 2.5 by the author using his professional judgment. The resulting table is intended to provide helpful information to teachers who desire to have some guidelines for students' reading rates. Because the norms are in words correct per minute (WCPM), comparing them to words per minute (WPM) as suggested in the Basic Reading Inventory means that there is a slightly different basis for comparison. Comparisons can still be done and used to make informal appraisals regarding students' rates of reading. Just remember that the rates in Table 2.5 are more conservative than the rates determined by the WPM method. The percentiles within each grade level can be used by teachers to informally track and monitor student progress in rate throughout the school year.

In recent years, there has been mention of desired reading rates for various instructional levels for students in various grades. Using the four sources of information previously described, Table 2.6 was developed to provide average rates for students at three points in the school year (fall, winter, and spring). These figures are less than the "challenging" rates created by Carnine, Silbert, Kame'enui, and Tarver (2004, pp. 192–93) based on students who were performing very well on standardized tests. They argue that helping students achieve high rates of fluency in the early grades leads to more reading by the student and makes school a more enjoyable experience. Keep in mind that the averages are best used to informally determine students' progress in comparison with so-called average students. Note in grade six and beyond that the rate for the spring of the year stays at 150 words correct per minute. Because of individual differences in student ability and learning rates, expecting all students to reach the target is unrealistic. Finally, do not consider rate to be the same as fluency (Johns & Berglund, 2010). See "Fluency Considerations" in Section 4 (page 87) for a discussion of the core elements of fluency.

Caution

TABLE 2.6
Mean Words Correct per Minute* for Average Students in Grades One through Eight

Grade	Fall	Winter	Spring
1	Not Applicable	20	50
2	50	70	90
3	70	90	110
4	95	110	125
5	110	125	140
6	125	140	150
7	125	140	150
8	130	140	150

*Reported in "round" numbers

Carver (1989, p. 165) has provided information on *silent* reading rates for students in grades one through twelve that "may be helpful to teachers who administer informal reading inventories." The figures he presents are the average rates of students in that *particular* grade who can *understand* material at *that* grade level. Although Carver's figures are in standard word lengths, they may be useful as a rough indication of the average rates at which average students in a particular grade read with understanding. Users of the Basic Reading Inventory, then, can use the figures presented in Table 2.7 when evaluating a student's silent reading ability.

TABLE 2.7

Silent Reading Rates for Students in Various Grades Who Understand the Material

Grade	1	2	3	4	5	6	7	8
WPM	<81	82–108	109–130	131–147	148–161	162–174	175–185	186–197

	9	10	11	12				
	198–209	210–224	225–240	241–255				

The Listening Level

In addition to the three reading levels, you may wish to get a rough estimate of the student's listening level or potential for substantial growth in reading. Intelligence tests are sometimes used to estimate potential for reading; however, their limitations have led some teachers to read graded passages to a student and determine the highest level of material that the student can understand. Undertaking such a procedure is known as determining the student's listening level. This procedure should **not** be used with students in the primary grades (Schell, 1982).

`Caution`

 Determining the Listening Level

Select a form of the Basic Reading Inventory that was not used for either oral or silent reading. The listening level is determined after *you* read increasingly difficult passages to the student. You should first read the title and develop a purpose for listening to the passage. Procedures similar to those used for oral and silent reading may be used: Invite the student to predict what the passage will be about and then have the student *listen* to the content in the passage as you read a passage *to* the student. After the passage has been read, assess the student's comprehension with the questions, a retelling strategy, or a combination of the two. The criteria for estimating the student's listening level is a comprehension score of three or fewer questions missed. You should also informally note the student's ability to use vocabulary and language structures as complex as those used in the passage read.

It is recommended that you begin reading a passage that is not higher than the student's instructional level. Then continue reading more difficult passages until the student misses more than three comprehension questions. The *highest* passage at which the student misses three or fewer questions is his or her listening level.

✏ Scoring Tom's Listening Level

Suppose, for example, that Tom is a fifth-grade student who has a fourth-grade instructional level for oral and silent reading. To determine his listening level or potential, you should choose a passage at the fourth-grade level from a form of the Basic Reading Inventory that Tom has not read orally or silently. After you read the passage aloud, Tom responds to the comprehension questions. If Tom misses three or fewer questions, continue reading increasingly difficult passages until Tom misses more than three questions. The highest level at which Tom meets this criterion is identified as his listening level. To illustrate this procedure, consider the data in Table 2.8.

TABLE 2.8
Data for Tom's Listening Level

Level of Passage	Comprehension Questions Missed
4 (C 5414)	0
5 (C 8595)	2
6 (C 6867)	3
7 (C 3717)	4

Based on these data, Tom's listening level would be sixth grade, because that was the highest level at which he missed three or fewer questions. Because his listening level (sixth grade) is higher than his instructional level (fourth grade), there is reason to believe that Tom has the potential to increase his reading ability. Harris and Sipay (1990) suggest a two-year discrepancy between the listening level and the instructional level as a rough criterion for practical significance. In this instance, Tom's listening comprehension can be viewed as a favorable prognostic sign; namely, Tom should be able to understand material at the sixth-grade level once he acquires the necessary reading competence.

There are some limitations for using the listening level as an indicator of reading potential. Limitations within the assessment process as well as a student's auditory handicaps and/or unfamiliarity with standard English reduce the importance that should be attached to a listening level. In addition, bright students in the middle and upper grades may have reading abilities that exceed their listening abilities. For these reasons, consider the listening level as a rough estimate of reading potential that needs to be supported from observation and the results of measures of intellectual capacity.

Caution

Figure 2-9 provides a summary of procedures for administering and scoring the Basic Reading Inventory. You will also find a helpful quick guide inside the front cover of this manual. The quick guide provides an easy-to-use reference with page numbers that will facilitate your administration of the Basic Reading Inventory.

Figure 2-9. Basic Reading Inventory Administration and Scoring Procedures

 # Basic Reading Inventory Administration and Scoring Procedures

To determine a student's independent, instructional, and frustration levels, administer the graded word lists and graded passages included in the Basic Reading Inventory as follows:

WORD RECOGNITION IN ISOLATION: Select a graded word list at a reading level that will be easy for the student. Ask the student to pronounce the words at a comfortable rate. Record the student's responses in the sight column beside the corresponding word list in the performance booklet. The enclosed CD provides downloadable versions of all performance booklets.

Return to mispronounced or unknown words for an attempt at analysis and note the student's responses in the analysis column. Administer successive word lists until the student is no longer able to achieve a total score of at least 14 correct words or until the student becomes frustrated.

Scoring: Total the correct responses in the sight and analysis columns. Consult the criteria on the scoring guide at the bottom of the word lists to determine a rough estimate of the reading level achieved on each graded word list. Record the number-correct scores and the reading levels on the summary sheet of the performance booklet.

WORD RECOGNITION IN CONTEXT: Ask the student to read aloud the passage graded one level below the highest independent level achieved on the graded word lists. If desired, time the student's reading. As the student reads the passage, record all miscues such as omissions, repetitions, substitutions, and the like on the corresponding copy of the passage found in the performance booklet.

Scoring: Count the number of total miscues or significant miscues (those that affect meaning) in each graded passage.

To determine reading levels from the word recognition in context scores, consult the criteria on the scoring guide at the bottom of the passage. Record the score and the reading levels on the summary sheet of the performance booklet.

COMPREHENSION: Ask the comprehension questions that accompany the passage in the performance booklet and record the student's responses. Continue administering graded passages until the student has many word recognition miscues or is unable to answer half the comprehension questions. Also, watch for behavior associated with frustration: lack of expression, word-by-word reading, excessive anxiety, and so on.

Scoring: Count the number of comprehension questions missed.

To convert these scores into reading levels, consult the criteria on the scoring guide at the bottom of the questions. (Judgment must be exercised at the pre-primer levels because the limited number of questions may not permit precise measurement of comprehension.) Record the scores and the reading levels on the summary sheet of the performance booklet.

FREQUENTLY ASKED QUESTIONS

1. Must every student be given the Basic Reading Inventory?

Many teachers use the inventory with all their students so they can differentiate instruction and monitor progress. Other teachers use the inventory with those students they believe need further assessment in reading: students who score very high or very low on state tests, other standardized reading tests, or students who need assessment of their word identification, fluency, or comprehension skills. The Basic Reading Inventory has also been used in response to intervention programs to help assess progress. It is also useful with students who have transferred into your school system. Remember that the basic assessment strategy described in this manual can be used with instructional materials in your classroom (such as trade books, literature-based readers, and language experience stories) to help make your instruction more responsive to students' needs.

2. Can the Basic Reading Inventory be used for progress monitoring in Response to Intervention (RTI)?

Yes, the Basic Reading Inventory can be an excellent tool as part of the progress-monitoring process in RTI. Depending on the schedule for progress monitoring for a specific student, the Basic Reading Inventory can be used in three different ways. First, because the Basic Reading Inventory has seven forms and measures word identification, fluency, and comprehension, it can be used as the primary tool for progress monitoring for students who need to be assessed on a quarterly or monthly basis. Second, the Basic Reading Inventory can be used in conjunction with other assessments such as Curriculum Based Measures (CBMs). CBMs may be administered weekly, and the Basic Reading Inventory can be administered on a quarterly basis to provide a more complete assessment of the student's reading and progress. Finally, the Basic Reading Inventory may be used as a pre-assessment and post-assessment to determine student growth related to a reading intervention.

3. Why do first graders sometimes have difficulty with the pre-primer and primer passages?

Generally, students at the early stages of reading, especially those taught with intensive phonic programs, literature-based readers, or trade books, are most familiar with the vocabulary used in such books. Because the Basic Reading Inventory is not designed for use with specific reading programs or materials, differences in vocabulary may exist, particularly in the pre-primer, primer, and first-grade passages. You should take this information into consideration when you assess reading and determine the student's three levels. You may also find the Early Literacy Assessments (ELA) in Part 3 to be especially helpful with emergent readers. Take a moment to look over these assessments (see page 349). You may find the following Early Literacy Assessments especially helpful with emergent and beginning readers: Literacy Knowledge, Caption Reading, and Wordless Picture Reading.

4. How should I assess the reading of students who are unable to read the easiest word lists and passages?

Remember that emergent readers and older students experiencing difficulty in reading may find the easiest word lists and pre-primer passages difficult. When this situation occurs, the language experience approach (LEA) is recommended. A concrete object, photograph, or experience is used to engage the student in discussion. Then the teacher writes down the student's dictation and has the student read the LEA story. This strategy can be used to probe what students have learned about how the reading process works. Walker (2004, pp. 266–67), Gillet, Temple, and Crawford (2004, pp. 413–15), McCormick (2006, pp. 162–63), and Lipson and Wixson (2003, pp. 488–91) offer some concise assistance for launching, maintaining, and using dictated stories. You may want to use Wordless Picture Reading in Part 3 (page 354) as the stimulus for a language experience story.

FREQUENTLY ASKED QUESTIONS

Part 3 of this manual contains a variety of Early Literacy Assessments. Included are informal ways to assess literacy knowledge, phoneme segmentation awareness, auditory discrimination, alphabet knowledge, picture reading, and so on. The informal assessment devices will be especially useful for students who are unable to read the easiest word lists and passages. Additional assessments and teaching strategies for the early stages of reading can be found in Elish-Piper, Johns, and Lenski (2006).

5. Why do illustrations accompany only the pre-primer passages of the reading inventory?

Illustrations can make reading material attractive. They can also capture the interest of a student. Pictures, however, sometimes provide clues to help the student understand the passage. Because the Basic Reading Inventory is designed to assess how a student uses language cues to construct meaning from print, illustrations are restricted to the pre-primer passages. For passages with illustrations at grade levels one and two, consult Elish-Piper, Johns, and Lenski (2006). Additional passages at grade levels one through eight (with illustrations) can be found in Johns and Berglund (2010).

6. Why are some passages literary (narrative) and others informational (expository)?

Literary passages generally tell a story. Informational passages inform by presenting information. Both types of literature are commonly found in schools, and students need to be able to read both types of texts. In recent years, informational books have become much more common in the primary grades.

Forms A, B, and LL of the Basic Reading Inventory contain literary passages. Form C contains mostly literary passages. Form D, starting in grade two, contains informational passages. Form A is designed for oral reading, and you can assess the student's ability to deal with literary discourse. Form LL contains longer literary passages (250 words) than Form A (100 words). You can use Form LL for oral or silent reading.

In the upper grades, the content areas become more important, so Forms D and LI contain informational passages at and above the second-grade level. Form E contains all informational passages. Because students often read their content area texts silently, Form D assesses silent reading with informational materials. Form LI contains longer informational passages and may be used for oral or silent reading. With these various forms, you have the resources to help you gain a more complete picture of the student's reading. Both teachers and research have found that informational (expository) passages can cause students greater difficulty. McCormick (1999) notes that informational text structures are commonly more difficult to comprehend than the story structures of literary materials. One reason such a situation exists may be a student's lack of experience with informational materials. Another reason may be the differences in structure between the two types of literature. If, for example, a student has difficulty with the informational passages, you may have gained valuable knowledge to use in your instructional program.

7. Should I help students with words they don't know?

Every time a student is told an unknown word is one less opportunity to gain insights into the student's reading. There will probably be some instances where you tell a student a word; nevertheless, the recommended procedure is to remain silent or to say, "Do the best you can." Then you can note the strategies (or lack of them) that the student uses frequently, occasionally, or not at all. There is some evidence (McNaughton, 1981) that students were less accurate and self-corrected a smaller proportion of their miscues when they received immediate, as compared with delayed, correction. You may, therefore, want to be very selective about telling students unknown words when administering the Basic Reading Inventory.

8. What should I do when the student mispronounces proper nouns?

First, do not include multiple mispronunciations of the same word in counting miscues. Count only one miscue. Second, encourage the student to use strategies to pronounce the word by saying, "Just do the best you can." Third, use the student's pronunciation if the word appears in a question. Finally, in some instances you may pronounce the word for the student because of the frustration that is evident. Be sure you make a note about the student's behavior (for example, "unable to go on until I pronounced the word"; "tried several pronunciations"; "is aware that the word is mispronounced but seems to have the basic meaning").

9. What are miscues and what's the difference between total miscues and significant miscues?

Miscues occur when a student's oral reading of the passage results in a version that differs from the printed passage. Common miscues include substitutions, omissions, and insertions. A miscue can be as minor as substituting *a* for *the* in the following sentence: I saw the squirrel run up *the* tree. Other miscues can be significant: substituting *horse* for *house* in the sentence, Dad parked the car in the garage and walked into the *house*. It is important to remember that miscues are a natural part of the reading process.

The number of miscues a student makes can merely be counted; this procedure is called quantitative analysis or total miscues. Such analysis does not take into account the quality of the student's miscues; therefore, all miscues are given equal weight.

A qualitative analysis counts significant miscues. It is a search to gain insights into a student's reading by making judgments about the student's miscues. In a qualitative analysis, some miscues are rated of higher quality than others. To determine significant miscues, evaluate each miscue in the passage in which it occurs and judge the extent to which the meaning of the sentence or passage is altered. Generally, significant miscues change the meaning of the passage. Whether you choose to count total miscues or significant miscues is up to you. The scoring guide contains both options. Consult page 35 for a method to determine which miscues are considered significant. Also, see question 9.

Below are some examples of miscues that teachers **considered significant** because of the change in meaning was substantial.

Student: Here comes a *cat*.
Text: Here comes a *car*.

Student: While gathered *above* the council fire . . .
Text: While gathered *about* the council fire . . .

Student: The summer had been a dry one, *usual* . . .
Text: The summer had been a dry one, *unusual* . . .

Student: The flower got its name from its *stage* habit . . .
Text: The flower got its name from its *strange* habit . . .

Student: They threw leaves into the *yard*.
Text: They threw leaves into the *air*.

Student: He unlocked the *bank* door.
Text: He unlocked the *back* door.

Student: He *sniffled* slowly down the street.
Text: He *shuffled* slowly down the street.

Student: Jim put the *bird* on the snow.
Text: Jim put the *bread* on the snow.

Student: Only he would know the amount in each dose.
Text: Only he would know the *correct* amount in each dose.

Here are some examples of miscues that were **not considered significant** because the essential meaning of the phrase or sentence was retained.

Student:	. . . sailing over the *middle* line . . .
Text:	. . . sailing over the *midline* . . .
Student:	. . . and scored. *The* game ended.
Text:	. . . and scored *as* the game ended.
Student:	*Ooh!* What fun!
Text:	*Wow!* What fun!
Student:	She went with her parents to the pet *store*.
Text:	She went with her parents to the pet *shop*.
Student:	. . . trees fell *on* the ground.
Text:	. . . trees fell *to* the ground.
Student:	Dale *was* the strongest player on the team *and* was up first.
Text:	Dale, the strongest player on the team, was up first.
Student:	The Tigers and *the* Jets were playing . . .
Text:	The Tigers and Jets were playing . . .

Finally, here are some **"gray area" examples** for which greater teacher judgment is needed to determine whether the miscues are significant.

Student:	The *kick* went sailing . . .
Text:	The *ball* went sailing . . .
Student:	The children helped by *carrying* bits of wood.
Text:	The children helped by *carting* bits of wood.
Student:	This is *funny*.
Text:	This is *fun*.
Student:	. . . some would take *the* wood and start . . .
Text:	. . . some would take *this* wood and start . . .

10. What guidelines should be used if I decide to count only significant miscues?

Miscues are generally significant when:
1. the meaning of the sentence or passage is significantly changed or altered, and the student does not correct the miscue.
2. a nonword is used in place of the word in the passage.
3. only a partial word is substituted for the word or phrase in the passage.
4. a word is pronounced for the student.

Miscues are generally *not* significant when:
1. the meaning of the sentence or passage undergoes no change or only minimal change.
2. they are self-corrected by the student.
3. they are acceptable in the student's dialect *(goed home* for *went home, idear* for *idea)*.
4. they are later read correctly in the same passage.

FREQUENTLY ASKED QUESTIONS

11. Are the answers provided with the comprehension questions the only acceptable answers?

No. You may decide that some students' responses are both logical and reasonable even though they differ from the "answer" in the parentheses under the question. In such cases, give the student credit. The age and grade of the student should also be taken into consideration when you are scoring responses. In essence, use your knowledge of students when scoring the comprehension questions.

Some "answers" in parentheses for the comprehension questions are separated by a semicolon. When two or more answers are separated by a semicolon, only one of the answers is necessary for full credit (unless other guidelines are specified).

12. What should I do if a student uses experience instead of information in the passage to correctly answer a factual question even though it is not the answer in parentheses?

After you acknowledge the student's response, ask what the passage said. You might say, "That's right, but what did it say in the passsage?" In essence, the student's answers to factual questions should be tied to information presented in the passage. If the student is unable to remember and the initial response (based on experience) was correct, you may want to give half credit.

13. What should I do when students fail to see that they should use their experience along with information in the passage to answer an inference or evaluative question?

Gently remind students that, based on what they read, you want to know what they think. When the student says, "It didn't say," you might respond, "That's right, but I want to know what you think." Feel free to encourage students to use their experience in conjunction with information in the passage (see question 16).

14. Is it acceptable to reword questions that the student doesn't seem to understand?

Yes. You should not, however, provide information that will help the student answer the question. In addition, if you find that many students experience difficulty with a particular question, you may want to develop a replacement question of your own.

15. May I omit some comprehension questions?

Yes, you may omit questions to shorten the administration time. It takes about ten seconds for each question to be asked and answered. Some teachers omit the vocabulary questions because they are least dependent on the passage. In other words, students are often able to use their backgrounds and experiences to give correct responses to the vocabulary questions. The evaluation and inference questions encourage students to integrate information in the passage with their background knowledge in order to give a satisfactory response. Because such responses are not based entirely on the text, some teachers may prefer to omit these questions. You can probably omit one question without changing the scoring guide at the bottom of each passage in the performance booklet.

Another alternative is replacing some of the questions with others that you believe are more important in assessing the student's comprehension. How you conceptualize the nature of comprehension will likely influence the types of questions you ask. The author's view is that if comprehension is assessed with questions, an effort should be made to tap the student's ability to recall the literal information *and* to reason beyond the information given in the passages. That is why evaluation and inference questions are also included.

16. Do some comprehension questions tap the student's background and experience?

For most of the questions in the Basic Reading Inventory, the student must recall or use information from the passage to answer the question. These types of questions are called passage dependent. Some questions, however, are not totally passage dependent. The most notable ones are the vocabulary questions. Two other types of questions (inference and experience/evaluation) encourage students to use their knowledge, background, and experience in conjunction with the information presented in the passage to engage in what some reading authorities identify as higher-level thinking. Raphael and Au (2005) refer to such questions as author and you. Such questions invite students to make explicit connections between the ideas in the passage and their own background knowledge and experience. Teachers are generally pleased with the variety of questions contained in the Basic Reading Inventory.

17. When I ask the first comprehension question, the student also answers other questions in his or her response. What should I do?

Just put a plus (+) next to the questions answered. There is no need to ask them again.

18. What should I do if a student mispronounces a word in the passage that happens to be the word used in the vocabulary question?

Ask the question as it is printed. You can then determine whether the student has meaning for the word even if he or she did not pronounce it correctly in the passage.

19. What should I do if a student finds a particular passage extremely easy or difficult?

The diversity of students' experiences and backgrounds may make a particular passage easier or more difficult than its assigned level. You can generally note this problem when the student's reading of a particular passage is much better or worse than would be predicted from the student's performance on previous passages. When you believe that a passage is inappropriate, the recommended procedure is to substitute a passage at the same level from a different form of the reading inventory. If this passage is still too difficult for the student to read, you may discontinue the assessment at that time. After a break, or on another day, you may wish to administer another passage at that same level from another form of the Basic Reading Inventory to see if the student is able to read it. If not, discontinue the assessment and use the total results from the student's reading to make your judgments about the student's reading levels.

20. Is it acceptable to give the student a break during administration of the Basic Reading Inventory?

Yes, if the student appears tired, bored, or frustrated, you can give the student a break. Doing so will help to ensure that the student is focused and performing to his or her true ability on the Basic Reading Inventory. For younger students or students who struggle a great deal, you may wish to plan to administer the Basic Reading Inventory over two or three days, with one day for the word lists, and one to two days for the passages and accompanying comprehension questions.

FREQUENTLY ASKED QUESTIONS

21. How do passages in the Basic Reading Inventory and the Early Literacy Assessments relate to levels for Guided Reading and Reading Recovery?

Using criteria summarized by Reutzel and Cooter (2004), the work of Gunning (2008), and an analysis by Ferroli and Turmo (2005–2006), the chart below contains approximations of the passages in the Basic Reading Inventory and Early Literacy Assessments. These approximations should be used along with your experience and professional judgment.

Grade Level	Early Literacy Assessments	Basic Reading Inventory Passage Code	Guided Reading Level	Reading Recovery Level
Caption Reading	Caption Reading	—	A	1–3
Easy Sight Word	EE-1	AAA, BBB, CCC, DDD, EEE (6 Passages)	A–B	4–6
Pre-primer	EE-2	AA, BB, CC, DD, EE (6 Passages)	B–E	7–8
Primer	—	A, B, C, D, E (5 Passages)	F–G	9–11
1	—	A, B, C, D, E 7141 (5 Passages)	H–I	12–17
2	—	A, B, C, D, E 8224 (5 Passages)	J–M	18–28
3	—	A, B, C, D, E, LL, LI 3183 (7 Passages)	N–P	30–38
4	—	A, B, C, D, E, LL, LI 5414 (7 Passages)	Q–T	39–40
5	—	A, B, C, D, E, LL, LI 8595 (7 Passages)	U–V	41–44
6	—	A, B, C, D, E, LL, LI 6867 (7 Passages)	X–Y	
7	—	A, B, C, D, E, LL, LI 3717 (7 Passages)	Z	
8	—	A, B, C, D, E, LL, LI 8183 (7 Passages)	Z	

22. Are informal reading inventory (IRI) results appropriate additions to my students' portfolios?

Certainly. One of the guiding principles for literacy portfolios is that assessment should be a multifaceted process (Valencia, 1990). Results and insights (both yours and the student's) from an IRI can help chronicle reading development. You can record or make a DVD of the student's reading and responses to the comprehension questions and include the recording or DVD in the portfolio. Teachers have used multiple indications of performance for many years. Continue using observations, your judgments, running records, daily work, and other informal and formal assessments. McCormick (1999) has provided an excellent discussion for beginning, maintaining, and evaluating portfolios. She has also included ideas for portfolio conferences.

23. What do I do when the student's scores within a particular level (word list, passage reading, and comprehension scores) don't indicate the same level?

McKenna and Stahl (2003) use the term *borderline results* to describe the situation and note that such results are a natural consequence of using reading inventories. The term *gray areas* also can be used to describe the situation. Basically, you have to make an overall judgment when results are in the gray areas as shown below.

Word Identification Percentages

100	99	98	97	96	95	94	93	92	91	90	<90
Ind.		Ind./Inst.			Inst.		Inst./Frust.				Frust.
100	90	85		80	75	70		60		50	<50

Comprehension Percentages

Section 3 contains examples of determining a student's reading levels when there are gray areas in the results. You should find that information helpful. There are also practice exercises in Section 3 that you can use to gain greater competence. The completed exercises can be found on the CD. The important point to remember is that your judgment must be used when there are gray areas. Some teachers also like to share and discuss their results with colleagues to help gather additional insights and perspectives.

A teacher in a Basic Reading Inventory workshop shared an idea for the gray areas. When scores fall in the ind./inst. or inst./frust. areas, circle the level closest to the numerical score. If the numerical score is in the middle, circle the slash (/). This procedure will help you know at a glance the level to which the numerical score was closest and should help you make a more informed decision as you determine the student's three reading levels.

24. Can students have a range of reading levels?

Yes and no. A student's instructional level can sometimes span two or more grades. The independent and frustration levels are always designated by a single number. For example, if a student is independent at first and second grade, you would record the student's **highest** independent level. On the other hand, if the student is frustrated at the fifth and sixth grades, you would record the **lowest** grade as the student's frustration level. For this particular student, third and fourth grade could be recorded as the instructional level range. The student's three reading levels would be: independent—second grade, instructional—third and fourth grade, and frustration—fifth grade. The reading levels you record should have no gaps or missing grades.

FREQUENTLY ASKED QUESTIONS

25. What other tips might be helpful as I learn to administer the Basic Reading Inventory (BRI)?

You need to be patient with yourself! Even with a careful reading and study of this manual, you may feel overwhelmed during your first administration. Cut yourself some slack! After a few administrations, you will gain greater confidence and competence. Below are some tips you may find useful.

- Gather all the materials you will need for the administration of the BRI.
- Arrange the materials in the order that they will be used.
- Review the directions for administration.
- Make a copy of page 47 which contains a concise summary of BRI administration and scoring procedures.
- Enjoy your time with the student—even if things get confusing from time to time.
- Refer to the examples in the manual as you determine the student's three reading levels.
- Learn from your experiences, and you will be on your way to becoming a BRI pro!

Note: In addition to the above questions, Felknor, Winterscheidt, and Benson (1999) and Paris and Carpenter (2003) provide thoughtful answers to many questions related to selecting, administering, scoring, and using informal reading inventories.

Determining the Student's Three Reading Levels

Is this book at the appropriate instructional level for this student?

Assimilating Jeff's Results

After you have summarized the results for graded word lists, words in context, and passage comprehension, estimates of the student's independent level, instructional level, and frustration level can be determined. Figure 3-1 contains a summary of Jeff's performance on Form A of the Basic Reading Inventory. The various scores and levels should correspond to your efforts to complete the examples that were presented in Figure 2-2 (page 26). You should check your results from Figure 2-2 with Figure 3-1 (page 58), check your answers, and resolve any discrepancies. Note that the circled items in Figure 3-1 indicate the level closest to Jeff's actual scores.

From the data presented in Figures 2-2 and 3-1, Jeff's independent levels are pre-primer, primer, and first grade. Because the independent level is the *highest* level at which Jeff can read books by himself, first grade would be his independent level. Materials at the second-grade level of difficulty should provide the basis for instruction because such materials are at his instructional level. At this level, Jeff should make maximum progress with teacher guidance. The third-grade level, according to the criteria, appears to be his frustration level. In summary, Jeff's three reading levels are: independent—first grade, instructional—second grade, and frustration—third grade.

Examples: Reading Levels for Bob and Pablo

It should be noted that most summary sheets, unlike Figure 3-1, will not provide such clear distinctions among the three reading levels. When discrepancies arise, you must use your judgment in conjunction with the results to determine the student's three reading levels. Frequently, it is

FIGURE 3-1. Summary of Jeff's Performance on Form A of the Basic Reading Inventory

| Grade | Word Recognition | | | | | | Comprehension | |
| | Isolation (Word Lists) | | | | Context (Passages) | | Form A | |
	Sight	Analy-sis	Total	Level	Miscues*	Level	Questions Missed	Level
PP2	15	4	19	Ind.	0	Ind.	0	Ind.
P	15	3	18	Inst.	1	Ind.	½	Ind.
1	16	4	20	Ind.	2	(Ind.)/Inst.	0	Ind.
2	14	2	16	Inst.	5	Inst.	1½	(Ind.)/Inst.
3	9	2	11	Frust.	10	Frust.	5	Frust.

*Refers to *total* miscues in this example

wise to consider the student's performance *preceding and following* the level in question, as well as the student's performance *within* a particular passage.

Generally, the recommended procedure is to place a bit more emphasis on comprehension if word identification on the graded word lists and in context is clearly instructional level or better. **Remember that the goal of reading is constructing meaning from print.** The ability to pronounce words automatically *is* important; nevertheless, word identification must always be judged with regard to the student's ability to understand the passage. In addition, give greater emphasis to silent reading comprehension in the upper grades.

It is also important to take reading rates (judged in words per minute and/or words correct per minute) and the behavioral characteristics of the student at each reading level into consideration to aid in proper placement. A student, for example, may have percentages high enough to read independently at a certain level of difficulty; however, the student may read very slowly, lack fluency, appear to be quite nervous, and/or exhibit other behavioral characteristics that lead you to conclude that such a level is too difficult for independent reading. It is prudent to exercise extreme care in determining a student's three reading levels. It is always best to give a student easier material than to give or recommend a book to the student that might be difficult and frustrating.

In most cases the three reading levels serve as a starting point for effective reading instruction. Because the reading levels are determined in a relatively short period of time, they may not be entirely accurate. You should not, therefore, consider a student's three reading levels to be rigid and static. If, in working with the student, you find that the student's various reading levels are not accurate, make the necessary adjustments. Keep in mind that the passages in the Basic Reading Inventory provide a limited sample of student reading behavior and that the assessment was done one on one. Adjustments, based on classroom performance and other relevant information, should be made when necessary.

Estimating Bob's Reading Levels

Interpreting the summary of Bob's reading, presented in Figure 3-2 on the next page, requires some judgment. The circled levels in Figure 3-2 indicate the levels to which the scores are closest. Note that *total* miscues are recorded for word recognition in context.

All the scores for the first- and third-grade levels present no problems because the numerals correspond to those given in Tables 2.1, 2.2, and 2.3. At the second-grade level, however, word recognition in context is below the criteria in Table 2.2 for a clear independent level. Because Bob's other two scores at the second-grade level are marked independent with strong scores, you

FIGURE 3-2. Summary of Bob's Performance on Form A of the Basic Reading Inventory

Grade	Word Recognition						Comprehension	
	Isolation (Word Lists)				Context (Passages)		Form A	
	Sight	Analy-sis	Total	Level	Miscues*	Level	Questions Missed	Level
1	20	0	20	Ind.	1	Ind.	1	Ind.
2	19	1	20	Ind.	3	Ind./Inst.	0	Ind.
3	13	3	16	Inst.	5	Inst.	2½	Inst.
4	8	3	11	Frust.	8	Inst./Frust.	6	Frust.

*Refers to *total* miscues in this example

may hypothesize that second grade is probably his independent level. For the fourth-grade level, Bob achieved the instructional/frustration level for word recognition in context and this score was closer to frustration than instructional. In addition, his scores for word recognition in isolation and comprehension are at the frustration level. Bob is unable to comprehend the material satisfactorily, so fourth grade is likely to be Bob's frustration level. Now, by analyzing Bob's performance *within* a given graded passage and *between* the four graded passages, you can verify earlier hypotheses and make a judgment that his three reading levels are: independent—second grade, instructional—third grade, and frustration—fourth grade.

You should also note that it is possible for some students to have a range of several grades within the instructional level. If, for example, Bob's scores in Figure 3-2 were changed so that the comprehension score at the second-grade level was two questions missed, his three reading levels would probably be: independent—first grade, instructional—second grade and third grade, and frustration—fourth grade. Given a range of instructional levels, where should Bob be placed for instruction? Place him in second-grade reading materials and carefully monitor his progress. If he does well at this level, you should consider a temporary placement in third-grade reading materials and monitor his reading at this level. Generally, it is easier to move a student to a higher level than to a lower level.

Estimating Pablo's Reading Levels

Another summary sheet that requires judgment is shown in Figure 3-3. Study the percentages and make a judgment with regard to Pablo's independent, instructional, and frustration levels before continuing. Remember that the circled levels in Figure 3-3 indicate the levels to which scores are closest. Note that *total* miscues are recorded for word recognition in context.

At the fourth-grade level, you must resolve Pablo's word recognition score in context. Two significant miscues could be either independent or instructional; however, by examining the other scores *within* that level, you should judge fourth grade as his independent level because of his near-perfect scores for word recognition in isolation and silent reading comprehension. The fifth-grade level requires judgment in oral reading comprehension. Because the score in comprehension is near the independent level and the other three scores at this grade level are independent, you should conclude that the fifth-grade level is also independent. At the sixth-grade level, the two significant miscues for word recognition in context are probably best identified as instructional (even though his word recognition is strong) because Pablo's other three scores are instructional.

FIGURE 3-3. Summary of Pablo's Performance on Form A and Form D of the Basic Reading Inventory

Grade	Word Recognition						Comprehension			
	Isolation (Word Lists)				Context (Passages)		Form A		Form D	
	Sight	Analy-sis	Total	Level	Mis-cues*	Level	Ques-tions Missed	Level	Ques-tions Missed	Level
4	20	0	20	Ind.	2	(Ind.)/Inst.	0	Ind.	1	Ind.
5	19	1	20	Ind.	1	Ind.	1½	(Ind.)/Inst.	1	Ind.
6	16	2	18	Inst.	2	(Ind.)/Inst.	2½	Inst.	2½	Inst.
7	16	1	17	Inst.	8	Inst./(Frust.)	4½	Inst./(Frust.)	5	Frust.
8	10	4	14	Inst.	5	Inst.	5	Frust.	6	Frust.

*Refers to *total* miscues in this example

The seventh-grade level requires judgment in two areas: word recognition in context and oral reading comprehension. Both of these scores, according to the scoring guide, appear to be nearer the frustration level, so a tentative judgment for the seventh-grade level is frustration. Judgment is required at the eighth-grade level because the words in isolation score and the words in context score are both instructional. Both comprehension scores, however, are clearly frustration. In addition, because the seventh-grade level was judged to be frustration, the eighth-grade level, by definition, would also be frustration.

You must now decide on Pablo's reading levels. From the earlier judgments, his three reading levels would probably be independent—fifth grade, instructional—sixth grade, and frustration—seventh grade. Although Pablo is quite good at pronouncing words at the seventh- and eighth-grade levels, considerable emphasis was placed on comprehension and these levels were considered to be too difficult.

Contrasting Examples: Reading Levels for Aaron and Hem

Those who have given reading inventories have noticed that some students make many miscues but are still able to answer many of the comprehension questions. Other students are able to recognize most of the words but have difficulty answering the comprehension questions. How are the reading levels of such students best estimated?

Estimating Aaron's Reading Levels

Aaron's reading performance is presented in Figure 3-4. Look at his performance in word recognition. It is clear in grades five and six that he is having difficulty pronouncing words in the word lists and graded passages. His comprehension, however, is not clearly frustration at grades five or six. Aaron appears to have great difficulty in word recognition, but his comprehension could be characterized as near instructional level at grade five and clearly instructional or better at grade six. Because the goal of reading is comprehension, some teachers may tend to emphasize Aaron's ability to comprehend in spite of many miscues. There is a problem with this sort of emphasis—it fails to acknowledge that both word recognition and comprehension must be taken into account when determining reading levels. An over-emphasis on comprehension may lead to placement in materials where Aaron would make many miscues, lack fluency, and likely regard reading as a frustrating experience. He would have to work so hard to construct meaning that the joys of reading would be lost.

FIGURE 3-4. Summary of Aaron's Performance on Form A of the Basic Reading Inventory

| Grade | Word Recognition | | | | | | Comprehension | |
| | Isolation (Word Lists) | | | | Context (Passages) | | Form A | |
	Sight	Analysis	Total	Level	Miscues*	Level	Questions Missed	Level
3	18	2	20	Ind.	1	Ind.	0	Ind.
4	15	3	18	Inst.	5	Inst.	2½	Inst.
5	11	2	13	Frust.	10	Frust.	3	(Inst.)/Frust.
6	9	1	10	Frust.	11	Frust.	2	Ind./(Inst.)

*Refers to *total* miscues in this example

Reflective teachers will recognize the need to help Aaron strengthen his sight vocabulary and word identification skills. Based on the data in Figure 3-4, Aaron's independent reading level is third grade. His instructional level is best characterized as grade four because his scores for words in isolation, words in context, and comprehension are all instructional level. Grade five would be Aaron's frustration level because of his great difficulty with word recognition. The teacher should realize that Aaron has the ability to comprehend at higher levels—possibly because his background knowledge and/or intelligence allow him to compensate for his limited abilities in word recognition. A systematic analysis of Aaron's miscues could provide the basis for specific instruction that is responsive to Aaron's needs. Responsive instruction, coupled with plenty of reading materials at Aaron's instructional level, will likely result in strengthening his sight vocabulary, fluency, and overall confidence in reading. It might then be appropriate to try materials at the fifth-grade level that are of interest to Aaron.

Estimating Hem's Reading Levels

In contrast to Aaron, Hem has the ability to recognize words (see Figure 3-5). His scores for words in isolation and words in context never reach the frustration level. Comprehension, however, is an entirely different matter. He has no clear independent level in comprehension. Even at second grade, Hem is experiencing difficulties with comprehension. Those difficulties persist with each of the subsequent passages Hem reads. The ability to pronounce words without adequate comprehension is often characterized as word calling or barking at print. Situations of this type suggest that a student may have limited background experiences, poor vocabulary knowledge, lowered mental abilities, and/or limited oral language skills in English.

Hem's teacher should explore possible explanations for his reading behavior. It is possible that his background experiences are limited. Based on the data available, Hem does not have a clear independent level, but second grade might be his independent level as long as he has the necessary background knowledge for the selection being read or the necessary background is built prior to reading. Third grade could be Hem's instructional level, but his teacher must be sure that needed concepts and ample background are built before reading. Materials at grades four and five should not be used for instruction unless adequate attention is devoted to ensure that Hem has the necessary background experiences. Hem's teacher will probably need to help him expand his meaning vocabulary, teach him that the goal of reading is comprehension, and develop strategies he can use for comprehension monitoring. See Johns and Lenski (2010) for teaching strategies in these areas. Plenty of easy reading in materials where Hem possesses the necessary background knowledge, coupled with retellings and discussions about the material, should help Hem strengthen his reading.

FIGURE 3-5. Summary of Hem's Performance on Form A of the Basic Reading Inventory

| Grade | Word Recognition | | | | | | Comprehension | |
| | Isolation (Word Lists) | | | | Context (Passages) | | Form A | |
	Sight	Analy-sis	Total	Level	Miscues*	Level	Questions Missed	Level
2	20	0	20	Ind.	0	Ind.	3	(Inst.)/Frust.
3	19	1	20	Ind.	1	Ind.	4	Inst./(Frust.)
4	17	2	19	Ind.	2	(Ind.)/Inst.	5	Frust.
5	16	1	17	Inst.	3	Ind./(Inst.)	5	Frust.

*Refers to *total* miscues in this example

Practice Exercises in Determining Reading Levels

To give you an opportunity to practice determining students' reading levels, Figures 3-6 (Nick), 3-7 (Antonio), and 3-8 (Corey) have been adapted from the research of Johns and L'Allier (2004). Two additional practice exercises (Figures 3-9 and 3-10) are also included. You should complete the three practice exercises by filling in the numerical and reading level data where necessary. In Figure 3-6, for example, Nick's grade two total for words in isolation and the corresponding reading level need to be determined. Nick's reading level for grade two comprehension and the grade three words in context also need to be determined. Then all the data should be carefully considered as you estimate Nick's three reading levels and write them in the space provided. You can check your results by looking on the CD for the Answers for Practice Exercises in Determining Reading Levels for Figures 3-6 through 3-10.

The practice exercises in Figures 3-7, 3-8, 3-9, and 3-10 each have more information that you need to complete before reading levels can be determined. The answers for these practice exercises can be found on the CD. These practice exercises consider only quantitative information; hence there is no opportunity to observe the students' behaviors and gather useful qualitative information. These exercises, nevertheless, should help you gain additional expertise in scoring the Basic Reading Inventory.

Figure 3-6. Practice Exercise to Determine Nick's Reading Levels

Eleventh Edition

BASIC READING INVENTORY PERFORMANCE BOOKLET

Jerry L. Johns, Ph.D.

Form A

Student _Nick_   Grade _____ Gender   M   F   Date of Test _____

School _____   Examiner _____   Date of Birth _____

Address _____   Current Book/Level _____   Age _____

SUMMARY OF STUDENT'S READING PERFORMANCE

Grade	Word Recognition						Comprehension		Reading Rate	
	Isolation (Word Lists)				Context (Passages)		Form F		Words per Minute (WPM)	Norm Group Percentile
	Sight	Analysis	Total	Level	Miscues	Level	Questions Missed	Level		
PP1										
PP2	16	3	19	Ind.	0	Ind.	0	Ind.		
P	15	3	18	Inst.	1	Ind.	1/2	Ind.		
1	16	4	20	Ind.	2	Ind./Inst.	1	Ind.		
2	14	2			5	Inst.	1 1/2			← Fill in.
3	9	2	11	Frust.	10		5	Frust.		
4										
5										
6										
7										
8										
9										
10										
11										
12										

ESTIMATE OF READING LEVELS

← Fill in.

Independent _____   Instructional _____   Frustration _____

Word Recognition Scoring Guide

Total Miscues	Level	Significant Miscues
0–1	Independent	0–1
2–4	Ind./Inst.	2
5	Instructional	3
6–9	Inst./Frust.	4
10 +	Frustration	5 +

Comprehension Scoring Guide

Questions Missed	Level
0–1	Independent
1 1/2–2	Ind./Inst.
2 1/2	Instructional
3–4 1/2	Inst./Frust.
5 +	Frustration

Scoring Guide for Graded Word Lists

Independent	Instructional	Inst./Frust.	Frustration
20 19	18 17 16	15 14	13 or less

1. **Complete the summary where necessary.**
2. **Study the overall results.**
3. **Estimate reading levels. Fill in the chart.**
   Remember:
   - **Reading levels generally go in order.**
   - **Only the instructional level can have a range of two or more levels.**

Figure 3-7. Practice Exercise to Determine Antonio's Reading Levels

BASIC READING INVENTORY PERFORMANCE BOOKLET

Jerry L. Johns, Ph.D.

Student _Antonio_____   Grade _____ Gender   M   F   Date of Test _____

School _____   Examiner _____   Date of Birth _____

Address _____   Current Book/Level _____   Age _____

SUMMARY OF STUDENT'S READING PERFORMANCE

| Grade | Word Recognition | | | | | | Comprehension | | Reading Rate | |
| | Isolation (Word Lists) | | | | Context (Passages) | | Form F | | Words per Minute (WPM) | Norm Group Percentile |
	Sight	Analysis	Total	Level	Miscues	Level	Questions Missed	Level		
PP1										
PP2										
P										
1	20	0	20	Ind.	1	Ind.	2	Ind./Inst.		
2	19	1			4		1			
3	13	2	15	Inst./Frust.	5	Inst.	2½	Inst.		
4	9	4			8		5½			
5	6	2	8	Frust.						
6										
7										
8										
9										
10										
11										
12										

Fill in. →

ESTIMATE OF READING LEVELS

← Fill in.

Independent _____   Instructional _____   Frustration _____

Word Recognition Scoring Guide		
Total Miscues	Level	Significant Miscues
0–1	Independent	0–1
2–4	Ind./Inst.	2
5	Instructional	3
6–9	Inst./Frust.	4
10 +	Frustration	5 +

Comprehension Scoring Guide	
Questions Missed	Level
0–1	Independent
1½–2	Ind./Inst.
2½	Instructional
3–4½	Inst./Frust.
5 +	Frustration

Scoring Guide for Graded Word Lists			
Independent	Instructional	Inst./Frust.	Frustration
20 19	18 17 16	15 14	13 or less

1. **Complete the summary where necessary.**
2. **Study the overall results.**
3. **Estimate reading levels. Fill in the chart. Remember:**
   - **Reading levels generally go in order.**
   - **Only the instructional level can have a range of two or more levels.**

Figure 3-8. Practice Exercise to Determine Corey's Reading Levels

Eleventh Edition

BASIC READING INVENTORY PERFORMANCE BOOKLET

Jerry L. Johns, Ph.D.

Form A

Student _Corey_

Grade _____ Gender M F

Date of Test _____

School _____

Examiner _____

Date of Birth _____

Address _____

Current Book/Level _____

Age _____

SUMMARY OF STUDENT'S READING PERFORMANCE

Grade	Word Recognition						Comprehension		Reading Rate	
	Isolation (Word Lists)				Context (Passages)		Form F		Words per Minute (WPM)	Norm Group Percentile
	Sight	Analysis	Total	Level	Miscues	Level	Questions Missed	Level		
PP1										
PP2										
P										
1										
2	18	1								
3	18	2			2		1			← Fill in.
4	15	3			6		2			
5	11	2			10		4			
6	9	1			12		6			
7										
8										
9										
10										
11										
12										

ESTIMATE OF READING LEVELS ← Fill in.

Independent _____ Instructional _____ Frustration _____

Word Recognition Scoring Guide

Total Miscues	Level	Significant Miscues
0–1	Independent	0–1
2–4	Ind./Inst.	2
5	Instructional	3
6–9	Inst./Frust.	4
10 +	Frustration	5 +

Comprehension Scoring Guide

Questions Missed	Level
0–1	Independent
1½–2	Ind./Inst.
2½	Instructional
3–4½	Inst./Frust.
5 +	Frustration

Scoring Guide for Graded Word Lists

Independent	Instructional	Inst./Frust.	Frustration
20 19	18 17 16	15 14	13 or less

1. **Complete the summary where necessary.**
2. **Study the overall results.**
3. **Estimate reading levels. Fill in the chart. Remember:**
   - **Reading levels generally go in order.**
   - **Only the instructional level can have a range of two or more levels.**

Figure 3-9. Practice Exercise to Determine Marcus' Reading Levels

Eleventh
Edition

BASIC READING INVENTORY PERFORMANCE BOOKLET

Form
A

Jerry L. Johns, Ph.D.

Student _Marcus_ 　　　　　　　　　Grade _____ Gender M F 　Date of Test _____

School _____ 　Examiner _____ 　Date of Birth _____

Address _____ 　Current Book/Level _____ 　Age _____

SUMMARY OF STUDENT'S READING PERFORMANCE

Grade	Word Recognition						Comprehension		Reading Rate	
	Isolation (Word Lists)				Context (Passages)		Form F		Words per Minute (WPM)	Norm Group Percentile
	Sight	Analysis	Total	Level	Miscues	Level	Questions Missed	Level		
PP1										
PP2										
P										
1	19	1								
2	17	1			3		0			
3	17	2			3		$1\frac{1}{2}$			⇐ Fill in.
4	14	4			4		1			
5	13	1			7		$1\frac{1}{2}$			
6	11	3			11		4			
7										
8										
9					ESTIMATE OF READING LEVELS					⇐ Fill in.
10										
11										
12					Independent _____ Instructional _____ Frustration _____					

Word Recognition Scoring Guide

Total Miscues	Level	Significant Miscues
0–1	Independent	0–1
2–4	Ind./Inst.	2
5	Instructional	3
6–9	Inst./Frust.	4
10 +	Frustration	5 +

Comprehension Scoring Guide

Questions Missed	Level
0–1	Independent
$1\frac{1}{2}$–2	Ind./Inst.
$2\frac{1}{2}$	Instructional
3–$4\frac{1}{2}$	Inst./Frust.
5 +	Frustration

Scoring Guide for Graded Word Lists

Independent	Instructional	Inst./Frust.	Frustration
20 19	18 17 16	15 14	13 or less

1. **Complete the summary where necessary.**
2. **Study the overall results.**
3. **Estimate reading levels. Fill in the chart. Remember:**
   - **Reading levels generally go in order.**
   - **Only the instructional level can have a range of two or more levels.**

Figure 3-10. Practice Exercise to Determine Kyle's Reading Levels

Eleventh Edition

BASIC READING INVENTORY PERFORMANCE BOOKLET

Jerry L. Johns, Ph.D.

Form A

Student _Kyle_   Grade _____ Gender M F   Date of Test _____

School _____   Examiner _____   Date of Birth _____

Address _____   Current Book/Level _____   Age _____

SUMMARY OF STUDENT'S READING PERFORMANCE

Grade	Word Recognition						Comprehension		Reading Rate	
	Isolation (Word Lists)				Context (Passages)		Form F		Words per Minute (WPM)	Norm Group Percentile
	Sight	Analysis	Total	Level	Miscues	Level	Questions Missed	Level		
PP1										
PP2	20				0		0			
P	19	1			2		2			
1	17	2			2		1			
2	14	3			6		3			
3	12	4			6		$2\frac{1}{2}$			⇐ Fill in.
4	11	2			9		$4\frac{1}{2}$			
5										
6										
7										
8										
9							ESTIMATE OF READING LEVELS			
10										⇐ Fill in.
11							Independent _____ Instructional _____ Frustration _____			
12										

Word Recognition Scoring Guide		
Total Miscues	Level	Significant Miscues
0–1	Independent	0–1
2–4	Ind./Inst.	2
5	Instructional	3
6–9	Inst./Frust.	4
10 +	Frustration	5 +

Comprehension Scoring Guide	
Questions Missed	Level
0–1	Independent
$1\frac{1}{2}$–2	Ind./Inst.
$2\frac{1}{2}$	Instructional
3–$4\frac{1}{2}$	Inst./Frust.
5 +	Frustration

Scoring Guide for Graded Word Lists			
Independent	Instructional	Inst./Frust.	Frustration
20 19	18 17 16	15 14	13 or less

1. **Complete the summary where necessary.**
2. **Study the overall results.**
3. **Estimate reading levels. Fill in the chart. Remember:**
   - **Reading levels generally go in order.**
   - **Only the instructional level can have a range of two or more levels.**

SECTION 4

Instructional Uses of Inventory Results

Sharing assessment results at a parent-student-teacher conference can be helpful.

In addition to using the Basic Reading Inventory to estimate a student's three reading levels, the results can also be used to study the student's reading behavior in order to provide responsive interventions (Haager, Klingnev, & Vaughn, 2007; Johns, L'Allier, & Johns, 2012). Kibby (1995) notes that a key question in a diagnostic decision-making model is determining which reading strategies and skills are strengths and limitations for the student. Carefully evaluating a student's performance on reading inventories cannot be surpassed for the wealth of useful diagnostic data that they provide. Three strategies for evaluating inventory results are suggested for word identification. Two strategies are provided for analyzing the student's comprehension. Fluency is also considered.

Determining Word Identification Strategies

Any system of analyzing the student's word identification strategies should be guided by a careful and thoughtful analysis of oral reading performance. Conrad and Shankin (1999) suggest helpful ways to use miscues to understand the student's reading. In addition, Johnson, Kress, and Pikulski (1987) provide several questions that may help guide the overall analysis:

- Does the student's oral reading reflect a balanced use of sight vocabulary, context clues, phonics, structural analysis, and syntactic clues? Do weaknesses appear to exist in any of these areas?

69

- Is the student's oral reading fluent or is the student's reading hesitant or word by word?

- To what extent do the student's miscues alter or interfere with the meaning of the passages read?

- When miscues occur, does the student appear to be monitoring his or her reading by rereading, correcting unacceptable miscues (those that adversely affect meaning), and/or noting that the passage is difficult? Are the miscues influenced by the student's dialect?

- Does the student's limited vocabulary, background, or concept development appear to be affecting oral reading?

- Are any patterns suggested by analyzing the student's miscues and oral reading behavior?

Strategy 1 Simple Error Analysis

Three Strategies for Evaluating Inventory Results

1—Simple Error Analysis: to quickly identify general patterns in a student's miscues for instructional interventions.

2—Miscue Analysis Tally: to analyze the patterns in miscues to determine areas where a student is likely to benefit from instruction.

3—Advanced Qualitative Analysis: to provide an in-depth analysis of a student's miscues to determine types of miscues, graphic similarity, acceptability in context, and self-corrections to help focus instruction.

Simple error analysis is one method for analyzing the miscues made during oral reading in an effort to find patterns. These patterns may indicate certain tendencies in word identification or general reading behavior. By recording a student's miscues from the reading inventory on a sheet similar to that in Figure 4-1, you may make hypotheses about a student's needs in reading. A reproducible master for your use is found in Appendix B. The recommended procedure is to **use miscues from passages that are at the student's independent, instructional, and instructional/frustration levels.** Suppose, for example, that Sam's errors from the oral reading passages revealed the information contained in Figure 4-1. Based on these data, it would appear that Sam is able to apply the initial sounds in the words he has difficulty pronouncing. He has difficulty, however, with the middle of words. After further analysis of his medial errors, it would seem that a lack of vowel knowledge may be contributing to his difficulties in word recognition. It is also evident that many of these miscues distort the meaning of the reading selection (*ran* for *rain*, *well* for *will*, *barn* for *burn*, and so on). Sam may be helped with the strategy lessons from Scenario 5 in Section 5 on page 121. Sam has also made several other substitutions; however, these substitutions (*a* for *the*; *road* for *street*, and so on) do not result in significant changes in the meaning of the passage and do not require any instruction. The repetitions Sam made may indicate a problem that requires the attention of the teacher or the implementation of an effective reading strategy. Evaluate such repetitions within the context of Scenario 1 in Section 5 on page 117.

A different student may show weaknesses in other areas. Pete, for example, may have many words under the section "Omissions." Perhaps he does not attempt to pronounce many of the words he does not recognize immediately. Pete may, therefore, need instruction in developing more effective strategies for anticipating words through the use of contextual and syntactic cues (see Scenarios 2 and 3 in Section 5 on pages 118–120).

Still another student may fail to recognize many word endings. Such miscues may be indicative of a possible problem in structural analysis (*s, es, ed, ing,* and so on). Remember, however, that some speakers of a particular dialect may omit word endings. Miscues of this type, as long as they make sense in the reader's dialect, should not be regarded as significant; furthermore, they do not require instructional intervention.

When analyzing word recognition by charting miscues, be careful to base conclusions on patterns of miscues, not just a few miscues in any given category. Remember that only miscues at the student's independent and instructional levels should be charted for analysis; the frustration level indicates that the reading process has broken down. Miscues noted at the student's frustration level may be used to verify tendencies noted at the student's independent and instructional levels. The graded word lists, if used in this type of analysis, should be kept separate because research (Allington & McGill-Franzen, 1980) has revealed that students made different miscues when reading the same words in a random order instead of in context.

Caution

Figure 4-1. Summary of Sam's Oral Reading Performance

SUBSTITUTIONS			
Different Beginnings	**Different Middles**	**Different Endings**	**Different in Several Parts**
	ran for rain naw – now well – will walk – work barn – burn	fly for flew had – have big – bigger in – into	a for the road – street big – huge
Insertions	**Omissions**	**Repetitions**	**Miscellaneous**
big always	she spider(s) many	/ / / /	

Your hypotheses regarding a student's tendencies in word identification should be considered tentative and verified or discounted through classroom instruction, observations, and other formal and informal assessment results. Also remember that word identification is not an end in itself; it is a means for constructing meaning of the text. It is often possible for a student to construct meaning from reading material even when he or she makes several miscues. Instruction in word identification, therefore, should be based on strategies that will help the student comprehend text and develop greater automaticity in word recognition.

Strategy 2 Miscue Analysis Tally

The teacher's passages for Forms A, B, C, D, and E have provisions to tally miscues and other reading behaviors as shown in Figure 4-2. The generic sheet for use with Forms LL and LI can be found in Appendix B. The tallies should be completed after the assessment session with the student has been completed.

The example in Figure 4-2 on the following page is based on Jeff's oral reading in Figure 2-5 (page 33). Each miscue should be considered and tallied accordingly. Jeff substituted *Bob* for *Bill* so a tally mark is placed in the substitution column. Because this miscue resulted in a meaning change, a tally mark is also placed under the meaning change column. The same columns were also marked for the miscue *so* because it was a substitution miscue that also changed the meaning. The miscue *trees* is an insertion, so a tally mark is placed in the insertion column on the appropriate line of the text. Jeff's teacher judged that this miscue did not change the meaning, so no other column is marked. The miscue *was* is a reversal, and a tally mark is placed in the reversal column. This miscue resulted in a meaning change, and a tally mark was placed in the meaning change column corresponding to the appropriate line of text. The miscue *minute*

Figure 4-2. Jeff's Miscue Tally and Reading Behavior on a Graded Passage

Student Booklet copy is on page 14.

A 8224 (Grade 2) Activating Background: Read the title to yourself; then tell me what you think will happen.

Background: Low |———+———| High

Bill at Camp

		MISCUES						
		Substitution	Insertion	Omission	Reversal	Repetition	Self-Correction of Unacceptable Miscue	Meaning Change (Significant Miscue)
It was the first time Bill went to *Bob*	8	1						1
camp. He was very happy to be there. Soon *So*	17	1						1
he went for a walk in the woods to look for	28							
many kinds of leaves. He found leaves	35							
from some maple ˇand oak trees. As Bill *trees*	43		1					
walked in the woods, he saw some animal *was*	51				1			1
tracks. At that moment, a mouse ran into *minute*	59	1						
a small hole by a tree. Bill wondered if the	69							
tracks were made by the mouse. He looked	77							
around for other animals. He did not see	85							
any. The last thing Bill saw was an old	94							
bird nest in a pine tree.	100							
TOTAL		3	1	0	1	0	0	3

good phrasing and intonation

Total Miscues [5]   Significant Miscues [3]

Word Recognition Scoring Guide		
Total Miscues	Level	Significant Miscues
0–1	Independent	0–1
2–4	Ind./Inst.	2
5	Instructional	3
6–9	Inst./Frust.	4
10 +	Frustration	5 +

Oral Reading Rate	Norm Group Percentile
65)6000 *92* WPM	☐ 90 ☐ 75 ☒ 50 ☐ 25 ☐ 10

for *moment* was a substitution that his teacher felt did not result in a significant meaning change; therefore, a tally mark was only placed in the substitution column corresponding to the line of text where the miscue was made.

Once the tallies for miscues and other reading behaviors are completed for **all** the passages read by the student, they can be summarized on the two sample charts shown below in Figure 4-3. These charts are also contained in Appendix B for your reproduction and use.

After completing the Miscue Tally and Reading Behavior Summary Charts, look for patterns in order to hypothesize areas where the student might profit from strategy lessons. In the sample charts shown in Figure 4-3, the student appears to have a pattern of omissions. You might offer responsive instruction for omissions by considering some of the ideas in Scenario 3 in Section 5 on page 119. The student in this example also corrected a number of miscues that changed the meaning. Behavior of this sort should be seen as a reading strength, and the student should be praised for monitoring reading and using correction strategies. Some effort should be made to increase the student's sight vocabulary to build greater automaticity with words encountered during reading.

Figure 4-3. Sample Miscue Tally and Reading Behavior Summary Charts

Total Miscues Across Passages Read	Type of Miscue			
	Substitution	Insertion	Omission	Reversal
	3	2	8	0

Other Reading Behaviors (Totals)	Repetition	Self-Correction of Unacceptable Miscues	Meaning Change
	2	6	2

Strategy 3 Advanced Qualitative Analysis

A more advanced system for analyzing miscues has been developed by Christie (1979) and is presented in Figure 4-4 on page 74. A reproducible master is found in Appendix B. This system draws upon the work of Goodman, Watson, and Burke (1987) and the suggestions of Williamson and Young (1974). The following qualitative analysis has been adapted, with permission, from Christie. For convenience, the procedure is presented in the following five-step outline.

Step 1—Select Miscues for Analysis

A. Select miscues from oral passages at the student's **independent** and **instructional** levels only. Record the following types of miscues on the Analysis Sheet:
 1. substitutions
 2. omissions
 3. insertions
 4. word-order reversals
 5. nonwords

Figure 4-4. System for the Qualitative Analysis of Miscues

MISCUE	TEXT	GRAPHIC SIMILARITY			CONTEXT		Self-Correction of Unacceptable Miscues
		Beginning	Middle	End	Acceptable	Unacceptable	
Column Total							
Number of Miscues Analyzed							
Percentage							

Profile Sheet

PREDICTION STRATEGY

Graphic Similarity
B   M   E

100%
90
80
70
60
50
40
30
20
10

___% ___% ___%

Miscues Acceptable in Context

100%
90
80
70
60
50
40
30
20
10

___%

CORRECTION STRATEGY

Unacceptable Miscues Self-Corrected

100%
90
80
70
60
50
40
30
20
10

___%

B. Do *not* use the following types of miscues:
   1. repetitions
   2. hestitations
   3. prompts
   4. disregard for punctuation
   5. omissions of entire lines of text
   6. variations in pronunciation involving dialect
   7. partial words

Step 2—Record Miscues on the Analysis Sheet

A. Record each type of miscue as follows:
   1. substitutions

   The girl was very ~~glad~~ sad.

MISCUE	TEXT
glad	sad

   2. omissions

   He went to ~~the~~ church.

MISCUE	TEXT
———	the

   3. insertions

   The road was *very* narrow.

MISCUE	TEXT
very	———

   4. word order reversals

   Jill sat quietly at her desk. (*at her desk quietly*)

MISCUE	TEXT
at her desk quietly	quietly at her desk

   5. nonwords

   The *redon* region was large.

MISCUE	TEXT
redon	region

B. Special Rules
   1. Record identical substitutions only once.
   2. If the reader makes several attempts at a word, record the first complete word or nonword substitution.

   Example: He went up
   2. stars
   1. st-
   the stairs.

MISCUE	TEXT
stars	stairs

   3. If a miscue causes the reader to immediately make another miscue in one apparent thought, record as one complex miscue.

   Example: He could *have danced* dance all night.

MISCUE	TEXT
have danced	dance

Step 3—Analyze Miscues

A. Graphic Similarity
   1. Miscues to Analyze
      a. Only substitutions of a single word or nonword for a single text item should be analyzed for graphic similarity.
      b. Do *not* analyze omissions, insertions, reversals, or substitutions that involve more than one word. In these cases, draw *Xs* through the three boxes under GRAPHIC SIMILARITY.
      c. Example:

         went
         He walked to ~~the~~ school.

MISCUE	TEXT	GRAPHIC SIMILARITY		
		Beginning	Middle	End
went	walked	✓		
————	the	✕	✕	✕

   2. Judging Graphic Similarity
      a. Compare the sequence and shape of the letters in the miscue with those in the text item. Place a check in the appropriate box if the beginning, middle, and/or end of the miscue is graphically similar to the corresponding part of the text item.
      b. Guidelines for judging graphic similarity
         (1) divide the miscue and text item into corresponding thirds.
         (2) Use the following criteria for judging the different thirds as being graphically similar:
            (a) *Beginning*—the first letter of the miscue and the first letter of the text item must be identical.
            (b) *Middle* and *End*—the letters in the miscue and text item need only be similar in sequence and configuration.
         (3) Special cases
            (a) Two-letter text items—place an *X* in the "Middle" box and judge only for beginning and ending similarity.

(b) One-letter text items—place an X in the "Middle" and "End" boxes and judge only for beginning similarity.

c. Examples:

MISCUE	TEXT	GRAPHIC SIMILARITY		
		Beginning	Middle	End
men	man	√	√	√
here	said		√	
his	this		√	√
walk	walked	√	√	
cub	carry	√		
meal	material	√		√
be	by	√	⊠	
if	it	√	⊠	
the	a		⊠	⊠
an	on		⊠	√

B. Acceptability in Context
  1. Judge all miscues recorded on the Analysis Sheet for acceptability in context. Refer to the graded passages that were coded to make these judgments.
  2. To judge the acceptability of a miscue, take the following two factors into consideration:
    a. *Syntax*—Is the miscue grammatically acceptable in the manner in which the sentence was read?
    b. *Semantics*—Does the miscue make sense in the context of the sentence and the preceding portion of the passage?
  3. Marking the Analysis Sheet
    a. If the miscue meets **both** criteria, check the box in the "Acceptable" column.
    b. If either criterion is not met, check the box in the "Unacceptable" column.
    c. If the unacceptable miscue is successfully self-corrected by the reader, place a check in the "Self-Correction of Unacceptable Miscues" column.

	CONTEXT		Self-Correction of Unacceptable Miscues
	Acceptable	Unacceptable	
Acceptable in context; no self-correction	√		
Unacceptable in context; no self-correction		√	
Unacceptable in context; self-correction		√	√

Step 4—Determine Totals and Percentages

A. Graphic Similarity
   1. Count the number of checks in each column (Beginning, Middle, and End) and place the totals in the boxes marked Column Total.
   2. For each column, count the number of boxes that do not have Xs in them. Place each total in the box marked Number of Miscues Analyzed.
   3. Determine the percentage for each column by dividing each Column Total by the Number of Miscues Analyzed and then multiplying by 100.

B. Acceptability in Context
   1. Count the number of checks in the "Acceptable" column and enter the total in the appropriate Column Total box.
   2. "Acceptable" column *only*
      a. Enter the total number of miscues analyzed for acceptability in context in the box marked Number of Miscues Analyzed. (This should equal the total number of miscues recorded on the Analysis Sheet.)
      b. Determine the percentage of miscues acceptable in context by dividing the Column Total by the Number of Miscues Analyzed and then multiplying by 100.

C. Percentage of Unacceptable Miscues That Were Self-Corrected
   1. Count the number of checks in the "Unacceptable" column and enter the total in the appropriate Column Total box.
   2. Count the number of miscues in the "Unacceptable" Column that were self-corrected. Be sure to count only self-corrections for **Unacceptable** miscues. Place this total in the Column Total box in the "Self-Correction of Unacceptable Miscues" column.

		GRAPHIC SIMILARITY			CONTEXT		
MISCUE	TEXT	Beginning	Middle	End	Acceptable	Unacceptable	Self-Correction of Unacceptable Miscues
men	man	√	√	√		√	√
here	said		√			√	√
his	this		√	√		√	
walk	walked	√	√		√		
cub	carry	√				√	√
meal	material	√		√		√	
be	by	√	✕			√	√
if	it	√	✕			√	
the	a		✕	✕	√		
an	on		✕	√		√	√
Column Total		6	4	4	2	8	5
Number of Miscues Analyzed		10	6	9	10		
Percentage		60	67	44	20		63

3. Determine the percentage of unacceptable miscues that were self-corrected by dividing the Column Total of "Self-Correction of Unacceptable Miscues" by the Column Total of "Unacceptable" miscues and then multiplying by 100. Place this percentage in the Percentage Column under "Self-Correction of Unacceptable Miscues."

Step 5—Complete Profile Sheet

A. Transfer the percentages from the Analysis Sheet to the blanks below the appropriate bar graphs as shown here.
B. Darken in the bar graphs.

Profile Sheet

Once the three parts of the Profile Sheet are completed, reading strategy lessons and interventions can be developed. The two Prediction Strategy graphs help to determine whether the student is relying on graphic cues, context cues, or both in predicting upcoming text and decoding unknown words. When both graphs are similar, the student has a balanced prediction strategy. If, on the other hand, the two graphs show a marked difference, the student may be depending excessively on one type of cue.

If the Graphic Similarity graph is high and the Context graph is low, the student may be relying excessively on graphic (letter) cues. If this is the case, intervention lessons that emphasize the use of context cues may be warranted. See Scenarios 3 (page 119) and 6 (page 123) in Section 5.

When the Graphic Similarity graph is low and the Context graph is high, the student may be relying heavily on context cues. Intervention lessons could include asking the student a question like, "What word do you know that begins like _____ that would make sense?"

The Correction Strategy graph shows the percentage of unacceptable miscues that were self-corrected by the student. When a large percentage of unacceptable miscues are not corrected (when the Correction Strategy graph is low), the student may need to be taught strategies for monitoring his or her reading. Intervention lessons to help the reader develop a sensitivity to correcting miscues that disrupt meaning may also be needed. Scenario 5 in Section 5 on page 121 contains some useful suggestions. Several additional resources for instructional techniques can be found in the work of Cooper and Kiger (2011), Gillet, Temple, Temple, and Crawford (2012), Gunning (2010), Johns and Lenski (2010), Elish-Piper, Johns, and Lenski (2006), and Walker (2008).

Analyzing Comprehension

To guide the overall assessment of the student's comprehension, the following questions should be considered:

- Does the student appear to know that comprehension is the goal of reading?
- Does the student appear to possess the background (concepts and vocabulary) necessary for understanding the passage?
- Are there significant differences between the student's oral and silent comprehension?
- Do significant comprehension differences exist between literary (narrative) and informational (expository) passages?
- Are there significant differences in comprehension between the shorter passages and the longer passages?
- Does the student appear to have difficulties with specific types of comprehension questions?
- What does the student do when comprehension becomes difficult?
- Does the student monitor his or her reading and use appropriate fix-up strategies?

Two Strategies
for Analyzing
Comprehension

1—Analysis of
comprehension
by question type
2—Analysis
by level of
comprehension

The Basic Reading Inventory contains five different types of comprehension questions coded as follows: (F) fact, (T) topic, (E) experience/evaluation, (I) inference, and (V) vocabulary. Two strategies are suggested for analyzing comprehension performance. For each strategy, **only comprehension questions at the student's independent, instructional, and instructional/frustration levels should be analyzed**. Comprehension questions at the student's frustration level may be used to verify tendencies at the student's independent and instructional levels.

These categories of comprehension questions, although widely used, have little or no empirical support (Schell & Hanna, 1981). In other words, many reading tests claim to measure comprehension skills that authorities cannot show to exist. Although such analysis lacks empirical support, Johnson, Kress, and Pikulski (1987) believe such a procedure is useful to help identify general tendencies in comprehension. Spache (1976) notes that comprehension is composed of three essential elements: (1) a word meaning factor, (2) a relationships-among-ideas factor, and (3) a reasoning factor. He goes on to say that "when the reading teacher has determined by repeated observations that the student apparently does not use a certain type of essential thinking, the remedial course is quite obvious. She may repeatedly ask the student to attempt to answer questions that appear to sample the missing cognitive process" (p. 269). The following strategies described for determining strengths and weaknesses in comprehension offer two systematic ways to gather preliminary evidence indicating that some aspect of a student's comprehension may need attention. You can then support or refute this tentative need through the student's performance in classroom activities, observations, and other assessment data. If a need exists, you can develop appropriate intervention lessons. Remember that the scheme for analyzing comprehension performance is intended to be used informally. It should aid your judgment, not replace it.

Caution

Strategy **1** **Analysis of Comprehension by Question Type**

You can analyze comprehension after recording the number and types of questions the student misses on each passage read at the independent, instructional, and instructional/frustration levels. An example of this procedure, using Dan's comprehension scores, is shown in Figure 4-5. A reproducible master for your use is found in Appendix B. Using such a procedure may enable you to discern patterns of possible difficulty in comprehension. Dan's performance on the comprehension questions marked in Figure 4-5 indicates possible strengths in answering topic and vocabulary questions. Areas of possible weakness include answering fact, evaluation, and inference questions. Because of the limited data upon which these hypotheses are based, Dan's silent reading should also be considered. These hypotheses should then be verified or discounted through observation, instruction, and other relevant data.

Figure 4-5. Summary of Dan's Comprehension Performance in Oral Reading

Grade	Fact (F-6)*	Topic (T-1)	Evaluation (E-1)	Inference (I-1)	Vocabulary (V-1)
	Oral	Oral	Oral	Oral	Oral
P	2/6	0/1	0/1	0/1	0/1
1	1/6	0/1	0/1	0/1	0/1
2	3/6	0/1	0/1	1/1	0/1
3	2/6	0/1	1/1	1/1	0/1
Ratio Missed	8/24	0/4	1/4	2/4	0/4
Percent Missed	33%	0%	25%	50%	0%

*Indicates the type of question and the number of questions in each graded paragraph. For example, F indicates a fact question and 6 signifies that each graded passage contains six F questions.

Now, consider Tony's errors on the comprehension questions. To determine Tony's tendencies in comprehension, complete Figure 4-6 by determining the ratios of comprehension questions missed and the corresponding percentages. First, record the number of questions missed for each question type. Second, determine the percent of errors by dividing the number of errors by the total number of that question type and multiplying by 100. For example, Tony responded to 30 fact questions and missed 4 of them. His error rate for the fact questions was 13 percent ($4 \div 30 = .13; .13 \times 100 = 13\%$). What are Tony's possible strengths and weaknesses in comprehension?

Figure 4-6. Tony's Comprehension Performance in Oral Reading

Grade	Fact (F-6) Oral	Topic (T-1) Oral	Evaluation (E-1) Oral	Inference (I-1) Oral	Vocabulary (V-1) Oral
4	1/6	0/1	0/1	0/1	0/1
5	0/6	0/1	1/1	1/1	0/1
6	1/6	1/1	0/1	0/1	0/1
7	0/6	1/1	0/1	0/1	1/1
8	2/6	1/1	0/1	0/1	1/1
Ratio Missed	4/30	__/__	__/__	__/__	__/__
Percent Missed	13%	__%	__%	__%	__%

During oral reading, Tony missed 4 of 30 fact questions (13%), 3 of 5 topic questions (60%), 1 of 5 evaluation questions (20%), 1 of 5 inference questions (20%), and 2 of 5 vocabulary questions (40%). Based on these percentages, answering topic questions may be hypothesized as an area of weakness. A possible strength is in the area of recalling facts. It seems most appropriate from this analysis to identify topic questions as a possible weakness and responses to fact questions as a possible strength. Whether the areas of evaluation, inference, and vocabulary warrant instructional interventions should be based on additional information gained from classroom observations and relevant performance on reading tasks.

When a student reads orally and silently, it is recommended that the results be combined for both sets of graded passages. This procedure enables you to use a larger sample of behavior on which to make hypotheses. Remember that the student may not always read the same number or level of oral and silent passages. A reproducible master is found in Appendix B. Figure 4-7 contains Tony's comprehension performance from the graded passages that were analyzed previously, as well as his silent reading performance on a different set of graded passages from the Basic Reading Inventory. Complete Figure 4-7 by determining the ratio of questions answered incorrectly and the corresponding percentages. First, total the ratio of questions missed for oral reading and silent reading separately. For the fact questions, Tony missed 4 of 30 questions in oral reading and 6 of 30 questions in silent reading. Second, add these numerals to complete the "Total Ratio Missed" column. Tony missed 10 of the 60 fact questions. Third, determine the percent of fact questions missed. ($10 \div 60 = .16$; $.16 \times 100 = 16\%$). After determining Tony's comprehension performance for topic, evaluation, inference, and vocabulary questions, compare the results to Table 4.1 on page 83.

A comparison of Tony's oral and silent reading comprehension is shown in Table 4.1. Check your work and resolve any discrepancies. Because the number of questions upon which the total percentages are calculated has increased, the hypotheses about Tony's strengths and weaknesses

Figure 4-7. Tony's Comprehension Performance in Oral and Silent Reading

Grade	Fact (F-6)		Topic (T-1)		Evaluation (E-1)		Inference (I-1)		Vocabulary (V-1)	
	Oral	Silent	Oral	Silent	Oral	Silent	Oral	Silent	Oral	Silent
4	1/6	0/6	0/1	0/1	0/1	0/1	0/1	1/1	0/1	0/1
5	0/6	0/6	0/1	0/1	1/1	0/1	1/1	0/1	0/1	0/1
6	1/6	1/6	1/1	1/1	0/1	0/1	0/1	0/1	0/1	1/1
7	0/6	3/6	1/1	0/1	0/1	0/1	0/1	0/1	1/1	0/1
8	2/6	2/6	1/1	1/1	0/1	0/1	0/1	0/1	1/1	1/1
Ratio Missed	4/30	6/30	3/5	___/___	1/5	___/___	1/5	___/___	2/5	___/___
Percent Missed	13%	20%	60%	___%	20%	___%	20%	___%	40%	___%
Total Ratio Missed	10/60		___/___		___/___		___/___		___/___	
Total Percent Missed	16%		___%		___%		___%		___%	

TABLE 4.1
Summary of Tony's Comprehension Performance in Oral and Silent Reading

	Fact		Topic		Evaluation		Inference		Vocabulary	
	Oral	Silent	Oral	Silent	Oral	Silent	Oral	Silent	Oral	Silent
Ratio Missed	4/30	6/30	3/5	2/5	1/5	0/5	1/5	1/5	2/5	2/5
Percent Missed	13%	20%	60%	40%	20%	0%	20%	20%	40%	40%
Total Ratio Missed	10/60		5/10		1/10		2/10		4/10	
Total Percent Missed	16%		50%		10%		20%		40%	

should have greater validity. His answers to fact, evaluation, and inference questions appear to be areas of strength. Errors on topic and vocabulary questions may be hypothesized as areas of weakness. Because these findings are generally consistent with those based on Tony's oral reading, the combined analysis should give the teacher greater confidence in the hypotheses made. See Johns and Lenski (2010) for over fifty teaching strategies to strengthen comprehension.

Strategy 2 Analysis by Level of Comprehension

A second way to analyze comprehension performance is by classifying the various types of comprehension questions into logical categories. Numerous classification schemes have been developed (Raphael, 1986; Tatham, 1978). It is recommended that two levels of comprehension be used. Category one, lower-level comprehension, is composed of the six fact questions. Category two, higher-level comprehension, is composed of topic, evaluation, inference, and vocabulary questions. The logic behind the two categories is that the first is based on literal or explicit information, whereas the second is based on thinking beyond the ideas stated in the graded passages. The student's ability to reason and use experiences is assessed in the latter category. Although the evaluation, inference, and vocabulary questions may not be completely passage dependent, they can be used to help evaluate a student's vocabulary and ability to reason beyond the printed text. Even some of the factual questions may not be totally passage dependent, depending on student's prior knowledge. Viewed from this perspective, comprehension is only partially contextual. Johnston (1983, p. 34) argues strongly that "since no two individuals will have identical prior knowledge, the construction of tests which are free of bias at the individual level is impossible. Furthermore, it can be argued that it would be undesirable in any case since a reading comprehension test uninfluenced by prior knowledge would certainly not be measuring comprehension as it is understood theoretically."

Other classification schemes are also possible; you are encouraged to modify the scheme suggested to conform to your own conception of comprehension. The two categories of comprehension suggested make it possible for comprehension to be viewed more holistically when planning instruction for students. Table 4.2 contains the results of such an analysis for Tony's scores that were reported earlier. A reproducible master is found in Appendix B.

The results of the global analysis reveal that Tony's major difficulties are in the higher-level comprehension area. Johns and Lenski (2010) provide instructional strategies for this area of comprehension. If a more detailed analysis of this area is desired, the comprehension questions may be arranged by type and analyzed as described previously.

TABLE 4.2
Summary of Tony's Two-Level Comprehension Performance

	Lower-Level Comprehension (Fact Questions Only)		Higher-Level Comprehension (All Other Questions)	
	Oral	Silent	Oral	Silent
Ratio Missed	4/30	6/30	7/20	5/20
Total Ratio	10/60		12/40	
Total Percent Missed	16%		30%	

Integrating the Concept of Engagement

Another way to enhance comprehension assessment is to use the "engagement" concept (Manzo & Manzo, 1993). In short, you determine whether the student's responses to comprehension questions are congruent or incongruent. All correct responses are congruent. Incorrect responses "may be congruent (related but incorrect) or incongruent (unrelated as well as incorrect). An increase of congruent responses is a sound sign that the student is engaged" (Manzo & Manzo, 1993, p. 92).

Those who plan to integrate the engagement concept while asking comprehension questions should follow two guidelines to record relevant data:

- All comprehension questions scored as correct (+) are a sign of engagement. For correct responses that are "especially full, fresh, or elaborated in some meaningful and appropriate way," circle the numeral beside the comprehension question (Manzo & Manzo, 1993, p. 467).

- For comprehension questions scored as incorrect (−), a decision needs to be made: Is the incorrect response congruent (related to the passage in some meaningful way) or incongruent (not related to the passage in some meaningful, logical way)? For incorrect responses that are incongruent, place an X on the numeral beside the comprehension question.

If these two pieces of data have been recorded on appropriate pages of the performance booklet, they can be used to informally assess engagement. A reproducible master is found in Appendix B. An example of this procedure, using Kendrick's responses to comprehension questions, is shown in Table 4.3. Kendrick had one response to the questions at the fourth-grade level that was elaborated in some meaningful and appropriate way. None of the questions on the fifth-grade passage were elaborated; however, one response was rated as incongruent. For the sixth-grade passage, two questions were elaborated. Kendrick had four incongruent responses for the seventh-grade passage.

TABLE 4.3
Summary of Kendrick's Comprehension Engagement

	Grade Level of Passage			
	4	5	6	7
Correct responses especially full, fresh, or elaborated (numerals circled)*	1	0	2	0
Incongruent incorrect responses **unrelated** to the passage in some meaningful, logical way (numerals with Xs)*	0	1	0	4

*Refers to numerals beside the comprehension questions in the performance booklet.

To evaluate a student's responses, the following guidelines should be used. First, more than one elaboration per passage may be "taken as evidence of an alert mind that is engaged and being driven by meaning" (Manzo & Manzo, 1993, p. 467). Second, more than three incongruent responses (illogical, far out) to questions "is an indication that engagement was weak and nonproductive" (Manzo & Manzo, 1993, p. 467). Based on these guidelines, Kendrick was quite engaged for the sixth-grade passage. For the seventh-grade passage, Kendrick's engagement was weak. You can use this information along with other qualitative criteria and observations to better understand a student's overall comprehension.

Now, consider Juan's engagement based on the data presented in Table 4.4. Using the guidelines just presented, what tentative conclusions regarding Juan's engagement are appropriate? For the second- and third-grade passages, Juan was engaged; however, on the fourth-grade passage, Juan's engagement was weak. No specific conclusions regarding engagement are appropriate for the fifth-grade passage.

According to Manzo and Manzo (1993, p. 467), "it is too soon to say if any significant meanings can be attached to the absence of elaborations." While future research is being conducted on the concept of engagement, teachers are encouraged to use the simple recording system in order to possibly add a richer interpretation of factors that may influence comprehension.

TABLE 4.4
Summary of Juan's Comprehension Engagement

	Grade Level of Passage				
	1	2	3	4	5
Correct responses especially full, fresh, or elaborated (numerals circled)*	0	2	3	0	1
Incongruent incorrect responses **unrelated** to the passage in some meaningful, logical way (numerals with Xs)*	0	0	0	4	2

*Refers to numerals beside the comprehension questions in the performance booklet.

Using Retelling to Evaluate Comprehension

You can also use the student's retelling to evaluate his or her comprehension. Retelling offers insight into the student's ability to recall specific information, to determine what is important, and to organize ideas from the text. A sample retelling rubric for a fifth-grade student, Maria, is provided in the figure below.

Figure 4-8. Maria's Retelling Performance

Level	Description	Retelling Notes
Excellent/Independent Level	Recalls central or key ideas Remembers important facts Retains the general sequence of events Relates most of the content in an organized manner	
Satisfactory/Instructional Level	Recalls most central or key ideas Remembers some important facts Retains the general sequence of events Relates an overall sense of the content	*Main idea, mystery figure, and solution included* *Included some facts, but forgot names* *Beginning, middle, and end accurate* *Included all big ideas—she clearly understood passage*
Unsatisfactory/Frustration Level	Recalls bits of information in a haphazard manner Little apparent organization	

To evaluate Maria's retelling, consider each of the criteria listed in the rubric and make an overall assessment of her level of comprehension by synthesizing her performance on each aspect of the retelling. Maria's retelling included the main idea of the passage, illustrated by her comment, "It is a mystery about a skateboarder." She also provided the solution to the mystery by explaining, "The kids found a skateboard and black hooded jacket by her house and a skateboard tricks book on her desk." The teacher noted this by recording her comments in the right column on the rubric. For the remaining criteria on the rubric, the teacher recorded Maria's performance by writing brief notes. Overall, Maria's retelling was satisfactory or instructional level because she included all of the key events, remembered some important facts, followed the general sequence of events, and demonstrated an overall sense of the content in the passage. Areas where Maria could use further instruction and development relate to identifying specific characters and settings.

Fluency Considerations

The Basic Reading Inventory offers an excellent means to gain insights into the student's reading fluency. The Report of the National Reading Panel (2000) identified fluency as one of the foundational areas for reading instruction. Fluency has several components, aspects, or elements (Harris & Hodges, 1995; Samuels, 2002). Johns and Berglund (2010) note that fluency is comprised of four components: rate, accuracy, expression, and comprehension. How you can gain insights in each of these four areas is explained below.

Rate refers to speed of reading. When the student begins reading a graded passage orally or silently, you can time the student's reading using a stopwatch or a watch with a second hand. There are two ways to determine the student's rate or speed of reading. These two methods are described in detail on pages 40–42. In short, the first method determines the number of seconds it takes the student to read the passage and uses the formula at the bottom of the passage to get the student's rate in words per minute (WPM). Then the student's rate can be compared to the norms in Table 2.5 on page 43. Figure 4-9 contains an example for Ethan, a third-grade student.

Figure 4-9. Ethan's Oral Reading Rate

Oral Reading Rate	Norm Group Percentile				
$120\overline{)6000}$ $\frac{50}{}$ WPM	☐ 90	☐ 75	☐ 50	☒ 25	☐ 10

The second way to determine reading rate is described on page 40. That method determines the student's reading for one minute. A line or slash is drawn after the last word read by the student at the end of one minute. An example of this procedure is shown in Figure 2-8 (page 40).

Once the student's oral rate of reading is determined with either of these methods, consult Table 2.5 (page 43) and check the percentile that most closely corresponds to the student's rate in WPM. Table 2.6 (page 44) could also be used to help determine how the student's reading rate compares to average students at various points in the school year. For Ethan, it can be seen that his rate is near the 25th percentile on a third-grade passage in the fall of the school year. Figure 4-9 shows Ethan's reading rate (50 WPM) and percentile rank (25).

Accuracy refers to the facility with which the student recognizes words. In terms of the Basic Reading Inventory, the word recognition in context score gives some indication of the student's automaticity with words. You can also observe the student's ability to pronounce words and the ease with which the student moves through the passage. Obviously, a student who makes many miscues (misses one word in ten) would likely be trying to read a passage that is too difficult. The word lists can also be used to assess the student's ability to pronounce words at sight (automatically).

Appropriate expression "means that the student uses phrasing, tone, and pitch so that oral reading sounds conversational" (Johns & Berglund, 2010, p. 3). As the student reads, you can note the appropriateness of the oral reading in flow, emphasis, and phrasing. There are also more formal fluency rubrics that can be used if desired (see Johns & Berglund, 2010).

Comprehension is the essence of reading and refers to understanding the passage. Comprehension of passages on the Basic Reading Inventory is typically assessed with questions, retelling, or a combination of the two. Without comprehension, the student is merely word calling. There are some students who are very good at pronouncing words who are not actively constructing meaning. On the surface, these students may seem like excellent readers because they sound so good. Unfortunately, these readers are really automatic word callers (Valencia & Buly, 2004). Ideas for such students can be found later in this section titled "Targeting Interventions and Instruction for Struggling Readers." Refer to Cluster 1—Automatic Word Callers on page 92.

Important Points to Remember about Fluency

Fluency is dependent upon a variety of factors; the most important is probably an adequate sight vocabulary. Slow, choppy reading can be the result of not knowing a number of the words in the passage. It has been noted that "inefficiency in identifying individual words is the most important factor in accounting for individual differences in text reading fluency in samples of students with reading disabilities" (Torgesen, 2004, p. 376). Viewed from this perspective, fluency is symptomatic of poor reading rather than the cause of it. Many students improve their fluency when they are given books to read where they can recognize 95 percent or more of the words (Allington, 2012). The interest and background the student has about the topic or content of the reading material can also impact fluency.

If a student's reading is not fluent, hypothesize the most basic reasons for the behavior. Those hypotheses should then be used as the basis for initial responsive instruction and interventions. For example, one student may have weak word identification skills and a limited sight vocabulary. These areas would be the logical focus for instruction. Another student may have accurate, slow reading with adequate comprehension. For this student, instruction to increase rate may be appropriate. A third student may use improper phrasing and ignore punctuation. This student could profit from Scenario 8 in Section 5.

Through experience with the Basic Reading Inventory and a careful analysis of the student's reading, you will learn to differentiate the need for instruction in fluency from other, more casual factors for the lack of fluent reading (e.g., limited sight vocabulary and inadequate skills for word identification). It should also be noted that after third grade, the number of less frequent words increases rapidly, so it is difficult for students who struggle in reading to catch up with average students (Torgesen, 2004). Many of these students would likely profit from focused instruction in needed areas and extensive periods of practice with easy materials that exceed that of average students.

Instructional Interventions Grid

To help make instruction more responsive to the student's needs using the results of the Basic Reading Inventory, classroom observations, and the student's daily work, there are numerous sources for ideas. The author and his colleagues have prepared several easy-to-use books to assist a wide range of professionals in their quest to enhance student achievement in reading.

Improving Reading: Strategies, Resources, and Common Core Connections (Johns & Lenski, 2014) contains a wealth of teaching strategies, practice activities, games, and reproducible materials to use with students—over 600 pages. The ideas in this resource book support a wide range of learners. Teachers from kindergarten through high school have used the strategies to energize their instruction with average students as well as with students who struggle in reading. The fifth edition of *Improving Reading* contains more strategies than earlier editions and has many resource materials that can be duplicated and readily used with students. A CD makes it even easier to use the reproducibles and resources. Refer to the instructional interventions grid on page 89 for a comprehensive overview of the areas included in *Improving Reading*.

Tip!

Instructional Interventions Grid for Responsive Instruction

Resource Book		Resource Book	
General Area Specific Interventions	*Improving Reading* (6th ed.)	**General Area** Specific Interventions	*Improving Reading* (6th ed.)

1. Motivation, Engagement, Interests, and Attitudes

Lack of Motivation and Engagement	1.1
Negative Attitude Toward Reading	1.2
Limited Reading Interests	1.3
Low Confidence in Reading Ability	1.4
Reluctant to Set Goals	1.5

2. Oral Language, Phonemic Awareness, and Beginning Reading

Oral Language	2.1
Concepts About the Nature and Purpose of Reading	2.2
Alphabet Knowledge	2.3
Auditory Discrimination	2.4
Concept of a Word	2.5
Rhyming	2.6
Syllabic Awareness	2.7
Alphabetic Principle	2.8
Onsets and Rimes	2.9
Phonemic Awareness	2.10
Visual Discrimination	2.11
Letter and Word Reversals	2.12
Sense of Story	2.13

3. Phonics, Decoding, and Word Recognition

Phonics: Consonants	3.1
Phonics: Vowels	3.2
Word Patterns and Word Building	3.3
Structural Analysis	3.4
High-Frequency Words	3.5
Sight Vocabulary	3.6
Using Context to Predict Known Words	3.7
Dictionary: Word Pronunciation	3.8
Lack of Flexible Word-Identification Strategies	3.9
Ineffective Use of Word-Identification Strategies	3.10

4. Fluency and Effective Oral Reading

General Lack of Fluency	4.1
Lack of Fluency: Poor Phrasing and Expression	4.2
Lack of Fluency: Ignoring Punctuation	4.3
Lack of Fluency: Repetitions of Words or Phrases	4.4
Lack of Expression	4.5
Overemphasis on Speed and Accuracy	4.6
Failure to Attempt Unknown Words	4.7
Meaning-Changing Substitutions	4.8
Nonmeaning-Changing Substitutions	4.9
Nonword Substitutions	4.10
Meaning-Changing Omissions	4.11

4. Fluency and Effective Oral Reading (continued)

Nonmeaning-Changing Omissions	4.12
Excessive Use of Phonics	4.13
Excessive Use of Experience	4.14

5. Vocabulary Acquisition and Use

Using Context Clues to Predict Meanings of Unknown Words or Phrases	5.1
Using Affixes to Determine Word Meanings	5.2
Using Root Words and Compound Words to Determine Word Meaning	5.3
Using a Dictionary to Determine Word Meaning	5.4
Understanding Figurative Language	5.5
Differentiating between Word Meanings	5.6
Extending Meaning Vocabulary	5.7
Using New Words in Speaking and Writing	5.8
Demonstrating Independence in Gathering Vocabulary Knowledge	5.9

6. Comprehension Strategies

Purpose for Reading	6.1
Activating Prior Knowledge	6.2
Making Predictions	6.3
Sequence	6.4
Monitoring Reading	6.5
Questioning	6.6
Making Inferences	6.7
Drawing Conclusions	6.8
Making Connections	6.9
Visualizing	6.10
Reading Flexibly	6.11

7. Comprehending Fictional Texts

Using Fictional Text Structure for Comprehension	7.1
Understanding Characters in Fiction	7.2
Determining Theme in Fiction	7.3
Determining Point of View in Fiction	7.4

8. Comprehending Informational Texts

Using Informational Text Structure for Comprehension	8.1
Identifying Main Ideas and Details	8.2
Identifying Textual Evidence	8.3
Reading Visual Displays	8.4
Summarizing Ideas	8.5
Evaluating Arguments	8.6

Teaching Reading Pre-K–Grade 3 (Elish-Piper, Johns, & Lenski, 2006) contains 28 different assessments in areas such as literacy knowledge, phoneme segmentation, phonics, decoding, retelling, sight words, fluency, passage reading, and writing. These assessments can be used with students who are emergent readers up to third grade. A unique feature of the book is the presentation of over 300 teaching strategies, ideas, and activities that are linked to the assessments. Also included are ideas to send home to help practice and reinforce needed skills and strategies. These home-school connections are presented in English and Spanish. A number of tips for English language learners are highlighted in an easy-to-use chart. To make this resource even easier to use, a CD is included. It contains a bonus chapter on writing and spelling, 40 instructional reproducibles, home-school connections, selected resources, and assessment record sheets.

Essential Comprehension Strategies for the Intermediate Grades (Johns, Lenski, & Berglund, 2011) contains over 20 comprehension strategies. A quick reference guide helps determine the text type, when to use the strategy, the group size, and which of the seven areas of comprehension are enhanced with each strategy. A step-by-step lesson that can be adapted follows the teaching goals related to expected student outcomes. There are one or more examples for each strategy along with ready-to-use reproducible masters for students.

Comprehension and Vocabulary Strategies for the Elementary Grades (Johns, Lenski, & Berglund, 2006) contains over 40 comprehension and vocabulary strategies neatly organized with a quick reference guide that shows when, why, and how to use the strategies. Also shown is the type of text (narrative and/or informational) with which the strategy is most useful. Teaching is enhanced with a step-by-step lesson format and numerous examples. Reproducible masters, which you can use for instructional purposes, are provided with each strategy. A CD contains over 120 of these reproducibles plus bonus reproducibles for selected strategies.

Fluency: Differentiated Strategies and Progress-Monitoring Assessments (Johns & Berglund, 2010) provides answers to questions teachers often ask about fluency and offers over 30 strategies to strengthen fluency. A brief description is provided for each strategy, followed by a numbered set of procedures on how to use the strategy with students. Literary (narrative) and informational (expository) passages for monitoring fluency in grades one through eight are also included. A unique and helpful feature is a chart that aligns the various fluency strategies to six types of readers so that interventions can be targeted to specific students.

Visualization: Using Mental Images to Strengthen Comprehension (Zeigler & Johns, 2005) offers answers to some basic questions about visualization and provides 60 lessons to help students realize what visualization is, understand how to use it, and then apply it in various subject areas. Also included are assessments with scoring rubrics.

Strategies for Content Area Learning: Vocabulary, Comprehension, and Response (Johns & Berglund, 2011) contains over 35 strategies, each accompanied with a reproducible. The strategies can be used with narrative and/or informational text. Like the other books described above, the lessons are well organized and presented in easy-to-use steps. In addition to some readily recognized strategies (like K-W-L), there are less well known, but effective, strategies (for example, concept circles, possible sentences, and STAR). A website contains all the reproducibles in the book as well as additional reproducibles.

Reading and Learning Strategies: Middle Grades through High School (Lenski, Wham, Johns, & Caskey, 2011) is also a user-friendly book that contains approximately 140 strategies that focus on reading engagement, vocabulary, word study, comprehension, critical reading, and studying. The strategies are aimed at helping students learn more effectively in the content areas where informational (expository) text is often used. An included CD contains over 200 reproducibles and content area examples.

Targeting Interventions and Instruction for Struggling Readers

A study of 108 fifth-grade students who scored below standard on a state reading test given at the end of fourth grade was undertaken by Valencia and Buly (2004). Approximately two hours were spent with each student over several days to administer additional assessments, including an informal reading inventory. After an analysis of all the data, the students' scores "fell into three statistically distinct and educationally familiar categories: word identification (word reading in isolation and context), meaning (comprehension and vocabulary), and fluency (rate and expression)" (Valencia & Buly, 2004, p. 522). In addition, six clusters characterized the students who scored below standard on the state test:

1. Automatic Word Callers (18% of the sample)
2. Struggling Word Callers (15%)
3. Word Stumblers (17%)
4. Slow Comprehenders (24%)
5. Slow Word Callers (17%)
6. Disabled Readers (9%)

Beginning on page 92, six clusters are described with particular focus on informal reading inventory results and instructional interventions that can be found in *Improving Reading: Interventions, Strategies, and Resources* (Johns & Lenski, 2010).

An investigation was undertaken by Lutes (2004) to study the impact of implementing numerous strategies from the third edition of *Improving Reading: Strategies and Resources*. Fifteen second graders enrolled in a Title I program participated in the study. There were twelve boys and three girls who received instruction twice a week over a four-month period. The Basic Reading Inventory was used as a pretest and posttest. Statistically significant ($p<.001$) gains were reported for word recognition, oral comprehension, and silent comprehension. Lutes (2004) noted that most students were reading at the primer or pre-primer levels at the beginning of the study and at first- or second-grade levels at the conclusion of the study. While acknowledging the small sample size, the researcher noted that students can learn specific reading and writing strategies; moreover, teaching strategies can help strengthen comprehension.

As the results from the Basic Reading Inventory are analyzed for students in the upper grades who struggle with reading, it should become apparent which clusters characterize various students. Students who have similar needs can then be instructed together using some of the intervention strategies for that cluster (Johns, L'Allier, & Johns, 2012). Be cautious and flexible in this approach so students receive the type of instruction they need to become better readers. The cluster approach should be thought of as a beginning to high-quality, differentiated instruction. The six clusters may also be used with students in the primary grades to help identify instructional needs and interventions.

Cluster 1 Automatic Word Callers (18%)

Word Identification (Isolation & Context)	Meaning (Comprehension & Vocabulary)	Fluency (Rate & Expression)
STRONG	WEAK	STRONG

The dominant characteristic of students in this cluster is their ability to recognize words quickly and accurately. Unfortunately, these students exhibit very poor comprehension. They may be characterized as word callers. Their rate of reading in words per minute (WPM) could be quite high compared to the rates of average students. The majority of students in this cluster qualify for free or reduced lunch, and they are English-language learners who no longer receive special services.

In terms of performance on a reading inventory, a typical student in this cluster may score far above grade level in the graded word lists and passages and below grade level in comprehension. Comprehension difficulties are more complex than individual word meanings.

Instructional Interventions

Students in this cluster should first be helped to understand text. They may also be asked to adjust rate (slow down), focus on meaning, and think about the ideas while reading. Because many of these students are English-language learners, opportunities for language and conceptual development (Antunez, 2002), listening to and discussing classroom read-alouds, and lots of independent reading would help build language and attention to understanding. Other ideas for explicit instruction can be found in *Improving Reading: Strategies, Resources, and Common Core Connections* (Johns & Lenski, 2014) and are listed in the chart below.

Possible Area of Instructional Need	Where to Look in *Improving Reading* (6th ed.)
Understanding the purpose of reading	Section 2.2, Strategy 6
Creating purposes for reading	Section 6.1, Strategies 1, 2, and 3
Self-monitoring and think-alouds	Section 6.5, Strategies 1, 2, and 3
Adjusting rate	Section 4.6 Section 6.11, Strategies 1, 2, and 3
Various areas of comprehension	Chapters, 6, 7 and 8, Choose appropriate interventions
Building vocabulary	Section 2.1, Strategy 3 Chapter 5, Choose appropriate interventions
Activate prior knowledge	Section 6.2, Strategies 1, 2, 3, and 4 Section 6.3, Strategies 1, 2, and 3
Understanding fictional text structure	Section 7.1
Understanding informational text structure	Section 8.1
Learning new words and concepts	Section 5.9, Strategies 1, 2, 3, and 4

Cluster 2 Struggling Word Callers (15%)

Word Identification (Isolation & Context)	Meaning (Comprehension & Vocabulary)	Fluency (Rate & Expression)
WEAK	WEAK	FAIR

The students in this cluster struggle with both decoding and meaning. Their rather high rate of reading may be deceiving, because they say words quickly whether or not they are correct. Furthermore, these students seldom self-correct or monitor their reading. Expression and phrasing are uneven.

In terms of performance on a reading inventory, students in this cluster may score near grade level on the graded word lists. Word identification difficulties on the graded passages are much more pronounced and contribute to difficulties in comprehension. In addition, these students are often in the lower percentiles of oral assessment of vocabulary knowledge. Because 56 percent of students in this cluster are English-language learners, a lack of oral vocabulary and language may contribute to students' struggles with reading.

Instructional Interventions

Students in this cluster require specific, focused instruction in word identification that is determined through an analysis of reading miscues (see pages 71–80). Instruction should take place at students' instructional levels, which will typically be below grade placement. Exposure to the content and vocabulary of grade-level texts can be achieved through teacher read-alouds, recorded texts, and partner reading so that students' conceptual understandings continue to grow. Lots of reading should be done at the independent level or with texts that take students' background knowledge and interests into account. A good deal of background building by the teacher may be required.

Possible Area of Instructional Need	Where to Look in *Improving Reading* (6th ed.)
Expanding oral language	Section 2.1, 1, 4, 5, 6, 7, 8, 9, 12, 13, 15, 17, and 18
Strengthening word identification	Chapters 2 and 3, Choose appropriate interventions
Building vocabulary	Chapter 5, Choose appropriate interventions
Self-correcting miscues	Sections 4.4, 4.8, 4.10, and 4.11
Self-monitoring	Section 6.5, Strategies 1, 2, and 3
Unifying word identification strategies	Sections 3.9 and 3.10
Strengthening sight vocabulary	Section 3.5, Strategies 1, 2, 3, and 4 Section 3.6, Strategies 1, 2, and 3 Section 3.7, Strategies 1 and 2
Activating prior knowledge	Section 6.2
Making predictions	Section 6.3

Cluster 3 Word Stumblers (17%)

Word Identification (Isolation & Context)	Meaning (Comprehension & Vocabulary)	Fluency (Rate & Expression)
WEAK	FAIR	WEAK

The students in this cluster have substantial difficulty with word recognition, but they still have surprisingly strong comprehension. Teachers may wonder how students can initially stumble on many words and repeat text, but still be able to comprehend so well.

In terms of performance on an informal reading inventory, word recognition in context may be a couple of years below grade level. When the impact of the students' miscues is taken into account, many of them are self-corrected. In addition, words substituted for those in the passage tend to preserve the meaning. Because of weak word identification strategies, students may over-rely on context. Self-corrections and rereading slow the students' reading rate and expression suffers. When the comprehension questions are asked, the students' comprehension scores may be independent at grade level, even though the word recognition in context score is at the frustration level. Such students generally understand that reading should make sense, self-monitoring strategies are important, and background knowledge is actively used in constructing meaning.

Instructional Interventions

Students in this cluster know that reading should make sense, and they use numerous strategies to compensate for difficulties in word identification. Specific systematic instruction in word identification should be coupled with wide reading at the students' independent and instructional levels to help build fluency and automaticity with words. Meaningful reading to younger students, repeated readings, and reader's theater will help strengthen word identification and fluency.

Possible Area of Instructional Need	Where to Look in *Improving Reading* (6th ed.)
Strengthening word recognition	Chapters 2 and 3, Choose appropriate interventions
Building sight vocabulary	Sections 3.5 and 3.6
Effective oral reading behaviors	Chapter 4, Choose appropriate interventions
Developing automaticity	Sections 4.1, 4.2, 4.3, 4.4, 4.5, and 4.6 Oral Reading as Performance, page 232

Cluster 4 Slow Comprehenders (24%)

Word Identification (Isolation & Context)	Meaning (Comprehension & Vocabulary)	Fluency (Rate & Expression)
FAIR	STRONG	WEAK

Students in this cluster have adequate to good word identification and strong comprehension but an extremely slow rate of reading. The student may experience some difficulty in decoding multisyllabic words efficiently.

In terms of performance on an informal reading inventory, these students may score above grade level on the graded word lists and have generally good word identification on the graded passages. What is readily apparent, however, is a rate of reading that is far below average students.

Instructional Interventions

These students can identify words and construct meaning; however, their slow rate of reading makes it quite unlikely that they will spend much time reading. As the amount of reading increases in the upper grades and middle school, such students are likely to encounter frustration in the amount of time it takes them to complete assigned readings. Instruction should focus on building fluency (see Johns & Berglund, 2010) and helping develop effective strategies for how to attack multisyllabic words. Supply materials of interest that can be completed in a relatively short period of time. Gradually increase the length of the materials. Through such activities, students may begin to choose reading as a leisure-time activity.

Possible Area of Instructional Need	Where to Look in *Improving Reading* (6th ed.)
Strengthening fluency	Section 4.1, 2, 4, and 10 for emergent readers, page 235 Section 4.1, 3, 4, and 5 for older readers, page 236 Section 4.1, Strategies 1, 2, and 3 Oral Reading as Performance, page 232
Facility with longer words	Section 3.4, Strategies 2, 3, 4, 5, 6, 7, 8, and 9
Increasing motivation	Section 1.1, Strategies 2, 4, and 5 Section 1.2, Strategies 3, 4, and 5 Section 1.3, Strategies 2 and 3 Section 1.4, Strategies 4 and 5 Section 1.5, Strategies 1 and 4

Cluster 5 Slow Word Callers (17%)

Word Identification (Isolation & Context)	Meaning (Comprehension & Vocabulary)	Fluency (Rate & Expression)
FAIR	WEAK	WEAK

The students in this cluster are a fairly even mix of English-language learners and native English speakers who have difficulty in comprehension and fluency.

In terms of performance on an informal reading inventory, these students generally score above grade level on the word lists and when reading the passages. Comprehension, however, is often significantly below grade level. These students may be experiencing significant difficulties with word meanings and a slow rate of reading in which phrasing and meaningful expression are lacking. To further understand the student's needs, try materials where the student has strong background knowledge so that word meanings and comprehension are unlikely to be a problem. If rate and expression improve with such materials, instruction should probably focus on meaning and building vocabulary. On the other hand, if rate and expression are still concerns under these conditions, instruction should focus on both meaning and fluency. This cluster of readers can have a wide range of needs, so prioritize student needs and select the most appropriate strategies for initial instruction and intervention.

Instructional Interventions

The specific instruction needed for these students will result from a careful appraisal of their reading. Extensive reading at the independent level and listening to teacher read-alouds (with discussion) are critical. Some typical areas for instruction are provided below. Choose specific strategies and interventions from the chapters and sections that are related to students' needs.

Possible Area of Instructional Need	Where to Look in *Improving Reading* (6th ed.)
Strengthening vocabulary	Chapter 5, Choose appropriate interventions
Building and expanding comprehension	Chapter 6, Choose appropriate interventions
Comprehending fictional texts	Chapter 7, Choose appropriate interventions
Comprehending informational texts	Chapter 8, Choose appropriate interventions
Improving fluency	Chapter 4, Choose appropriate interventions Oral Reading as Performance, page 232
Activating prior knowledge	Section 6.2

Cluster 6 — Disabled Readers (9%)

Word Identification (Isolation & Context)	Meaning (Comprehension & Vocabulary)	Fluency (Rate & Expression)
VERY WEAK	VERY WEAK	VERY WEAK

The students in this cluster experience significant difficulties with all areas of reading. The dominant characteristic of students in this cluster is an extremely limited ability in word identification.

In terms of performance on an informal reading inventory, these students typically score far below grade level on all measures. Even high-frequency word knowledge is minimal. These students possess average receptive language, so there is an adequate knowledge base for reading. What is missing is a sufficient level of decoding ability and sight words, so fluency and comprehension are significantly impacted.

Instructional Interventions

These students, regardless of their grade placement, are really at the early stages of reading instruction. A primary need is intensive, systematic instruction in word identification that includes needed elements of phonics along with building sight vocabulary. Reading materials should be easy and provide successful experiences with print. These students are likely to benefit from additional instruction with a reading specialist, interventionist, or coach. A concerted effort with the combined talents of the classroom teacher and a reading specialist, along with support at home, will provide a solid foundation for growth in reading. Major areas for instruction are listed below. Begin interventions in decoding and word identification by selecting strategies most needed by students.

Possible Area of Instructional Need	Where to Look in *Improving Reading* (6th ed.)
Decoding and word recognition	Chapters 2 and 3, Choose appropriate interventions
Building sight vocabulary	Sections 3.5 and 3.6
Developing fluency	Sections 4.1, 4.2, 4.3, 4.4, and 4.5
Motivating reading	Sections 1.1, 1.2, and 1.4
Comprehension skills and strategies	Chapter 6, Choose appropriate interventions

A Teacher's Administration of the Basic Reading Inventory

Over the years, I have had the privilege of conducting many Basic Reading Inventory training workshops for classroom teachers, reading coaches, special education teachers, reading specialists, and interventionists. During the workshops, I have often done live demonstrations with students. These sample administrations have been well received by workshop participants; nevertheless, it is not always possible to secure a student. That's one reason I developed a DVD (Johns, 2012a).

In several of my workshops, I had the good fortune to have a local classroom teacher or reading teacher administer the Basic Reading Inventory before the workshop and share the results with me. Then, during the workshop, I used the student's performance along with input from the teacher who did the administration.

Joelle was one teacher who agreed to administer the Basic Reading Inventory. It was her first administration, and I was really pleased with her results and analysis. The results, which you are about to see, were shared in a large workshop of over one hundred teachers, specialists, and administrators. Then, at a later workshop, the results were shared with teachers in her school. Now you have a chance to see the big picture of how the Basic Reading Inventory can be used to determine a student's three reading levels and offer insights for instruction.

About the Student

Logan (not his real name) entered Joelle's school in second grade as a struggling reader. His motivation was low, and he exhibited immaturity. He began receiving Tier II instruction for weak decoding and word identification skills. By the end of second grade, improvement in reading ability increased. The Title I teacher indicated that focused small group instruction and highly structured motivational incentives helped Logan's progress. Near the middle of third grade, Joelle assessed Logan with the Basic Reading Inventory. Her purpose was to evaluate his progress and to determine the type of instruction and interventions that would help Logan strengthen his reading.

Results of the Basic Reading Inventory

Beginning with the performance booklet summary sheet, Logan's results are shown followed by his actual performance on the word lists and passages he read. Refer to these pages as you read the commentary below.

Logan's Word List Performance. Logan read word lists ranging from first grade through sixth grade. He made minimal miscues on all the lists through fifth grade and was able to correct some of the words he initially mispronounced. By sixth grade, however, Logan had great difficulty with the words, but he demonstrated a willingness to try to pronounce a number of the words. Logan also demonstrated a strong ability to pronounce words at and above his grade placement. It would appear that his weak decoding skills in second grade improved significantly because of the Tier II instructional interventions he received that year.

Logan's Passage Reading, Comprehension, and Rate. Logan read passages ranging from first through fifth grade. On the first-grade passage, Logan made two miscues, had excellent comprehension, and demonstrated excellent rate (90th percentile). On the second-grade passage, his miscue count was slightly higher (4), he missed parts of two comprehension questions, and his rate was average (50th percentile). His performance on the third-grade passage demonstrated adequate word identification, excellent comprehension, and a reading rate at the 25th percentile. Except for his rate, Logan demonstrated very good performance at his grade level. On the fourth-grade passage, Logan maintained good word identification but had lower comprehension (he missed three questions) and an oral reading rate at the 10th percentile. On the fifth-grade passage, Logan made many miscues, but he still understood much of the passage. His oral reading rate, however, was below the 10th percentile.

Logan's Reading Strengths and Weaknesses. The area of comprehension appears to be Logan's strength. He did not reach a clear frustration level in comprehension on any passage. Word recognition in isolation was stronger than words in context, but both areas were fully satisfactory at the fourth-grade level. An informal analysis of Logan's miscues revealed a preponderance of substitutions that had little impact on meaning. His overall abilities in word recognition indicate that the earlier interventions in decoding were very successful. Reading rate, however, reveals a consistent decline as increasingly difficult passages are read. Logan's reading rate at grade level is below average in spite of his strong abilities in word identification and comprehension.

Suggestions to Strengthen Logan's Reading. It seems clear that the Tier II instruction Logan received in decoding successfully strengthened his overall ability to recognize words. His current instructional level is fourth grade, a year above his grade placement. It is possible that he is quite focused on using various word attack skills and has not fully achieved automaticity in his passage reading. This focus can influence reading rate as clearly shown.

To help target instruction, it could be helpful to see if Logan's overall reading fits one of the clusters of struggling readers found on pages 92–97. After a careful comparison of his overall performance on the Basic Reading Inventory to the six clusters, it appears that Cluster 4 on page 95 is the best fit for Logan. Logan has adequate to good word recognition, strong comprehension, but an extremely slow rate of reading.

Tier II intervention and small-group instruction needs to focus on building fluency. Because Joelle noted Logan's low motivation, there may also be a need to use motivational incentives to encourage his engagement in reading. The instructional interventions grid on page 89 provides numerous ideas found in *Improving Reading* (Johns & Lenski, 2010). Some specific suggestions are listed below:

- Encourage plenty of easy reading using materials of interest that are at or below Logan's instructional level of fourth grade. Materials that are easy to read will help foster automaticity with words and build Logan's confidence.

- Commend Logan for the strong gains he has made in reading and offer him personal encouragement.

- Support Logan's rereading of favorite books and stories.

- Invite Logan to prepare a story to read orally to younger students. Ensure that the experience will be a positive one by providing plenty of practice prior to the sharing. Videotape and/or digital recordings could provide one basis for monitoring his progress.

- Use structured repeated reading (Johns & Lenski, 2010, p. 326) to increase motivation and use a Reading Progress Chart as a visible means of demonstrating progress.

- Secure scripts for readers theater (www.aaronshep.com), assign an appropriate part for Logan and other students, have students practice over several days, and then perform the script for an appropriate audience.

In Conclusion

Joelle's first administration of the Basic Reading Inventory helped her see Logan's progress and the need for focused instructional interventions in fluency, specifically rate of reading. I hope this example will encourage you to do the same with your students so they can become better readers. Be patient with yourself as you learn how to administer the Basic Reading Inventory and use the results to energize instruction and to provide appropriate, high-quality interventions.

BASIC READING INVENTORY PERFORMANCE BOOKLET

Jerry L. Johns, Ph.D.

Student _Logan_   Grade _3_   Gender (M) F   Date of Test _Jan. 4_

School _____   Examiner _Joelle_   Date of Birth _____

Address _____   Current Book/Level _____   Age _____

SUMMARY OF STUDENT'S READING PERFORMANCE

| Grade | Word Recognition | | | | | | Comprehension | | Reading Rate | |
| | Isolation (Word Lists) | | | | Context (Passages) | | Form A | | Words Group Minute (WPM) | Norm Per-centile |
	Sight	Analy-sis	Total	Level	Mis-cues	Level	Ques-tions Missed	per Level		
PP1										
PP2										
P										
1	19	1	20	Ind.	2	Ind./Inst.	0	Ind.	71	90
2	20		20	Ind.	4	Ind./Inst.	1	Ind.	79	50
3	19	1	20	Ind.	3	Ind./Inst.	1	Ind.	53	25
4	17	1	18	Inst.	3	Ind./Inst.	3	Inst./Frust.	52	10
5	18	1	19	Ind.	10	Frust.	4	Inst./Frust.	41	<10
6	10	3	13	Frust.						
7										
8										
9										
10										
11										
12										

ESTIMATE OF READING LEVELS

Independent _3_   Instructional _4_   Frustration _5_

LISTENING LEVEL

Form _____

Grade	Questions Missed	Level
1		
2		
3		
4		
5		
6		
7		
8		

ESTIMATED LEVEL: _____

GENERAL OBSERVATIONS

– Hard-working student
– Improved word recognition skills since second grade
– Strong comprehension skills

INFORMAL ANALYSIS OF ORAL READING

| Oral Reading Behaviors | Frequency of Occurrence | | | General Impact on Meaning | | |
	Seldom	Sometimes	Frequently	No Change	Little Change	Much Change
Substitutions			✔		✔	
Insertions	✔			✔		
Omissions	✔					
Reversals						
Repetitions						

QUALITATIVE ANALYSIS OF BASIC READING INVENTORY INSIGHTS

General Directions: Note the degree to which the student shows behavior or evidence in the following areas. Space is provided for additional items.

Seldom / Weak / Poor ———→ Always / Strong / Excellent

COMPREHENSION

Seeks to construct meaning
Makes predictions
Activates background knowledge
Possesses appropriate concepts and vocabulary
Monitors reading
Varies reading rate as needed
Understands topic and major ideas
Remembers facts or details
Makes and supports appropriate inferences
Evaluates ideas from passages
Understands vocabulary used
Provides appropriate definitions of words
Engages with passages

WORD IDENTIFICATION

Possesses numerous strategies
Uses strategies flexibly
Uses graphophonic information
Uses semantic information
Uses syntactic information
Knows basic sight words automatically
Possesses sight vocabulary

ORAL AND SILENT READING

Reads fluently
Reads with expression
Attends to punctuation
Keeps place while reading
Reads at appropriate rate
Reads silently without vocalization *NA*

ATTITUDE AND CONFIDENCE

Enjoys reading
Demonstrates willingness to risk
Possesses positive self-concept
Chooses to read
Regards himself/herself as a reader
Exhibits persistence

Form A • Graded Word Lists • Performance Booklet • Student Booklet copy is on page 3.

List A 7141 (Grade 1)	Sight	Analysis	List A 8224 (Grade 2)	Sight	Analysis
1. here*	+		1. ten*	+	
2. down*	+		2. poor	+	
3. then*	+		3. city	+	
4. how*	+		4. teacher	+	
5. saw*	+		5. turn*	+	
6. pocket	*pack*	+	6. fight	+	
7. hello	+		7. because*	+	
8. aunt	+		8. soft	+	
9. never*	+		9. open*	+	
10. puppy	+		10. winter	+	
11. could*	+		11. joke	+	
12. after*	+		12. different	+	
13. hill	+		13. say*	+	
14. men	+		14. quiet	+	
15. gone*	+		15. sister	+	
16. ran*	+		16. above	+	
17. gave*	+		17. seed	+	
18. or*	+		18. thought*	+	
19. way	+		19. such	+	
20. coat	+		20. chase	+	

*denotes basic sight word from Revised Dolch List

*denotes basic sight word from Revised Dolch List

Number Correct ___19___ ___1___   Number Correct ___20___ _____

Total _____20_____   Total _____20_____

Scoring Guide for Graded Word Lists			
Independent	Instructional	Inst./Frust.	Frustration
20 19	18 17 16	15 14	13 or less

Form A • Graded Word Lists • Performance Booklet • Student Booklet copy is on page 4.

List A 3183 (Grade 3)	Sight	Analysis	List A 5414 (Grade 4)	Sight	Analysis
1. trail	+		1. stove	+	
2. stream	+		2. government	govenment	x
3. beach	+		3. program	+	
4. snake	+		4. grape	+	
5. lift	+		5. favorite	+	
6. cabin	+		6. blizzard	+	
7. bless	+		7. noon	+	
8. rooster	+		8. greet	+	
9. journey	+		9. sport	+	
10. treasure	+		10. rumble	+	
11. hero	+		11. tropical	+	
12. beyond	+		12. language	+	
13. moan	+		13. expert	+	
14. glitter	+		14. nervous	+	
15. impossible	+		15. starve	stāry	x
16. shot	+		16. voyage	+	
17. island	izland	+	17. silence	sĭlence	+
18. manage	+		18. scamper	+	
19. receive	+		19. prairie	+	
20. automobile	+		20. moccasin	+	
Number Correct	19	1	Number Correct	17	1
Total		20	Total		18

Scoring Guide for Graded Word Lists			
Independent	Instructional	Inst./Frust.	Frustration
20 19	18 17 16	15 14	13 or less

Form A • Graded Word Lists • Performance Booklet • Student Booklet copy is on page 5.

List A 8595 (Grade 5)	Sight	Analysis
1. lizard	+	
2. double	+	
3. scarlet	+	
4. helmet	+	
5. dusk	+	
6. bandit	+	
7. loyal	+	
8. choice	+	
9. furnish	+	
10. century	+	
11. kindergarten	+	
12. entrance	+	
13. dentist	+	
14. celebration	+	
15. blister	+	
16. symbol	+	
17. drowsy	+	
18. attach	autŭch	x
19. rehearse	rĕh-	+
20. terrace	+	
Number Correct	18	1
Total	19	

List A 6867 (Grade 6)	Sight	Analysis
1. bleed	+	
2. accomplishment	pass	pass
3. whimper	+	
4. marriage	+	
5. frisky	+	
6. seam	+	
7. backward	pass	+
8. location	pass	pass
9. nightmare	+	
10. gently	+	
11. employ	employee	employee
12. broadcast	+	
13. kennel	+	
14. pulp	+	
15. satisfaction	pass	+
16. cushion	cŭshion	+
17. graduate	pass	gratitude
18. harmonica	pass	harmon passs
19. definite	definit	pass
20. yacht	pass	yăcht
Number Correct	10	3
Total	13	

Scoring Guide for Graded Word Lists			
Independent	Instructional	Inst./Frust.	Frustration
20 19	18 17 16	15 14	13 or less

Student Booklet copy is on page 13.

A 7141 (Grade 1) Activating Background: Read the title to yourself. Then tell me what you think this might be about. *A dog is going to learn how to swim.*

Background: Low ├────+─✗───┤ High

Spotty Swims

		MISCUES						
	Substitution	Insertion	Omission	Reversal	Repetition	Self-Correction of Unacceptable Miscue	Meaning Change (Significant Miscue)	
One day Spotty went for a walk.	7							
The sun was warm. Spotty walked to	14							
where the pond! There he saw a frog. The	22	*1*						
frog was on a log. Spotty wanted to	30							
play. Spotty began to bark. The frog	37							
jumped into the water.	41							
Then Spotty jumped into the water.	47							
But poor Spotty did not know what to	55							
do. The water was very deep. The water	63							
went way over his head. Spotty moved	70							
his legs. Soon his head came out of the	79							
water. He kept on moving. He came to	87							
the other side of the pond. That is how	96							
how Spotty learned to swim.	100		*1*					
TOTAL		*1*	*1*					

Word Recognition Scoring Guide		
Total Miscues	Level	Significant Miscues
0–1	Independent	0–1
2–4	Ind./Inst.	2
5	Instructional	3
6–9	Inst./Frust.	4
10 +	Frustration	5 +

Total Miscues [2]   Significant Miscues [ ]

Oral Reading Rate	Norm Group Percentile
84)6000 = 71 WPM	☒ 90 ☐ 75 ☐ 50 ☐ 25 ☐ 10

A 7141 (Grade 1)
Comprehension Questions

T 1. __+__ What is this story about?
             (Spotty and a frog; how Spotty
   A dog   learned to swim)

F 2. __+__ Where did Spotty go?
             (to the pond; for a walk)

F 3. __+__ What did Spotty see?
             (a frog)

F 4. __+__ What happened when Spotty saw
             the frog?
             (he barked; he wanted to play; he
             jumped into the water [any 1])

F 5. __+__ What did the frog do when Spotty
             barked?
             (the frog jumped into the water)

F 6. __+__ What did Spotty do when the water
             went over his head?
             (moved his legs; he didn't know
             what to do)

F 7. __+__ What did Spotty learn in this story?
             (how to swim)

I 8. __+__ Who was Spotty?
             (any logical response; a dog)

E 9. __+__ Why do you think Spotty wanted to
             play with the frog?
             (any logical response; he was
             lonesome) *Dogs like to play.*

V 10. __+__ What is a "pond"?
              (like a lake; water) *but ponds are
              smaller*

0	Questions Missed

Comprehension Scoring Guide	
Questions Missed	Level
0–1	Independent
1½–2	Ind./Inst.
2½	Instructional
3–4½	Inst./Frust.
5 +	Frustration

Retelling Notes

Retelling Rubric for the Three Reading Levels

Independent Level/Excellent
Recalls central or key ideas
Remembers important facts
Retains the general sequence of events
Relates most of the content in an organized manner

Instructional Level/Satisfactory
Recalls most central or key ideas
Remembers some important facts
Retains the general sequence of events
Relates an overall sense of the content

Frustration Level/Unsatisfactory
Recalls bits of information in a haphazard manner
Little apparent organization

Student Booklet copy is on page 14.

A 8224 (Grade 2) Activating Background: Read the title to yourself. Then tell me what you think this might be about. *A guy named Billy who goes to camp.*

Background: Low ├──────┼─✗──┤ High

Bill at Camp

		MISCUES						
		Substitution	Insertion	Omission	Reversal	Repetition	Self-Correction of Unacceptable Miscue	Meaning Change (Significant Miscue)
Billy It was the first time Bill went to	8	1						
camp. He was very happy to be there. Soon	17							
he went for a walk in the woods to look for	28							
many kinds of leaves. He found leaves	35							
from some maple and oak trees. As Bill	43							
walked in the woods, he saw some animal *s*	51		1					
tracks. At that moment, a mouse ran into	59							
the a small hole by a tree. Bill wondered if the	69	1						
tracks were made by the mouse. He looked	77							
around for other animals. He did not see	85							
any. The last thing Bill saw was an old	94							
the bird nest in a pine tree.	100	1						
TOTAL		**3**	**1**					

Total Miscues **4**   Significant Miscues ☐

Word Recognition Scoring Guide		
Total Miscues	Level	Significant Miscues
0–1	Independent	0–1
2–4	Ind./Inst.	2
5	Instructional	3
6–9	Inst./Frust.	4
10 +	Frustration	5 +

Oral Reading Rate	Norm Group Percentile
$\overset{79}{76\overline{)6000}}$ WPM	☐ 90 ☐ 75 ☒ 50 ☐ 25 ☐ 10

A 8224 (Grade 2)
Comprehension Questions

T 1. _+_ What is this story about?
(a boy at camp; Bill's walk in the woods) *A guy goes to camp and then into the words.*

F 2. _1/2_ Did Bill enjoy going to camp? How do you know?
(yes, the story said he was happy there) *It said so in the story.*

F 3. _+_ Why did Bill go walking in the woods?
(to look for leaves) *to find leaves*

F 4. _1/2_ What kinds of leaves did Bill find in the woods?
(maple and oak leaves) *maple and pine*

F 5. _+_ What else did Bill see besides the mouse? *beside a tree*
(a bird nest; animal tracks)

F 6. _+_ Where did the mouse go?
(into a small hole by or in a tree)

F 7. _+_ What other animals did Bill see?
(none; he didn't see any)

I 8. _+_ Do you think Bill went on this walk by himself? What makes you think so?
(any logical response) *No other names were mentioned.*

E 9. _+_ What other animals might Bill see if he goes for another walk?
(any logical response) *squirrel in a tree; deer*

V 10. _+_ What are "tracks"?
(footprints made in the dirt; something made by animals when they walk or run) *like footprints you leave somewhere when you walk*

[1] Questions Missed

Comprehension Scoring Guide	
Questions Missed	Level
0–1	Independent
1½–2	Ind./Inst.
2½	Instructional
3–4½	Inst./Frust.
5 +	Frustration

Retelling Notes

Retelling Rubric for the Three Reading Levels
Independent Level/Excellent
Recalls central or key ideas
Remembers important facts
Retains the general sequence of events
Relates most of the content in an organized manner
Instructional Level/Satisfactory
Recalls most central or key ideas
Remembers some important facts
Retains the general sequence of events
Relates an overall sense of the content
Frustration Level/Unsatisfactory
Recalls bits of information in a haphazard manner
Little apparent organization

Student Booklet copy is on page 15.

A 3183 (Grade 3) Activating Background: Read the title to yourself. Then tell me what you think this might be about. *A bear goes into the forest to hunt for food.*

Background: Low |————|——X——| High

The Hungry Bear

		MISCUES						
	Substitution	Insertion	Omission	Reversal	Repetition	Self-Correction of Unacceptable Miscue	Meaning Change (Significant Miscue)	
buzzy The busy bees had been making honey all — 8	1							
dump day. That night it was cool and damp. I had — 18	1							
me (sc) slept well until I heard a loud noise near my — 28	1							
window. It sounded as if someone were — 35								
a (sc) trying to break into my cabin. As I moved — 44	1							
from my cot, I could see something black — 52								
standing near the window. In fright I knocked — 60								
on the window. Very slowly and quietly the — 68								
great shadow moved back and went away. — 75								
The next day we found huge bear tracks. — 83		1						
The bear had come for the honey the bees — 92								
were making in the attic of the cabin. — 100								
TOTAL	4	1						

Total Miscues 3*   Significant Miscues [ ]

*did not count self-corrections
(*me* for *my* and *a* for *I*)

Word Recognition Scoring Guide		
Total Miscues	Level	Significant Miscues
0–1	Independent	0–1
2–4	Ind./Inst.	2
5	Instructional	3
6–9	Inst./Frust.	4
10 +	Frustration	5 +

Oral Reading Rate	Norm Group Percentile
53 / 114)6000 WPM	☐ 90 ☐ 75 ☐ 50 ☒ 25 ☐ 10

A 3183 (Grade 3)
Comprehension Questions

T 1. __+__ What is this story about?
(a bear trying to get honey; being scared) *A hungry bear*

F 2. __+__ What had the bees been doing?
(making honey)

F 3. __−__ Where were the bees making honey?
(in the attic of the cabin)
in their hive

F 4. __+__ Who or what woke the person in this story?
(a bear; a loud noise at the window)

F 5. __+__ What was near the window?
(blackness; a shadow; a bear)

F 6. __+__ What was found the next day?
(bear tracks)

F 7. __+__ What did the bear want?
(honey)

I 8. __+__ Why do you think the bear walked away?
(any logical response; it heard the knock) *Because he could tell there was a person inside*

E 9. __+__ What might you do to keep the bear away?
(any logical response; remove the honey) *I'd get a shot gun!*

V 10. __+__ What is an "attic"?
(a place way upstairs in your house where you put junk and stuff)
It's upstairs and there's a lot of old stuff. We have an attic.

_1_	Questions Missed

Comprehension Scoring Guide	
Questions Missed	Level
0–1	Independent
1½–2	Ind./Inst.
2½	Instructional
3–4½	Inst./Frust.
5 +	Frustration

Retelling Notes

Retelling Rubric for the Three Reading Levels
Independent Level/Excellent
Recalls central or key ideas
Remembers important facts
Retains the general sequence of events
Relates most of the content in an organized manner
Instructional Level/Satisfactory
Recalls most central or key ideas
Remembers some important facts
Retains the general sequence of events
Relates an overall sense of the content
Frustration Level/Unsatisfactory
Recalls bits of information in a haphazard manner
Little apparent organization

Student Booklet copy is on page 16.

A 5414 (Grade 4) Activating Background: Read the title to yourself. Then tell me what you think this might be about. *There might be a fire close to an animal colony.*

Background: Low |————+—X——| High

Fire and Animals

	MISCUES						
	Substitution	Insertion	Omission	Reversal	Repetition	Self-Correction of Unacceptable Miscue	Meaning Change (Significant Miscue)
The summer was a dry one, ~~unusual~~ 7			1				
for this area. Trees and bushes in the forest 16							
wilted and died. One afternoon a storm *strom* (SC) 23	1						
came to the forest. Thunder was heard and 31							
lightning was seen. Then it began to 38							
rain. A spark touched the leaves *leaf* and a 46	1						
fire began. The fire spread quickly. The *And* 53	1						
animals warned each other as they hurried 60							
to escape the flames. As the fire came 68							
closer, trees fell to the ground. Their 75							
branches were yellow, orange, and red. 81							
The smoke was so thick that the animals 89							
could hardly breathe. Many couldn't 94							
escape the danger of the flames. 100							
TOTAL	3		1				

Word Recognition Scoring Guide		
Total Miscues	Level	Significant Miscues
0–1	Independent	0–1
2–4	Ind./Inst.	2
5	Instructional	3
6–9	Inst./Frust.	4
10 +	Frustration	5 +

Total Miscues $3*$ Significant Miscues [ ]

*did not count self-correction (*strom* for *storm*)

Oral Reading Rate	Norm Group Percentile
52 WPM 116)6000	☐ 90 ☐ 75 ☐ 50 ☐ 25 ☒ 10

A 5414 (Grade 4)
Comprehension Questions

T 1. __+__ What is this story about?
(a forest fire) *A spark touched a leaf and there was a fire.*

F 2. __+__ What did the animals try to do?
(<u>escape</u>; warn each other)

F 3. __−__ What was unusual about this summer?
(it had been a dry one)
It rained.

F 4. __−__ What was heard and seen in the woods before the fire began?
(<u>thunder</u> and <u>lightning</u>)
I don't remember.

F 5. __+__ What started the fire?
(a <u>spark</u>; lightning)

F 6. __+__ What colors were the trees in this story?
(<u>yellow</u>, <u>orange</u>, and <u>red</u> [any 2])

F 7. __+__ Why was it difficult for the animals to breathe?
(<u>smoke filled the air</u>; the fire)

I 8. __−__ Why do you think the fire spread quickly?
(any logical response; it had been a dry summer)
It was thick.

E 9. __+__ What problems do you think the animals that survived the fire might have?
(any logical response)
cuts, scars

V 10. __+__ What does "escape" mean?
(<u>get away</u>; any logical response)

3	Questions Missed

Comprehension Scoring Guide	
Questions Missed	Level
0–1	Independent
1½–2	Ind./Inst.
2½	Instructional
3–4½	Inst./Frust.
5 +	Frustration

Retelling Notes

Retelling Rubric for the Three Reading Levels
Independent Level/Excellent
Recalls central or key ideas
Remembers important facts
Retains the general sequence of events
Relates most of the content in an organized manner
Instructional Level/Satisfactory
Recalls most central or key ideas
Remembers some important facts
Retains the general sequence of events
Relates an overall sense of the content
Frustration Level/Unsatisfactory
Recalls bits of information in a haphazard manner
Little apparent organization

Student Booklet copy is on page 17.

A 8595 (Grade 5) Activating Background: Read the title to yourself. Then tell me what you think this might be about. *It might have a surprise ending or a big secret.*

Background: Low |————+——✗—| High

The Mystery		**MISCUES**						Self-Correction of Unacceptable Miscue	Meaning Change (Significant Miscue)
		Substitution	Insertion	Omission	Reversal	Repetition			
Everyone turned to stare as a black *(back)*	7	1							
hooded *(hode)* figure whizzed *(wized)* by on a skateboard.	14	2							
It was a mystery because no one knew	22								
who the talented person was. Ken saw	29								
the skateboarder slide *(slid)* down the library	35	1							
railing and disappear *(disappoint)* into the alley. Nita	42	1							
followed the person *(persons)* from school and	48		1						
watched as a curb was jumped and a	56								
three hundred sixty degree *(de/gree)* turn was	62	1							
completed *(complicate)* with ease. One day Ken	68	1							
noticed a skateboard and a black hooded *(hōded)*	75	1							
jacket next to Rose's house. He also saw	83								
a library book called *Skateboarding Tips*	89								
in her desk at school. Ken had solved *(slaved)*	97	1							
the challenging mystery.	100								
TOTAL		9	1						

Total Miscues [10]   Significant Miscues [ ]

Word Recognition Scoring Guide		
Total Miscues	Level	Significant Miscues
0–1	Independent	0–1
2–4	Ind./Inst.	2
5	Instructional	3
6–9	Inst./Frust.	4
10 +	Frustration	5 +

Oral Reading Rate	Norm Group Percentile
147)6000 = 41 WPM	☐ 90 ☐ 75 ☐ 50 ☐ 25 ☒ 10

A 8595 (Grade 5)
Comprehension Questions

T 1. __+__ What is this story about?
(a skateboarder; finding out who the
skateboarder was) *and a mystery*

F 2. __−__ What did the mystery person look
like?
(wore a black hood; rode a
skateboard)
ordinary

F 3. __−__ Why was this person such a
mystery?
(no one knew who the person was)
He skateboarded so fast.

F 4. __+__ Who saw the skateboarder?
(everyone; Ken and Nita)

F 5. __+__ What kind of stunts did the mystery
person do?
(slide down a railing; three hundred
sixty degree turn; jump a curb
[any 1])

F 6. __+__ Who solved the mystery?
(Ken)

F 7. __+__ What items did Ken see that helped
him solve the mystery?
(hooded jacket; skateboard; book
[any 2])

I 8. __−__ Who was the mystery person?
(Rose) *Someone at Rose's house*

E 9. __−__ If you were Ken, how might you
have solved the mystery differently?
(any logical response)
I'm not sure.

V 10. __+__ What does "talented" mean?
(good at something; gifted)
do stuff real good

<table>
<tr><td>4</td><td>Questions
Missed</td></tr>
</table>

Comprehension Scoring Guide	
Questions Missed	Level
0–1	Independent
1½–2	Ind./Inst.
2½	Instructional
3–4½	Inst./Frust.
5 +	Frustration

Retelling Notes

Retelling Rubric for the Three Reading Levels
Independent Level/Excellent
Recalls central or key ideas
Remembers important facts
Retains the general sequence of events
Relates most of the content in an organized manner
Instructional Level/Satisfactory
Recalls most central or key ideas
Remembers some important facts
Retains the general sequence of events
Relates an overall sense of the content
Frustration Level/Unsatisfactory
Recalls bits of information in a haphazard manner
Little apparent organization

How the Basic Reading Inventory Helps Your Students

The results of the Basic Reading Inventory can be used as a valuable basis for instruction. The insights can be used to inform instruction, prepare strategy lessons, and determine and provide appropriate interventions. The *total* results from the Basic Reading Inventory must be used to help plan effective instruction, taking into account each student's *specific* strengths and needs in word identification, comprehension, and/or fluency.

Assessments like the Basic Reading Inventory play a substantial role in providing data for

- placing students in appropriate instructional materials,
- assessing reading behavior,
- providing helpful and appropriate interventions,
- differentiating instruction,
- developing reading strategy lessons
- helping students strengthen their reading, and
- monitoring progress.

Caution

Unless Basic Reading Inventory results are used in conjunction with observation, cumulative records, portfolios, and other evaluative techniques, serious errors may result. One should not underestimate the importance of the Basic Reading Inventory for classroom, resource room, and clinical use; however, the results should be used to *guide* your responses to a student's reading. Results should not be used to dictate your actions, thereby dominating your professional knowledge and experience. Professionals who use the Basic Reading Inventory as suggested in this manual will help ensure that students are placed in appropriate reading materials, taught needed reading strategies, and given appropriate interventions.

The professional who places students in reading materials at their appropriate instructional levels and provides responsive instructional interventions for specific areas of need will help students become better readers. That's the essence of realizing and acting upon "the point that individual differences are a fact of life in schools and classrooms" (Pearson, 2007, p. 155). Using the Basic Reading Inventory to discover students' instructional levels and needs in reading, coupled with responsive teaching and interventions, is an appropriate way to design and implement high-quality reading instruction.

SECTION 5

Targeted Interventions for Reading Difficulties

Focused instructional interventions help students become better readers.

- Scenario 1: The Student Repeats Words, Phrases, or Sentences 117
- Scenario 2: The Student Waits to Be Told Unknown Words 118
- Scenario 3: The Student Produces a Nonword or Omits Unknown Words 119
- Scenario 4: The Student Substitutes Words That Make Sense 120
- Scenario 5: The Student Substitutes Words That Do Not Make Sense 121
- Scenario 6: The Student Habitually Tries to Sound Out Unknown Words 123

- Scenario 7: The Student Ignores Punctuation, Adds Punctuation, or Uses Inappropriate Intonation 125
- Scenario 8: The Student Overrelies on Context While Reading 126
- Scenario 9: The Student's Oral Reading Lacks Fluency 126
- Scenario 10: The Student is Overly Concerned with Rate When Reading Is Timed 127
- Scenario 11: The Student Does Not Read for Meaning 128

The Student Repeats Words, Phrases, or Sentences

SCENARIO 1

Repetitions may help the student understand what he or she has read. You must decide whether the student is anticipating a "hard" word, making a legitimate effort to have the reading make sense, or merely repeating from habit. Consider the following:

- If the student's repetitions are frequent, it is possible that the reading material is too difficult. If this is the case, provide the student with reading materials at his or her instructional level.
- Repetitions that are "stalls" may provide additional time to unlock an unknown word. This behavior may be a normal part of the reading process. Excessive use of the "stall" technique, however, may indicate that the reading material is too difficult and/or that more effective reading strategies are needed. It may also indicate a need to teach how context and language cues can be used to anticipate words (see Johns & Lenski, 2010). Many repetitions can also impact rate of reading, one aspect of fluency.

117

- Praise the student when a word, phrase, or sentence is repeated to preserve ongoing meaning. Tell the student that such behavior is fully acceptable when reading doesn't make sense. Provide examples from students' reading similar to the following that a student and/or class could discuss and evaluate. Note that the miscues distorted the meaning in the first two examples, and the student went back and corrected them.

1. *They grew* ©
   He knew he must try to save the woods he loved so much.

2. © *in*
   He jumped on the high wall perfectly.

3. Jack woke up Saturday morning.

4. *saved*
   Ken had solved the mystery.

- If repetitions are merely a habit (as in the third example above), it may be helpful to have the student record his or her reading and then discuss it with you. The student should then be guided to realize that the majority of the repetitions are a habit that generally detract from effective reading. Such repetitions also reduce fluency.

- Sometimes a student repeatedly overcorrects to ensure word-for-word accuracy. Such students should be encouraged not to repeat and break the flow when the miscue does not significantly alter the meaning (such as substituting *the* for *a*). Have the student follow along as you read and model the process.

SCENARIO 2

The Student Waits to Be Told Unknown Words

The reluctance of some students to attempt unknown words may be due to several factors. First, students may not have been taught a functional strategy for word identification, or they do not have a variety of strategies to use when confronted with an unknown word. Although students may have been taught phonics and the use of context, they do not apply these strategies during reading. Second, students may often be told unknown words, thereby reducing their need to acquire or use an internal strategy for word identification. Third, students who struggle in reading may be reluctant to take risks. Instead, they frequently reply on you or other students to tell them unknown words. The following strategies may be helpful:

- Stress that you want the student to attempt unknown words without help.

- Wait 5 or 10 seconds and see whether this will suggest to the student that you expect him or her to attempt to pronounce the word.

- Discuss what the student thinks should be done when confronted with an unknown word. Guide the student toward effective strategies that have been taught to help identify unknown words.

- Have the student continue reading to see whether subsequent textual information will help with the unknown word.

- Ask the student to go back a line and see whether the preceding sentence and the words around the "unknown" word suggest the word. If the student does not suggest a word, ask him or her to reread the sentence until a good guess is made.

- Ask the student to reread the sentence and try to guess a word that begins with the initial sound of the "unknown" word and makes sense.

- Provide oral examples where the student uses the information provided to anticipate the missing word.

  I saw a _____.

  I would like to play _____.

  It's time to go _____.

  I found a _____ in the lawn.

- Use easy cloze exercises where the student is asked to say or write in a word that makes sense. Discuss various choices offered by a group of students. Gradually include some graphic information, as in the third example, about the exact word the author used.

  I like _____.

  I like to go to the _____.

  I like to go to the s_____.

- If the student encounters several unknown words in a line of print, it is probable that the reading material is too difficult. Provide reading material at the student's instructional level.

- Teach a functional set of strategies for word identification. The following chart might be adapted and taught.

FIGURING OUT UNKNOWN WORDS

1. Use the words around the unknown word to help think of a word that makes sense in the sentence.
2. Use the letters, and the sounds associated with the letters, along with the words around the unknown word, to say a word that makes sense in the sentence.
3. Look for root words, prefixes, suffixes, and endings. Try to pronounce the various word parts to see whether you have heard it before. Try various pronunciations, especially for the vowels.
4. Continue reading. Later sentences may help you figure out the unfamiliar word.
5. As a last resort, use the dictionary, ask someone, or skip the unknown word.

The Student Produces a Nonword or Omits Unknown Words

SCENARIO

3

The student must be helped to realize that reading is a meaningful process and words pronounced should make sense. In short, reading should sound like oral language. Try the following strategies:

- Ask the student what the nonword means. It is possible that the student knows the meaning but has mispronounced the word.

- Share oral and written examples where the student attempts to predict the appropriate word that has been omitted. Discuss the student's choices and the clues that the student used to predict the omitted word.

  I will mail the _____.

  The horse _____ over the fence.

  Jack and Tom _____ into the kitchen.

- Provide examples that contain a nonword and ask the student to tell what the nonword could mean. Have the student share clues in the sentence that were helpful in predicting the meaning of the unknown word.

  He drank a glass of *fax*.

  The *zop* bought some candy.

  I went swimming in the *tos*.

- Place opaque white tape over certain words in the student's reading material that can be easily predicted. Encourage the student to supply a real word that makes sense. Then compare the student's word to the word in the reading material. If the words are different, encourage the student to evaluate his or her choice in light of the actual word. Help the student to transfer this prediction strategy to identifying unknown words when reading.

- Many nonwords may indicate that the reading material is too difficult. Provide materials at the student's independent or instructional level.

- If the student omits an unknown word, ask questions such as:

  Does that sound like language to you?

  What word do you think could go in this spot?

  Why do you think so?

  What word do you know that begins like _____ that would make sense?

  If the student is unable to produce a word with the same beginning sound, ask the student to try a word that he or she thinks would make sense.

  The goal should be to have the student produce a word or nonword rather than omitting the word. Remember that there are times when a word can be omitted without any or much loss in meaning.

SCENARIO 4

The Student Substitutes Words That Make Sense

The most important strategy must be enacted by you: remain silent. Try to keep other students from breaking the thought line. You might tell students that readers will sometimes substitute words that make sense. Only substitutions that do not make sense or alter the meaning should be corrected. To help students decide whether substitutions do or do not make sense, try the following strategies:

- Provide sentences that contain a substituted word written above the text. Have students discuss whether or not the substituted word makes sense. You could also read a text and make substitution miscues that students could evaluate.

  before
  He tried to make up for it by shocking people with his rude behavior.

  they
  They went to the zoo because there were many things to see.

  big
  He put the bag down.

- Provide exercises that contain substitutions two different readers made in the same sentence. Discuss which substitution, if either, appears to be closer to the author's intended meaning.

  the
  Billy decided to ride along a little road.

  walk
  Billy decided to ride along a little road.

- Develop lessons where students can discuss the subtle differences in words even though such differences are unlikely to significantly influence the author's intended meaning. For example, what is the difference between *street* and *road*, *house* and *home*, *tall* and *big*, *little* and *small*?

  NOTE: Similar strategies may also be used with omissions. For example:

  He knew that there were ~~so~~ many things to see. He remembered how bare and black it ~~had~~ looked.

  He gave the boy twenty-~~five~~ cents.

  He found leaves from ~~some~~ maple and oak trees.

  Dad went out to get your sleds. First we will eat.

  In the sky I saw a ~~strange~~ object.

The Student Substitutes Words That Do Not Make Sense

Tell the student that reading is a process of constructing meaning. (Did that sound right to you?) The student must be taught to use semantic (contextual) cues. Try the following strategies:

- Remind the student to think while reading so that he or she will stop and reread the material if it is not making sense. This student may view reading primarily as a "word-calling" process. You may need to help the student develop a concept of reading that involves meaning as the crucial element.

- Give the student oral exercises in which he or she identifies words that do not make sense in the context of the sentences or the story. Discuss why the word or words do not make sense. Do similar written exercises. For example:

    I like to drink apples.

    The postman delivered the groceries.

    He set his calendar so he would wake up at seven o'clock.

    Bill went to the store to buy some candy for her sister.

    She likes to eat books.

- Provide the student with oral and written exercises containing closure tasks in which the student anticipates omitted words that make sense. Use the cloze procedure as a teaching technique. Develop the notion that language dictates that only certain types of words can be placed after certain language structures.

    After playing, the children _____.

    I will see you after _____.

    He was reading a _____.

    "I lost my money," _____ Bill.

    The _____ climbed the tree.

- Use small group activities where certain key words in a story are covered. Elicit responses from the group and have students evaluate the responses. The ultimate criterion is: "Does the word you suggest make sense in the phrase (sentence, paragraph)?" Demonstrate how the flow of the story helps the reader to predict certain words. Think out loud so students can "see" you model the process. Be sure some of your predictions do not match the text and take time to have students explain why they are inappropriate in the context.

- Keep track of the student's substitutions to see whether certain words are habitually associated with other words. Write selections where the grammatical structures make it highly unlikely for the habitual associations to occur. For example:

    was and saw

Once upon a time there was a girl named Ebony. Her hair was long and black. Ebony liked to wear beads in her hair. One day, while she was walking downtown, she saw some beads in a store window. She saw blue, yellow, and pink beads.

    in and on

Jim liked to collect insects. He kept the spiders in a jar on top of his dresser. One Friday, his mother invited some friends to come over for coffee. They were talking in the kitchen. Jim took his jar of spiders into the kitchen and set it on the table. When one lady reached for a cup on the table, she bumped the jar. It landed on the floor. What do you think happened next?

    when and then

José and his mother had some errands to do. His mother said, "I will get my coat; <u>then</u> I will be ready to go. <u>When</u> you find your jacket, come out to the car. First, we will go to the market; <u>then</u> we can go to the pet shop to find out <u>when</u> the puppy will be ready to come home. <u>When</u> we bring the puppy home, you will get the basket out of the closet."

● Provide sentences that contain a substituted word written above the text. Have students discuss whether the substituted word makes sense. Be sure that students give reasons or explain their responses. For example:

  then
  Sam did not see them.

  they
  They went to the zoo because there were many things to see.

  radius
  The key to success was in the radium reaction.

● Provide exercises that contain substitutions two different readers made in the same sentence. Discuss which substitution appears to be closer to the author's intended meaning. For example:

  the
  Billy decided to ride along a little road.

  walk
  Billy decided to ride along a little road.

● Tape-record the student's reading. Have the student listen to the reading and note substitutions that resulted in a partial or significant loss of meaning. Discuss and use some of the appropriate strategies already presented. In addition, encourage the student to monitor his or her reading by asking, "Does that make sense?" Ask this question from time to time when the reading makes sense so students are not automatically cued by the question that there is a significant miscue.

● If there are many substitutions that distort the author's intended meaning, the book may be too difficult. Choose materials at the student's instructional level. Books at this level should contain words that are usually within the student's meaning vocabulary. In other words, the student should have the necessary background, experiences, and concepts to understand the words.

NOTE: Similar strategies may also be used with omissions that distort the meaning.

The Student Habitually Tries to Sound Out Unknown Words

SCENARIO
6

Some students may have been taught or think that the only appropriate strategy is to sound out words when they are unknown. Other students may not have been taught any strategies that can be applied in such a situation. In either case, help students use their knowledge of language (syntax) and teach the value of context (semantic) cues. The following strategies represent an appropriate beginning:

- Show the student that a word in oral language can often be predicted correctly before it is heard. Model the process. Then, help the student use this same knowledge in reading. The following examples may be useful:

    He gave the kitten some _____.

    Put a stamp on the _____.

    Five pennies make a _____.

    The bird began to _____ to the tree.

- Offer examples where two readers have come across the same unknown word. Discuss the responses of the two readers in an attempt to decide which reader has been most effective and why.

    Text: The car went down the old *street*.
    Reader 1:   The car went down the old *road*.
    Reader 2:   The car went down the old *stream*.

- Provide words that the student is probably able to pronounce but that are not familiar in meaning. Then provide a sentence that builds meaning for the word. Have students identify and explain which clues in the sentence were helpful. For example:

    kingcups   He picked some kingcups for his mother because she likes flowers.

    kipper   The kipper is not usually caught by fishermen.

- Provide words in the student's meaning vocabulary that he or she is unable to pronounce. Such words can then be placed in a context that builds meaning for the words. Through such exercises the student should realize that meaning can be achieved without always sounding out words.

- Teach the student a set of strategies for word identification. A chart or bookmark could be adapted from the items listed below.

FIGURING OUT UNKNOWN WORDS

1. What makes sense here?
2. What sound does it start with?
3. Chunk the sounds.
4. Are there root words, prefixes, or endings?
5. Keep reading to try to figure it out.
6. Use these last:
   - dictionary
   - someone's help
   - skip it

The Student Ignores Punctuation, Adds Punctuation, or Uses Inappropriate Intonation

SCENARIO 7

Try the following strategies to rectify misuses of punctuation and intonation:

- The student should be shown examples where punctuation is ignored or substituted. In some cases meaning may not be disturbed; in other cases a change in meaning may occur. Discuss whether or not the reader should have paid attention to the punctuation. The following examples may be useful:

  He woke up ∧ *and* got ready for school.   *. He*

  Billy looked ahead ∧ *and* saw smoke coming out of a pile of dry brush.   *. He*

  Even as Billy looked, *at* the flames burst out.

  But Blaze scrambled up the bank, and Billy held on somehow, ∧ *with* his arms around the pony's neck.

  Down Blaze went to his knees, ∧ *and* Billy slipped out of the saddle.

  Model similar oral examples using classroom materials.

- Read plays and write experience stories or journals. Help the student see the role of punctuation.

- Teach the basic marks of punctuation, as needed, in a natural writing situation.

- Discuss reading that has been recorded and ask the student to point out areas where it can be improved.

- Remember that some intonation patterns may be the result of the student's dialect. In such cases, no interventions are necessary.

- Use slash marks to indicate appropriate phrasing (for instance, Bill,/my brother,/ has gone away.). Reduce the number of slash marks as the student's phrasing and attention to punctuation improve. Students can also be encouraged to mark appropriate phrases in reproduced copies of selected reading selections.

- Use pattern books. Each time the pattern is repeated, ask the student to read it. Stress that the pattern should sound like speech.

- List phrases on cards and have the student read the phrases as they would sound naturally.

at school	at home	near my house	by the school
on the table	by my house	in the box	near the tree

- Model correct phrasing and punctuation in a passage that is easy for the student. Invite the student to read it like you do. Then have the student read along with you. Finally, have the student read the passage independently.

The Student Overrelies on Context While Reading

Some students read fluently, but they often add a number of words that were not written by the author. These same students may also omit a number of words. The result is often an interesting story that is quite different from the one in print. These students seem to rely heavily on their background knowledge to the partial exclusion of graphophonic knowledge. Because effective reading requires the use of context, language cues, and graphophonic cues, the following strategies and interventions may be helpful:

- Tell the student that background knowledge is important to help predict words while reading, but other cues should also be used. Model how initial sounds, along with context clues, can be used to help pronounce words. Possible responses are provided in parentheses.

  The leaves on the tree are g_____. (green)

  To write, you need p_____ and p_____. (pencil, paper)

  Jamie is my best f_____. (friend)

  The h_____ has a roof and ch_____. (house, chimney)

- Record the student's reading, listen to it, and mark any miscues. Then review selected miscues with the student and discuss how meaning is changed even though the miscue may make sense in the sentence. Model how graphic cues can be used along with the context to determine the actual word used by the author.

  quietly
  She quickly dashed down the hill.

  perplexed
  The soft buzz of the computer relaxed Anthony.

- Present sentences where the student can make initial predictions of a missing word. Then provide a series of graphic cues to help the student correctly identify the word used by the author.

  I must put the _____ away.

  I must put the d_____ away.

  I must put the de_____s away.

  I must put the decor_____s away.

  I must put the decorations away.

- Tell the student that all readers make miscues, but stress the importance of trying to pay attention to the words written by the author. Relate the situation to a piece of the student's writing. The expectation is that the reader will read the words that were written.

The Student's Oral Reading Lacks Fluency

Students at the beginning stages of reading are seldom fluent readers (National Reading Panel, 2000). This situation is to be expected and no intervention is required. Such students are beginning to acquire a sight vocabulary and learn strategies such as phonics so they can identify unknown words. Such is the case for most beginning readers, whatever their age. If, however, students remain in a stage where they continue to read word for word, the following strategies may be considered.

● Be sure students are placed in materials at an appropriate instructional level. At the instructional level, the student will generally miss no more than one word in twenty.

● Recognize that reading is a developmental process. Fluency will usually improve as sight vocabularies and word-identification strategies develop.

● Encourage the repeated readings of pattern books and books at the student's independent and instructional levels.

● Use echo reading. Have the student echo your phrasing and expression from a book.

● Promote wide reading and oral reading of plays and jokes.

● Engage students in choral reading and reader's theater.

● Have older students practice "easy" books that can be read orally to younger students. Practice sessions can include tape recording the reading and evaluating the fluency and expression.

● Provide books on tape so students can listen and follow along.

● Remember that a lack of fluency may be symptomatic of limited word-identification strategies, poor sight vocabulary, and/or insufficient meaningful practice. Consider these areas carefully when evaluating the student's fluency.

Johns and Berglund (2010) have prepared a compact book on fluency that answers common questions often asked by teachers and offers over 30 strategies to strengthen fluency. Each strategy contains a brief description followed by an easy-to-use lesson plan.

The Student Is Overly Concerned with Rate When Reading Is Timed

The increased emphasis on fluency has resulted in progress monitoring, usually with timed readings. While the ability to read with appropriate speed, accuracy, and expression are worthwhile instructional goals, some students may focus so much on speed that meaning is forgotten. If instruction in fluency is perceived only as fast reading, there is the real risk of students becoming word-callers, not meaning seekers (Marcell, 2007). The following strategies may help students develop, embrace, and maintain a concept of fluency that embodies much more than "faster is better."

● Help students realize that fluency involves comprehension, accuracy, speed, and expression. Put a fluency diamond on poster board to remind students of the four components that make up fluency. Model each of these aspects of fluency during read alouds and in the ongoing instructional program.

- Compare and contrast multiple readings of a portion of text where 1) it is read without expression, 2) many errors are made, and 3) it is read quickly without attending to meaning. Stress a broad concept of fluency when oral reading and progress monitoring occurs.

- Create purposes prior to reading and have students read to answer the purpose-setting questions.

- Incorporate retelling or summarizing into fluency assessments so students will realize that comprehension is important. Questions can also be asked.

- If the student reads fast and does not understand what was read, stress that the reason to read is to construct meaning, gain information, and make sense of the reading material. Provide examples of various types of reading materials and have the student explain what the reader would probably like to achieve. Use or adapt the examples below.

a recipe for a favorite treat	the ingredients on a food label
comics in the newspaper	a book about various sports
a Harry Potter book	the directions inside a model car kit
a joke or riddle book	receiving a postcard from a friend
directions in a new game	the school newspaper

- If the student makes many miscues in an effort to increase rate, stop the reading and remind the student that accuracy is an important part of reading. Have the student practice the selection so it can be read accurately.

- If the student reads without expression or with inappropriate expression in an effort to increase rate, model appropriate expression in a portion of the selection for the student. Then have the student reread the same selection in an effort to emulate the modeled expression.

- Use reader's theater scripts to help students practice appropriate rate and expression to help convey meaning to the audience.

- Remind students that oral reading should sound a lot like conversations that people have with each other. Have students prepare written "conversations" between two classmates. Then have partners practice the "conversations" using appropriate phrasing, rate, and expression.

- Strive to have progress monitoring in the classroom "reflect a more comprehensive model of fluency in which comprehension and expression join speed and accuracy" (Johns, 2007, p. 18).

SCENARIO 11 The Student Does Not Read for Meaning

Some students are so focused on decoding words accurately that they do not focus on comprehending what they read. Many younger readers and struggling readers may believe that the purpose of reading is to identify the words rather than to construct meaning from those words. Because the purpose of all reading is comprehension, it is essential that students be taught to read for meaning at all times. The following strategies may help students understand that the purpose of reading is to construct meaning.

- Explain to the student that there are many purposes for reading. These include learning, enjoyment, and to solve problems. Explain that all of these purposes require the student to understand what has been read.

- Model the importance of reading for meaning by reading a short set of instructions aloud. Complete some of the steps correctly and some incorrectly. Ask the student why it is important to read for meaning in this situation.

- Explain that sometimes the purpose for reading is enjoyment. Read a short text aloud to the student. Do a brief think-aloud to demonstrate your understanding and enjoyment of the text. Ask the student to think of a text he or she enjoyed reading. Discuss the importance of reading for meaning to promote enjoyment.

- Tell the student that the purpose of many school reading assignments is to read for information. Using a science or social studies textbook, show the student the questions that appear at the end of each section. Read these questions together and explain that they can set a purpose for reading that section. In other words, clarify that the student should be thinking about these questions while reading, and that after reading, he or she should be able to answer them.

- Prior to reading, help the student set a specific purpose for reading to focus attention on understanding the text. These purposes may include answering specific questions, stating the main idea, checking to see if predictions were accurate, or enjoying the text. When the student has read the text, have him or her reflect and discuss whether the purpose was met.

- Teach the student to use the Read-Cover-Remember-Retell strategy. First, the student will read a piece of text that is no larger than can be covered by his or her hand. Next, the student covers the text and consciously remembers what was read. Finally, the student retells what was just read to a partner. If he or she can't retell accurately, he or she can go back and read the text again. Once the student understands the Read-Cover-Remember-Retell strategy, ask him or her to apply it while reading independently or with a partner.

SECTION 6

Development, Reliability, and Validity Data for the Basic Reading Inventory

Sharing information from books with others can strengthen understanding.

- Basis for the Graded Word Lists   131
- Selection of the Graded Word Lists   134
- Reliability Studies of the Word Lists   135
- Validity of Graded Word List Criteria   137
- Reliability of Graded Passages   138
- Strengthening the Manual, Graded Passages, and Comprehension Questions   140

- Development of Forms LL and LI   141
- Development of Form E and New Pre-Primer Levels   142
- Reliability Studies   143
- Validity Considerations   144

Basis for the Graded Word Lists

The word lists were selected from two sources: *EDL Core Vocabularies in Reading, Mathematics, Science, and Social Studies* (Taylor et al., 1979) and *Basic Skills Word List: Grades 1–12* (IOX, 1980). These two word lists and their development are described here.

The first source was the Reading Core Vocabulary portion from the *EDL Core Vocabularies.* Fourteen graded word lists, from pre-primer through grade thirteen, are included. The lists are composed of words "introduced in the more widely used basal reading series and/or found on frequency lists" (p. 1). Originally published in 1949, the EDL Reading Core Vocabulary was revised in 1951, 1955, 1969, and 1979. In the 1979 revision, several procedures were used to select words for the 14 graded word lists for each of the three forms.

The lists through grade three were developed by determining the level at which words were introduced in nine different basal reader series. A word was included if it was introduced at the same level in at least three of the nine basal series.

In selecting words for the fourth-, fifth-, and sixth-grade lists, words occurring in at least three basals on the same level or below were judged to be suitable for that level. In addition, words occurring in two readers at the same level were checked against the Rinsland (1945) list and the Thorndike and Lorge (1944) list. The Rinsland list was used to confirm student knowledge of the word at that particular level. The Thorndike-Lorge list was used to determine whether a word occurred with sufficient frequency to justify its inclusion.

131

For grades seven and eight, words used in basal readers in grades four through six that did not occur with sufficient frequency to be included in earlier lists were checked against the Rinsland and Thorndike-Lorge lists for frequency. If warranted, these words were included in the Reading Core Vocabulary. The remaining words for grades seven and eight were derived, for the most part, from frequency on these same two word lists.

Nine of the Reading Core Vocabulary graded lists were used for the graded word lists on the Basic Reading Inventory: pre-primer through grade eight. The pre-primer list contained 68 different words; the eighth-grade word list contained over 700 different words.

The second source, *Basic Skills Word List: Grades 1–12* (IOX, 1980), contains lists of words for grades one through twelve. The graded word lists contain key words that students need to master in each grade and were designed as a resource for reading teachers and for the development of tests.

To select the words for the Basic Skills Word List, three criteria were used:

1. the frequency of words in basal readers
2. the frequency of words in general reading materials
3. students' demonstrated familiarity with particular words.

The initial source of words, the *EDL Core Vocabularies*, was described earlier. All the words on the *EDL Core Vocabularies* were checked for their familiarity to children by using *The Living Word Vocabulary—The Words We Know* (Dale & O'Rourke, 1976). To determine students' knowledge of commonly encountered words, Dale and O'Rourke administered three-option, multiple-choice test items to students. Students were given a word and asked to choose the correct definition for it. *The Living Word Vocabulary* provides a "familiarity percentage" for each word listed. This index reflects the percentage of students who answered that word's multiple-choice test item correctly. In order to assign a word to a particular grade level, Dale and O'Rourke aimed for each tested word to have a familiarity percentage for a given grade level that was within the range of 67 percent to 84 percent. Therefore, if a word was tested at the sixth grade and only 66 percent of the students at that grade were familiar with it, then the word was retested at the eighth grade. Conversely, if a word tested at the eighth grade received a familiarity score higher than 84 percent, it was retested at the sixth grade. The familiarity percentage supplied with each word in *The Living Word Vocabulary* reflects the percentage of correct student responses at the grade level to which the word was ultimately assigned.

The authors of *The Living Word Vocabulary* did not begin testing words until the fourth grade; after that, they tested words only at alternate grades. Thus, familiarity percentages appear only for grades four, six, eight, and so on. Therefore, EDL words through grade four were checked for their familiarity to students according to the fourth-grade Dale-O'Rourke familiarity percentages. Fifth-grade EDL words were checked against both fourth- and sixth-grade familiarity percentages. Words in all subsequent grade lists were checked for familiarity ratings at either the grade level at which they appeared in EDL or at a lower grade.

Words that were not familiar to at least 65 percent of students at a given grade on the basis of the Dale-O'Rourke study were moved to a higher grade level in the Basic Skills Word List. The exact familiarity percentages necessary for an EDL word to be retained at the same grade level on the Basic Skills Word List varied slightly from grade to grade. These percentages were adjusted in order to meet the requirements of a predetermined word load for each grade. (This word load factor will be described subsequently.) Table 6.1 contains the minimum familiarity percentages used through grade twelve.

The rationale for employing a stringent familiarity criterion was straightforward: even if a word is found in several reading series at a given grade level, it may still be unfamiliar to many students and therefore should not be assigned to that grade level. The effect of this student fa-

TABLE 6.1

Minimum Familiarity Percentages: Pre-Primer through Twelfth Grade

Grade at Which Word Appeared in EDL	Grade to Which Word Was Assigned in Dale-O'Rourke Study*	Minimum Familiarity Percentage Required for Retention in Same Grade Level as EDL on Basic Skills Word List
Pre-Primer and First	Fourth	80%
Second	Fourth	83%
Third	Fourth	76%
Fourth	Fourth	65%
	Sixth	75%
Fifth	Fourth	65%
	Sixth	75%
Sixth	Fourth	65%
	Sixth	84%
Seventh	Fourth and Sixth	65%
Eighth	Fourth and Sixth	65%
	Eighth	80%
Ninth	Sixth and Eighth	65%
Tenth	Sixth and Eighth	65%
	Tenth	75%
Eleventh	Eighth and Tenth	65%
Twelfth	Eighth and Tenth	65%
	Twelfth	75%

*This study did not include words from the pre-primer through third grade.

miliarity screen was to move some words from each of the graded EDL word lists to higher grade levels.

For instructional purposes, it is desirable to allocate words to grade levels on a proportional basis. It would make little sense to assign 200 words to one grade level and 2,000 words to another. One of the best guides to the determination of an appropriate word load per grade level is the average number of words introduced per grade level by publishers of reading textbook series. These commercially published textbooks, many of them revised more than once, provide an experience-based estimate of how many new words can be reasonably introduced at each grade level. In the process of researching the background for their core vocabularies, developers of the EDL word lists calculated the average number of words introduced at grades one through six for nine different textbook series. These textbook-derived word loads were the following:

Grade	1	2	3	4	5	6
Word Load	341	440	708	787	1,063	1,077

The word loads for the Basic Skills Word List at grades one through four were designed to coincide as closely as possible with these textbook-derived word loads. The word loads for the Basic Skills Word List at grades one through four are as follows:

Grade	1	2	3	4
Word Load	341	439	708	785

In grades five through twelve, students' familiarity with words, as reflected by the Dale-O'Rourke study, became a major determinant of grade level word load for the Basic Skills Word List. Students at these grade levels displayed insufficient familiarity with many potentially includable words, thus reducing the word loads—particularly in grades nine through twelve. The word loads for the Basic Skills Word List in grades five through twelve are as follows:

Grade	5	6	7	8	9	10	11	12
Word Load	971	846	884	874	325	407	393	345

The final step in the selection of words for the Basic Skills Word List was based on a massive study by Carroll, Davies, and Richman (1971). This study analyzed 5,000,000 running words of text. These 5,000,000 words were taken from approximately 10,000 samples of 500 words excerpted from textbooks in 17 different curriculum areas in grades three through nine, plus magazines, books, newspapers, and poetry. The result of the study is a list of 87,000 words, accompanied by the frequency with which each of those words appears in print. Unfortunately, this enormous set of words is listed alphabetically rather than in the order of each word's frequency of usage. Hence, one cannot readily determine the most frequently encountered words. Sakiey and Fry (1979), however, have drawn on the 87,000 words to provide a list of the 3,000 most frequently occurring words ranked according to their frequency of usage in print. These words, in order of decreasing frequency of appearance, were added at each grade level of the Basic Skills Word List if they were not already listed. This ensured that words appearing very frequently in general reading materials were not overlooked because they did not have a high enough familiarity percentage.

Selection of the Graded Word Lists

Fourteen graded word lists accompany Forms A, B, and C of the Basic Reading Inventory. Each list contains 20 words. The lists range in difficulty from pre-primer through the twelfth-grade level.

The general rule for selecting words for inclusion in the graded word lists for grades one through eight was that the word had to be assigned to the same grade on both the Reading Core Vocabulary and the Basic Skills Word List. Words from an earlier edition of the Basic Reading Inventory were used when they met the criterion. The remaining words to complete each list were selected at random within each grade level designation of the published word lists. Once a word was selected, it was checked for inclusion on the other list. If the word appeared on both lists it was included; otherwise, another word was randomly selected and the checking procedure was repeated until 20 words were secured for each word list.

A slight modification was used to select words for the pre-primer and primer graded word lists because neither published word list used the term *primer*. Words selected at the pre-primer and primer levels had to appear on either the pre-primer or first-grade list of the Reading Core Vocabulary *and* on the first-grade level of the Basic Skills Word List. After the words were selected, they were assigned to one of the three forms of the Basic Reading Inventory.

Fieldtesting the pre-primer through grade eight word lists involved 309 students in grades one through eight from the United States and Canada. The vast majority of the students were identified as average readers by their teachers. As the students pronounced the words on the graded word lists, examiners marked the words that were mispronounced. The major change resulting from fieldtesting the graded word lists was moving some of the words from one form to another form. Equivalence of forms was accomplished by the initial selection of words from large scale vocabulary studies and fieldtesting to help ensure that the more difficult words were evenly distributed among the three forms of word lists at each grade level. In addition, the words on each list are arranged from easier to more difficult based on fieldtest results.

A three-phase process was used to develop the graded word lists for grades nine through twelve. First, all words common to both the Reading Core Vocabulary and the Basic Skills Word List for grades nine through twelve were listed. A total of 66 words was randomly selected from each graded list.

Next, the 66 words were randomly divided into three forms and fieldtested with 334 students in ninth grade, 544 students in tenth grade, 301 students in eleventh grade, and 207 students in twelfth grade. The students attended schools in Washington, South Carolina, and Illinois. The students marked each word they could read with a plus sign (+) and used a minus sign (–) for each word they thought they couldn't read. Students were instructed not to mark a word if they were in doubt. All words marked with a minus sign were tallied across forms for each grade level. Then, using the student responses, three new forms were devised. Words were ranked and distributed among the three forms. Six words were deleted from each grade level because students' responses indicated that the words were either very easy or very difficult.

Finally, the revised forms were given to 330 students in grade nine, 276 students in grade ten, 231 students in grade eleven, and 263 students in grade twelve who crossed out any words they were unable to pronounce. The students attended high schools in New York or Illinois. Research assistants then asked 65 students in grade nine, 61 students in grade ten, 75 students in grade eleven, and 157 students in grade twelve to respond individually to the words that were not crossed out. Based on an analysis of student responses, several words were rearranged so the words at the end of each list were the most difficult.

Reliability Studies of the Word Lists

In the late spring of the 2003 school year, the author and five assistants who had classroom teaching experience undertook two studies with the word lists. All the assistants had advanced degrees, and two assistants were working on doctoral degrees. Training sessions were conducted by the author to familiarize the assistants with the word lists and how the data would be gathered. The training session lasted about an hour, and debriefing sessions were held at the end of each school day to address any additional questions or concerns. The data were collected during one school week near the end of the school year.

The students in this Midwest K–5 elementary school, according to the school's 2003 state report card, represented various racial/ethnic backgrounds: White, 85%; Black; 9%; Hispanic, 5%; and Asian/Pacific Islander, 1%. The mobility rate was 26%, and 25% of the students were from low-income families. Overall, approximately 77% of the students in grade three met or exceeded state standards in reading. Approximately 73% of the students in grade five met or exceeded state standards in reading.

The first study undertaken was an alternate-form reliability study for the three forms of the graded word lists in the Basic Reading Inventory. A total of 115 students participated in the study: African American, 6; Asian/Pacific Islander, 2; Hispanic, 6; and White, 101. Table 6.2 contains a breakdown of number and sex of students in the study. Boys represented 56% of the sample;

TABLE 6.2

Number and Sex of Students in Basic Reading Inventory Alternate-Form Reliability Study

Grade	Boys	Girls	Total
K	6	7	13
1	9	5	14
2	10	7	17
3	8	10	18
4	9	9	18
5	22	13	35
Totals	64	51	115

African American, 6; Asian, 2; Hispanic, 6; White, 101

girls represented 44% of the sample. Teachers in grades one through five who agreed to participate in the study had all their students assessed, except those who were absent. For kindergarten, the teacher recommended students for assessment who were most likely to be able to read some of the words on the lists.

Students were tested in an area reasonably free of distractions. Usually, an empty classroom was used, but some students were also assessed in the hall. The first word list used was at grade level. The form initially presented was determined randomly. The same procedure was used with the two remaining forms at the same level. Students read lists until they reached a frustration level or the grade eight word list. If the initial list was too difficult, easier lists were used. The raw scores (number of words correct) were entered into a database and analyzed by an SPSS program to determine the reliability of Forms A and B, Forms A and C, and Forms B and C. Two analyses were completed. Table 6.3 shows the alternate-form reliability for the ten different word lists (pre-primer through grade eight). The constant was the graded list, but students who read the lists were from different grades. In this analysis, the N indicates that students from various grades read lists at several levels, especially students in the upper grades. The overall reliability coefficient for each of the comparisons was .84 or higher. The lower reliability coefficients were .42 for Forms B and C in grade five and .47 for Forms A and B in grade 5. All the remaining reliability coefficients were .61 or higher. In addition, all the Pearson r coefficients in Table 6.3 are statistically significant ($p<.0001$).

Another analysis of the data was done to determine the alternate-form reliability for the students' grade placements. The constant was the grade in which the student was enrolled. The actual administration of the Basic Reading Inventory often involves a student reading various word lists until his or her frustration level is reached. This analysis may be a more realistic indication of the alternate-form reliability of the word lists. The results of this analysis are presented in Table 6.4. The alternate-form reliability coefficients ranged from .52 to .97, with a majority of the coefficients .80 or higher. Overall, the results demonstrate moderate to high alternate-form reliability for almost all of the comparisons.

The second study examined test-retest differences by using a random sample of 30 students from the first study. Table 6.5 reports the number of students at each grade in this study. Each student selected was asked to read some of the same word lists read the day before. Lists where students got all the words correct in each form were not used. The order in which each list was presented was random. The student rolled a die, and each specific number corresponded to a particular form of the graded word lists. The student's raw scores (number of words correct) for

TABLE 6.3
Basic Reading Inventory Word List Alternate-Form Reliability by Level

Level	N	Form A & B	A & C	B & C
PP	17	.95	.95	.95
P	8	.79	.90	.79
1	17	.87	.79	.95
2	32	.93	.89	.94
3	37	.86	.80	.91
4	59	.87	.78	.76
5	67	.47	.65	.42
6	67	.81	.78	.74
7	47	.76	.73	.79
8	37	.84	.63	.61
Overall r		.85	.84	.85

All paired correlations are statistically significant ($p<.0001$).

TABLE 6.4
Basic Reading Inventory Word List Alternate-Form Reliability by Grade

Grade	N*	Form		
		A & B	A & C	B & C
K	19	.97	.98	.97
1	52	.80	.71	.88
2	72	.82	.82	.87
3	55	.88	.83	.84
4	75	.73	.68	.67
5	117	.53	.71	.52

*Refers to number of word lists read by students. Range of Word Lists Read: K (PP–1), 1 (PP–7), 2 (PP–8), 3 (1–6), 4 (3–8), 5 (2–8). All paired correlations are statistically significant ($p<.0001$).

each of the lists read on day one and day two were entered into a database and analyzed using dependent t-tests with an SPSS program. The analysis compared the day one scores to the day two scores to find any differences and to determine whether any of the differences were statistically significant at the .05 level. Table 6.6 contains the results of this analysis. In all the comparisons, there were no significant test-retest differences for these 30 students a day after the initial lists were read. Although the sample size is small, the results indicate that K–5 students will perform very similarly on the same word lists if they are re-administered within a day.

TABLE 6.5
Number of Students in Basic Reading Inventory Test-Retest Study

Grade	Total
K	4
1	4
2	5
3	7
4	6
5	4
Totals	30

African American, 3; Asian, 1; Hispanic, 2; White, 24
Females, 12; Males, 18

Validity of Graded Word List Criteria

Ferroli (2008) conducted a series of studies over five consecutive summers to help establish and validate criteria for the reading levels associated with untimed scores on the graded word lists. Ninety-six students were involved in the studies. The students were struggling in reading and represented a variety of grade levels. Graduate students who had completed two diagnostic and clinical reading courses used the Basic Reading Inventory and other data (developmental spelling tests, phonics inventories, standardized measures, interest inventories, and the students' responses to several hours of tutoring) to determine each student's instructional reading level. Af-

TABLE 6.6
Basic Reading Inventory Word List Mean Test-Retest Differences in Alternate Forms

Grade	N*	Form		
		A & B	A & C	B & C
K	8	1.25	.25	1.00
1	8	.88	1.38	.50
2	10	.20	.10	.30
3	14	.43	.29	.71
4	12	.00	.67	.67
5	8	1.13	.75	.37

*Refers to the pairs of word lists read by students. There were no significant differences in any of the forms for the various grades.

ter the student's instructional reading level was determined, the word list scores were examined and analyzed for the level identified as instructional and the next higher word list. After combining and analyzing the data for all the students, Ferroli concluded that untimed scores of 16, 17, and 18 were closely associated with students' overall instructional levels. Scores of 14 and 15 could be thought of as being in a gray area between instructional and frustration levels. Scoring guides reflecting these findings were included in the tenth edition of the Basic Reading Inventory.

The revised graded word list criteria should be especially helpful with students who struggle in reading. The inclusion of a gray area for scores of 14 and 15 provide additional flexibility for teachers as they assess so-called average students. These criteria, along with the results of the student's word recognition in context score, comprehension score, and overall fluency should help in determining an appropriate instructional level for initial instruction.

Reliability of Graded Passages

A recent study of the Basic Reading Inventory was conducted to determine technical adequacy for use of the BRI as a universal screening and progress monitoring assessment for oral reading fluency and comprehension (Bieber, 2011a). A total of 149 students (i.e., 55 third-grade students, 50 fourth-grade students, and 44 fifth-grade students) participated in the study which examined the third-, fourth-, and fifth-grade passages from Forms A–E.

Alternate forms reliability analyses were conducted for accuracy on Forms A–E of the third-, fourth-, and fifth-grade passages. These analyses provided results regarding the equivalence or interchangeability of the various forms of the third-, fourth-, and fifth-grade passages. Adequate alternate forms reliability requires a coefficient of .80 or higher (Sattler, 2001).

For the third-grade passages, reliability coefficients ranged from .82 to .92 with a median of .90. Results for each of the forms are provided in Table 6.7 below.

TABLE 6.7
Third Grade Accuracy Alternate Forms Reliability (N=55) for the Basic Reading Inventory

Form	Pearson Correlations for Passages			
	B	C	D	E
A	.91	.89	.86	.92
B		.92	.87	.90
C			.82	.91
D				.90

Note: All correlations p<.001; Pearson r=.82–.92 (Median=.90)
[Bieber, G. A. (2011b). *Basic Reading Inventory: Accuracy data tables.* Unpublished manuscript.]
Copyright © by Gregg Bieber. Reprinted by permission of the author.

For the fourth-grade passages, reliability coefficients ranged from .88 to .95 with a median of .93. Results for each of the forms included in the analysis for the fourth-grade passages are provided in Table 6.8.

TABLE 6.8
**Fourth Grade Accuracy Alternate Forms Reliability ($N=50$)
for the Basic Reading Inventory**

	Pearson Correlations for Passages			
Form	B	C	D	E
A	.94	.92	.91	.93
B		.95	.90	.92
C			.92	.93
D				.88

Note: All correlations $p<.001$; Pearson $r=.88-.95$ (Median=.93)
[Bieber, G. A. (2011b). *Basic Reading Inventory: Accuracy data tables*. Unpublished manuscript.]
Copyright © by Gregg Bieber. Reprinted by permission of the author.

For the fifth-grade passages, reliability coefficients ranged from .62 to .82 with a median of .77. Results for the fifth-grade passages are provided in Table 6.9.

TABLE 6.9
**Fifth Grade Accuracy Alternate Forms Reliability ($N=44$)
for the Basic Reading Inventory**

	Pearson Correlations for Passages			
Form	B	C	D	E
A	.75	.62	.82	.82
B		.80	.69	.79
C			.73	.74
D				.81

Note: All correlations $p<.001$; Pearson $r=.62-.82$ (Median=.77)
[Bieber, G. A. (2011b). *Basic Reading Inventory: Accuracy data tables*. Unpublished manuscript.]
Copyright © by Gregg Bieber. Reprinted by permission of the author.

Test-retest reliability was calculated in relation to oral reading accuracy on the third-, fourth-, and fifth-grade passages. Pearson correlations ranged from .75 to .84 for the third-grade passages; from .77 to .89 for the fourth-grade passages; and from .71 to .90 for the fifth-grade passages. The median across all passages in the study was calculated at .80. Results for test-retest reliability are provided in Table 6.10.

TABLE 6.10
**Accuracy Test-Retest Reliability Pearson Correlations ($N=35$)
for the Basic Reading Inventory**

Passage	Third Grade Retest	Fourth Grade Retest	Fifth Grade Retest
A	.80	.77	.76
B	.80	.86	.71
C	.75	.81	.72
D	.81	.80	.90
E	.84	.89	.86

Note: All correlations $p<.001$; Pearson $r=.71-.90$ (Median=.80)
[Bieber, G. A. (2011b). *Basic Reading Inventory: Accuracy data tables*. Unpublished manuscript.]
Copyright © by Gregg Bieber. Reprinted by permission of the author.

Accuracy and fluency correlations were also calculated for Forms A–E. Results are provided in Table 6.11.

TABLE 6.11
Accuracy and Fluency Pearson Correlations for the Basic Reading Inventory

| Passages | | Third Grade | Fourth Grade | Fifth Grade |
Accuracy	Fluency	$(N=55)$	$(N=50)$	$(N=44)$
A	A	.73	.76	.62
B	B	.70	.75	.73
C	C	.74	.76	.69
D	D	.68	.76	.66
E	E	.75	.78	.72

Note: All correlations $p<.001$
[Bieber, G. A. (2011b). *Basic Reading Inventory: Accuracy data tables*. Unpublished manuscript.]
Copyright © by Gregg Bieber. Reprinted by permission of the author.

Bieber (2011a) also calculated the correlations for fluency rates on the Basic Reading Inventory and the Dynamic Indicators of Basic Early Literacy (DIBELS) Oral Reading Fluency (ORF). This analysis was undertaken to determine if adequate criterion-related concurrent validity was present when comparing the Basic Reading Inventory fluency rates to the DIBELS-ORF. All correlations were above .80 indicating a high level of criterion-related concurrent validity. The results are provided in Table 6.12.

TABLE 6.12
DIBELS-ORF Pearson Correlations with the Basic Reading Inventory

Passage	Third Grade $(N=53)$	Fourth Grade $(N=49)$	Fifth Grade $(N=42)$
A	.96	.93	.88
B	.97	.89	.85
C	.95	.93	.87
D	.96	.92	.90
E	.93	.92	.86

Note: All correlations $p<.001$
[Bieber, G. A. (2011b). *Basic Reading Inventory: Accuracy data tables*. Unpublished manuscript.]
Copyright © by Gregg Bieber. Reprinted by permission of the author.

Strengthening the Manual, Graded Passages, and Comprehension Questions

The passages in the Basic Reading Inventory were evaluated by one or more readability formulas (Spache, Fry, & Dale-Chall). A readability computer program (Hardy & Jerman, 1985; Micro Power & Light Co., 1995) was used to help assess the appropriateness of passages for assigned grade levels. The passages were also analyzed to determine placement on the Lexile scale. The results are shown in Table 6.13. Remember that Lexile measures do not translate specifically to grade levels.

To revise the graded passages for the Basic Reading Inventory, data and input were gathered from a wide variety of sources. First, users of the inventory in the United States and Canada were invited to share reactions based on use of the inventory in their particular educational setting. Second, undergraduate and graduate students at Northern Illinois University who used the inventory in classroom and clinical situations critiqued the passages and questions. Third, letters and e-mails sent to the author that contained suggestions for improving the passages and questions were given careful consideration. Fourth, relevant articles and research studies pertaining to informal reading inventories were critically reviewed. Fifth, several reading professionals who used the Basic Reading Inventory provided input for revision of the manual, word lists, passages, questions, and related

TABLE 6.13

Lexile® Measures for the Seven Forms of the Basic Reading Inventory Passages

Grade Level	Form of the Basic Reading Inventory						
	A	B	C	D	E	LL	LI
Pre-Primer 1	100	220	140	130	100	—	—
Pre-Primer 2	BR*	BR*	BR*	60	BR*	—	—
Primer	60	220	100	210	130	—	—
1	190	70	230	290	50	—	—
2	540	390	500	490	420	—	—
3	640	400	590	630	520	630	640
4	440	690	550	770	570	450	570
5	930	770	690	680	870	620	610
6	900	810	740	920	800	800	700
7	1040	890	870	1020	1010	800	720
8	900	930	920	1130	1020	1090	1040
9	—	—	—	—	—	960	1130
10	—	—	—	—	—	1150	1220
11	—	—	—	—	—	1080	1000
12	—	—	—	—	—	1200	1120

*BR = Beginning Reader

features. Finally, the author's use of the Basic Reading Inventory with students and in numerous workshops provided still more input. Based on findings from Bieber (2011a), the third-grade passage in Form E was replaced. The topic, Necco Wafers, was unfamiliar to many students in the study, and their oral fluency rate was slower than on any of the other third-grade passages. In addition, the students scored significantly lower on the comprehension questions on this passage than any of the other forms at the third-grade level. For these reasons, the third-grade passage in Form D was substituted for Necco Wafers and a new passage, Big Star, for third-grade Form D was added to the eleventh edition after field testing with 73 students of diverse backgrounds in public and private schools in Illinois and Florida.

Development of Forms LL and LI

In late 1987, the development of two new forms for grades three through eight was begun. In 1990, the development of longer passages for grades nine and ten was undertaken. The longer passages for grades eleven and twelve used in the seventh edition were adapted from an inventory developed by Johns (1990b). The forms were developed to (1) provide additional passages for initial assessment, (2) provide for assessment of the student's ability to read longer narrative and expository passages, (3) allow posttesting with different passages, and (4) give teachers greater flexibility in using the Basic Reading Inventory.

Written or adapted drafts of the initial passages were based on topics that would be interesting and appropriate for average readers in grades three through eight. The initial passages were analyzed by a readability program (Hardy & Jerman, 1985) to help assess their appropriateness for a particular grade level. Comprehension questions were prepared for each passage. Numerous changes in the passages and questions were made based on an initial limited fieldtesting and critical reviews of the passages and questions by 26 teachers and graduate students enrolled in an advanced reading course.

Fieldtesting for grade three through grade eight passages began in 1989 and continued into 1990. Classroom teachers, reading teachers, and research assistants participated in the fieldtests. The fieldtests took place in Illinois, Missouri, and Michigan. Average, above-average, and below-average students in grades three through eight participated in the fieldtesting. A total of 537 students read Form LN and LE passages, now referred to as LL and LI respectively.

In 1990, two new grade levels (nine and ten) were developed for forms LL and LI using the general procedures just described. Both comprehension questions and passages underwent numerous revisions based on limited fieldtesting and the critical analysis by several reading professionals.

Actual fieldtesting was carried out early in 1993 with the cooperation of a local high school and two research assistants. Table 6.14 contains the number of students who read each passage in grades three through ten. As mentioned earlier, the passages for grades eleven and twelve were adapted from Johns (1990b).

During the process of fieldtesting, a number of changes were suggested. These changes were incorporated into subsequent fieldtests. The nature of the changes involved some changes in the vocabulary used in the passages and, in one instance, modification in the organization of the passage. Other changes included revisions in the wording of comprehension questions. Students initially responded to more than 10 questions, and their answers were very useful in the selection of the final comprehension questions.

TABLE 6.14
Number of Students Involved in Fieldtesting Forms LL and LI

Passage	Form	
	LL	LI
3	51	47
4	47	50
5	48	55
6	41	48
7	36	40
8	34	40
9	48	50
10	51	49
Totals	356	379

Development of Form E and New Pre-Primer Levels

The development of Form E began in 1992. The passages were used in the Reading Clinic at Northern Illinois University for two years and then revised. These revised passages were then shared with teachers in two states for use with students. Feedback for the passages and questions were used to finalize the passages and questions. The passages were also evaluated with two readability formulas. The Fry formula was used for all the passages. The Spache formula was appropriate to use with the passages through grade three. The grade levels of the passages in Form E are presented in Table 6.15. Readability formulas and fieldtest results were used to assign passages to grade levels. For Lexile results, refer to Table 6.13 found on page 141. Teachers should also remember that expository passages could be more difficult for students to read, because of a heavier vocabulary load and text structure that may be less familiar to students.

New Pre-Primer Passages

Reports from teachers indicated that the pre-primer passages in the eighth edition were quite challenging for students at the beginning of first grade. Many students are in the emergent stage of learning to read, so this finding is not surprising. The length of the passages (approximately 50 words) was also thought to contribute to the challenge. To help teachers more accurately assess students who are beginning to process text, five new passages were developed for Forms A,

TABLE 6.15
Readability Ratings for Form E

Readability Formula	Graded Passage									
	PP	P	1	2	3	4	5	6	7	8
Fry	P	1	1	3	3	4	4	6	7	8
Spache	1.2	1.5	1.5	2.2	2.8	—	—	—	—	—

B, C, D, and E. An experienced first-grade teacher was invited to draft some initial passages that could be read by students in the early stages of formal reading instruction.

The passages were designed with simple, helpful illustrations to help convey the story or information. After initial tryouts with a small sample of first graders, the revised passages were fieldtested by teachers in two states. Their feedback was used to create the final passages. The Fry readability formula was applied to each of the passages, and the results were all in the pre-primer or primer area with the exception of a passage about apples (a two-syllable word). Because of the helpful illustrations and the positive results from the field trials, the passage was judged to be appropriate for the pre-primer level.

Reliability Studies

Several studies have been reported which involve the Basic Reading Inventory. Bristow, Page, and Pikulski (1983) conducted a study involving 72 students, 24 each from grades two, four, and six. One part of the study compared the results of the Basic Reading Inventory to the students' actual placement in books. The comparison revealed the Basic Reading Inventory and book placement were identical 35% of the time, within one level 76% of the time, and within two levels 92% of the time.

An alternate-form reliability study reported by Helgren-Lempesis and Mangrum (1986) involved 75 fourth-grade students who were randomly assigned to one of three commercially-prepared reading inventories, one of which was the Basic Reading Inventory. Pearson r coefficients were .64 for the independent level, .72 for the instructional level, and .73 for the frustration level. According to estimated variance components from the generalizability analysis, little error could be directly attributed to the forms, as the students were the source of the greatest variance.

Pikulski and Shanahan (1982) studied 33 students who were evaluated at the Reading Center at the University of Delaware. The students represented a wide range in terms of chronological age (7 yrs., 2 mos. to 15 yrs., 11 mos.) and reading ability (pre-primer through sixth grade). Comparisons of the Basic Reading Inventory with a clinician constructed informal reading inventory resulted in "an outstanding amount of agreement between the two forms of the IRI" (p. 110). The two reading inventories were remarkably similar: 22 or 66% of the students were placed at the same instructional level; the remaining 11 students (33%) were within one grade level of each other.

Three recent studies examined how reliably participants scored the Basic Reading Inventory. In the first study, Johns and L'Allier (2003) investigated how reliably 31 practicing teachers completed summary sheets and interpreted data regarding three students' performances on the Basic Reading Inventory. After basic instruction in the administration, scoring, and interpretation of the Basic Reading Inventory, teachers completed summary sheets and interpreted those results to determine the independent, instructional, and frustration reading levels for each student. The teachers were able to reliably complete the summary sheet, showing 98% agreement with the experts. With respect to determining the students' three reading levels (independent, instructional, and frustration), there was an 89% average agreement rate.

In the second study, Johns and L'Allier (2004) examined how reliably preservice teachers scored and interpreted the Basic Reading Inventory with respect to word recognition, oral miscues, and comprehension. The 49 preservice teachers were enrolled in their second undergraduate reading course. After instruction in the Basic Reading Inventory, they completed four scoring and interpretation tasks. Results indicated that the preservice teachers were highly reliable with the scoring related to word lists (92% agreement) and total miscues (86% and 90% agreement on the two passages). They had some difficulty with the scoring of comprehension (79% and 81% agreement on the two sets of comprehension questions), and they had the most difficulty in identifying significant miscues (68% and 72% on the two passages). The researchers recommended that preservice teachers who use reading inventories in early clinical experiences rely on total miscues to help them determine the three reading levels and that they receive additional instruction in scoring significant miscues.

The third study (Johns & L'Allier, 2007) examined whether additional targeted instruction enabled preservice teachers to more reliably score a student's oral miscues on an informal reading inventory. Participants ($N=94$) enrolled in their second undergraduate reading course were randomly divided into an experimental group ($N=43$) and a control group ($N=51$). All participants received instruction in the administration, scoring, and interpretation of the Basic Reading Inventory. One week after the initial instruction, all participants scored the oral miscues on a reading passage. Errors in scoring were analyzed and additional instruction, based on common errors, was planned for the experimental group. Teacher think alouds, explicit explanation regarding significant miscues, and additional guided practice in the scoring of oral miscues were included in the forty-minute instructional session. One week later, all participants scored the oral reading miscues on a second reading passage.

Results after initial instruction indicated that the two groups were similar in their accuracy in scoring total miscues and significant miscues, and they had particular difficulty identifying significant miscues. On average, they had 77% agreement with the consensus responses of three experts. Results from the scored passages after the experimental group had received additional instruction indicated that both groups had improved in their ability to score total and significant miscues; they had 87% agreement with the experts. No significant differences between the two groups were found. The fact that both groups had access to a concise set of guidelines while scoring the passages and the relatively short amount of additional instruction and practice for the experimental group may have influenced the results. The results suggest that preservice and beginning teachers should frequently refer to the scoring guidelines when scoring informal reading inventories, use total miscues, rather than significant miscues, when determining reading levels, and review their scoring of significant miscues with a more experienced user of informal reading inventories in order to gain more skill in this area.

Validity Considerations

Validity can be considered in a variety of ways. Face and content validity are two ways to consider whether the Basic Reading Inventory looks like it is measuring what it purports to measure and that those factors are important components of reading. Numerous professionals have reported that the Basic Reading Inventory contains a representative sample of word lists, passages, and comprehension questions that are helpful in assessing students' reading behavior. Bieber's (2011a) study of the Basic Reading Inventory concluded that it did measure what it purported to measure—word identification (accuracy), fluency, and comprehension. These areas are generally regarded as core components of reading and appropriate and important areas for assessment. Concurrent validity data were reported by Bieber (2011a) by correlating the percentages of comprehension in the Basic Reading Inventory with the Scholastic Reading Inventory (SRI) Lexiles which provide an overall achievement level. Most of the correlations for students in grades three, four, and five were significant but below the level required for technical adequacy. The SRI is a computer test that uses a branching program to determine a student's achievement level in Lexiles. It may be inappropriate to compare an overall reading achievement score from the SRI to a single passage of the Basic Reading Inventory that may or may not accurately represent the student's instructional level. A more helpful approach could be determining a student's three reading levels with the Basic Reading Inventory and then making comparisons to an assessment that provides grade levels.

Based upon numerous studies of the Basic Reading Inventory (Bieber, 2011a; Bristow, Pikulski, & Pelosi, 1983; Cunningham, Hall, & Defee, 1991; Helgren-Lempesis, & Mangrum, 1986; Nilsson, 2008; Pikulski, 1983; Pikulski & Shanahan, 1982), it can be concluded that the BRI exhibits reasonable validity to informally assess students' reading.

PART TWO

Basic Reading Inventory Performance Booklets

Form

Performance Booklet

Teacher Copy

Form A

Primary Uses:

- Oral Reading
- Initial Assessment

Other Uses:

- Silent Reading
- Listening Level

 Note: This Performance Booklet is on the CD that accompanies the Basic Reading Inventory.

BASIC READING INVENTORY PERFORMANCE BOOKLET

Jerry L. Johns, Ph.D.

Student _____   Grade _____   Gender   M   F   Date of Test _____

School _____   Examiner _____   Date of Birth_____

Address _____   Current Book/Level_____   Age_____

SUMMARY OF STUDENT'S READING PERFORMANCE

| Grade | Word Recognition | | | | | | Comprehension | | Reading Rate | |
| | Isolation (Word Lists) | | | | Context (Passages) | | Form A | | Words per Minute (WPM) | Norm Group Percentile |
	Sight	Analysis	Total	Level	Miscues	Level	Questions Missed	Level		
PP1										
PP2										
P										
1										
2										
3										
4										
5										
6										
7										
8										
9										
10										
11										
12										

ESTIMATE OF READING LEVELS

Independent _____   Instructional _____   Frustration _____

LISTENING LEVEL

Form _____

Grade	Questions Missed	Level
1		
2		
3		
4		
5		
6		
7		
8		

ESTIMATED LEVEL: _____

GENERAL OBSERVATIONS

INFORMAL ANALYSIS OF ORAL READING

Oral Reading Behaviors	Frequency of Occurrence			General Impact on Meaning		
	Seldom	Sometimes	Frequently	No Change	Little Change	Much Change
Substitutions						
Insertions						
Omissions						
Reversals						
Repetitions						

QUALITATIVE ANALYSIS OF BASIC READING INVENTORY INSIGHTS

General Directions: Note the degree to which the student shows behavior or evidence in the following areas. Space is provided for additional items.

Seldom / Weak / Poor — Always / Strong / Excellent

COMPREHENSION

Seeks to construct meaning
Makes predictions
Activates background knowledge
Possesses appropriate concepts
 and vocabulary
Monitors reading
Varies reading rate as needed
Understands topic and major ideas
Remembers facts or details
Makes and supports appropriate
 inferences
Evaluates ideas from passages
Understands vocabulary used
Provides appropriate definitions
 of words
Engages with passages

WORD IDENTIFICATION

Possesses numerous strategies
Uses strategies flexibly
Uses graphophonic information
Uses semantic information
Uses syntactic information
Knows basic sight words
 automatically
Possesses sight vocabulary

ORAL AND SILENT READING

Reads fluently
Reads with expression
Attends to punctuation
Keeps place while reading
Reads at appropriate rate
Reads silently without vocalization

ATTITUDE AND CONFIDENCE

Enjoys reading
Demonstrates willingness to risk
Possesses positive self-concept
Chooses to read
Regards himself/herself as a reader
Exhibits persistence

Form A • Graded Word Lists • Performance Booklet • Student Booklet copy is on page 2.

List AA (Pre-Primer)	Sight	Analysis	List A (Primer)	Sight	Analysis
1. me*			1. show		
2. get*			2. play*		
3. home			3. be*		
4. not*			4. eat*		
5. he*			5. did*		
6. tree			6. brown		
7. girl			7. is*		
8. take*			8. boat		
9. book			9. call*		
10. milk			10. run*		
11. dog			11. what*		
12. all*			12. him*		
13. apple			13. wagon		
14. like*			14. over*		
15. go*			15. but*		
16. farm			16. on*		
17. went*			17. had*		
18. friend			18. this*		
19. about*			19. around*		
20. some*			20. sleep		

*denotes basic sight word from Revised Dolch List

*denotes basic sight word from Revised Dolch List

Number Correct _____ _____

Number Correct _____ _____

Total _____

Total _____

Scoring Guide for Graded Word Lists			
Independent	Instructional	Inst./Frust.	Frustration
20 19	18 17 16	15 14	13 or less

Form A • Graded Word Lists • Performance Booklet • Student Booklet copy is on page 3.

List A 7141 (Grade 1)	Sight	Analysis	List A 8224 (Grade 2)	Sight	Analysis
1. here*			1. ten*		
2. down*			2. poor		
3. then*			3. city		
4. how*			4. teacher		
5. saw*			5. turn*		
6. pocket			6. fight		
7. hello			7. because*		
8. aunt			8. soft		
9. never*			9. open*		
10. puppy			10. winter		
11. could*			11. joke		
12. after*			12. different		
13. hill			13. say*		
14. men			14. quiet		
15. gone*			15. sister		
16. ran*			16. above		
17. gave*			17. seed		
18. or*			18. thought*		
19. way			19. such		
20. coat			20. chase		

*denotes basic sight word from Revised Dolch List   *denotes basic sight word from Revised Dolch List

Number Correct _____ _____   Number Correct _____ _____

Total _____   Total _____

Scoring Guide for Graded Word Lists			
Independent	Instructional	Inst./Frust.	Frustration
20 19	18 17 16	15 14	13 or less

Form A • Graded Word Lists • Performance Booklet • Student Booklet copy is on page 4.

List A 3183 (Grade 3)	Sight	Analysis	List A 5414 (Grade 4)	Sight	Analysis
1. trail			1. stove		
2. stream			2. government		
3. beach			3. program		
4. snake			4. grape		
5. lift			5. favorite		
6. cabin			6. blizzard		
7. bless			7. noon		
8. rooster			8. greet		
9. journey			9. sport		
10. treasure			10. rumble		
11. hero			11. tropical		
12. beyond			12. language		
13. moan			13. expert		
14. glitter			14. nervous		
15. impossible			15. starve		
16. shot			16. voyage		
17. island			17. silence		
18. manage			18. scamper		
19. receive			19. prairie		
20. automobile			20. moccasin		
Number Correct			Number Correct		
Total			Total		

Scoring Guide for Graded Word Lists			
Independent	Instructional	Inst./Frust.	Frustration
20 19	18 17 16	15 14	13 or less

154

Form A • Graded Word Lists • Performance Booklet • Student Booklet copy is on page 5.

List A 8595 (Grade 5)	Sight	Analysis	List A 6867 (Grade 6)	Sight	Analysis
1. lizard			1. bleed		
2. double			2. accomplishment		
3. scarlet			3. whimper		
4. helmet			4. marriage		
5. dusk			5. frisky		
6. bandit			6. seam		
7. loyal			7. backward		
8. choice			8. location		
9. furnish			9. nightmare		
10. century			10. gently		
11. kindergarten			11. employ		
12. entrance			12. broadcast		
13. dentist			13. kennel		
14. celebration			14. pulp		
15. blister			15. satisfaction		
16. symbol			16. cushion		
17. drowsy			17. graduate		
18. attach			18. harmonica		
19. rehearse			19. definite		
20. terrace			20. yacht		
Number Correct			Number Correct		
Total			Total		

Scoring Guide for Graded Word Lists			
Independent	Instructional	Inst./Frust.	Frustration
20 19	18 17 16	15 14	13 or less

155

Form A • Graded Word Lists • Performance Booklet • Student Booklet copy is on page 6.

List A 3717 (Grade 7)	Sight	Analysis	List A 8183 (Grade 8)	Sight	Analysis
1. dwell			1. quote		
2. slogan			2. ventilate		
3. knapsack			3. surgeon		
4. administration			4. analyze		
5. gangster			5. masterpiece		
6. flatter			6. disinfectant		
7. incredible			7. extraordinary		
8. algebra			8. camouflage		
9. bachelor			9. ruthless		
10. vocabulary			10. perpendicular		
11. longitude			11. juvenile		
12. saliva			12. vacancy		
13. peninsula			13. dictator		
14. monarch			14. negative		
15. feminine			15. honorary		
16. quench			16. custody		
17. competition			17. maneuver		
18. pollute			18. faculty		
19. ambitious			19. pneumonia		
20. orchid			20. embassy		
Number Correct			Number Correct		
Total			Total		

Scoring Guide for Graded Word Lists			
Independent	Instructional	Inst./Frust.	Frustration
20 19	18 17 16	15 14	13 or less

Form A • Graded Word Lists • Performance Booklet • Student Booklet copy is on page 7.

List A 4959 (Grade 9)	Sight	Analysis	List A 1047 (Grade 10)	Sight	Analysis
1. random			1. displacement		
2. disrupt			2. heritage		
3. autobiography			3. exponent		
4. expire			4. variable		
5. contestant			5. preliminary		
6. strategy			6. embryo		
7. crave			7. sterile		
8. detach			8. gratify		
9. apprehend			9. maternity		
10. idolize			10. incorporate		
11. consecutive			11. gore		
12. vacate			12. illogical		
13. debatable			13. radiate		
14. combustion			14. forum		
15. famished			15. predominant		
16. detract			16. fictitious		
17. crochet			17. cuticle		
18. insomnia			18. panorama		
19. siesta			19. inquisitive		
20. bayonet			20. artisan		
Number Correct			Number Correct		
Total			Total		

Scoring Guide for Graded Word Lists			
Independent	Instructional	Inst./Frust.	Frustration
20 19	18 17 16	15 14	13 or less

157

Form A • Graded Word Lists • Performance Booklet • Student Booklet copy is on page 8.

List A 1187 (Grade 11)	Sight	Analysis	List A 1296 (Grade 12)	Sight	Analysis
1. insensible			1. denote		
2. beneficiary			2. hallowed		
3. spectrum			3. transcend		
4. idealism			4. affiliate		
5. epic			5. obtuse		
6. composite			6. recipient		
7. informant			7. consensus		
8. ransack			8. concentric		
9. interlude			9. postulate		
10. suede			10. impel		
11. renaissance			11. collateral		
12. dissociate			12. repugnant		
13. commemorate			13. promissory		
14. populous			14. meticulous		
15. fraudulent			15. flippant		
16. inquisition			16. sardonic		
17. dexterity			17. indemnity		
18. lenient			18. adamant		
19. dilapidated			19. effigy		
20. disheveled			20. tithe		
Number Correct			Number Correct		
Total			Total		

Scoring Guide for Graded Word Lists			
Independent	Instructional	Inst./Frust.	Frustration
20 19	18 17 16	15 14	13 or less

Student Booklet copy is on page 10.

AAA (Pre-Primer 1) Activating Background: Look at the picture and read the title to yourself. Then tell me what you think this might be about.

Background: Low ├────┼────┤ High

A Green Frog

	MISCUES						
	Substitution	Insertion	Omission	Reversal	Repetition	Self-Correction of Unacceptable Miscue	Meaning Change (Significant Miscue)
A green frog sits on a rock. 7							
It has big back legs. 12							
It can jump up. 16							
It can swim in the pond. 22							
It gets wet. 25							
TOTAL							

Total Miscues ☐   Significant Miscues ☐

Word Recognition Scoring Guide		
Total Miscues	Level	Significant Miscues
0	Independent	0
1	Ind./Inst.	—
2	Instructional	1
3	Inst./Frust.	2
4 +	Frustration	3 +

Oral Reading Rate	Norm Group Percentile
───── WPM √1500	☐ 90 ☐ 75 ☐ 50 ☐ 25 ☐ 10

159

AAA (Pre-Primer 1)
Comprehension Questions

F 1. _____ Where is the frog sitting?
            (on a rock)

F 2. _____ Where does it swim?
            (in the pond)

E 3. _____ What does a frog like to do?
            (any logical response; jump; hop; swim)

I 4. _____ What helps a frog jump up high?
            (any logical response; it has big hind
            legs)

V 5. _____ What is a "frog"?
            (an animal)

<table>
<tr><td colspan="2">Retelling Notes</td></tr>
<tr><td></td></tr>
</table>

☐ Questions
   Missed

Comprehension Scoring Guide	
Questions Missed	Level
0	Independent
1	Ind./Inst.
1½	Instructional
2	Inst./Frust.
2½ +	Frustration

Retelling Rubric for the Three Reading Levels
Independent Level/Excellent
Recalls central or key ideas
Remembers important facts
Retains the general sequence of events
Relates most of the content in an organized manner
Instructional Level/Satisfactory
Recalls most central or key ideas
Remembers some important facts
Retains the general sequence of events
Relates an overall sense of the content
Frustration Level/Unsatisfactory
Recalls bits of information in a haphazard manner
Little apparent organization

Student Booklet copy is on page 11.

AA (Pre-Primer 2) Activating Background: Look at the picture and read the title to yourself. Then tell me what you think this might be about.

Background: Low ⊢———+———⊣ High

A Walk in the Fall

MISCUES							
Substitution	Insertion	Omission	Reversal	Repetition	Self-Correction of Unacceptable Miscue	Meaning Change (Significant Miscue)	

It was fall. Pat went for a walk. She	9							
took her dog Sam. They liked to walk.	17							
They walked for a long time. They saw	25							
trees. Some were red. Some were green.	32							
They were pretty. Pat and Sam saw birds	40							
too. Sam did not run after them. He was	49							
good.	50							
TOTAL								

Total Miscues ☐   Significant Miscues ☐

Word Recognition Scoring Guide		
Total Miscues	Level	Significant Miscues
0	Independent	0
1–2	Ind./Inst.	1
3	Instructional	2
4	Inst./Frust.	3
5 +	Frustration	4+

Oral Reading Rate	Norm Group Percentile
)3000 WPM	☐ 90 ☐ 75 ☐ 50 ☐ 25 ☐ 10

AA (Pre-Primer 2)
Comprehension Questions

F 1. _____ What time of the year or season was it?
(fall)

F 2. _____ What did Pat do?
(went for a walk; took her dog for a walk)

E 3. _____ Why do you think Pat took her dog on the walk?
(any logical response; for company; she liked him)

I 4. _____ Why do you think Sam didn't run after the birds?
(any logical response)

V 5. _____ What does "pretty" mean?
(nice; any logical response)

Retelling Notes

Questions Missed

Comprehension Scoring Guide	
Questions Missed	Level
0	Independent
1	Ind./Inst.
1½	Instructional
2	Inst./Frust.
2½ +	Frustration

Retelling Rubric for the Three Reading Levels
Independent Level/Excellent
Recalls central or key ideas
Remembers important facts
Retains the general sequence of events
Relates most of the content in an organized manner
Instructional Level/Satisfactory
Recalls most central or key ideas
Remembers some important facts
Retains the general sequence of events
Relates an overall sense of the content
Frustration Level/Unsatisfactory
Recalls bits of information in a haphazard manner
Little apparent organization

Student Booklet copy is on page 12.

A (Primer) Activating Background: Read the title to yourself. Then tell me what you think this might be about.

Background: Low ├──────┼──────┤ High

The First Snow

	MISCUES						
	Substitution	Insertion	Omission	Reversal	Repetition	Self-Correction of Unacceptable Miscue	Meaning Change (Significant Miscue)
Jack woke up Saturday morning. He 6							
looked out of the window. The ground was 14							
white. The trees were white. 19							
"Oh boy," said Jack, "snow." 24							
"What did you say?" asked Tom, 30							
opening his eyes. 33							
"It snowed last night. Get up and 40							
see," said Jack. 43							
Both boys ran to the window. 49							
"Look at that!" said Tom. "Come on. 56							
Let's get dressed." 59							
Jack and Tom ran into the kitchen. 66							
"Mom!" they said. "It snowed last 72							
night." 73							
"Yes," said Mom. "Dad went out to 80							
get your sleds. First we will eat breakfast. 88							
Then we can have some fun. The first snow 97							
is the best!" 100							
TOTAL							

Word Recognition Scoring Guide

Total Miscues	Level	Significant Miscues
0–1	Independent	0–1
2–4	Ind./Inst.	2
5	Instructional	3
6–9	Inst./Frust.	4
10 +	Frustration	5 +

Total Miscues [　]　　Significant Miscues [　]

Oral Reading Rate	Norm Group Percentile
6000)⎯⎯ WPM	☐ 90　☐ 75　☐ 50　☐ 25　☐ 10

A (Primer)
Comprehension Questions

T 1. _____ What is this story about?
(boys getting ready to play in the snow)

F 2. _____ On what day of the week does the story
take place?
(Saturday)

F 3. _____ What happened when the boys woke
up?
(they ran to the window; they saw
snow)

F 4. _____ Who woke up first?
(Jack)

F 5. _____ What was Dad doing?
(getting the sleds)

F 6. _____ How did the trees look in this story?
(white)

F 7. _____ What did the boys have to do before
playing in the snow?
(eat breakfast)

I 8. _____ Why do you think the boys were so
excited?
(any logical response; they will play in
the snow)

E 9. _____ What things do you think the family
will do outside?
(any logical response; make snowballs;
go sledding, and so on)

V 10. _____ What is "ground"?
(dirt; something you walk on; any
logical response)

☐ Questions
Missed

Comprehension Scoring Guide	
Questions Missed	Level
0–1	Independent
1½–2	Ind./Inst.
2½	Instructional
3–4½	Inst./Frust.
5 +	Frustration

Retelling Notes

Retelling Rubric for the Three Reading Levels
Independent Level/Excellent
Recalls central or key ideas
Remembers important facts
Retains the general sequence of events
Relates most of the content in an organized manner
Instructional Level/Satisfactory
Recalls most central or key ideas
Remembers some important facts
Retains the general sequence of events
Relates an overall sense of the content
Frustration Level/Unsatisfactory
Recalls bits of information in a haphazard manner
Little apparent organization

Student Booklet copy is on page 13.

A 7141 (Grade 1) Activating Background: Read the title to yourself. Then tell me what you think this might be about.

Background: Low ├─────┼─────┤ High

Spotty Swims

MISCUES					Self-Correction of Unacceptable Miscue	Meaning Change (Significant Miscue)
Substitution	Insertion	Omission	Reversal	Repetition		

One day Spotty went for a walk.	7						
The sun was warm. Spotty walked to	14						
the pond. There he saw a frog. The	22						
frog was on a log. Spotty wanted to	30						
play. Spotty began to bark. The frog	37						
jumped into the water.	41						
Then Spotty jumped into the water.	47						
But poor Spotty did not know what to	55						
do. The water was very deep. The water	63						
went way over his head. Spotty moved	70						
his legs. Soon his head came out of the	79						
water. He kept on moving. He came to	87						
the other side of the pond. That is how	96						
Spotty learned to swim.	100						
TOTAL							

Word Recognition Scoring Guide		
Total Miscues	Level	Significant Miscues
0–1	Independent	0–1
2–4	Ind./Inst.	2
5	Instructional	3
6–9	Inst./Frust.	4
10 +	Frustration	5 +

Total Miscues ☐   Significant Miscues ☐

Oral Reading Rate	Norm Group Percentile
)6000 WPM	☐ 90 ☐ 75 ☐ 50 ☐ 25 ☐ 10

165

A 7141 (Grade 1)
Comprehension Questions

T 1. _____ What is this story about?
           (Spotty and a frog; how Spotty learned
           to swim)

F 2. _____ Where did Spotty go?
           (to the pond; for a walk)

F 3. _____ What did Spotty see?
           (a frog)

F 4. _____ What happened when Spotty saw the
           frog?
           (he barked; he wanted to play; he
           jumped into the water [any 1])

F 5. _____ What did the frog do when Spotty
           barked?
           (the frog jumped into the water)

F 6. _____ What did Spotty do when the water
           went over his head?
           (moved his legs; he didn't know what
           to do)

F 7. _____ What did Spotty learn in this story?
           (how to swim)

I 8. _____ Who was Spotty?
           (any logical response; a dog)

E 9. _____ Why do you think Spotty wanted to play
           with the frog?
           (any logical response; he was lonesome)

V 10. _____ What is a "pond"?
           (like a lake; water)

Retelling Notes

___ Questions Missed

Comprehension Scoring Guide	
Questions Missed	Level
0–1	Independent
1½–2	Ind./Inst.
2½	Instructional
3–4½	Inst./Frust.
5 +	Frustration

Retelling Rubric for the Three Reading Levels
Independent Level/Excellent
Recalls central or key ideas
Remembers important facts
Retains the general sequence of events
Relates most of the content in an organized manner
Instructional Level/Satisfactory
Recalls most central or key ideas
Remembers some important facts
Retains the general sequence of events
Relates an overall sense of the content
Frustration Level/Unsatisfactory
Recalls bits of information in a haphazard manner
Little apparent organization

Student Booklet copy is on page 14.

A 8224 (Grade 2) Activating Background: Read the title to yourself. Then tell me what you think this might be about.

Background: Low ⊢——————⊣ High

Bill at Camp

		MISCUES						
		Substitution	Insertion	Omission	Reversal	Repetition	Self-Correction of Unacceptable Miscue	Meaning Change (Significant Miscue)
It was the first time Bill went to	8							
camp. He was very happy to be there. Soon	17							
he went for a walk in the woods to look for	28							
many kinds of leaves. He found leaves	35							
from some maple and oak trees. As Bill	43							
walked in the woods, he saw some animal	51							
tracks. At that moment, a mouse ran into	59							
a small hole by a tree. Bill wondered if the	69							
tracks were made by the mouse. He looked	77							
around for other animals. He did not see	85							
any. The last thing Bill saw was an old	94							
bird nest in a pine tree.	100							
TOTAL								

Total Miscues ☐   Significant Miscues ☐

Word Recognition Scoring Guide		
Total Miscues	Level	Significant Miscues
0–1	Independent	0–1
2–4	Ind./Inst.	2
5	Instructional	3
6–9	Inst./Frust.	4
10 +	Frustration	5 +

Oral Reading Rate	Norm Group Percentile
$\dfrac{}{\overline{)6000}}$ WPM	☐ 90 ☐ 75 ☐ 50 ☐ 25 ☐ 10

167

A 8224 (Grade 2)
Comprehension Questions

T 1. _____ What is this story about?
(a boy at camp; Bill's walk in the woods)

F 2. _____ Did Bill enjoy going to camp? How do you know?
(yes, the story said he was happy there)

F 3. _____ Why did Bill go walking in the woods?
(to look for leaves)

F 4. _____ What kinds of leaves did Bill find in the woods?
(maple and oak leaves)

F 5. _____ What else did Bill see besides the mouse?
(a bird nest; animal tracks)

F 6. _____ Where did the mouse go?
(into a small hole by or in a tree)

F 7. _____ What other animals did Bill see?
(none; he didn't see any)

I 8. _____ Do you think Bill went on this walk by himself? What makes you think so?
(any logical response)

E 9. _____ What other animals might Bill see if he goes for another walk?
(any logical response)

V 10. _____ What are "tracks"?
(footprints made in the dirt; something made by animals when they walk or run)

	Retelling Notes

☐ Questions Missed

Comprehension Scoring Guide	
Questions Missed	Level
0–1	Independent
1½–2	Ind./Inst.
2½	Instructional
3–4½	Inst./Frust.
5 +	Frustration

Retelling Rubric for the Three Reading Levels
Independent Level/Excellent
Recalls central or key ideas
Remembers important facts
Retains the general sequence of events
Relates most of the content in an organized manner
Instructional Level/Satisfactory
Recalls most central or key ideas
Remembers some important facts
Retains the general sequence of events
Relates an overall sense of the content
Frustration Level/Unsatisfactory
Recalls bits of information in a haphazard manner
Little apparent organization

Student Booklet copy is on page 15.

A 3183 (Grade 3) Activating Background: Read the title to yourself. Then tell me what you think this might be about.

Background: Low ├──────┼──────┤ High

The Hungry Bear

		MISCUES					
	Substitution	Insertion	Omission	Reversal	Repetition	Self-Correction of Unacceptable Miscue	Meaning Change (Significant Miscue)
The busy bees had been making honey all — 8							
day. That night it was cool and damp. I had — 18							
slept well until I heard a loud noise near my — 28							
window. It sounded as if someone were — 35							
trying to break into my cabin. As I moved — 44							
from my cot, I could see something black — 52							
standing near the window. In fright I knocked — 60							
on the window. Very slowly and quietly the — 68							
great shadow moved back and went away. — 75							
The next day we found huge bear tracks. — 83							
The bear had come for the honey the bees — 92							
were making in the attic of the cabin. — 100							
TOTAL							

Total Miscues ☐   Significant Miscues ☐

Word Recognition Scoring Guide		
Total Miscues	Level	Significant Miscues
0–1	Independent	0–1
2–4	Ind./Inst.	2
5	Instructional	3
6–9	Inst./Frust.	4
10 +	Frustration	5 +

Oral Reading Rate	Norm Group Percentile
)6000 WPM	☐ 90 ☐ 75 ☐ 50 ☐ 25 ☐ 10

A 3183 (Grade 3)
Comprehension Questions

T 1. _____ What is this story about?
(a bear trying to get honey; being scared)

F 2. _____ What had the bees been doing?
(making honey)

F 3. _____ Where were the bees making honey?
(in the attic of the cabin)

F 4. _____ Who or what woke the person in this story?
(a bear; a loud noise at the window)

F 5. _____ What was near the window?
(blackness; a shadow; a bear)

F 6. _____ What was found the next day?
(bear tracks)

F 7. _____ What did the bear want?
(honey)

I 8. _____ Why do you think the bear walked away?
(any logical response; it heard the knock)

E 9. _____ What might you do to keep the bear away?
(any logical response; remove the honey)

V 10. _____ What is an "attic"?
(a place way upstairs in your house where you put junk and stuff)

[ ] Questions Missed

Comprehension Scoring Guide	
Questions Missed	Level
0–1	Independent
1½–2	Ind./Inst.
2½	Instructional
3–4½	Inst./Frust.
5 +	Frustration

Retelling Notes

Retelling Rubric for the Three Reading Levels
Independent Level/Excellent
Recalls central or key ideas
Remembers important facts
Retains the general sequence of events
Relates most of the content in an organized manner
Instructional Level/Satisfactory
Recalls most central or key ideas
Remembers some important facts
Retains the general sequence of events
Relates an overall sense of the content
Frustration Level/Unsatisfactory
Recalls bits of information in a haphazard manner
Little apparent organization

Student Booklet copy is on page 16.

A 5414 (Grade 4) Activating Background: Read the title to yourself. Then tell me what you think this might be about.

Background: Low ├──────┼──────┤ High

Fire and Animals

		MISCUES					
Substitution	Insertion	Omission	Reversal	Repetition	Self-Correction of Unacceptable Miscue	Meaning Change (Significant Miscue)

		Substitution	Insertion	Omission	Reversal	Repetition	Self-Correction of Unacceptable Miscue	Meaning Change (Significant Miscue)
The summer was a dry one, unusual	7							
for this area. Trees and bushes in the forest	16							
wilted and died. One afternoon a storm	23							
came to the forest. Thunder was heard and	31							
lightning was seen. Then it began to	38							
rain. A spark touched the leaves and a	46							
fire began. The fire spread quickly. The	53							
animals warned each other as they hurried	60							
to escape the flames. As the fire came	68							
closer, trees fell to the ground. Their	75							
branches were yellow, orange, and red.	81							
The smoke was so thick that the animals	89							
could hardly breathe. Many couldn't	94							
escape the danger of the flames.	100							
TOTAL								

Word Recognition Scoring Guide		
Total Miscues	Level	Significant Miscues
0–1	Independent	0–1
2–4	Ind./Inst.	2
5	Instructional	3
6–9	Inst./Frust.	4
10 +	Frustration	5 +

Total Miscues [ ]   Significant Miscues [ ]

Oral Reading Rate	Norm Group Percentile
⎯⎯⎯ WPM ⎵6000	☐ 90 ☐ 75 ☐ 50 ☐ 25 ☐ 10

171

A 5414 (Grade 4)
Comprehension Questions

T   1. _____   What is this story about?
(a forest fire)

F   2. _____   What did the animals try to do?
(escape; warn each other)

F   3. _____   What was unusual about this summer?
(it had been a dry one)

F   4. _____   What was heard and seen in the woods before the fire began?
(thunder and lightning)

F   5. _____   What started the fire?
(a spark; lightning)

F   6. _____   What colors were the trees in this story?
(yellow, orange, and red [any 2])

F   7. _____   Why was it difficult for the animals to breathe?
(smoke filled the air; the fire)

I   8. _____   Why do you think the fire spread quickly?
(any logical response; it had been a dry summer)

E   9. _____   What problems do you think the animals that survived the fire might have?
(any logical response)

V   10. _____   What does "escape" mean?
(get away; any logical response)

☐ Questions Missed

Comprehension Scoring Guide	
Questions Missed	Level
0–1	Independent
1½–2	Ind./Inst.
2½	Instructional
3–4½	Inst./Frust.
5 +	Frustration

Retelling Notes

Retelling Rubric for the Three Reading Levels

Independent Level/Excellent
Recalls central or key ideas
Remembers important facts
Retains the general sequence of events
Relates most of the content in an organized manner

Instructional Level/Satisfactory
Recalls most central or key ideas
Remembers some important facts
Retains the general sequence of events
Relates an overall sense of the content

Frustration Level/Unsatisfactory
Recalls bits of information in a haphazard manner
Little apparent organization

Student Booklet copy is on page 17.

A 8595 (Grade 5) Activating Background: Read the title to yourself. Then tell me what you think this might be about.

Background: Low ├────┼────┤ High

The Mystery

	MISCUES						
	Substitution	Insertion	Omission	Reversal	Repetition	Self-Correction of Unacceptable Miscue	Meaning Change (Significant Miscue)
Everyone turned to stare as a black — 7							
hooded figure whizzed by on a skateboard. — 14							
It was a mystery because no one knew — 22							
who the talented person was. Ken saw — 29							
the skateboarder slide down the library — 35							
railing and disappear into the alley. Nita — 42							
followed the person from school and — 48							
watched as a curb was jumped and a — 56							
three hundred sixty degree turn was — 62							
completed with ease. One day Ken — 68							
noticed a skateboard and a black hooded — 75							
jacket next to Rose's house. He also saw — 83							
a library book called *Skateboarding Tips* — 89							
in her desk at school. Ken had solved — 97							
the challenging mystery. — 100							
TOTAL							

Word Recognition Scoring Guide		
Total Miscues	Level	Significant Miscues
0–1	Independent	0–1
2–4	Ind./Inst.	2
5	Instructional	3
6–9	Inst./Frust.	4
10 +	Frustration	5 +

Total Miscues ☐   Significant Miscues ☐

Oral Reading Rate	Norm Group Percentile
6000) ___ WPM	☐ 90 ☐ 75 ☐ 50 ☐ 25 ☐ 10

173

A 8595 (Grade 5)
Comprehension Questions

T   1. _____   What is this story about?
(a skateboarder; finding out who the skateboarder was)

F   2. _____   What did the mystery person look like?
(wore a black hood; rode a skateboard)

F   3. _____   Why was this person such a mystery?
(no one knew who the person was)

F   4. _____   Who saw the skateboarder?
(everyone; Ken and Nita)

F   5. _____   What kind of stunts did the mystery person do?
(slide down a railing; three hundred sixty degree turn; jump a curb [any 1])

F   6. _____   Who solved the mystery?
(Ken)

F   7. _____   What items did Ken see that helped him solve the mystery?
(hooded jacket; skateboard; book [any 2])

I   8. _____   Who was the mystery person?
(Rose)

E   9. _____   If you were Ken, how might you have solved the mystery differently?
(any logical response)

V   10. _____   What does "talented" mean?
(good at something; gifted)

Retelling Notes

[ ] Questions Missed

Comprehension Scoring Guide	
Questions Missed	Level
0–1	Independent
1½–2	Ind./Inst.
2½	Instructional
3–4½	Inst./Frust.
5 +	Frustration

Retelling Rubric for the Three Reading Levels

Independent Level/Excellent
Recalls central or key ideas
Remembers important facts
Retains the general sequence of events
Relates most of the content in an organized manner

Instructional Level/Satisfactory
Recalls most central or key ideas
Remembers some important facts
Retains the general sequence of events
Relates an overall sense of the content

Frustration Level/Unsatisfactory
Recalls bits of information in a haphazard manner
Little apparent organization

174

Student Booklet copy is on page 18.

A 6867 (Grade 6) Activating Background: Read the title to yourself. Then tell me what you think this might be about.

Background: Low ├─────┼─────┤ High

Keep Your Distance

	MISCUES						
	Substitution	Insertion	Omission	Reversal	Repetition	Self-Correction of Unacceptable Miscue	Meaning Change (Significant Miscue)
Elwood was considered a tough 5							
guy at Anderson School. Everybody 10							
called him Sky. They didn't dare 16							
call him by his full name because 23							
that riled him. He was colossal in 30							
size. From far away Elwood looked 36							
like Mr. Wilson, a teacher, but the 43							
moment you saw Elwood's shoes 48							
and faded, torn jeans, you knew it 55							
could only be Elwood. He felt 61							
inferior because of his clothing, so 67							
he tried to make up for it by 75							
shocking people with his rude 80							
behavior and toughness. Elwood 84							
didn't have many friends, except for 90							
Bob who lived in the same old brick 98							
apartment building. 100							
TOTAL							

Total Miscues ☐   Significant Miscues ☐

Word Recognition Scoring Guide		
Total Miscues	Level	Significant Miscues
0–1	Independent	0–1
2–4	Ind./Inst.	2
5	Instructional	3
6–9	Inst./Frust.	4
10 +	Frustration	5 +

Oral Reading Rate	Norm Group Percentile
6000)‾‾ WPM	☐ 90 ☐ 75 ☐ 50 ☐ 25 ☐ 10

A 6867 (Grade 6)
Comprehension Questions

T 1. _____ What is this story about?
           (a boy named Elwood)

F 2. _____ What was Elwood considered?
           (a tough guy)

F 3. _____ What school did he attend?
           (Anderson School)

F 4. _____ What did Elwood look like?
           (a teacher; Mr. Wilson; colossal in size;
           big; tough)

F 5. _____ What kind of clothes did Elwood wear?
           (faded, torn jeans; old clothes)

F 6. _____ What did everybody call him?
           (Sky)

F 7. _____ How did Elwood shock people?
           (rude behavior; toughness)

I 8. _____ Why do you think Bob was Elwood's
           friend?
           (any logical response; he lived in the
           same apartment building)

E 9. _____ Would you be Elwood's friend if you
           went to Anderson School? Why?
           (any logical response)

V 10. _____ What does "riled" mean?
           (irritated; made angry)

Retelling Notes

Questions Missed

Comprehension Scoring Guide	
Questions Missed	Level
0–1	Independent
1½–2	Ind./Inst.
2½	Instructional
3–4½	Inst./Frust.
5 +	Frustration

Retelling Rubric for the Three Reading Levels
Independent Level/Excellent
Recalls central or key ideas
Remembers important facts
Retains the general sequence of events
Relates most of the content in an organized manner
Instructional Level/Satisfactory
Recalls most central or key ideas
Remembers some important facts
Retains the general sequence of events
Relates an overall sense of the content
Frustration Level/Unsatisfactory
Recalls bits of information in a haphazard manner
Little apparent organization

Student Booklet copy is on page 19.

A 3717 (Grade 7) Activating Background: Read the title to yourself. Then tell me what you think this might be about.

Background: Low ├──────┼──────┤ High

Looming Danger

	Substitution	Insertion	Omission	Reversal	Repetition	Self-Correction of Unacceptable Miscue	Meaning Change (Significant Miscue)
	MISCUES						
The foreheads of the soldiers 5							
glistened with sweat as they struggled 11							
forward under the blazing sun of the 18							
tropics. This small band of soldiers 24							
sincerely felt that their leader was the 31							
salvation of their country. Their objective 37							
was to reach a distant army fort where they 46							
hoped to fire a rocket into the storeroom of 55							
the fort. This would cause the gunpowder 62							
to erupt like a tinderbox. A huge person 70							
bellowed an order from the leader as they 78							
trudged across the uninhabited land. The 84							
soldiers hoped their attack would 89							
scare enemy soldiers and impress more 95							
local people to join them. 100							
TOTAL							

Word Recognition Scoring Guide		
Total Miscues	Level	Significant Miscues
0–1	Independent	0–1
2–4	Ind./Inst.	2
5	Instructional	3
6–9	Inst./Frust.	4
10 +	Frustration	5 +

Total Miscues ☐   Significant Miscues ☐

Oral Reading Rate	Norm Group Percentile
6000 ⟌ _____ WPM	☐ 90 ☐ 75 ☐ 50 ☐ 25 ☐ 10

A 3717 (Grade 7)
Comprehension Questions

T 1. _____ What is this story about?
(soldiers planning to raid an army fort)

F 2. _____ What was the weather like?
(blazing sun; tropical; hot and sunny)

F 3. _____ How did the soldiers feel about their
leader?
(they felt the leader was the salvation of
their country; they liked him)

F 4. _____ What kind of land were they traveling in?
(uninhabited; tropics)

F 5. _____ What was the soldiers objective?
(to reach a distant fort; to fire a rocket
into the storeroom)

F 6. _____ What would be used to destroy the
storeroom?
(a rocket)

F 7. _____ What did they hope their attack would
accomplish?
(scare enemy soldiers; impress local
people to join them)

I 8. _____ In what country do you think this story
took place? Why?
(any logical response that suggests a
tropical climate)

E 9. _____ What dangers do you think might be
involved for the soldiers in their attack?
(any logical response)

V 10. _____ What does "glistened" mean?
(to shine; to sparkle)

[ ] Questions Missed

Comprehension Scoring Guide	
Questions Missed	Level
0–1	Independent
1½–2	Ind./Inst.
2½	Instructional
3–4½	Inst./Frust.
5 +	Frustration

Retelling Notes

Retelling Rubric for the Three Reading Levels
Independent Level/Excellent
Recalls central or key ideas
Remembers important facts
Retains the general sequence of events
Relates most of the content in an organized manner
Instructional Level/Satisfactory
Recalls most central or key ideas
Remembers some important facts
Retains the general sequence of events
Relates an overall sense of the content
Frustration Level/Unsatisfactory
Recalls bits of information in a haphazard manner
Little apparent organization

Student Booklet copy is on page 20.

A 8183 (Grade 8) Activating Background: Read the title to yourself. Then tell me what you think this might be about.

Background: Low ├──────┼──────┤ High

A Scientist's Search

	MISCUES						
	Substitution	Insertion	Omission	Reversal	Repetition	Self-Correction of Unacceptable Miscue	Meaning Change (Significant Miscue)
Chris, a scientist, worked hard at $\quad$ 6							
the lab bench. Chris had been given a $\quad$ 14							
very stimulating suggestion in a letter $\quad$ 20							
from an unknown person. The key to $\quad$ 27							
success was in the radium reaction that $\quad$ 34							
would activate the needed medicine. $\quad$ 39							
From that point, it was simply a matter $\quad$ 47							
of reducing different compounds to find $\quad$ 53							
the right one. Ultimately, it would be $\quad$ 60							
found, and then Chris would have a $\quad$ 67							
monopoly on the medicine that could $\quad$ 73							
make people immortal. Only Chris would $\quad$ 79							
know the correct amount in each tablet. $\quad$ 86							
The disappearance of death and disease $\quad$ 92							
would make Chris the most powerful $\quad$ 98							
person alive. $\quad$ 100							
TOTAL							

Word Recognition Scoring Guide		
Total Miscues	Level	Significant Miscues
0–1	Independent	0–1
2–4	Ind./Inst.	2
5	Instructional	3
6–9	Inst./Frust.	4
10 +	Frustration	5 +

Total Miscues [ ]   Significant Miscues [ ]

Oral Reading Rate	Norm Group Percentile
$\overline{)6000}$ WPM	☐ 90 ☐ 75 ☐ 50 ☐ 25 ☐ 10

A 8183 (Grade 8)
Comprehension Questions

T   1. _____   What is this story about?
               (a scientist searching for a medicine to
               make people immortal)

F   2. _____   Where did the scientist get the idea for
               the formula?
               (in a letter from an unknown person)

F   3. _____   What was the key to the
               experiment?
               (the radium reaction)

F   4. _____   What would the radium reaction do?
               (activate the medicine)

F   5. _____   What would the medicine do?
               (make people immortal)

F   6. _____   Why would Chris be powerful?
               (only he or she would know the right
               amount in each tablet)

F   7. _____   What would disappear because of the
               medicine?
               (death and disease)

I   8. _____   How do you think people would react
               to this discovery? Why?
               (any logical response)

E   9. _____   Do you think Chris might be placed in
               a dangerous position? Why?
               (any logical response)

V 10. _____   What does "immortal" mean?
               (to live forever; not to die)

⬚ Questions
   Missed

Comprehension Scoring Guide	
Questions Missed	Level
0–1	Independent
1½–2	Ind./Inst.
2½	Instructional
3–4½	Inst./Frust.
5 +	Frustration

Retelling Notes

Retelling Rubric for the Three Reading Levels
Independent Level/Excellent
Recalls central or key ideas
Remembers important facts
Retains the general sequence of events
Relates most of the content in an organized manner
Instructional Level/Satisfactory
Recalls most central or key ideas
Remembers some important facts
Retains the general sequence of events
Relates an overall sense of the content
Frustration Level/Unsatisfactory
Recalls bits of information in a haphazard manner
Little apparent organization

Form B

Performance Booklet

Teacher Copy

Form B

Primary Uses:
- Oral Reading
- Later Assessment

Other Uses:
- Silent Reading
- Listening Level
- Progress Monitoring

 Note: This Performance Booklet is on the CD that accompanies the Basic Reading Inventory.

BASIC READING INVENTORY PERFORMANCE BOOKLET

Jerry L. Johns, Ph.D.

Form B

Student _____ Grade _____ Gender M F Date of Test _____

School _____ Examiner _____ Date of Birth_____

Address _____ Current Book/Level_____ Age_____

SUMMARY OF STUDENT'S READING PERFORMANCE

Grade	Word Recognition						Comprehension		Reading Rate	
	Isolation (Word Lists)				Context (Passages)		Form B		Words per Minute (WPM)	Norm Group Percentile
	Sight	Analysis	Total	Level	Miscues	Level	Questions Missed	Level		
PP1										
PP2										
P										
1										
2										
3										
4										
5										
6										
7										
8										
9										
10										
11										
12										

ESTIMATE OF READING LEVELS

Independent _____ Instructional _____ Frustration _____

LISTENING LEVEL

Form _____

Grade	Questions Missed	Level
1		
2		
3		
4		
5		
6		
7		
8		

ESTIMATED LEVEL: _____

GENERAL OBSERVATIONS

INFORMAL ANALYSIS OF ORAL READING

Oral Reading Behaviors	Frequency of Occurrence			General Impact on Meaning		
	Seldom	Sometimes	Frequently	No Change	Little Change	Much Change
Substitutions						
Insertions						
Omissions						
Reversals						
Repetitions						

QUALITATIVE ANALYSIS OF BASIC READING INVENTORY INSIGHTS

General Directions: Note the degree to which the student shows behavior or evidence in the following areas. Space is provided for additional items.

Seldom / Weak / Poor .... Always / Strong / Excellent

COMPREHENSION

Seeks to construct meaning
Makes predictions
Activates background knowledge
Possesses appropriate concepts and vocabulary
Monitors reading
Varies reading rate as needed
Understands topic and major ideas
Remembers facts or details
Makes and supports appropriate inferences
Evaluates ideas from passages
Understands vocabulary used
Provides appropriate definitions of words
Engages with passages

WORD IDENTIFICATION

Possesses numerous strategies
Uses strategies flexibly
Uses graphophonic information
Uses semantic information
Uses syntactic information
Knows basic sight words automatically
Possesses sight vocabulary

ORAL AND SILENT READING

Reads fluently
Reads with expression
Attends to punctuation
Keeps place while reading
Reads at appropriate rate
Reads silently without vocalization

ATTITUDE AND CONFIDENCE

Enjoys reading
Demonstrates willingness to risk
Possesses positive self-concept
Chooses to read
Regards himself/herself as a reader
Exhibits persistence

183

Form B • Graded Word Lists • Performance Booklet • Student Booklet copy is on page 22.

List BB (Pre-Primer)	Sight	Analysis		List B (Primer)	Sight	Analysis
1. we*	_____	_____		1. they*	_____	_____
2. and*	_____	_____		2. she*	_____	_____
3. house	_____	_____		3. will*	_____	_____
4. the*	_____	_____		4. of*	_____	_____
5. duck	_____	_____		5. blue*	_____	_____
6. one*	_____	_____		6. it*	_____	_____
7. street	_____	_____		7. are*	_____	_____
8. happy	_____	_____		8. his*	_____	_____
9. lost	_____	_____		9. now*	_____	_____
10. first*	_____	_____		10. dress	_____	_____
11. do*	_____	_____		11. if*	_____	_____
12. at*	_____	_____		12. from*	_____	_____
13. very*	_____	_____		13. morning	_____	_____
14. find*	_____	_____		14. father	_____	_____
15. out*	_____	_____		15. ask*	_____	_____
16. party	_____	_____		16. back	_____	_____
17. goat	_____	_____		17. green*	_____	_____
18. wish	_____	_____		18. time	_____	_____
19. know*	_____	_____		19. who*	_____	_____
20. sing	_____	_____		20. cookie	_____	_____

*denotes basic sight word from Revised Dolch List   *denotes basic sight word from Revised Dolch List

Number Correct   _____   _____   Number Correct   _____   _____

Total   _____   Total   _____

Scoring Guide for Graded Word Lists			
Independent	Instructional	Inst./Frust.	Frustration
20 19	18 17 16	15 14	13 or less

Form B • Graded Word Lists • Performance Booklet • Student Booklet copy is on page 23.

List B 7141 (Grade 1)	Sight	Analysis	List B 8224 (Grade 2)	Sight	Analysis
1. little*			1. feel		
2. next*			2. drink		
3. reads			3. wave		
4. my*			4. gray		
5. make*			5. start*		
6. old*			6. horn		
7. mother			7. across*		
8. bed			8. warm*		
9. grow*			9. bad		
10. laugh			10. even*		
11. near*			11. feed		
12. before*			12. always*		
13. lamb			13. round*		
14. ride			14. country		
15. store			15. enough*		
16. high*			16. able		
17. began*			17. should*		
18. made*			18. bottom		
19. cry			19. crawl		
20. her*			20. machine		

*denotes basic sight word from Revised Dolch List   *denotes basic sight word from Revised Dolch List

Number Correct _____ _____   Number Correct _____ _____

Total _____   Total _____

Scoring Guide for Graded Word Lists			
Independent	Instructional	Inst./Frust.	Frustration
20 19	18 17 16	15 14	13 or less

Form B • Graded Word Lists • Performance Booklet • Student Booklet copy is on page 24.

List B 3183 (Grade 3)	Sight	Analysis	List B 5414 (Grade 4)	Sight	Analysis
1. star			1. bike		
2. net			2. castle		
3. doctor			3. jungle		
4. spoon			4. bullet		
5. trap			5. factory		
6. valley			6. stripe		
7. shirt			7. problem		
8. meet			8. target		
9. chuckle			9. capture		
10. gaze			10. sleeve		
11. rib			11. pump		
12. discover			12. sausage		
13. hundred			13. electric		
14. reason			14. business		
15. conductor			15. instant		
16. coast			16. balance		
17. escape			17. surround		
18. thirty			18. invention		
19. prepare			19. accident		
20. nation			20. rifle		
Number Correct			Number Correct		
Total			Total		

Scoring Guide for Graded Word Lists			
Independent	Instructional	Inst./Frust.	Frustration
20 19	18 17 16	15 14	13 or less

186

Form B • Graded Word Lists • Performance Booklet • Student Booklet copy is on page 25.

List B 8595 (Grade 5)	Sight	Analysis	List B 6867 (Grade 6)	Sight	Analysis
1. science			1. painful		
2. blush			2. raspberry		
3. marvelous			3. medical		
4. index			4. label		
5. panther			5. household		
6. grace			6. foreman		
7. boss			7. catalog		
8. emergency			8. solar		
9. blond			9. unexpected		
10. nugget			10. beggar		
11. terrific			11. thermometer		
12. effort			12. portable		
13. observe			13. distrust		
14. mammoth			14. dandelion		
15. transportation			15. charity		
16. liberty			16. graduation		
17. balcony			17. species		
18. scar			18. variety		
19. confidence			19. contribute		
20. admiral			20. jagged		
Number Correct			Number Correct		
Total			Total		

Scoring Guide for Graded Word Lists			
Independent	Instructional	Inst./Frust.	Frustration
20 19	18 17 16	15 14	13 or less

187

List B 3717 (Grade 7)	Sight	Analysis	List B 8183 (Grade 8)	Sight	Analysis
1. focus			1. skyscraper		
2. turnpike			2. reaction		
3. harmony			3. horsepower		
4. uranium			4. justify		
5. merchandise			5. garlic		
6. irregular			6. omit		
7. humidity			7. divorce		
8. enlarge			8. exception		
9. expel			9. flounder		
10. remainder			10. comedian		
11. industrious			11. nomination		
12. pamphlet			12. barbarian		
13. geologist			13. molecule		
14. rayon			14. recruit		
15. novel			15. imperfect		
16. survival			16. upholster		
17. meteorite			17. authentic		
18. dormitory			18. variation		
19. mahogany			19. mortgage		
20. chauffeur			20. brigade		
Number Correct			Number Correct		
Total			Total		

Scoring Guide for Graded Word Lists			
Independent	Instructional	Inst./Frust.	Frustration
20 19	18 17 16	15 14	13 or less

Form B • Graded Word Lists • Performance Booklet • Student Booklet copy is on page 27.

List B 4959 (Grade 9)	Sight	Analysis	List B 1047 (Grade 10)	Sight	Analysis
1. disapprove			1. immature		
2. data			2. reorganize		
3. texture			3. evaluate		
4. disqualify			4. visualize		
5. compress			5. grim		
6. slur			6. patronize		
7. gruesome			7. rupture		
8. deceased			8. chronic		
9. transaction			9. exploit		
10. misconduct			10. obituary		
11. sarcasm			11. saturate		
12. momentary			12. induce		
13. ingenious			13. recuperate		
14. mechanism			14. pictorial		
15. audible			15. phenomenal		
16. embezzle			16. portal		
17. robust			17. centennial		
18. luminous			18. silhouette		
19. heathen			19. boisterous		
20. ecstasy			20. impertinent		
Number Correct			Number Correct		
Total			Total		

Scoring Guide for Graded Word Lists			
Independent	Instructional	Inst./Frust.	Frustration
20 19	18 17 16	15 14	13 or less

Form B • Graded Word Lists • Performance Booklet • Student Booklet copy is on page 28.

List B 1187 (Grade 11)	Sight	Analysis	List B 1296 (Grade 12)	Sight	Analysis
1. discredit			1. invalidate		
2. habitat			2. metabolism		
3. profane			3. metamorphosis		
4. intern			4. advert		
5. intimidate			5. impotent		
6. inseparable			6. predatory		
7. binder			7. protocol		
8. bilingual			8. prodigy		
9. jurisdiction			9. derivative		
10. stilt			10. zealous		
11. metropolis			11. debase		
12. preposterous			12. pretentious		
13. pollinate			13. regurgitate		
14. patronage			14. herbivorous		
15. reminiscent			15. maritime		
16. secede			16. aesthetic		
17. knoll			17. blasphemy		
18. promenade			18. extemporaneous		
19. catechism			19. agrarian		
20. cavalcade			20. colloquial		
Number Correct			Number Correct		
Total			Total		

Scoring Guide for Graded Word Lists			
Independent	Instructional	Inst./Frust.	Frustration
20 19	18 17 16	15 14	13 or less

190

Student Booklet copy is on page 30.

BBB (Pre-Primer 1) Activating Background:
Look at the picture and read the title to yourself.
Then tell me what you think this might be about.

Background: Low ├──────┼──────┤ High

The Pink Pig		Substitution	Insertion	Omission	Reversal	Repetition	Self-Correction of Unacceptable Miscue	Meaning Change (Significant Miscue)
		MISCUES						
The pink pig ran to the wet mud.	8							
It was a big, fat pig.	14							
The pig was hot.	18							
It just sat in the wet mud.	25							
TOTAL								

Total Miscues [ ]   Significant Miscues [ ]

Word Recognition Scoring Guide		
Total Miscues	Level	Significant Miscues
0	Independent	0
1	Ind./Inst.	—
2	Instructional	1
3	Inst./Frust.	2
4 +	Frustration	3 +

Oral Reading Rate	Norm Group Percentile
$\frac{\quad}{)1500}$ WPM	☐ 90 ☐ 75 ☐ 50 ☐ 25 ☐ 10

BBB (Pre-Primer 1)
Comprehension Questions

F 1. _____ What color was the pig?
(pink)

F 2. _____ Where did the pig go in the story?
(to the mud)

E 3. _____ Why did the pig like the mud?
(any logical response; to get cool; to
play in)

I 4. _____ Why was the pig hot?
(any logical response; it was a hot day;
the sun was shining)

V 5. _____ What is "mud"?
(wet dirt)

Retelling Notes

☐ Questions
Missed

Comprehension Scoring Guide	
Questions Missed	Level
0	Independent
1	Ind./Inst.
1½	Instructional
2	Inst./Frust.
2½ +	Frustration

Retelling Rubric for the Three Reading Levels
Independent Level/Excellent
Recalls central or key ideas
Remembers important facts
Retains the general sequence of events
Relates most of the content in an organized manner
Instructional Level/Satisfactory
Recalls most central or key ideas
Remembers some important facts
Retains the general sequence of events
Relates an overall sense of the content
Frustration Level/Unsatisfactory
Recalls bits of information in a haphazard manner
Little apparent organization

Student Booklet copy is on page 31.

BB (Pre-Primer 2) Activating Background: Look at the picture and read the title to yourself. Then tell me what you think this might be about.

Background: Low ├────┼────┤ High

I Like Birds

		MISCUES					
	Substitution	Insertion	Omission	Reversal	Repetition	Self-Correction of Unacceptable Miscue	Meaning Change (Significant Miscue)
I can look for birds. I look up in 9							
a tree. I see a big bird. It is brown. 19							
I see a baby bird. It is little. It is 29							
brown too. 31							
The big bird can fly. The baby 38							
bird can not fly. It is little. I like to 48							
see birds. 50							
TOTAL							

Total Miscues [ ]   Significant Miscues [ ]

Word Recognition Scoring Guide		
Total Miscues	Level	Significant Miscues
0	Independent	0
1–2	Ind./Inst.	1
3	Instructional	2
4	Inst./Frust.	3
5 +	Frustration	4 +

Oral Reading Rate	Norm Group Percentile
‾‾‾‾‾ WPM)3000	☐ 90 ☐ 75 ☐ 50 ☐ 25 ☐ 10

BB (Pre-Primer 2)
Comprehension Questions

F 1. _____ Where did the person in the story look
                 for the birds?
                 (in a tree)

F 2. _____ What kinds of birds did the person see?
                 (big bird; baby bird; brown; little bird
                 [any 2])

E 3. _____ Besides being too little, why do you
                 think the baby bird could not fly?
                 (any logical response)

I 4. _____ Why do you think the person looked up
                 in a tree to find birds?
                 (any logical response; birds live there)

V 5. _____ What does "little" mean?
                 (small; tiny; baby)

Retelling Notes

☐ Questions
  Missed

Comprehension Scoring Guide	
Questions Missed	Level
0	Independent
1	Ind./Inst.
1½	Instructional
2	Inst./Frust.
2½ +	Frustration

Retelling Rubric for the Three Reading Levels
Independent Level/Excellent
Recalls central or key ideas
Remembers important facts
Retains the general sequence of events
Relates most of the content in an organized manner
Instructional Level/Satisfactory
Recalls most central or key ideas
Remembers some important facts
Retains the general sequence of events
Relates an overall sense of the content
Frustration Level/Unsatisfactory
Recalls bits of information in a haphazard manner
Little apparent organization

Student Booklet copy is on page 32.

B (Primer) Activating Background: Read the title to yourself. Then tell me what you think this might be about.

Background: Low |————|————| High

The Box

	MISCUES						
	Substitution	Insertion	Omission	Reversal	Repetition	Self-Correction of Unacceptable Miscue	Meaning Change (Significant Miscue)
Ben went to see his friend Nan. He — 8							
had a blue box. Nan saw the box. She — 17							
said, "What is in the blue box?" — 24							
"I can not tell you," said Ben. — 31							
Nan asked, "Is it a ball?" — 37							
"No, it is not a ball," said Ben. — 45							
"Is it a car?" asked Nan. — 51							
"No, it is not a car," said Ben. — 59							
"I know, it is an apple," said Nan. — 67							
Ben looked in the box. There were — 74							
two apples. One apple was green. One — 81							
apple was red. He gave the red apple to — 90							
Nan. Nan liked the apple. Ben was a — 98							
good friend. — 100							
TOTAL							

Word Recognition Scoring Guide		
Total Miscues	Level	Significant Miscues
0–1	Independent	0–1
2–4	Ind./Inst.	2
5	Instructional	3
6–9	Inst./Frust.	4
10 +	Frustration	5 +

Total Miscues [ ]   Significant Miscues [ ]

Oral Reading Rate	Norm Group Percentile
6000)‾‾‾ WPM	☐ 90 ☐ 75 ☐ 50 ☐ 25 ☐ 10

B (Primer)
Comprehension Questions

T 1. _____ What is this story about?
            (Ben's box; Nan guessing about the box)

F 2. _____ Who did Ben see?
            (Nan)

F 3. _____ What did Ben have with him?
            (a box; apples)

F 4. _____ What color was the box?
            (blue)

F 5. _____ What things did Nan think were in the box?
            (ball, car, apple [any 2])

F 6. _____ How many apples were in the box?
            (two)

F 7. _____ How did Nan feel about the apple?
            (she liked it)

I 8. _____ What color was the apple that Ben kept?
            (green)

E 9. _____ Would you like Ben as your friend? Why?
            (any logical response)

V 10. _____ What does "good" mean?
            (nice; friendly; kind)

	Retelling Notes

☐ Questions Missed

Comprehension Scoring Guide	
Questions Missed	Level
0–1	Independent
1½–2	Ind./Inst.
2½	Instructional
3–4½	Inst./Frust.
5 +	Frustration

Retelling Rubric for the Three Reading Levels
Independent Level/Excellent
Recalls central or key ideas
Remembers important facts
Retains the general sequence of events
Relates most of the content in an organized manner
Instructional Level/Satisfactory
Recalls most central or key ideas
Remembers some important facts
Retains the general sequence of events
Relates an overall sense of the content
Frustration Level/Unsatisfactory
Recalls bits of information in a haphazard manner
Little apparent organization

Student Booklet copy is on page 33.

B 7141 (Grade 1) Activating Background: Read the title to yourself. Then tell me what you think this might be about.

Background: Low ├────┼────┤ High

Up a Tree

MISCUES							
Substitution	Insertion	Omission	Reversal	Repetition	Self-Correction of Unacceptable Miscue	Meaning Change (Significant Miscue)	

Jeff likes to play with his cat Boots.	8							
One day a dog walked by. Boots ran up a	18							
big tree.	20							
Jeff said, "Come down Boots." The cat	27							
did not come down. Jeff did not know what	36							
to do. He called his mom.	42							
His mom said, "Here Boots. Come	48							
here." The cat did not come.	54							
Then Jeff went home. He came back	61							
with a bag. He put the bag down. He took	71							
out some milk. He walked to the tree with	80							
the milk. He said, "Here Boots. Come get	88							
some milk." Boots came down and had	95							
some milk. Jeff was happy.	100							
TOTAL								

Word Recognition Scoring Guide		
Total Miscues	Level	Significant Miscues
0–1	Independent	0–1
2–4	Ind./Inst.	2
5	Instructional	3
6–9	Inst./Frust.	4
10 +	Frustration	5 +

Total Miscues [ ]   Significant Miscues [ ]

Oral Reading Rate	Norm Group Percentile
‾‾‾)6000 WPM	☐ 90 ☐ 75 ☐ 50 ☐ 25 ☐ 10

197

B 7141 (Grade 1)
Comprehension Questions

T   1. _____   What is this story about?
                  (Boots; getting Boots down from a tree;
                  a cat)

F   2. _____   Why did Boots run up the tree?
                  (a dog walked by; the dog scared the
                  cat)

F   3. _____   At first, how did Jeff try to get Boots
                  down?
                  (called the cat; called mom)

F   4. _____   Where did Jeff go after mom came?
                  (home)

F   5. _____   What did he bring from home?
                  (a bag; milk)

F   6. _____   How did Jeff finally get Boots down?
                  (he brought milk and told Boots to get
                  the milk)

F   7. _____   How did Jeff feel at the end of the
                  story?
                  (happy)

I   8. _____   Why didn't Boots come down when Jeff
                  and his mom called?
                  (any logical response; it was scared of
                  the dog; it didn't want to)

E   9. _____   How would you feel if your cat ran up a
                  tree? Why?
                  (any logical response; sad; scared)

V 10. _____   What is a "bag"?
                  (a sack; something to put things in)

Retelling Notes

☐ Questions Missed

Comprehension Scoring Guide	
Questions Missed	Level
0–1	Independent
1½–2	Ind./Inst.
2½	Instructional
3–4½	Inst./Frust.
5 +	Frustration

Retelling Rubric for the Three Reading Levels
Independent Level/Excellent
Recalls central or key ideas
Remembers important facts
Retains the general sequence of events
Relates most of the content in an organized manner
Instructional Level/Satisfactory
Recalls most central or key ideas
Remembers some important facts
Retains the general sequence of events
Relates an overall sense of the content
Frustration Level/Unsatisfactory
Recalls bits of information in a haphazard manner
Little apparent organization

Student Booklet copy is on page 34.

B 8224 (Grade 2) Activating Background: Read the title to yourself. Then tell me what you think this might be about.

Background: Low |———|———| High

The Strange Object

	Substitution	Insertion	Omission	Reversal	Repetition	Self-Correction of Unacceptable Miscue	Meaning Change (Significant Miscue)
MISCUES							
It was a breezy day in March. I was — 9							
walking home thinking about my day at — 16							
school. In the sky I saw a strange object. — 25							
At first, I thought it was an airplane. — 33							
I climbed up a hill to get a better view. — 43							
As I got closer, I saw it diving through the — 53							
air in a strange way. It was brown and had — 63							
wings. Maybe it was a bird. — 69							
Then the wind stopped, and the object — 76							
came crashing toward me. I ran to get away. — 85							
Then I heard a friendly laugh. My friend — 93							
Max came to get his hawk kite. — 100							
TOTAL							

Total Miscues ☐   Significant Miscues ☐

Word Recognition Scoring Guide		
Total Miscues	Level	Significant Miscues
0–1	Independent	0–1
2–4	Ind./Inst.	2
5	Instructional	3
6–9	Inst./Frust.	4
10 +	Frustration	5 +

Oral Reading Rate	Norm Group Percentile
6000) ___ WPM	☐ 90 ☐ 75 ☐ 50 ☐ 25 ☐ 10

B 8224 (Grade 2)
Comprehension Questions

T　1. _____　What is this story about?
(a kite in the sky; a strange object)

F　2. _____　What month was it?
(March)

F　3. _____　What was the person thinking about
before seeing the object?
(the day at school)

F　4. _____　What did the person think the object
was?
(an airplane; a large bird)

F　5. _____　What did the person do to get a better
view?
(climbed a hill)

F　6. _____　How did the object look?
(like a bird; brown and had wings)

F　7. _____　To whom did the object belong?
(Max)

I　8. _____　Why was the breeze important in this
passage?
(any logical response; it kept the kite in
the air)

E　9. _____　How do you think the person felt when
seeing Max and his kite? Why?
(any logical response; angry; happy;
relieved)

V　10. _____　What does "strange" mean?
(unusual; different; weird)

☐ Questions
Missed

Comprehension Scoring Guide	
Questions Missed	Level
0–1	Independent
1½–2	Ind./Inst.
2½	Instructional
3–4½	Inst./Frust.
5 +	Frustration

Retelling Notes

Retelling Rubric for the Three Reading Levels
Independent Level/Excellent
Recalls central or key ideas
Remembers important facts
Retains the general sequence of events
Relates most of the content in an organized manner
Instructional Level/Satisfactory
Recalls most central or key ideas
Remembers some important facts
Retains the general sequence of events
Relates an overall sense of the content
Frustration Level/Unsatisfactory
Recalls bits of information in a haphazard manner
Little apparent organization

Student Booklet copy is on page 35.

B 3183 (Grade 3) Activating Background: Read the title to yourself. Then tell me what you think this might be about.

Background: Low ├────────┼────────┤ High

The Night Noise

		MISCUES					
	Substitution	Insertion	Omission	Reversal	Repetition	Self-Correction of Unacceptable Miscue	Meaning Change (Significant Miscue)
Fred was lying in bed trying to go to sleep. 10							
He had a big test the next day. He kept hearing 21							
a soft whistle, so he went into the kitchen and 31							
checked the tea kettle. The stove was off. 39							
Then he stood outside his parents' room to 47							
listen for snoring. Everyone was sleeping 53							
quietly. He returned to his room and noticed 61							
some wind. It wasn't the fan. It was off. He 71							
heard a dog bark outside and saw that his 80							
window was open a little. He closed it and the 90							
noise stopped. He climbed into bed and fell 98							
asleep quickly. 100							
TOTAL							

Total Miscues [ ]   Significant Miscues [ ]

Word Recognition Scoring Guide		
Total Miscues	Level	Significant Miscues
0–1	Independent	0–1
2–4	Ind./Inst.	2
5	Instructional	3
6–9	Inst./Frust.	4
10 +	Frustration	5 +

Oral Reading Rate	Norm Group Percentile
$\overline{)6000}$ WPM	☐ 90 ☐ 75 ☐ 50 ☐ 25 ☐ 10

201

B 3183 (Grade 3)
Comprehension Questions

T   1. _____   What is this story about?
(a night noise that kept Fred awake;
Fred looking for a noise)

F   2. _____   What was Fred trying to do at the
beginning of the story?
(sleep)

F   3. _____   What did Fred have to do the next day?
(take a test)

F   4. _____   How did the noise sound?
(like a soft whistle)

F   5. _____   Where did Fred look for the noise?
(the kitchen; his parents' room
[either 1])

F   6. _____   What did Fred hear from the window?
(a dog barking)

F   7. _____   How did Fred make the noise go away?
(he closed the window)

I   8. _____   What was probably causing the soft
whistle?
(any logical response; the wind)

E   9. _____   How would you feel if you heard a soft
whistle when you were trying to sleep?
Why?
(any logical response; scared; frustrated;
mad)

V 10. _____   What does "listen" mean?
(try to hear)

Retelling Notes

Questions Missed		Comprehension Scoring Guide	

Comprehension Scoring Guide	
Questions Missed	Level
0–1	Independent
1½–2	Ind./Inst.
2½	Instructional
3–4½	Inst./Frust.
5 +	Frustration

Retelling Rubric for the Three Reading Levels
Independent Level/Excellent
Recalls central or key ideas
Remembers important facts
Retains the general sequence of events
Relates most of the content in an organized manner
Instructional Level/Satisfactory
Recalls most central or key ideas
Remembers some important facts
Retains the general sequence of events
Relates an overall sense of the content
Frustration Level/Unsatisfactory
Recalls bits of information in a haphazard manner
Little apparent organization

Student Booklet copy is on page 36.

B 5414 (Grade 4) Activating Background: Read the title to yourself. Then tell me what you think this might be about.

Background: Low ⊢———┼———⊣ High

The Purse Detectives

	MISCUES					Self-Correction of Unacceptable Miscue	Meaning Change (Significant Miscue)
	Substitution	Insertion	Omission	Reversal	Repetition		
It had been raining. Kate and her brother 8							
Michael were looking for something 13							
entertaining to do. Aunt Sue came into the 21							
living room and announced, "I can't find my 29							
purse." 30							
The children looked for the missing 36							
purse in various parts of the house. Michael 44							
looked in the den where his aunt wrote 52							
checks, but no purse. Kate searched the 59							
bedroom carefully because the purse was 65							
last seen there. It wasn't there, but Kate 73							
recalled that her aunt had been shopping 80							
earlier that day. She ran outside. Just as she 89							
arrived, Michael was opening the trunk and 96							
Kate saw the purse. 100							
TOTAL							

Word Recognition Scoring Guide		
Total Miscues	Level	Significant Miscues
0–1	Independent	0–1
2–4	Ind./Inst.	2
5	Instructional	3
6–9	Inst./Frust.	4
10 +	Frustration	5 +

Total Miscues [ ]   Significant Miscues [ ]

Oral Reading Rate	Norm Group Percentile
‾‾‾‾)6000 WPM	☐ 90 ☐ 75 ☐ 50 ☐ 25 ☐ 10

B 5414 (Grade 4)
Comprehension Questions

T   1. _____   What is this story about?
              (looking for Aunt Sue's purse)

F   2. _____   What were Kate and Michael doing at
              the beginning of the story?
              (thinking of something entertaining
              to do)

F   3. _____   Why were Kate and Michael inside?
              (it had been raining)

F   4. _____   Where did Kate and Michael look for
              the purse?
              (den; bedroom; trunk [any 2])

F   5. _____   Why did Michael go into the den to
              look for the purse?
              (that is where his aunt wrote checks)

F   6. _____   Besides the house, where had Aunt Sue
              been that day?
              (shopping)

F   7. _____   Where was the purse found?
              (in Aunt Sue's trunk)

I   8. _____   Why do you think this story is called
              "The Purse Detectives"?
              (any logical response)

E   9. _____   What qualities made Kate and Michael
              good detectives? Why?
              (any logical response)

V 10. _____   What does "various" mean?
              (several; different; many)

	Retelling Notes

Questions Missed	

Comprehension Scoring Guide	
Questions Missed	Level
0–1	Independent
1½–2	Ind./Inst.
2½	Instructional
3–4½	Inst./Frust.
5 +	Frustration

Retelling Rubric for the Three Reading Levels

Independent Level/Excellent
Recalls central or key ideas
Remembers important facts
Retains the general sequence of events
Relates most of the content in an organized manner

Instructional Level/Satisfactory
Recalls most central or key ideas
Remembers some important facts
Retains the general sequence of events
Relates an overall sense of the content

Frustration Level/Unsatisfactory
Recalls bits of information in a haphazard manner
Little apparent organization

Student Booklet copy is on page 37.

B 8595 (Grade 5) Activating Background: Read the title to yourself. Then tell me what you think this might be about.

Background: Low ├────────┼────────┤ High

The Strange Gift

		MISCUES						
		Substitution	Insertion	Omission	Reversal	Repetition	Self-Correction of Unacceptable Miscue	Meaning Change (Significant Miscue)
Cheryl sat quietly, staring at the tiny	7							
black and green slip of paper in her hand.	16							
She was remembering how moved she had	23							
been when Marlene first gave it to her.	31							
Cheryl knew her best friend was poor.	38							
Marlene couldn't afford even a small gift for	46							
Cheryl's twelfth birthday. She was surprised	52							
when Marlene pulled her aside and timidly	59							
handed her a pretty, gift-wrapped box with a	68							
bow on it. Inside there was a ticket. Cheryl	77							
was touched by her friend's gesture. She	84							
never imagined that the slip of paper would	92							
be the winning ticket for their classroom	99							
drawing.	100							
TOTAL								

Word Recognition Scoring Guide		
Total Miscues	Level	Significant Miscues
0–1	Independent	0–1
2–4	Ind./Inst.	2
5	Instructional	3
6–9	Inst./Frust.	4
10 +	Frustration	5 +

Total Miscues ☐   Significant Miscues ☐

Oral Reading Rate	Norm Group Percentile
6000 ⟌‾‾‾‾ WPM	☐ 90 ☐ 75 ☐ 50 ☐ 25 ☐ 10

B 8595 (Grade 5)
Comprehension Questions

T   1. _____   What is this story about?
              (a birthday gift; a winning ticket)

F   2. _____   Who is Cheryl's best friend?
              (Marlene)

F   3. _____   How old is Cheryl?
              (eleven or twelve)

F   4. _____   Why did Cheryl receive a gift?
              (it was her birthday)

F   5. _____   Why was Cheryl surprised?
              (She didn't think Marlene could afford
              a gift)

F   6. _____   What was the ticket for?
              (a classroom drawing)

F   7. _____   What color was the ticket?
              (black and green)

I   8. _____   Why do you think Marlene pulled her
              aside to give her the gift?
              (any logical response; she was
              embarrassed)

E   9. _____   How would you feel if you were
              Cheryl?
              (any logical response; happy; surprised)

V 10. _____   What does "timidly" mean?
              (shy)

☐ Questions
  Missed

Comprehension Scoring Guide	
Questions Missed	Level
0–1	Independent
1½–2	Ind./Inst.
2½	Instructional
3–4½	Inst./Frust.
5 +	Frustration

Retelling Notes

Retelling Rubric for the Three Reading Levels
Independent Level/Excellent
Recalls central or key ideas
Remembers important facts
Retains the general sequence of events
Relates most of the content in an organized manner
Instructional Level/Satisfactory
Recalls most central or key ideas
Remembers some important facts
Retains the general sequence of events
Relates an overall sense of the content
Frustration Level/Unsatisfactory
Recalls bits of information in a haphazard manner
Little apparent organization

Student Booklet copy is on page 38.

B 6867 (Grade 6) Activating Background: Read the title to yourself. Then tell me what you think this might be about.

Background: Low |————|————| High

Stranger at Willowbrook

		MISCUES					Self-Correction of Unacceptable Miscue	Meaning Change (Significant Miscue)
		Substitution	Insertion	Omission	Reversal	Repetition		
Phil entered Willowbrook School	4							
for the first time. The five-minute bell	12							
rang. As he hurried to math class, an	20							
unfamiliar voice asked, "How's it	25							
going, Phil?" Startled, Phil responded	30							
with a quick wave and continued on to	38							
room 203. During lunch, Phil saw the	45							
stranger in the cafeteria, but he	51							
pretended not to notice. During the last	58							
period, Mr. Nichols was taking	63							
attendance when Phil heard a familiar	69							
name called. "Zack Wilson," thought	74							
Phil. "I remember when we used to	81							
build block houses in kindergarten."	86							
Phil turned to find Zack and realized	93							
that the stranger was a forgotten friend.	100							
TOTAL								

Word Recognition Scoring Guide		
Total Miscues	Level	Significant Miscues
0–1	Independent	0–1
2–4	Ind./Inst.	2
5	Instructional	3
6–9	Inst./Frust.	4
10 +	Frustration	5 +

Total Miscues [ ]   Significant Miscues [ ]

Oral Reading Rate	Norm Group Percentile
6000)‾‾‾‾ WPM	☐ 90 ☐ 75 ☐ 50 ☐ 25 ☐ 10

B 6867 (Grade 6)
Comprehension Questions

T 1. _____ What is this passage about?
(Phil meets a forgotten friend; Phil figures out who the stranger is)

F 2. _____ What was the name of Phil's school?
(Willowbrook)

F 3. _____ What startled Phil?
(an unfamiliar voice; Zack; someone saying "How's it going?" [any 1])

F 4. _____ Where was Phil going when he first heard the stranger?
(math class; room 203)

F 5. _____ Where else did Phil see the stranger?
(in the cafeteria; in the last period)

F 6. _____ When did Phil recognize the stranger?
(during last hour; during Mr. Nichols' class; during attendance)

F 7. _____ What did Phil and Zack do in kindergarten?
(build block houses)

I 8. _____ Why do you think Phil had trouble remembering Zack?
(any logical response; he hadn't seen him since kindergarten)

E 9. _____ How would you feel if you met a forgotten friend? Why?
(any logical response; happy)

V 10. _____ What does "familiar" mean?
(known; accustomed to; friendly)

☐ Questions Missed

Comprehension Scoring Guide	
Questions Missed	Level
0–1	Independent
1½–2	Ind./Inst.
2½	Instructional
3–4½	Inst./Frust.
5 +	Frustration

Retelling Notes

Retelling Rubric for the Three Reading Levels
Independent Level/Excellent
Recalls central or key ideas
Remembers important facts
Retains the general sequence of events
Relates most of the content in an organized manner
Instructional Level/Satisfactory
Recalls most central or key ideas
Remembers some important facts
Retains the general sequence of events
Relates an overall sense of the content
Frustration Level/Unsatisfactory
Recalls bits of information in a haphazard manner
Little apparent organization

Student Booklet copy is on page 39.

B 3717 (Grade 7) Activating Background: Read the title to yourself. Then tell me what you think this might be about.

Background: Low ├────────┼────────┤ High

Black Out

		MISCUES						
	Substitution	Insertion	Omission	Reversal	Repetition	Self-Correction of Unacceptable Miscue	Meaning Change (Significant Miscue)
The soft buzz of the computer relaxed 7							
Anthony as he worked on his yearly report 15							
for his anxious employer. He typed the 22							
final sentence, sighed in relief, and saved 29							
the computer file. The office lights 35							
flickered, the computer screen went black, 41							
and New York City was silent. Sirens 48							
sounded in the area. Emergency workers 54							
guided employees from several departments 59							
down the stairwell. An hour later, the police 67							
chief announced through his loud speaker, 73							
"All is clear." The workers filed into the 81							
elevators like clockwork, returning to their 87							
projects. One observer commented, "All in 93							
a day's work in New York City." 100							
TOTAL							

Word Recognition Scoring Guide		
Total Miscues	Level	Significant Miscues
0–1	Independent	0–1
2–4	Ind./Inst.	2
5	Instructional	3
6–9	Inst./Frust.	4
10 +	Frustration	5 +

Total Miscues [   ]   Significant Miscues [   ]

Oral Reading Rate	Norm Group Percentile
‾‾‾‾ WPM)6000	☐ 90 ☐ 75 ☐ 50 ☐ 25 ☐ 10

209

B 3717 (Grade 7)
Comprehension Questions

T	1. ___	What is this passage about?
		(the electricity going off in a building; people leaving a building after the electricity went off)

T 1. ___ What is this passage about?
(the electricity going off in a building; people leaving a building after the electricity went off)

F 2. ___ What relaxed Anthony?
(the soft buzz of the computer; the computer noises; having finished his report)

F 3. ___ What was Anthony working on for his employer?
(a yearly report; paper; report)

F 4. ___ Where did the story take place?
(New York City; office building; skyscraper)

F 5. ___ Who announced that it was safe to enter the building?
(the police chief; police)

F 6. ___ Who guided the employees down the stairs?
(emergency workers)

F 7. ___ How long did the workers wait before they heard the all clear announcement?
(an hour)

I 8. ___ What time of day did the story take place? How do you know?
(any logical response)

E 9. ___ How do you think you would feel if you were in a large building when the electricity went off? Why?
(any logical response)

V 10. ___ What is an "observer"?
(someone who watches or notices something)

Retelling Notes

☐ Questions Missed

Comprehension Scoring Guide	
Questions Missed	Level
0–1	Independent
1½–2	Ind./Inst.
2½	Instructional
3–4½	Inst./Frust.
5 +	Frustration

Retelling Rubric for the Three Reading Levels
Independent Level/Excellent
Recalls central or key ideas
Remembers important facts
Retains the general sequence of events
Relates most of the content in an organized manner
Instructional Level/Satisfactory
Recalls most central or key ideas
Remembers some important facts
Retains the general sequence of events
Relates an overall sense of the content
Frustration Level/Unsatisfactory
Recalls bits of information in a haphazard manner
Little apparent organization

Student Booklet copy is on page 40.

B 8183 (Grade 8) Activating Background: Read the title to yourself. Then tell me what you think this might be about.

Background: Low |———+———| High

Sunset Surprise

		MISCUES					
	Substitution	Insertion	Omission	Reversal	Repetition	Self-Correction of Unacceptable Miscue	Meaning Change (Significant Miscue)
Alex was enjoying the sunset from — 6							
Daisy Hill. The magnificent display of — 12							
bright orange, red, and yellow appeared to — 19							
be a sweet, ripe mango slowly sinking into — 27							
the earth. Alex was again surrounded by — 34							
the beautiful colors of falling leaves as she — 42							
reluctantly headed home for dinner. — 47							
Turning east toward the house, she — 53							
witnessed a horrible sight; her greenhouse — 59							
was enveloped in flames! She quickly — 65							
dashed down the hill and across a field of — 74							
drying corn stalks. A few yards before she — 82							
arrived, she realized the fire was only a — 90							
reflection of the sunset on the glass of the — 99							
greenhouse. — 100							
TOTAL							

Word Recognition Scoring Guide		
Total Miscues	Level	Significant Miscues
0–1	Independent	0–1
2–4	Ind./Inst.	2
5	Instructional	3
6–9	Inst./Frust.	4
10 +	Frustration	5 +

Total Miscues [ ]   Significant Miscues [ ]

Oral Reading Rate	Norm Group Percentile
6000)⎯⎯ WPM	☐ 90 ☐ 75 ☐ 50 ☐ 25 ☐ 10

B 8183 (Grade 8)
Comprehension Questions

<table>
<tr><td>T</td><td>1. _____</td><td>What is this passage about?
(an exciting sunset; Alex being fooled by a sunset; a greenhouse that appears to be on fire)</td></tr>
<tr><td>F</td><td>2. _____</td><td>Where was Alex enjoying the sunset?
(Daisy Hill)</td></tr>
<tr><td>F</td><td>3. _____</td><td>What did the sun resemble as it was setting?
(a mango)</td></tr>
<tr><td>F</td><td>4. _____</td><td>Why did Alex first decide to go home?
(to eat dinner)</td></tr>
<tr><td>F</td><td>5. _____</td><td>Which direction did she head to go home?
(east)</td></tr>
<tr><td>F</td><td>6. _____</td><td>How was the greenhouse described when Alex first saw it?
(enveloped in flames)</td></tr>
<tr><td>F</td><td>7. _____</td><td>Why did the greenhouse appear to be on fire?
(the glass reflected the sunset, which is the color of fire)</td></tr>
<tr><td>I</td><td>8. _____</td><td>Why didn't Alex notice the greenhouse sooner?
(any logical response; she was facing west; the sun sets in the west)</td></tr>
<tr><td>E</td><td>9. _____</td><td>How do you think Alex felt when she realized her mistake? Why?
(any logical response; relieved; embarrassed)</td></tr>
<tr><td>V</td><td>10. _____</td><td>What does "reluctantly" mean?
(hesitated; not sure at first; cautiously)</td></tr>
</table>

Retelling Notes

☐ Questions Missed

Comprehension Scoring Guide	
Questions Missed	Level
0–1	Independent
1½–2	Ind./Inst.
2½	Instructional
3–4½	Inst./Frust.
5 +	Frustration

Retelling Rubric for the Three Reading Levels

Independent Level/Excellent
Recalls central or key ideas
Remembers important facts
Retains the general sequence of events
Relates most of the content in an organized manner

Instructional Level/Satisfactory
Recalls most central or key ideas
Remembers some important facts
Retains the general sequence of events
Relates an overall sense of the content

Frustration Level/Unsatisfactory
Recalls bits of information in a haphazard manner
Little apparent organization

Form

Performance Booklet

Teacher Copy

Form C

Primary Uses:
- Oral Reading
- Initial Assessment

Other Uses:
- Silent Reading
- Listening Level
- Progress Monitoring

 Note: This Performance Booklet is on the CD that accompanies the Basic Reading Inventory.

BASIC READING INVENTORY PERFORMANCE BOOKLET

Jerry L. Johns, Ph.D.

Student _____   Grade _____ Gender   M   F   Date of Test _____

School _____   Examiner _____   Date of Birth_____

Address _____   Current Book/Level_____   Age_____

SUMMARY OF STUDENT'S READING PERFORMANCE

Grade	Word Recognition						Comprehension		Reading Rate	
	Isolation (Word Lists)				Context (Passages)		Form C		Words per Minute (WPM)	Norm Group Percentile
	Sight	Analysis	Total	Level	Miscues	Level	Questions Missed	Level		
PP1										
PP2										
P										
1										
2										
3										
4										
5										
6										
7										
8										
9										
10										
11										
12										

ESTIMATE OF READING LEVELS

Independent _____   Instructional _____   Frustration _____

LISTENING LEVEL

Form _____

Grade	Questions Missed	Level
1		
2		
3		
4		
5		
6		
7		
8		

ESTIMATED LEVEL: _____

GENERAL OBSERVATIONS

INFORMAL ANALYSIS OF ORAL READING

Oral Reading Behaviors	Frequency of Occurrence			General Impact on Meaning		
	Seldom	Sometimes	Frequently	No Change	Little Change	Much Change
Substitutions						
Insertions						
Omissions						
Reversals						
Repetitions						

QUALITATIVE ANALYSIS OF BASIC READING INVENTORY INSIGHTS

General Directions: Note the degree to which the student shows behavior or evidence in the following areas. Space is provided for additional items.

Seldom   Always
Weak   Strong
Poor   Excellent

COMPREHENSION

Seeks to construct meaning
Makes predictions
Activates background knowledge
Possesses appropriate concepts
    and vocabulary
Monitors reading
Varies reading rate as needed
Understands topic and major ideas
Remembers facts or details
Makes and supports appropriate
    inferences
Evaluates ideas from passages
Understands vocabulary used
Provides appropriate definitions
    of words
Engages with passages

WORD IDENTIFICATION

Possesses numerous strategies
Uses strategies flexibly
Uses graphophonic information
Uses semantic information
Uses syntactic information
Knows basic sight words
    automatically
Possesses sight vocabulary

ORAL AND SILENT READING

Reads fluently
Reads with expression
Attends to punctuation
Keeps place while reading
Reads at appropriate rate
Reads silently without vocalization

ATTITUDE AND CONFIDENCE

Enjoys reading
Demonstrates willingness to risk
Possesses positive self-concept
Chooses to read
Regards himself/herself as a reader
Exhibits persistence

215

Form C • Graded Word Lists • Performance Booklet • Student Booklet copy is on page 42.

List CC (Pre-Primer)	Sight	Analysis		List C (Primer)	Sight	Analysis
1. see*	_____	_____		1. red*	_____	_____
2. you*	_____	_____		2. day	_____	_____
3. school	_____	_____		3. in*	_____	_____
4. to*	_____	_____		4. for*	_____	_____
5. can*	_____	_____		5. have*	_____	_____
6. good*	_____	_____		6. walk*	_____	_____
7. soon*	_____	_____		7. boy	_____	_____
8. into*	_____	_____		8. cake	_____	_____
9. up*	_____	_____		9. your*	_____	_____
10. big*	_____	_____		10. again*	_____	_____
11. man	_____	_____		11. bee	_____	_____
12. look*	_____	_____		12. come*	_____	_____
13. away*	_____	_____		13. picture	_____	_____
14. stop*	_____	_____		14. said*	_____	_____
15. that*	_____	_____		15. put*	_____	_____
16. yard	_____	_____		16. word	_____	_____
17. train	_____	_____		17. baby	_____	_____
18. truck	_____	_____		18. car	_____	_____
19. black*	_____	_____		19. no*	_____	_____
20. white*	_____	_____		20. funny	_____	_____

*denotes basic sight word from Revised Dolch List

*denotes basic sight word from Revised Dolch List

Number Correct _____ _____   Number Correct _____ _____

Total _____   Total _____

Scoring Guide for Graded Word Lists			
Independent	Instructional	Inst./Frust.	Frustration
20 19	18 17 16	15 14	13 or less

Form C • Graded Word Lists • Performance Booklet • Student Booklet copy is on page 43.

List C 7141 (Grade 1)	Sight	Analysis	List C 8224 (Grade 2)	Sight	Analysis
1. ball			1. brave		
2. new*			2. top		
3. fast*			3. it's		
4. has*			4. follow		
5. with*			5. gold		
6. children			6. front		
7. work*			7. family		
8. pet			8. knock		
9. ready			9. count		
10. much*			10. smell		
11. came*			11. afraid		
12. parade			12. done*		
13. hen			13. silver		
14. live			14. face		
15. hear			15. visit		
16. far*			16. mountain		
17. thing			17. track		
18. year			18. pile		
19. hurry			19. been*		
20. met			20. through*		

*denotes basic sight word from Revised Dolch List   *denotes basic sight word from Revised Dolch List

Number Correct _____   _____   Number Correct _____   _____

Total _____   Total _____

Scoring Guide for Graded Word Lists			
Independent	Instructional	Inst./Frust.	Frustration
20 19	18 17 16	15 14	13 or less

Form C • Graded Word Lists • Performance Booklet • Student Booklet copy is on page 44.

List C 3183 (Grade 3)	Sight	Analysis	List C 5414 (Grade 4)	Sight	Analysis
1. pack			1. thunder		
2. matter			2. friendship		
3. hang			3. crickets		
4. center			4. yesterday		
5. chew			5. dozen		
6. rule			6. telescope		
7. pound			7. whiskers		
8. danger			8. skunk		
9. force			9. amount		
10. history			10. nature		
11. spend			11. level		
12. wisdom			12. husky		
13. mind			13. sight		
14. adventure			14. distance		
15. mental			15. hunger		
16. harbor			16. figure		
17. fault			17. medicine		
18. pilot			18. ashamed		
19. usually			19. saddle		
20. though			20. anxious		
Number Correct			Number Correct		
Total			Total		

Scoring Guide for Graded Word Lists			
Independent	Instructional	Inst./Frust.	Frustration
20 19	18 17 16	15 14	13 or less

218

Form C • Graded Word Lists • Performance Booklet • Student Booklet copy is on page 45.

List C 8595 (Grade 5)	Sight	Analysis	List C 6867 (Grade 6)	Sight	Analysis
1. brag			1. youngster		
2. college			2. activity		
3. tend			3. research		
4. ditch			4. grizzly		
5. bully			5. tornado		
6. journal			6. ruffle		
7. public			7. judgment		
8. goblin			8. nylon		
9. ransom			9. fable		
10. remarkable			10. exact		
11. ankle			11. decay		
12. social			12. substitute		
13. gym			13. wealthy		
14. education			14. communicate		
15. darling			15. assemble		
16. muscle			16. economics		
17. pouch			17. biscuit		
18. barley			18. forbid		
19. petticoat			19. attractive		
20. invitation			20. pliers		
Number Correct			Number Correct		
Total			Total		

Scoring Guide for Graded Word Lists			
Independent	Instructional	Inst./Frust.	Frustration
20 19	18 17 16	15 14	13 or less

219

Form C • Graded Word Lists • Performance Booklet • Student Booklet copy is on page 46.

List C 3717 (Grade 7)	Sight	Analysis	List C 8183 (Grade 8)	Sight	Analysis
1. jazz			1. motive		
2. puncture			2. function		
3. fantastic			3. transplant		
4. publication			4. impressive		
5. derby			5. encircle		
6. terminal			6. linoleum		
7. hemisphere			7. investment		
8. paralyze			8. fortify		
9. environment			9. maximum		
10. cantaloupe			10. detain		
11. blockade			11. leaflet		
12. ornamental			12. privacy		
13. warrant			13. lubricant		
14. bombard			14. oblong		
15. typhoon			15. liberal		
16. hypnotize			16. identification		
17. browse			17. energetic		
18. nasal			18. carburetor		
19. tuberculosis			19. antiseptic		
20. lacquer			20. infuriate		
Number Correct			Number Correct		
Total			Total		

Scoring Guide for Graded Word Lists			
Independent	Instructional	Inst./Frust.	Frustration
20 19	18 17 16	15 14	13 or less

220

Form C • Graded Word Lists • Performance Booklet • Student Booklet copy is on page 47.

List C 4959 (Grade 9)	Sight	Analysis	List C 1047 (Grade 10)	Sight	Analysis
1. nationality			1. organism		
2. complex			2. tart		
3. bleach			3. ashtray		
4. comparable			4. consultant		
5. overwhelm			5. intolerable		
6. contraction			6. synthetic		
7. equivalent			7. conclusive		
8. conservative			8. diverse		
9. bewitch			9. premature		
10. insignificant			10. insufferable		
11. earthy			11. cater		
12. monogram			12. reformatory		
13. redeem			13. demolition		
14. amputate			14. disintegrate		
15. disastrous			15. hoax		
16. disband			16. granulate		
17. coronation			17. necessitate		
18. barracks			18. illegitimate		
19. abolition			19. gaseous		
20. vestibule			20. revue		
Number Correct			Number Correct		
Total			Total		

Scoring Guide for Graded Word Lists			
Independent	Instructional	Inst./Frust.	Frustration
20 19	18 17 16	15 14	13 or less

221

Form C • Graded Word Lists • Performance Booklet • Student Booklet copy is on page 48.

List C 1187 (Grade 11)	Sight	Analysis	List C 1296 (Grade 12)	Sight	Analysis
1. nonexistent			1. fusion		
2. recession			2. modulate		
3. prohibition			3. infectious		
4. collaborate			4. delusion		
5. philosophy			5. marginal		
6. franchise			6. vulnerable		
7. essence			7. inalienable		
8. flagrant			8. fiscal		
9. replenish			9. convene		
10. anesthetic			10. avid		
11. monotone			11. platitude		
12. instigate			12. predecessor		
13. cataract			13. amity		
14. sedative			14. detonate		
15. memoir			15. caste		
16. dubious			16. atrophy		
17. premonition			17. amenable		
18. libel			18. omnibus		
19. maladjustment			19. arable		
20. claimant			20. meritorious		
Number Correct			Number Correct		
Total			Total		

Scoring Guide for Graded Word Lists			
Independent	Instructional	Inst./Frust.	Frustration
20 19	18 17 16	15 14	13 or less

Student Booklet copy is on page 50.

CCC (Pre-Primer 1) Activating Background: Look at the picture and read the title to yourself. Then tell me what you think this might be about.

Background: Low ├────┼────┤ High

Apples		MISCUES						
		Substitution	Insertion	Omission	Reversal	Repetition	Self-Correction of Unacceptable Miscue	Meaning Change (Significant Miscue)
I like apples.	3							
I like red and yellow apples.	9							
Apples can be green.	13							
I like to eat big apples.	19							
An apple is a fun snack.	25							
TOTAL								

Total Miscues [ ]   Significant Miscues [ ]

Word Recognition Scoring Guide		
Total Miscues	Level	Significant Miscues
0	Independent	0
1	Ind./Inst.	—
2	Instructional	1
3	Inst./Frust.	2
4 +	Frustration	3 +

Oral Reading Rate	Norm Group Percentile	
$\overline{)1500}$ WPM	☐ 90 ☐ 75 ☐ 50 ☐ 25 ☐ 10	

CCC (Pre-Primer 1)
Comprehension Questions

F 1. _____ What does the person in the story like?
(apples)

F 2. _____ What three colors can apples be?
(red, yellow, and green)

E 3. _____ Why are apples good to eat?
(any logical response; taste good;
healthy snack)

I 4. _____ What food can you make from apples?
(any logical response; pie; applesauce;
cider; juice)

V 5. _____ What is an "apple"?
(fruit; food; something to eat)

Retelling Notes

☐ Questions
Missed

Comprehension Scoring Guide	
Questions Missed	Level
0	Independent
1	Ind./Inst.
1½	Instructional
2	Inst./Frust.
2½ +	Frustration

Retelling Rubric for the Three Reading Levels
Independent Level/Excellent
Recalls central or key ideas
Remembers important facts
Retains the general sequence of events
Relates most of the content in an organized manner
Instructional Level/Satisfactory
Recalls most central or key ideas
Remembers some important facts
Retains the general sequence of events
Relates an overall sense of the content
Frustration Level/Unsatisfactory
Recalls bits of information in a haphazard manner
Little apparent organization

Student Booklet copy is on page 51.

CC (Pre-Primer 2) Activating Background: Look at the picture and read the title to yourself. Then tell me what you think this might be about.

Background: Low ├───────┼───────┤ High

A Fun Day

		MISCUES						
	Substitution	Insertion	Omission	Reversal	Repetition	Self-Correction of Unacceptable Miscue	Meaning Change (Significant Miscue)
"Here it comes!" said Tom. 5							
"I can see it," said Dan. "Here comes 13							
the band!" 15							
Tom jumped up and down. "Look at 22							
the man. He is tall. I can see his red hat." 33							
"Look!" said Dan. "I see a dog. The 41							
dog is big. The dog is brown and white." 50							
TOTAL							

Total Miscues ▢   Significant Miscues ▢

Word Recognition Scoring Guide		
Total Miscues	Level	Significant Miscues
0	Independent	0
1–2	Ind./Inst.	1
3	Instructional	2
4	Inst./Frust.	3
5 +	Frustration	4 +

Oral Reading Rate	Norm Group Percentile
⟌3000 WPM	▢ 90 ▢ 75 ▢ 50 ▢ 25 ▢ 10

225

CC (Pre-Primer 2)
Comprehension Questions

F   1. _____   What were the children's names?
(Tom and Dan)

F   2. _____   What was the first thing they saw?
(the band; a man)

E   3. _____   Why did Tom jump up and down?
(any logical response; he was excited;
he couldn't see)

I   4. _____   What were the children probably doing?
(any logical response; having fun;
listening to music; watching a parade)

V   5. _____   What is a "hat"?
(something you wear; something you
put on your head)

Retelling Notes

☐ Questions
Missed

Comprehension Scoring Guide	
Questions Missed	Level
0	Independent
1	Ind./Inst.
1½	Instructional
2	Inst./Frust.
2½ +	Frustration

Retelling Rubric for the Three Reading Levels
Independent Level/Excellent
Recalls central or key ideas
Remembers important facts
Retains the general sequence of events
Relates most of the content in an organized manner
Instructional Level/Satisfactory
Recalls most central or key ideas
Remembers some important facts
Retains the general sequence of events
Relates an overall sense of the content
Frustration Level/Unsatisfactory
Recalls bits of information in a haphazard manner
Little apparent organization

Student Booklet copy is on page 52.

C (Primer) Activating Background: Read the title to yourself. Then tell me what you think this might be about.

Background: Low ├────┼────┤ High

Food for Birds

	MISCUES						
	Substitution	Insertion	Omission	Reversal	Repetition	Self-Correction of Unacceptable Miscue	Meaning Change (Significant Miscue)
"See the small birds," said Jim. 6							
"They are looking in the snow. They want 14							
food." 15							
"The snow is deep," said Sue. "They 22							
cannot find food." 25							
Jim said, "Let's help them." 30							
"Yes," said Sue. "We can get bread 37							
for them." 39							
Jim and Sue ran home. They asked 46							
Mother for bread. Mother gave bread to 53							
them. Then they ran to find the birds. 61							
"There are the birds," said Sue. 67							
"Give them the bread." 71							
Jim put the bread on the snow. 78							
Sue said, "Look at the birds! They 85							
are eating the bread." 89							
"They are happy now," said Jim. 95							
"They are fat and happy." 100							
TOTAL							

Word Recognition Scoring Guide		
Total Miscues	Level	Significant Miscues
0–1	Independent	0–1
2–4	Ind./Inst.	2
5	Instructional	3
6–9	Inst./Frust.	4
10 +	Frustration	5 +

Total Miscues ☐   Significant Miscues ☐

Oral Reading Rate	Norm Group Percentile
6000) ___ WPM	☐ 90 ☐ 75 ☐ 50 ☐ 25 ☐ 10

C (Primer)
Comprehension Questions

T 1. _____ What is this story about?
   (feeding the hungry birds)

F 2. _____ Who was in this story?
   (Jim and Sue; two children; mother)

F 3. _____ What did the children see in the snow?
   (birds)

F 4. _____ What did the birds want?
   (food)

F 5. _____ Why couldn't the birds find any food?
   (the snow was deep)

F 6. _____ Where did the children get bread for the birds?
   (from their mother)

F 7. _____ Where did Jim put the bread?
   (on the snow)

I 8. _____ What season of the year is it?
   (winter)

E 9. _____ How do you think the children felt about the hungry birds? Why?
   (any logical response)

V 10. _____ What does "fat" mean?
   (big; large)

Retelling Notes

☐ Questions Missed

Comprehension Scoring Guide	
Questions Missed	Level
0–1	Independent
1½–2	Ind./Inst.
2½	Instructional
3–4½	Inst./Frust.
5 +	Frustration

Retelling Rubric for the Three Reading Levels
Independent Level/Excellent
Recalls central or key ideas
Remembers important facts
Retains the general sequence of events
Relates most of the content in an organized manner
Instructional Level/Satisfactory
Recalls most central or key ideas
Remembers some important facts
Retains the general sequence of events
Relates an overall sense of the content
Frustration Level/Unsatisfactory
Recalls bits of information in a haphazard manner
Little apparent organization

Student Booklet copy is on page 53.

C 7141 (Grade 1) Activating Background: Read the title to yourself. Then tell me what you think this might be about.

Background: Low ├──────┼──────┤ High

Fun with Leaves

	Substitution	Insertion	Omission	Reversal	Repetition	Self-Correction of Unacceptable Miscue	Meaning Change (Significant Miscue)
	MISCUES						
Bill had many leaves in his yard. He — 8							
raked them into a big pile. Pat helped. — 16							
Then Bill got a very good idea. — 23							
He ran and jumped in that pile of leaves. — 32							
"Wow! What fun!" — 35							
"Let me jump," said Pat. He — 41							
jumped in the leaves. — 45							
Soon both boys were jumping. — 50							
They threw leaves up into the air. — 57							
Mother looked out and said, "I see — 64							
two boys having fun. Come in for — 71							
something to eat." — 74							
"See our big pile!" said Bill. — 80							
"Where?" asked Mother. — 83							
The boys looked around. The pile was — 90							
not big now. The leaves were all over the — 99							
yard. — 100							
TOTAL							

Total Miscues ☐   Significant Miscues ☐

Word Recognition Scoring Guide		
Total Miscues	Level	Significant Miscues
0–1	Independent	0–1
2–4	Ind./Inst.	2
5	Instructional	3
6–9	Inst./Frust.	4
10 +	Frustration	5 +

Oral Reading Rate	Norm Group Percentile
6000)‾‾‾ WPM	☐ 90 ☐ 75 ☐ 50 ☐ 25 ☐ 10

C 7141 (Grade 1)
Comprehension Questions

T 1. _____ What is the story about?
(boys raking and playing or jumping in leaves)

F 2. _____ Who was in this story?
(Bill and Pat; two boys; Mother)

F 3. _____ What was in the yard?
(leaves)

F 4. _____ What did the boys do with the leaves?
(raked them; jumped or dived in them; threw them about)

F 5. _____ What did Pat do?
(he jumped into the pile too; he helped to rake the leaves)

F 6. _____ What did Mother want the boys to do?
(come in to eat)

F 7. _____ What happened to the pile of leaves?
(it was all over the yard; the boys messed it up)

I 8. _____ What season do you think it was? Why?
(fall; any logical response)

E 9. _____ How do you think Mother felt about what the boys were doing?
(any logical response)

V 10. _____ What is "jumping"?
(to go up and down)

Retelling Notes

☐ Questions Missed

Comprehension Scoring Guide	
Questions Missed	Level
0–1	Independent
1½–2	Ind./Inst.
2½	Instructional
3–4½	Inst./Frust.
5 +	Frustration

Retelling Rubric for the Three Reading Levels
Independent Level/Excellent
Recalls central or key ideas
Remembers important facts
Retains the general sequence of events
Relates most of the content in an organized manner
Instructional Level/Satisfactory
Recalls most central or key ideas
Remembers some important facts
Retains the general sequence of events
Relates an overall sense of the content
Frustration Level/Unsatisfactory
Recalls bits of information in a haphazard manner
Little apparent organization

Student Booklet copy is on page 54.

C 8224 (Grade 2) Activating Background: Read the title to yourself. Then tell me what you think this might be about.

Background: Low ├──────┼──────┤ High

Zoo Work

	MISCUES						
	Substitution	Insertion	Omission	Reversal	Repetition	Self-Correction of Unacceptable Miscue	Meaning Change (Significant Miscue)
Bob works at the zoo. He takes care — 8							
of all kinds of animals. The animals are — 16							
brought to the zoo from all over the world. — 25							
Bob gives hay to the elephants. He feeds — 33							
raw meat to the lions and fresh fish to the — 43							
seals. He knows just what to give every — 51							
animal. Each day Bob washes the cages in — 59							
the zoo. When an animal gets sick, Bob — 67							
takes it to the zoo doctor. He will make it — 77							
well. Bob keeps the zoo keys. When the — 85							
people go home, Bob locks the gates to the — 94							
zoo. Then he can go home. — 100							
TOTAL							

Total Miscues [ ]   Significant Miscues [ ]

Word Recognition Scoring Guide		
Total Miscues	Level	Significant Miscues
0–1	Independent	0–1
2–4	Ind./Inst.	2
5	Instructional	3
6–9	Inst./Frust.	4
10 +	Frustration	5 +

Oral Reading Rate	Norm Group Percentile
‾‾‾‾‾)6000 WPM	☐ 90 ☐ 75 ☐ 50 ☐ 25 ☐ 10

C 8224 (Grade 2)
Comprehension Questions

T   1. _____   What is this story about?
(Bob and the zoo; Bob's work at the zoo)

F   2. _____   What does Bob do?
(works at the zoo; takes care of animals; washes cages)

F   3. _____   Where do the animals come from?
(all over the world)

F   4. _____   What did Bob feed the lions and what did he feed the seals?
(meat to the lions and fish to the seals)

F   5. _____   How often does Bob wash the cages?
(each day; every day)

F   6. _____   Who takes care of sick animals?
(zoo doctor)

F   7. _____   What does Bob do when the people go home?
(locks the gates and goes home)

I   8. _____   How does Bob know what to feed the animals?
(any logical response)

E   9. _____   Why do you think Bob locks the gates to the zoo?
(any logical response; so no one can take animals)

V   10. _____   What is "raw" meat?
(meat that is not cooked)

Retelling Notes

Questions Missed

Comprehension Scoring Guide	
Questions Missed	Level
0–1	Independent
1½–2	Ind./Inst.
2½	Instructional
3–4½	Inst./Frust.
5 +	Frustration

Retelling Rubric for the Three Reading Levels
Independent Level/Excellent
Recalls central or key ideas
Remembers important facts
Retains the general sequence of events
Relates most of the content in an organized manner
Instructional Level/Satisfactory
Recalls most central or key ideas
Remembers some important facts
Retains the general sequence of events
Relates an overall sense of the content
Frustration Level/Unsatisfactory
Recalls bits of information in a haphazard manner
Little apparent organization

Student Booklet copy is on page 55.

C 3183 (Grade 3) Activating Background: Read the title to yourself. Then tell me what you think this might be about.

Background: Low |——————+——————| High

The Pet Shop

		MISCUES					
	Substitution	Insertion	Omission	Reversal	Repetition	Self-Correction of Unacceptable Miscue	Meaning Change (Significant Miscue)
Maria really wanted a little dog. One 7							
day she went with her parents to the pet 16							
shop. They looked at the fish, turtles, 23							
parrots, and many kinds of dogs. Maria 30							
and her parents saw one nice puppy that 38							
acted very lively. It looked like a small, 46							
bouncing, black ball of fur. The puppy was 54							
a fluffy black poodle. It jumped around in 62							
its cage. When Maria petted the puppy, it 70							
sat up and begged. Maria and her parents 78							
laughed because the poodle looked so cute. 85							
They decided to buy the poodle. After all, 93							
who could resist such a cute dog? 100							
TOTAL							

Total Miscues [ ]   Significant Miscues [ ]

Word Recognition Scoring Guide		
Total Miscues	Level	Significant Miscues
0–1	Independent	0–1
2–4	Ind./Inst.	2
5	Instructional	3
6–9	Inst./Frust.	4
10 +	Frustration	5 +

Oral Reading Rate	Norm Group Percentile				
� 6000 — WPM	☐ 90	☐ 75	☐ 50	☐ 25	☐ 10

233

C 3183 (Grade 3)
Comprehension Questions

T 1. _____ What is this story about?
(Maria and her parents buying a poodle;
a trip to the pet shop)

F 2. _____ Where did Maria and her parents go?
(to the pet shop)

F 3. _____ What did Maria and her parents see?
(fish; turtles; parrots; dogs [any 2])

F 4. _____ What did the poodle look like?
(small; furry; black; fluffy;
bouncing ball of fur; cute [any 2])

F 5. _____ What did the poodle do when Maria
petted it?
(it sat up; it begged)

F 6. _____ Why did Maria and her parents laugh?
(the poodle looked so cute)

F 7. _____ What happened to the poodle?
(Maria and her parents bought it)

I 8. _____ Why do you think Maria wanted a dog?
(any logical response; she liked dogs;
she didn't have anyone to play with)

E 9. _____ What do you think they will do with the
dog once they get it home?
(any logical response; play with it)

V 10. _____ What does "bouncing" mean?
(to spring back; to go up and down)

[ ] Questions Missed

Comprehension Scoring Guide	
Questions Missed	Level
0–1	Independent
1½–2	Ind./Inst.
2½	Instructional
3–4½	Inst./Frust.
5 +	Frustration

Retelling Notes

Retelling Rubric for the Three Reading Levels
Independent Level/Excellent
Recalls central or key ideas
Remembers important facts
Retains the general sequence of events
Relates most of the content in an organized manner
Instructional Level/Satisfactory
Recalls most central or key ideas
Remembers some important facts
Retains the general sequence of events
Relates an overall sense of the content
Frustration Level/Unsatisfactory
Recalls bits of information in a haphazard manner
Little apparent organization

234

Student Booklet copy is on page 56.

C 5414 (Grade 4) Activating Background: Read the title to yourself. Then tell me what you think this might be about.

Background: Low ├──────┼──────┤ High

The Soccer Game

		MISCUES						
	Substitution	Insertion	Omission	Reversal	Repetition	Self-Correction of Unacceptable Miscue	Meaning Change (Significant Miscue)	
There were only two minutes to go	7								
in the big soccer game between the	14								
Jets and the Bombers. The score was	21								
tied. The ball was in the Jets' area	29								
dangerously close to their goal. Rosa, a	36								
Jets midfielder, ran for the ball. She got	44								
to the ball and delivered a great kick.	52								
The ball went sailing over the midline	59								
into Bomber territory.	62								
With a yell, Kim got the ball and	70								
dribbled toward the Bomber goal.	75								
There was no time for a mistake. The	83								
shot must be true. Kim faked right.	90								
Then Kim kicked left and scored as the	98								
game ended.	100								
TOTAL									

Word Recognition Scoring Guide		
Total Miscues	Level	Significant Miscues
0–1	Independent	0–1
2–4	Ind./Inst.	2
5	Instructional	3
6–9	Inst./Frust.	4
10 +	Frustration	5 +

Total Miscues ☐   Significant Miscues ☐

Oral Reading Rate	Norm Group Percentile
⟌6000 WPM	☐ 90 ☐ 75 ☐ 50 ☐ 25 ☐ 10

C 5414 (Grade 4)
Comprehension Questions

T 1. _____ What is this story about?
(a soccer game)

F 2. _____ How much time was left in the game?
(2 minutes)

F 3. _____ What was the score near the end of the game?
(it was tied)

F 4. _____ What was the name of the team Rosa was on?
(Jets)

F 5. _____ What position did Rosa play?
(midfielder)

F 6. _____ When Rosa kicked the ball, where did it go?
(over the midline; into Bomber territory)

F 7. _____ Who scored the final goal of the game?
(Kim)

I 8. _____ Which team lost the game?
(the Bombers)

E 9. _____ If you were the coach, what would you tell your players to do with two minutes to go in the game?
(any logical response; try your hardest; try to get in a goal)

V 10. _____ What does "sailing" mean in this story?
(in the air; flying; soaring; to glide through the air)

	Retelling Notes

Retelling Rubric for the Three Reading Levels

Independent Level/Excellent
Recalls central or key ideas
Remembers important facts
Retains the general sequence of events
Relates most of the content in an organized manner

Instructional Level/Satisfactory
Recalls most central or key ideas
Remembers some important facts
Retains the general sequence of events
Relates an overall sense of the content

Frustration Level/Unsatisfactory
Recalls bits of information in a haphazard manner
Little apparent organization

[ ] Questions Missed

Comprehension Scoring Guide	
Questions Missed	Level
0–1	Independent
1½–2	Ind./Inst.
2½	Instructional
3–4½	Inst./Frust.
5 +	Frustration

Student Booklet copy is on page 57.

C 8595 (Grade 5) Activating Background: Read the title to yourself. Then tell me what you think this might be about.

Background: Low |———|———| High

Pioneer House Building

		MISCUES					
	Substitution	Insertion	Omission	Reversal	Repetition	Self-Correction of Unacceptable Miscue	Meaning Change (Significant Miscue)
When the first pioneers came to 6							
America, there were no special people 12							
to build houses, so they did the work 20							
together. All the people in the area 27							
would come and help. Some people 33							
would cut trees. Other people would take 40							
this wood and start forming the frame 47							
of the house. The older children 53							
helped by carting bits of wood or 60							
cutting the limbs. Younger children 65							
played. The work was difficult and 71							
long and gave the people enormous 77							
appetites. Large quantities of food 82							
were prepared and set outside on long 89							
wooden tables. Then everyone gathered 94							
around the table and feasted joyfully. 100							
TOTAL							

Word Recognition Scoring Guide		
Total Miscues	Level	Significant Miscues
0–1	Independent	0–1
2–4	Ind./Inst.	2
5	Instructional	3
6–9	Inst./Frust.	4
10 +	Frustration	5 +

Total Miscues [ ] Significant Miscues [ ]

Oral Reading Rate	Norm Group Percentile
⎯⎯ WPM)6000	☐ 90 ☐ 75 ☐ 50 ☐ 25 ☐ 10

C 8595 (Grade 5)
Comprehension Questions

T 1. _____ What is this passage about?
         (work the pioneers did to build a house)

F 2. _____ Why did the pioneers have to build their
         own houses?
         (there were no special people to do it)

F 3. _____ Who came and helped?
         (all the people in the area)

F 4. _____ What did the younger children do?
         (play)

F 5. _____ What did the older children do?
         (carted bits of wood; cut the limbs)

F 6. _____ What other jobs did people do?
         (cut trees; form frames; prepare food)

F 7. _____ Where was the food placed and eaten?
         (on wooden tables outside)

I 8. _____ What do you think was the hardest job?
         Why?
         (any logical response)

E 9. _____ Which job would you pick? Why?
         (any logical response)

V 10. _____ What does "enormous" mean?
         (large; big)

☐ Questions Missed

Comprehension Scoring Guide	
Questions Missed	Level
0–1	Independent
1½–2	Ind./Inst.
2½	Instructional
3–4½	Inst./Frust.
5 +	Frustration

Retelling Notes

Retelling Rubric for the Three Reading Levels
Independent Level/Excellent
Recalls central or key ideas
Remembers important facts
Retains the general sequence of events
Relates most of the content in an organized manner
Instructional Level/Satisfactory
Recalls most central or key ideas
Remembers some important facts
Retains the general sequence of events
Relates an overall sense of the content
Frustration Level/Unsatisfactory
Recalls bits of information in a haphazard manner
Little apparent organization

Student Booklet copy is on page 58.

C 6867 (Grade 6) Activating Background: Read the title to yourself. Then tell me what you think this might be about.

Background: Low ├────────┼────────┤ High

Museum Visit

		MISCUES						
		Substitution	Insertion	Omission	Reversal	Repetition	Self-Correction of Unacceptable Miscue	Meaning Change (Significant Miscue)
On our field trip we visited the new	8							
museum. We saw different exhibits about	14							
science and the world around us. The	21							
telephone exhibit was definitely the most	27							
interesting. Phones from the early days	33							
were made of wood and metal. People	40							
had to ring the operator to make a call.	49							
The exhibit displayed many other types of	56							
phones. Some had televisions so that you	63							
could see the person you were talking to.	71							
There were also wireless phones for people	78							
and cars that transmitted calls through tower	85							
signals. We saw movies that showed us	92							
how telephones help us in our everyday	99							
lives.	100							
TOTAL								

Word Recognition Scoring Guide		
Total Miscues	Level	Significant Miscues
0–1	Independent	0–1
2–4	Ind./Inst.	2
5	Instructional	3
6–9	Inst./Frust.	4
10 +	Frustration	5 +

Total Miscues ☐   Significant Miscues ☐

Oral Reading Rate	Norm Group Percentile
⁾6000 ___ WPM	☐ 90 ☐ 75 ☐ 50 ☐ 25 ☐ 10

C 6867 (Grade 6)
Comprehension Questions

T 1. _____ What is this passage about?
(a field trip to the museum; a telephone exhibit)

F 2. _____ What were some of the exhibits?
(science; telephone; world around us [any 2])

F 3. _____ Which exhibit was the most interesting?
(telephone)

F 4. _____ What materials were used to make the early phones?
(wood and metal)

F 5. _____ What did you have to do to make a phone call with early phones?
(call the operator)

F 6. _____ What other types of phones were mentioned?
(phones with televisions; car phones; wireless phones [any 2])

F 7. _____ How do wireless phones transmit messages?
(through tower signals)

I 8. _____ Do you think our phones are better than the early phones? Why?
(any logical response)

E 9. _____ Do you think telephones have made our lives better? Why?
(any logical response)

V 10. _____ What is an "exhibit"?
(any logical response; a display of objects)

Retelling Notes

Questions Missed		

Comprehension Scoring Guide	
Questions Missed	Level
0–1	Independent
1½–2	Ind./Inst.
2½	Instructional
3–4½	Inst./Frust.
5 +	Frustration

Retelling Rubric for the Three Reading Levels
Independent Level/Excellent
Recalls central or key ideas
Remembers important facts
Retains the general sequence of events
Relates most of the content in an organized manner
Instructional Level/Satisfactory
Recalls most central or key ideas
Remembers some important facts
Retains the general sequence of events
Relates an overall sense of the content
Frustration Level/Unsatisfactory
Recalls bits of information in a haphazard manner
Little apparent organization

Student Booklet copy is on page 59.

C 3717 (Grade 7) Activating Background: Read the title to yourself. Then tell me what you think this might be about.

Background: Low ├────┼────┤ High

The Rescue

	MISCUES						
	Substitution	Insertion	Omission	Reversal	Repetition	Self-Correction of Unacceptable Miscue	Meaning Change (Significant Miscue)
One of the most beloved tales is of the — 9							
princess and a knight. The princess, — 15							
shackled to a rock, caught the eye of the — 24							
wandering knight. He galloped over and, — 30							
with a single stroke of his sword, freed — 38							
her from the iron chain. Taking her hand, — 46							
he led her away from the dreadful — 53							
confinement of the rock. While relaxing in — 60							
a sunny meadow, he comforted her with — 67							
reassuring words. The princess told him — 73							
that she had been seized by pirates. These — 81							
pirates had brought her to this savage — 88							
island as a peace offering to the terrible — 96							
monsters of the sea. — 100							
TOTAL							

Word Recognition Scoring Guide		
Total Miscues	Level	Significant Miscues
0–1	Independent	0–1
2–4	Ind./Inst.	2
5	Instructional	3
6–9	Inst./Frust.	4
10 +	Frustration	5 +

Total Miscues ☐   Significant Miscues ☐

Oral Reading Rate	Norm Group Percentile
────) 6000 WPM	☐ 90 ☐ 75 ☐ 50 ☐ 25 ☐ 10

241

C 3717 (Grade 7)
Comprehension Questions

T   1. _____   What is this story about?
(a princess and her knight)

F   2. _____   How was the princess held captive?
(she was shackled to a rock)

F   3. _____   Who saw the princess?
(a knight)

F   4. _____   How did the knight free the princess?
(with his sword; he cut the chain)

F   5. _____   What did the knight do after freeing the princess?
(comforted her with reassuring words; led her away)

F   6. _____   Who took the princess to this island?
(the pirates)

F   7. _____   Why was the princess taken to this island?
(as a peace offering to the monsters)

I   8. _____   Why do you think the pirates used her as a peace offering?
(any logical response; she was beautiful, powerful, etc.)

E   9. _____   What qualities do you think a knight should have?
(any logical response; bravery; courage)

V   10. _____   What does "savage" mean?
(wild; rugged)

	Retelling Notes

[ ] Questions Missed

Comprehension Scoring Guide	
Questions Missed	Level
0–1	Independent
1½–2	Ind./Inst.
2½	Instructional
3–4½	Inst./Frust.
5 +	Frustration

Retelling Rubric for the Three Reading Levels

Independent Level/Excellent
Recalls central or key ideas
Remembers important facts
Retains the general sequence of events
Relates most of the content in an organized manner

Instructional Level/Satisfactory
Recalls most central or key ideas
Remembers some important facts
Retains the general sequence of events
Relates an overall sense of the content

Frustration Level/Unsatisfactory
Recalls bits of information in a haphazard manner
Little apparent organization

Student Booklet copy is on page 60.

C 8183 (Grade 8) Activating Background: Read the title to yourself. Then tell me what you think this might be about.

Background: Low ⊢————┼————⊣ High

Mount Kilarma

	MISCUES						
	Substitution	Insertion	Omission	Reversal	Repetition	Self-Correction of Unacceptable Miscue	Meaning Change (Significant Miscue)
The large mountain loomed ominously 5							
in the foreground. Many had tried to 12							
defeat this magnificent creation of nature, 18							
but to date no one had. There it was, the 28							
lonely unconquered giant, Mount Kilarma. 33							
In sheer size, there was nothing imposing 40							
about the 15,000 foot height of Mount 47							
Kilarma. The dangers rested in the skirt 54							
of glaciers around the steep sides of the 62							
mountain and in the fiercely changing 68							
winds that tore at the summit. The small 76							
band of mountaineers stared at the huge 83							
mass of ice. Could they reach the 90							
mountain's peak and do what no one had 98							
ever accomplished? 100							
TOTAL							

Word Recognition Scoring Guide		
Total Miscues	Level	Significant Miscues
0–1	Independent	0–1
2–4	Ind./Inst.	2
5	Instructional	3
6–9	Inst./Frust.	4
10 +	Frustration	5 +

Total Miscues ☐   Significant Miscues ☐

Oral Reading Rate	Norm Group Percentile
⎯⎯ WPM ⟌6000	☐ 90 ☐ 75 ☐ 50 ☐ 25 ☐ 10

C 8183 (Grade 8)
Comprehension Questions

T 1. _____ What is this passage about?
(a mountain; Mount Kilarma)

F 2. _____ How tall is Mount Kilarma?
(15,000 feet)

F 3. _____ What are the two dangers of Mount
Kilarma?
(the glaciers and changing winds at the
summit)

F 4. _____ How many people had reached the
mountain's peak?
(no one)

F 5. _____ What covered the mountain?
(ice; glaciers)

F 6. _____ On what parts of the mountain were the
glaciers?
(the steep sides)

F 7. _____ What tore at the summit?
(winds)

I 8. _____ Why do you think these people would
risk their lives to climb the mountain?
(any logical response; no one had ever
scaled the mountain)

E 9. _____ What do you believe the mountaineers
were thinking as they stared at Mount
Kilarma?
(any logical response; whether they
would be successful in the climb)

V 10. _____ What does "ominously" mean?
(threatening; menacing)

Retelling Notes

Questions Missed

Comprehension Scoring Guide	
Questions Missed	Level
0–1	Independent
1½–2	Ind./Inst.
2½	Instructional
3–4½	Inst./Frust.
5 +	Frustration

Retelling Rubric for the Three Reading Levels
Independent Level/Excellent
Recalls central or key ideas
Remembers important facts
Retains the general sequence of events
Relates most of the content in an organized manner
Instructional Level/Satisfactory
Recalls most central or key ideas
Remembers some important facts
Retains the general sequence of events
Relates an overall sense of the content
Frustration Level/Unsatisfactory
Recalls bits of information in a haphazard manner
Little apparent organization

Form D

Performance Booklet

Teacher Copy

Form D

Primary Use:
- Silent Reading (Informational)

Other Uses:
- Oral Reading
- Progress Monitoring

 Note: This Performance Booklet is on the CD that accompanies the Basic Reading Inventory.

BASIC READING INVENTORY PERFORMANCE BOOKLET

Jerry L. Johns, Ph.D.

Form D

Student _____ Grade _____ Gender M F Date of Test _____

School _____ Examiner _____ Date of Birth_____

Address _____ Current Book/Level_____ Age_____

SUMMARY OF STUDENT'S READING PERFORMANCE

Grade	Word Recognition						Comprehension		Reading Rate	
	Isolation (Word Lists)				Context (Passages)		Form D		Words per Minute (WPM)	Norm Group Percentile
	Sight	Analysis	Total	Level	Miscues	Level	Questions Missed	Level		
PP1										
PP2										
P										
1										
2										
3										
4										
5										
6										
7										
8										
9										
10										
11										
12										

ESTIMATE OF READING LEVELS

Independent _____ Instructional _____ Frustration _____

LISTENING LEVEL

Form _____

Grade	Questions Missed	Level
1		
2		
3		
4		
5		
6		
7		
8		

ESTIMATED LEVEL: _____

GENERAL OBSERVATIONS

INFORMAL ANALYSIS OF ORAL READING

Oral Reading Behaviors	Frequency of Occurrence			General Impact on Meaning		
	Seldom	Sometimes	Frequently	No Change	Little Change	Much Change
Substitutions						
Insertions						
Omissions						
Reversals						
Repetitions						

QUALITATIVE ANALYSIS OF BASIC READING INVENTORY INSIGHTS

General Directions: Note the degree to which the student shows behavior or evidence in the following areas. Space is provided for additional items.

Seldom / Weak / Poor ←→ Always / Strong / Excellent

COMPREHENSION
Seeks to construct meaning
Makes predictions
Activates background knowledge
Possesses appropriate concepts and vocabulary
Monitors reading
Varies reading rate as needed
Understands topic and major ideas
Remembers facts or details
Makes and supports appropriate inferences
Evaluates ideas from passages
Understands vocabulary used
Provides appropriate definitions of words
Engages with passages

WORD IDENTIFICATION
Possesses numerous strategies
Uses strategies flexibly
Uses graphophonic information
Uses semantic information
Uses syntactic information
Knows basic sight words automatically
Possesses sight vocabulary

ORAL AND SILENT READING
Reads fluently
Reads with expression
Attends to punctuation
Keeps place while reading
Reads at appropriate rate
Reads silently without vocalization

ATTITUDE AND CONFIDENCE
Enjoys reading
Demonstrates willingness to risk
Possesses positive self-concept
Chooses to read
Regards himself/herself as a reader
Exhibits persistence

Student Booklet copy is on page 62.

DDD (Pre-Primer 1) Activating Background: Look at the picture and read the title to yourself. Then tell me what you think this might be about.

Background: Low |———+———| High

Ted's Dog

		MISCUES						
		Substitution	Insertion	Omission	Reversal	Repetition	Self-Correction of Unacceptable Miscue	Meaning Change (Significant Miscue)
Ted has a dog.	4							
His name is Ben.	8							
Ben is a big dog.	13							
He can jump up.	17							
Ted pets Ben.	20							
He is a fun dog.	25							
TOTAL								

Oral Rereading:
Find and read out loud the sentence that tells what the dog can do.

Total Miscues ☐   Significant Miscues ☐

Word Recognition Scoring Guide		
Total Miscues	Level	Significant Miscues
0	Independent	0
1	Ind./Inst.	—
2	Instructional	1
3	Inst./Frust.	2
4 +	Frustration	3 +

Oral Reading Rate	Norm Group Percentile
WPM ⟌1500	☐ 90 ☐ 75 ☐ 50 ☐ 25 ☐ 10

248

DDD (Pre-Primer 1)
Comprehension Questions

T   1. _____ What was the dog's name?
             (Ben)

F   2. _____ What size was Ben?
             (big)

E   3. _____ Why was Ben a fun dog?
             (any logical response; he jumps up; he
             lets Ben pet him)

I   4. _____ What else might Ben be able to do?
             (any logical response; run; fetch; play
             ball)

V   5. _____ What does it mean to "pet" a dog?
             (you reach out and touch it with your
             hand)

Retelling Notes

☐ Questions Missed

Comprehension Scoring Guide	
Questions Missed	Level
0	Independent
1	Ind./Inst.
1½	Instructional
2	Inst./Frust.
2½ +	Frustration

Retelling Rubric for the Three Reading Levels
Independent Level/Excellent
Recalls central or key ideas
Remembers important facts
Retains the general sequence of events
Relates most of the content in an organized manner
Instructional Level/Satisfactory
Recalls most central or key ideas
Remembers some important facts
Retains the general sequence of events
Relates an overall sense of the content
Frustration Level/Unsatisfactory
Recalls bits of information in a haphazard manner
Little apparent organization

Student Booklet copy is on page 63.

DD (Pre-Primer 2) Activating Background: Look at the picture and read the title to yourself. Then tell me what you think this might be about.

Background: Low |———|———| High

Pete's Red Ball

		MISCUES					Self-Correction of Unacceptable Miscue	Meaning Change (Significant Miscue)
	Substitution	Insertion	Omission	Reversal	Repetition		
"I can not find my ball," said Pete. 8							
"My ball is a big ball. **It is red**." 17							
"Here is a ball," Rose said. "The ball is 26							
blue. It is little. It is not red." 34							
"I see a ball," said Pete. "It is red. It 44							
is big. It is my ball." 50							
TOTAL							

Oral Rereading:
Find and read out loud the sentence that tells what color Pete's ball is.

Total Miscues [ ]   Significant Miscues [ ]

Word Recognition Scoring Guide		
Total Miscues	Level	Significant Miscues
0	Independent	0
1–2	Ind./Inst.	1
3	Instructional	2
4	Inst./Frust.	3
5 +	Frustration	4 +

Oral Reading Rate	Norm Group Percentile
⎯⎯⎯ WPM)3000	☐ 90 ☐ 75 ☐ 50 ☐ 25 ☐ 10

DD (Pre-Primer 2)
Comprehension Questions

T 1. _____ What happened to Pete?
             (he lost his ball)

F 2. _____ What did the ball Rose found look like?
             (blue and little)

E 3. _____ What kind of game do you think Pete
             might play with his ball?
             (any logical response)

I 4. _____ How did Pete know that the ball Rose
             found wasn't his?
             (any logical response; it was little and
             blue; it wasn't red or big)

V 5. _____ What is a "ball"?
             (any logical response; something you
             play with; it is round)

Retelling Notes

| [ ] | Questions Missed |

Comprehension Scoring Guide	
Questions Missed	Level
0	Independent
1	Ind./Inst.
1½	Instructional
2	Inst./Frust.
2½ +	Frustration

Retelling Rubric for the Three Reading Levels
Independent Level/Excellent
Recalls central or key ideas
Remembers important facts
Retains the general sequence of events
Relates most of the content in an organized manner
Instructional Level/Satisfactory
Recalls most central or key ideas
Remembers some important facts
Retains the general sequence of events
Relates an overall sense of the content
Frustration Level/Unsatisfactory
Recalls bits of information in a haphazard manner
Little apparent organization

Student Booklet copy is on page 64.

D (Primer) Activating Background: Read the title to yourself. Then tell me what you think this might be about.

Background: Low ├──────┼──────┤ High

Jill's Egg

	Substitution	Insertion	Omission	Reversal	Repetition	Self-Correction of Unacceptable Miscue	Meaning Change (Significant Miscue)
	MISCUES						
A white house was in the woods. Jill 8							
lived there. The sun made Jill happy. The 16							
air smelled clean. She took a walk. 23							
Jill found something along the road 29							
in the grass. It was round and white. 37							
"Oh!" said Jill. "What a nice egg. 44							
I'll take it home." 48							
Mother was home. 51							
She said, **"Jill, you must keep the** 58							
egg warm." 60							
Jill filled a box with rags. She set the 69							
egg in it. She put it near the stove. 78							
The next day Jill heard a sound 85							
she did not know. 89							
"Cheep." A baby bird was born. Jill 96							
had a new pet. 100							
TOTAL							

Oral Rereading: Find and read out loud the sentence that tells what mother told Jill to do with the egg.

Total Miscues [ ]   Significant Miscues [ ]

Word Recognition Scoring Guide		
Total Miscues	Level	Significant Miscues
0–1	Independent	0–1
2–4	Ind./Inst.	2
5	Instructional	3
6–9	Inst./Frust.	4
10 +	Frustration	5 +

Oral Reading Rate	Norm Group Percentile
‾‾‾‾‾ WPM)6000	☐ 90 ☐ 75 ☐ 50 ☐ 25 ☐ 10

D (Primer)
Comprehension Questions

T	1. _____	What is this story about? (a girl named Jill who found an egg that hatched)
F	2. _____	Where did Jill live? (in the woods; in a white house)
F	3. _____	What made Jill happy? (the sun; finding an egg)
F	4. _____	What happened to Jill? (she took a walk; she found an egg)
F	5. _____	Where did Jill find the egg? (along the road in the grass)
F	6. _____	What happened to the egg? (it hatched; a baby chick was born)
F	7. _____	What did Jill do to make the egg hatch? (put it near the stove in a box; kept it warm)
I	8. _____	How do you think the egg got in the grass along the road? (any logical response)
E	9. _____	What other things might Jill have found on her walk? (any logical response; tracks, leaves, rocks, and so on.)
V	10. _____	What is a "pet"? (an animal to love, play with, and so on.)

⬜ Questions Missed

Comprehension Scoring Guide

Questions Missed	Level
0–1	Independent
1½–2	Ind./Inst.
2½	Instructional
3–4½	Inst./Frust.
5 +	Frustration

Retelling Notes

Retelling Rubric for the Three Reading Levels

Independent Level/Excellent
Recalls central or key ideas
Remembers important facts
Retains the general sequence of events
Relates most of the content in an organized manner

Instructional Level/Satisfactory
Recalls most central or key ideas
Remembers some important facts
Retains the general sequence of events
Relates an overall sense of the content

Frustration Level/Unsatisfactory
Recalls bits of information in a haphazard manner
Little apparent organization

Student Booklet copy is on page 65.

D 7141 (Grade 1) Activating Background: Read the title to yourself. Then tell me what you think this might be about.

Background: Low ├───┼───┤ High

At the Zoo

MISCUES							
Substitution	Insertion	Omission	Reversal	Repetition	Self-Correction of Unacceptable Miscue	Meaning Change (Significant Miscue)	

Dan wanted to go to the zoo. He	8							
asked his mother. She said, "Yes."	14							
Dan had fun at the zoo. There were many	23							
animals he liked. One animal looked like it	31							
had two tails. It was an elephant. One had	40							
a nice back to ride on. It was a big turtle.	51							
Dan looked at many things. He saw many	59							
furry animals. He liked seeing them.	65							
It got dark. "Where is my mother?"	72							
he asked. Dan looked and looked for his	80							
mother. He was lost! **He sat down and**	88							
cried. Then Dan looked up. He saw	95							
his mother running to him!	100							
TOTAL								

Oral Rereading:
Find and read out loud the sentence that tells what Dan did when he was lost.

Total Miscues [ ]   Significant Miscues [ ]

Word Recognition Scoring Guide		
Total Miscues	Level	Significant Miscues
0–1	Independent	0–1
2–4	Ind./Inst.	2
5	Instructional	3
6–9	Inst./Frust.	4
10 +	Frustration	5 +

Oral Reading Rate	Norm Group Percentile
_____ WPM 6000⟌	☐ 90 ☐ 75 ☐ 50 ☐ 25 ☐ 10

D 7141 (Grade 1)
Comprehension Questions

T   1. _____ What is this story about?
                  (a boy's trip to the zoo)

F   2. _____ Who went with Dan?
                  (his mother)

F   3. _____ What did Dan think he could do with
                  the turtle?
                  (ride it)

F   4. _____ What other kinds of animals did Dan
                  see at the zoo?
                  (furry animals; elephant)

F   5. _____ How did Dan think the elephant looked?
                  (like it had two tails)

F   6. _____ Why did Dan cry?
                  (he was lost; he was scared)

F   7. _____ What did Dan see when he looked up?
                  (his mother running to him)

I   8. _____ What do you think the furry animals
                  were?
                  (any logical response; monkeys; bears;
                  lions; tigers)

E   9. _____ What did you think the furry animals
                  did?
                  (any logical response; ate; slept)

V 10. _____ What does "furry" mean?
                  (covered with fur; soft)

Retelling Notes

☐ Questions Missed

Comprehension Scoring Guide	
Questions Missed	Level
0–1	Independent
1½–2	Ind./Inst.
2½	Instructional
3–4½	Inst./Frust.
5 +	Frustration

Retelling Rubric for the Three Reading Levels
Independent Level/Excellent
Recalls central or key ideas
Remembers important facts
Retains the general sequence of events
Relates most of the content in an organized manner
Instructional Level/Satisfactory
Recalls most central or key ideas
Remembers some important facts
Retains the general sequence of events
Relates an overall sense of the content
Frustration Level/Unsatisfactory
Recalls bits of information in a haphazard manner
Little apparent organization

Student Booklet copy is on page 66.

D 8224 (Grade 2) Activating Background: Read the title to yourself. Then tell me what you think this might be about.

Background: Low ├────┼────┤ High

A Spider Friend

		MISCUES						
	Substitution	Insertion	Omission	Reversal	Repetition	Self-Correction of Unacceptable Miscue	Meaning Change (Significant Miscue)
A spider sat down by a boy. The — 8							
boy was afraid of it. He should not have — 17							
been scared. The spider would not hurt — 24							
him. Most spiders are friendly. Spiders — 30							
belong to a group of animals that have — 38							
eight legs. Spiders are not insects. — 44							
In the fall the mother spider lays — 51							
about 500 eggs. Only the strong baby — 58							
spiders live. **When spring comes they** — 64							
leave their nest. They eat flies, bugs, and — 72							
ants. They also eat insects that harm our — 80							
crops. Some large spiders eat mice and — 87							
birds. You should be able to find a — 95							
spider web where you live. — 100							
TOTAL							

Oral Rereading:
Find and read out loud the sentence that tells what spiders do in the spring.

Total Miscues [ ]   Significant Miscues [ ]

Word Recognition Scoring Guide		
Total Miscues	Level	Significant Miscues
0–1	Independent	0–1
2–4	Ind./Inst.	2
5	Instructional	3
6–9	Inst./Frust.	4
10 +	Frustration	5 +

Oral Reading Rate	Norm Group Percentile
___ WPM ⟌6000	☐ 90 ☐ 75 ☐ 50 ☐ 25 ☐ 10

D 8224 (Grade 2)
Comprehension Questions

T   1. _____ What is this story about?
(spiders)

F   2. _____ What did the spider do first in this story?
(sat by a little boy)

F   3. _____ How many legs does a spider have?
(eight)

F   4. _____ When do mother spiders lay their eggs?
(in the fall)

F   5. _____ How many eggs does a mother spider lay?
(about 500)

F   6. _____ When do baby spiders leave their nest?
(in the spring)

F   7. _____ What do large spiders eat?
(mice and birds [either 1])

I   8. _____ What happens to weak baby spiders?
(any logical response; they die)

E   9. _____ Why do you think some people are afraid of spiders?
(any logical response)

V   10. _____ What are "crops"?
(any logical response; what farmers grow; corn; beans)

Retelling Notes

☐ Questions Missed

Comprehension Scoring Guide	
Questions Missed	Level
0–1	Independent
1½–2	Ind./Inst.
2½	Instructional
3–4½	Inst./Frust.
5 +	Frustration

Retelling Rubric for the Three Reading Levels
Independent Level/Excellent
Recalls central or key ideas
Remembers important facts
Retains the general sequence of events
Relates most of the content in an organized manner
Instructional Level/Satisfactory
Recalls most central or key ideas
Remembers some important facts
Retains the general sequence of events
Relates an overall sense of the content
Frustration Level/Unsatisfactory
Recalls bits of information in a haphazard manner
Little apparent organization

Student Booklet copy is on page 67.

D 3183 (Grade 3) Activating Background: Read the title to yourself. Then tell me what you think this might be about.

Background: Low ├────┼────┤ High

Big Star

	MISCUES							
	Substitution	Insertion	Omission	Reversal	Repetition	Self-Correction of Unacceptable Miscue	Meaning Change (Significant Miscue)	
The sun is important for life on earth. 8								
We need the sun for light, heat, and energy. 17								
If there was no sun, life on our planet earth 27								
would not exist. The sun is a star. It looks 37								
much larger than the stars you can see in the 47								
night sky. It seems larger because it is a lot 57								
closer to the earth than the other stars. **It is** 67								
actually about the same size as other stars. 75								
Stars are big balls of energy in the form of 85								
gas. Our earth will continue to get energy 93								
from the sun for billions of years. 100								
TOTAL								

Oral Rereading:
Find and read out loud the sentence that tells how the sun compares to other stars.

Total Miscues ☐   Significant Miscues ☐

Word Recognition Scoring Guide		
Total Miscues	Level	Significant Miscues
0–1	Independent	0–1
2–4	Ind./Inst.	2
5	Instructional	3
6–9	Inst./Frust.	4
10 +	Frustration	5 +

Oral Reading Rate	Norm Group Percentile
⟌6000 WPM	☐ 90 ☐ 75 ☐ 50 ☐ 25 ☐ 10

D 3183 (Grade 3)
Comprehension Questions

T 1. _____ What is this story about?
(the sun)

F 2. _____ What does the sun give the earth?
(light, heat, energy [any 2])

F 3. _____ What would happen to life on earth
without the sun?
(it would not exist)

F 4. _____ What kind of object is the sun?
(a star)

F 5. _____ Why does the sun look larger than other
stars?
(because it is closer to the earth)

F 6. _____ What are stars made of?
(gas; big balls of energy)

F 7. _____ How long will earth get energy from the
sun?
(for billions of years)

I 8. _____ What would the earth be like without
the sun?
(any logical response; there would be no
life; cold; dark)

E 9. _____ Do you like the sun? Why?
(any logical response; it makes warm
days; it gives light)

V 10. _____ What does it mean to "exist"?
(to live; to be; to be real)

	Retelling Notes

[ ] Questions Missed

Comprehension Scoring Guide	
Questions Missed	Level
0–1	Independent
1½–2	Ind./Inst.
2½	Instructional
3–4½	Inst./Frust.
5 +	Frustration

Retelling Rubric for the Three Reading Levels

Independent Level/Excellent
Recalls central or key ideas
Remembers important facts
Retains the general sequence of events
Relates most of the content in an organized manner

Instructional Level/Satisfactory
Recalls most central or key ideas
Remembers some important facts
Retains the general sequence of events
Relates an overall sense of the content

Frustration Level/Unsatisfactory
Recalls bits of information in a haphazard manner
Little apparent organization

Student Booklet copy is on page 68.

D 5414 (Grade 4) Activating Background: Read the title to yourself. Then tell me what you think this might be about.

Background: Low ├───────┼──────┤ High

Amazing Plants

		MISCUES						
	Substitution	Insertion	Omission	Reversal	Repetition	Self-Correction of Unacceptable Miscue	Meaning Change (Significant Miscue)
There are over three hundred 5							
thousand different kinds of plants. The 11							
oxygen in the air we breathe comes from 19							
plants. Some plants grow bigger and live 26							
longer than animals. Plants grow in many 33							
sizes and shapes. Some are smaller than 40							
the period at the end of this sentence. 48							
These plants can only be seen with a 56							
microscope. Other plants, like the giant 62							
pine, tower high in the sky. Most plants 70							
have stems and leaves. Plants can live in 78							
a variety of places. Some even seem to 86							
grow out of rocks. Others live in water, 94							
old bread, and even old shoes! 100							
TOTAL							

Oral Rereading:
Find and read out loud the sentence that tells how to see very small plants.

Total Miscues ☐   Significant Miscues ☐

Word Recognition Scoring Guide		
Total Miscues	Level	Significant Miscues
0–1	Independent	0–1
2–4	Ind./Inst.	2
5	Instructional	3
6–9	Inst./Frust.	4
10 +	Frustration	5 +

Oral Reading Rate	Norm Group Percentile
___)6000 WPM	☐ 90 ☐ 75 ☐ 50 ☐ 25 ☐ 10

D 5414 (Grade 4)
Comprehension Questions

T   1. _____   What is this passage about?
              (plants)

F   2. _____   How many plants are there?
              (over 300,000)

F   3. _____   Why are plants important to people?
              (they provide oxygen)

F   4. _____   How small can plants be?
              (smaller than a period at the end
              of a sentence; so small you need a
              microscope)

F   5. _____   What do most plants have?
              (stems and leaves)

F   6. _____   According to the passage, where can
              plants live?
              (rocks; water; bread; shoes [any 2] or a
              variety of places)

F   7. _____   What is used to see small plants?
              (a microscope)

I   8. _____   Name a plant that would probably live
              longer than most animals.
              (any logical response; trees)

E   9. _____   What do you think would happen if all
              the plants died? Why?
              (any logical response; there would be no
              life on earth; no oxygen)

V 10. _____   What is a "microscope"?
              (a thing that makes small things seem
              larger)

Retelling Notes

☐ Questions
  Missed

Comprehension Scoring Guide	
Questions Missed	Level
0–1	Independent
1½–2	Ind./Inst.
2½	Instructional
3–4½	Inst./Frust.
5 +	Frustration

Retelling Rubric for the Three Reading Levels

Independent Level/Excellent
Recalls central or key ideas
Remembers important facts
Retains the general sequence of events
Relates most of the content in an organized manner

Instructional Level/Satisfactory
Recalls most central or key ideas
Remembers some important facts
Retains the general sequence of events
Relates an overall sense of the content

Frustration Level/Unsatisfactory
Recalls bits of information in a haphazard manner
Little apparent organization

Student Booklet copy is on page 69.

D 8595 (Grade 5) Activating Background: Read the title to yourself. Then tell me what you think this might be about.

Background: Low ├────┼────┤ High

Plane Flight

		MISCUES						
		Substitution	Insertion	Omission	Reversal	Repetition	Self-Correction of Unacceptable Miscue	Meaning Change (Significant Miscue)
Older airplanes were moved through	5							
the air by the use of propellers. Now, most	14							
planes are driven by large jet engines.	21							
Some fly faster than sound. **The first thing**	29							
you may notice about a plane is the wings	38							
that stick out on either side of its long	47							
body. Today jet planes land and take off	55							
from major airports every few seconds.	61							
People can travel several hundred miles	67							
in less than an hour. It can take travelers	76							
longer to retrieve their luggage than to fly	84							
to their destination. Planes have been	90							
much improved since the Wright brothers	96							
first flew in 1903.	100							
TOTAL								

Oral Rereading:
Find and read out loud the sentence that tells what you might first notice about a plane.

Total Miscues ☐   Significant Miscues ☐

Word Recognition Scoring Guide		
Total Miscues	Level	Significant Miscues
0–1	Independent	0–1
2–4	Ind./Inst.	2
5	Instructional	3
6–9	Inst./Frust.	4
10 +	Frustration	5 +

Oral Reading Rate	Norm Group Percentile
⎯⎯⎯ WPM)6000	☐ 90 ☐ 75 ☐ 50 ☐ 25 ☐ 10

262

D 8595 (Grade 5)
Comprehension Questions

T   1. _____   What is this passage about?
(airplanes; the development of planes through the years)

F   2. _____   What kind of engines do most airplanes have today?
(jet engines)

F   3. _____   How fast can some planes fly?
(faster than sound)

F   4. _____   How were older planes moved through the air?
(propellers)

F   5. _____   In what year did the Wright brothers fly?
(1903)

F   6. _____   According to this passage, how long does it take for people to fly several hundred miles?
(less than an hour)

F   7. _____   According to the passage, how often do airplanes land and take off from major airports?
(every few seconds)

I   8. _____   How do you think the Wright brothers felt after the first flight? Why?
(any logical response; happy)

E   9. _____   Do you think jet airplanes have changed our lives for the better? Why?
(any logical response)

V 10. _____   What is a "destination"?
(a place you are trying to get to)

Retelling Notes

Questions Missed

Comprehension Scoring Guide	
Questions Missed	Level
0–1	Independent
1½–2	Ind./Inst.
2½	Instructional
3–4½	Inst./Frust.
5 +	Frustration

Retelling Rubric for the Three Reading Levels
Independent Level/Excellent
Recalls central or key ideas
Remembers important facts
Retains the general sequence of events
Relates most of the content in an organized manner
Instructional Level/Satisfactory
Recalls most central or key ideas
Remembers some important facts
Retains the general sequence of events
Relates an overall sense of the content
Frustration Level/Unsatisfactory
Recalls bits of information in a haphazard manner
Little apparent organization

Student Booklet copy is on page 70.

D 6867 (Grade 6) Activating Background: Read the title to yourself. Then tell me what you think this might be about.

Background: Low |———+———| High

Sunflowers		MISCUES						
		Substitution	Insertion	Omission	Reversal	Repetition	Self-Correction of Unacceptable Miscue	Meaning Change (Significant Miscue)
One of the most amazing flowers	6							
found in the Midwest is the sunflower.	13							
Legend states that the flower got its name	21							
from its strange habit of "turning" its head	29							
in order to face the sun. The sunflower is	38							
a very strong plant. It ranges in height	46							
from three to fifteen feet. The head of the	55							
sunflower is similar to that of a daisy. Both	64							
have an outer circle of wide petals and	72							
an inner circle of small brown flowers.	79							
Seeds later form from these small flowers.	86							
These seeds produce some of the most	93							
unique patterns found in the plant world.	100							
TOTAL								

Oral Rereading:
Find and read out loud the sentence that tells what happens to the brown flowers.

Total Miscues ☐   Significant Miscues ☐

Word Recognition Scoring Guide		
Total Miscues	Level	Significant Miscues
0–1	Independent	0–1
2–4	Ind./Inst.	2
5	Instructional	3
6–9	Inst./Frust.	4
10 +	Frustration	5 +

Oral Reading Rate	Norm Group Percentile
___)6000 WPM	☐ 90 ☐ 75 ☐ 50 ☐ 25 ☐ 10

D 6867 (Grade 6)
Comprehension Questions

T 1. _____ What is this passage about?
(sunflowers)

F 2. _____ How did the sunflower get its name?
(turning its head to face the sun)

F 3. _____ How tall is the sunflower?
(three to fifteen feet)

F 4. _____ What is on the outside of the sunflower?
(wide petals)

F 5. _____ What color is the inner circle of the
sunflower?
(brown)

F 6. _____ What is the head of the sunflower
similar to?
(daisy)

F 7. _____ What comes from the small flowers in
the middle?
(seeds)

I 8. _____ Would some sunflowers be taller than
you are? Why?
(any logical response)

E 9. _____ Why do you think a sunflower would be
considered a strong plant?
(any logical response; thick stem; tall)

V 10. _____ What does "unique" mean?
(any logical response; different)

	Retelling Notes

☐ Questions Missed

Comprehension Scoring Guide	
Questions Missed	Level
0–1	Independent
1½–2	Ind./Inst.
2½	Instructional
3–4½	Inst./Frust.
5 +	Frustration

Retelling Rubric for the Three Reading Levels

Independent Level/Excellent
Recalls central or key ideas
Remembers important facts
Retains the general sequence of events
Relates most of the content in an organized manner

Instructional Level/Satisfactory
Recalls most central or key ideas
Remembers some important facts
Retains the general sequence of events
Relates an overall sense of the content

Frustration Level/Unsatisfactory
Recalls bits of information in a haphazard manner
Little apparent organization

265

Student Booklet copy is on page 71.

D 3717 (Grade 7) Activating Background: Read the title to yourself. Then tell me what you think this might be about.

Background: Low ├────┼────┤ High

Native American Celebrations

		MISCUES						
	Substitution	Insertion	Omission	Reversal	Repetition	Self-Correction of Unacceptable Miscue	Meaning Change (Significant Miscue)	
Native American Indians worshipped 4								
the power in natural things, such as the stars, 13								
moon, and the sun. At various times during 21								
the year, they would hold celebrations in 28								
honor of this power that they named the 36								
Great Spirit. On these occasions, they would 43								
have ceremonies of dancing and feasting. 49								
They would decorate their bodies and faces 56								
and dress themselves in their best clothes. 63								
A medicine man would lead them in the 71								
celebration that continued for several days. 77								
Native Americans gathered about the 82								
council fire and prayed that the Great 89								
Spirit's wish for them would be revealed 96								
by a natural sign. 100								
TOTAL								

Oral Rereading:
Find and read out loud the sentence that tells who led the celebration.

Total Miscues ☐   Significant Miscues ☐

Word Recognition Scoring Guide		
Total Miscues	Level	Significant Miscues
0–1	Independent	0–1
2–4	Ind./Inst.	2
5	Instructional	3
6–9	Inst./Frust.	4
10 +	Frustration	5 +

Oral Reading Rate	Norm Group Percentile
WPM ⟌6000	☐ 90 ☐ 75 ☐ 50 ☐ 25 ☐ 10

266

D 3717 (Grade 7)
Comprehension Questions

T 1. _____ What is this passage about?
(Indian worship; how Native Americans celebrated)

F 2. _____ What did the Native American Indians worship?
(the power in natural things; sun, moon, stars)

F 3. _____ Why did the Native Americans hold celebrations?
(to honor the Great Spirit)

F 4. _____ How did they decorate themselves for the celebrations?
(painted their faces and bodies; wore their best clothes)

F 5. _____ What did the medicine man do during the celebration?
(led them)

F 6. _____ What were the Native Americans doing at their celebrations?
(dancing, feasting, decorating themselves, and praying [any 2])

F 7. _____ What did they pray for?
(a sign from the Great Spirit)

I 8. _____ What sign do you think the Native Americans wanted from the Great Spirit?
(any logical response)

E 9. _____ Why do you think the Native Americans worshipped things of nature?
(any logical response)

V 10. _____ What is meant by "reveal"?
(show; make known)

Retelling Notes

[ ] Questions Missed

Comprehension Scoring Guide	
Questions Missed	Level
0–1	Independent
1½–2	Ind./Inst.
2½	Instructional
3–4½	Inst./Frust.
5 +	Frustration

Retelling Rubric for the Three Reading Levels
Independent Level/Excellent
Recalls central or key ideas
Remembers important facts
Retains the general sequence of events
Relates most of the content in an organized manner
Instructional Level/Satisfactory
Recalls most central or key ideas
Remembers some important facts
Retains the general sequence of events
Relates an overall sense of the content
Frustration Level/Unsatisfactory
Recalls bits of information in a haphazard manner
Little apparent organization

Student Booklet copy is on page 72.

D 8183 (Grade 8) Activating Background: Read the title to yourself. Then tell me what you think this might be about.

Background: Low |———+———| High

Our Environment

		MISCUES				Repetition	Self-Correction of Unacceptable Miscue	Meaning Change (Significant Miscue)
		Substitution	Insertion	Omission	Reversal			
Besides using plants and animals for	6							
food, people use the hides of animals for	14							
shoes, the wood from trees to build houses,	22							
the fiber from the cotton plant to make	30							
skirts and shirts, and the wool from sheep	38							
to make suits and coats. Even the synthetic	46							
fibers that people use are made from	53							
matter found in the environment.	58							
People and the environment are	63							
interdependent, but that is not the whole	70							
story. **Modern people can do much more;**	77							
they can use science and technology	83							
to change their environment. Because	88							
of their advanced brains, people can	94							
investigate and manipulate their	98							
precious environment.	100							
TOTAL								

Oral Rereading:
Find and read out loud the sentence that tells what two things people use to change their environment.

Total Miscues [   ]   Significant Miscues [   ]

Word Recognition Scoring Guide		
Total Miscues	Level	Significant Miscues
0–1	Independent	0–1
2–4	Ind./Inst.	2
5	Instructional	3
6–9	Inst./Frust.	4
10 +	Frustration	5 +

Oral Reading Rate	Norm Group Percentile				
WPM)6000	☐ 90	☐ 75	☐ 50	☐ 25	☐ 10

D 8183 (Grade 8)
Comprehension Questions

T	1. _____	What is this passage about? (people's interdependence with their environment; how people use their environment)	

T   1. _____   What is this passage about?
(people's interdependence with their environment; how people use their environment)

F   2. _____   What do modern people use to change the environment?
(science and technology)

F   3. _____   Why are people able to investigate their environment?
(they have a brain)

F   4. _____   What are synthetic fibers made from?
(matter found in the environment)

F   5. _____   What are some of the things in the environment which people use?
(plants; animals; wood; cotton; wool [any 2])

F   6. _____   What does the passage say people use to make skirts and shirts?
(fiber from the cotton plant)

F   7. _____   According to the passage, what are the hides of animals used for?
(shoes)

I   8. _____   What are some of the ways in which people have changed the environment?
(any logical response)

E   9. _____   Do you think it's a good thing for people to change their environment? Why?
(any logical response)

V   10. _____   What does "synthetic" mean?
(fake; unnatural; made from several things put together)

Retelling Notes

[ ] Questions Missed

Comprehension Scoring Guide	
Questions Missed	Level
0–1	Independent
1½–2	Ind./Inst.
2½	Instructional
3–4½	Inst./Frust.
5 +	Frustration

Retelling Rubric for the Three Reading Levels
Independent Level/Excellent
Recalls central or key ideas
Remembers important facts
Retains the general sequence of events
Relates most of the content in an organized manner
Instructional Level/Satisfactory
Recalls most central or key ideas
Remembers some important facts
Retains the general sequence of events
Relates an overall sense of the content
Frustration Level/Unsatisfactory
Recalls bits of information in a haphazard manner
Little apparent organization

Form E

Performance Booklet

Teacher Copy

Form E

Primary Use:

- Oral Reading (Informational)

Other Uses:

- Silent Reading
- Progress Monitoring

 Note: This Performance Booklet is on the CD that accompanies the Basic Reading Inventory.

271

Eleventh Edition

BASIC READING INVENTORY PERFORMANCE BOOKLET

Jerry L. Johns, Ph.D.

Form E

Student _____   Grade _____   Gender   M   F   Date of Test _____

School _____   Examiner _____   Date of Birth_____

Address _____   Current Book/Level_____   Age_____

SUMMARY OF STUDENT'S READING PERFORMANCE

Grade	Word Recognition						Comprehension		Reading Rate	
	Isolation (Word Lists)				Context (Passages)		Form E		Words per Minute (WPM)	Norm Group Percentile
	Sight	Analysis	Total	Level	Miscues	Level	Questions Missed	Level		
PP1										
PP2										
P										
1										
2										
3										
4										
5										
6										
7										
8										

Grade	Sight	Analysis	Total	Level
9				
10				
11				
12				

ESTIMATE OF READING LEVELS

Independent _____   Instructional _____   Frustration _____

LISTENING LEVEL

Form _____

Grade	Questions Missed	Level
1		
2		
3		
4		
5		
6		
7		
8		

ESTIMATED LEVEL: _____

GENERAL OBSERVATIONS

INFORMAL ANALYSIS OF ORAL READING

Oral Reading Behaviors	Frequency of Occurrence			General Impact on Meaning		
	Seldom	Sometimes	Frequently	No Change	Little Change	Much Change
Substitutions						
Insertions						
Omissions						
Reversals						
Repetitions						

QUALITATIVE ANALYSIS OF BASIC READING INVENTORY INSIGHTS

General Directions: Note the degree to which the student shows behavior or evidence in the following areas. Space is provided for additional items.

	Seldom / Weak / Poor			Always / Strong / Excellent

COMPREHENSION

Seeks to construct meaning

Makes predictions

Activates background knowledge

Possesses appropriate concepts and vocabulary

Monitors reading

Varies reading rate as needed

Understands topic and major ideas

Remembers facts or details

Makes and supports appropriate inferences

Evaluates ideas from passages

Understands vocabulary used

Provides appropriate definitions of words

Engages with passages

_____

_____

WORD IDENTIFICATION

Possesses numerous strategies

Uses strategies flexibly

Uses graphophonic information

Uses semantic information

Uses syntactic information

Knows basic sight words automatically

Possesses sight vocabulary

_____

_____

ORAL AND SILENT READING

Reads fluently

Reads with expression

Attends to punctuation

Keeps place while reading

Reads at appropriate rate

Reads silently without vocalization

_____

_____

ATTITUDE AND CONFIDENCE

Enjoys reading

Demonstrates willingness to risk

Possesses positive self-concept

Chooses to read

Regards himself/herself as a reader

Exhibits persistence

_____

_____

Student Booklet copy is on page 74.

EEE (Pre-Primer 1) Activating Background: Look at the picture and read the title to yourself. Then tell me what you think this might be about.

Background: Low ├———┼———┤ High

A Spider		MISCUES							
		Substitution	Insertion	Omission	Reversal	Repetition	Self-Correction of Unacceptable Miscue	Meaning Change (Significant Miscue)	
A spider can be big or little.	7								
It has eight legs.	11								
It has a head and tummy.	17								
It can spin a web. It eats bugs.	25								
TOTAL									

Total Miscues ☐   Significant Miscues ☐

Word Recognition Scoring Guide		
Total Miscues	Level	Significant Miscues
0	Independent	0
1	Ind./Inst.	—
2	Instructional	1
3	Inst./Frust.	2
4 +	Frustration	3 +

Oral Reading Rate	Norm Group Percentile
$\frac{}{)1500}$ WPM	☐ 90 ☐ 75 ☐ 50 ☐ 25 ☐ 10

EEE (Pre-Primer 1)
Comprehension Questions

T   1. _____ How many legs does a spider have?
             (eight)

F   2. _____ What can a spider spin?
             (a web)

E   3. _____ What kind of bug does a spider eat?
             (any logical response; fly; mosquito)

I   4. _____ What is the biggest part of a spider?
             (its tummy; stomach; abdomen)

V   5. _____ What is a "web"?
             (something a spider makes to catch
             bugs; something a spider makes to walk
             on or hang from)

Retelling Notes

[ ] Questions
    Missed

Comprehension Scoring Guide	
Questions Missed	Level
0	Independent
1	Ind./Inst.
1½	Instructional
2	Inst./Frust.
2½ +	Frustration

Retelling Rubric for the Three Reading Levels
Independent Level/Excellent
Recalls central or key ideas
Remembers important facts
Retains the general sequence of events
Relates most of the content in an organized manner
Instructional Level/Satisfactory
Recalls most central or key ideas
Remembers some important facts
Retains the general sequence of events
Relates an overall sense of the content
Frustration Level/Unsatisfactory
Recalls bits of information in a haphazard manner
Little apparent organization

275

Student Booklet copy is on page 75.

EE (Pre-Primer 2) Activating Background: Look at the picture and read the title to yourself. Then tell me what you think this might be about.

Background: Low ⊢————┼————⊣ High

The Sun

		MISCUES						
		Substitution	Insertion	Omission	Reversal	Repetition	Self-Correction of Unacceptable Miscue	Meaning Change (Significant Miscue)
The sun helps plants grow. The	6							
sun makes them green. The sun	12							
helps them get food. People eat	18							
plants.	19							
The sun helps people. It gives	25							
them light. They can see.	30							
The sun helps animals. It helps	36							
keep them warm. Some animals eat	42							
in the day. It helps them see food.	50							
TOTAL								

Total Miscues [ ]   Significant Miscues [ ]

Word Recognition Scoring Guide		
Total Miscues	Level	Significant Miscues
0	Independent	0
1–2	Ind./Inst.	1
3	Instructional	2
4	Inst./Frust.	3
5 +	Frustration	4 +

Oral Reading Rate	Norm Group Percentile
$\overline{)3000}$ WPM	☐ 90 ☐ 75 ☐ 50 ☐ 25 ☐ 10

EE (Pre-Primer 2)
Comprehension Questions

T   1. _____ How does the sun help plants?
              (helps them grow; makes them green;
              helps them get food [any 1])

F   2. _____ What else does the sun help?
              (people; animals [either 1])

E   3. _____ How does the sun help keep animals
              warm?
              (any logical response; the light heats
              their fur; rays of sun come down)

I   4. _____ Do you like the sun? Why?
              (any logical response)

V   5. _____ What is "food"?
              (something to eat; plants; meat)

Retelling Notes

Questions Missed

Comprehension Scoring Guide	
Questions Missed	Level
0	Independent
1	Ind./Inst.
1½	Instructional
2	Inst./Frust.
2½ +	Frustration

Retelling Rubric for the Three Reading Levels
Independent Level/Excellent
Recalls central or key ideas
Remembers important facts
Retains the general sequence of events
Relates most of the content in an organized manner
Instructional Level/Satisfactory
Recalls most central or key ideas
Remembers some important facts
Retains the general sequence of events
Relates an overall sense of the content
Frustration Level/Unsatisfactory
Recalls bits of information in a haphazard manner
Little apparent organization

Student Booklet copy is on page 76.

E (Primer) Activating Background: Read the title to yourself. Then tell me what you think this might be about.

Background: Low ├────┼────┤ High

The Pig Farm

	Substitution	Insertion	Omission	Reversal	Repetition	Self-Correction of Unacceptable Miscue	Meaning Change (Significant Miscue)
	MISCUES						
It was hot. Dad and Lisa went to a farm. The	11						
farm was a pig farm.	16						
"Look at the pigs!" said Dad.	22						
Lisa said, "I see a pig with white spots. It is	33						
white and black."	36						
Dad said, "This one is red."	42						
"Look Lisa," said Dad. "This one has a funny	51						
tail."	52						
"The pigs like to play," said Lisa.	59						
Pigs like mud. They play in it. The mud helps	69						
keep them cool on hot days.	75						
A farm man talks to us. He says pigs cannot see	86						
well. But pigs have good noses.	92						
Lisa said, "My nose helps me find pigs."	100						
TOTAL							

Word Recognition Scoring Guide		
Total Miscues	Level	Significant Miscues
0–1	Independent	0–1
2–4	Ind./Inst.	2
5	Instructional	3
6–9	Inst./Frust.	4
10 +	Frustration	5 +

Total Miscues ☐   Significant Miscues ☐

Oral Reading Rate	Norm Group Percentile
⎯⎯⎯ WPM ⟌6000	☐ 90 ☐ 75 ☐ 50 ☐ 25 ☐ 10

E (Primer)
Comprehension Questions

T 1. _____ What is this story about?
(a pig farm; different kinds of pigs)

F 2. _____ What was the weather like in this story?
(hot)

F 3. _____ Who went to the pig farm?
(Lisa and Dad)

F 4. _____ What colors were the pigs?
(red; white and black [either 1])

F 5. _____ Where do the pigs like to play?
(in the mud)

F 6. _____ What did the farm man tell Lisa and Dad?
(pigs can't see well; pigs have good noses [either 1])

F 7. _____ Why did Lisa say her nose helps her find pigs?
(any logical response; pigs smell)

I 8. _____ How could mud help pigs stay cool?
(any logical response; the mud is cool)

E 9. _____ What would you do if you went to a pig farm?
(any logical response)

V 10. _____ What are "spots"?
(dots; circles of color)

[ ] Questions Missed

Comprehension Scoring Guide	
Questions Missed	Level
0–1	Independent
1½–2	Ind./Inst.
2½	Instructional
3–4½	Inst./Frust.
5 +	Frustration

Retelling Notes

Retelling Rubric for the Three Reading Levels
Independent Level/Excellent
Recalls central or key ideas
Remembers important facts
Retains the general sequence of events
Relates most of the content in an organized manner
Instructional Level/Satisfactory
Recalls most central or key ideas
Remembers some important facts
Retains the general sequence of events
Relates an overall sense of the content
Frustration Level/Unsatisfactory
Recalls bits of information in a haphazard manner
Little apparent organization

Student Booklet copy is on page 77.

E 7141 (Grade 1) Activating Background: Read the title to yourself. Then tell me what you think this might be about.

Background: Low |———+———| High

The Moon

		MISCUES					
	Substitution	Insertion	Omission	Reversal	Repetition	Self-Correction of Unacceptable Miscue	Meaning Change (Significant Miscue)
The moon has a face. My friend says it is — 10							
a man. I asked Miss Green. She said the — 19							
moon face was made by big rocks that bumped — 28							
and bumped. This made big holes. At night — 36							
the holes look like a face. No one lives on the — 47							
moon. It is too hot or cold to live there. It is — 59							
hard to walk on the moon, too. I would be too — 70							
light. I would go up into the sky. — 78							
The moon seems to change from big to — 86							
little and back again. I like to see it before — 96							
I go to sleep. — 100							
TOTAL							

Total Miscues ☐   Significant Miscues ☐

Word Recognition Scoring Guide		
Total Miscues	Level	Significant Miscues
0–1	Independent	0–1
2–4	Ind./Inst.	2
5	Instructional	3
6–9	Inst./Frust.	4
10 +	Frustration	5 +

Oral Reading Rate	Norm Group Percentile
_____ WPM 6000⟌	☐ 90 ☐ 75 ☐ 50 ☐ 25 ☐ 10

E 7141 (Grade 1)
Comprehension Questions

T   1. _____   What is this story about?
(how the moon looks and changes)

F   2. _____   What did the friend say about the moon?
(it is a man)

F   3. _____   Who told the person in the story how the face was made?
(Miss Green)

F   4. _____   How were the holes in the moon made?
(big rocks bumped and bumped)

F   5. _____   What did the story say about why we can't live on the moon?
(it is too hot or cold; it is hard to walk [either 1])

F   6. _____   How does the moon seem to change?
(from big to little and back again)

F   7. _____   Why does the friend probably think the moon is a man?
(any logical response; it has a face)

I   8. _____   Why might it be too hot on the moon?
(any logical response; too close to the sun)

E   9. _____   What would you do if you could visit the moon in a spaceship?
(any logical response)

V   10. _____   What does "light" mean in this story?
(not heavy; doesn't weigh a lot)

Retelling Notes

Questions Missed

Comprehension Scoring Guide	
Questions Missed	Level
0–1	Independent
1½–2	Ind./Inst.
2½	Instructional
3–4½	Inst./Frust.
5 +	Frustration

Retelling Rubric for the Three Reading Levels
Independent Level/Excellent
Recalls central or key ideas
Remembers important facts
Retains the general sequence of events
Relates most of the content in an organized manner
Instructional Level/Satisfactory
Recalls most central or key ideas
Remembers some important facts
Retains the general sequence of events
Relates an overall sense of the content
Frustration Level/Unsatisfactory
Recalls bits of information in a haphazard manner
Little apparent organization

Student Booklet copy is on page 78.

E 8224 (Grade 2) Activating Background: Read the title to yourself. Then tell me what you think this might be about.

Background: Low ├───────┼───────┤ High

Colors and Light

		MISCUES						
		Substitution	Insertion	Omission	Reversal	Repetition	Self-Correction of Unacceptable Miscue	Meaning Change (Significant Miscue)
The sky is blue and the grass is green. Colors	10							
help make the world beautiful. Light helps us see	19							
colors. You may have seen water waves while	27							
swimming. Light makes waves that we cannot	34							
see. Different parts of the waves make different	42							
colors.	43							
Sometimes the sun shines when it is raining and	52							
makes a rainbow. The rain bends the light from the	62							
sun. You can see red, orange, yellow, green, blue,	71							
and purple at the same time. You can make a	81							
rainbow. On a sunny day, spray water into the air.	91							
Look closely and you may see a nice rainbow.	100							
TOTAL								

Total Miscues ☐   Significant Miscues ☐

Word Recognition Scoring Guide		
Total Miscues	Level	Significant Miscues
0–1	Independent	0–1
2–4	Ind./Inst.	2
5	Instructional	3
6–9	Inst./Frust.	4
10 +	Frustration	5 +

Oral Reading Rate	Norm Group Percentile
___ WPM)6000	☐ 90 ☐ 75 ☐ 50 ☐ 25 ☐ 10

E 8224 (Grade 2)
Comprehension Questions

T 1. _____ What is this story about?
(how we see colors; how light makes colors)

F 2. _____ What helps make the world beautiful?
(colors)

F 3. _____ What helps us see color?
(light)

F 4. _____ What waves in the story can be seen?
(water)

F 5. _____ What does rain do with the light from the sun?
(bends it)

F 6. _____ What colors are in a rainbow?
(red, orange, yellow, green, blue, and purple [any 3])

F 7. _____ How can you make a rainbow?
(spray water when it's sunny)

I 8. _____ Why can't we see rainbows in the sky every day?
(any logical response; the sun needs rain to bend the light; it doesn't rain every day)

E 9. _____ Where have you seen a rainbow?
(any logical response)

V 10. _____ What does "bend" mean?
(twist; change shape; curve)

Retelling Notes

☐ Questions Missed

Comprehension Scoring Guide	
Questions Missed	Level
0–1	Independent
1½–2	Ind./Inst.
2½	Instructional
3–4½	Inst./Frust.
5 +	Frustration

Retelling Rubric for the Three Reading Levels
Independent Level/Excellent
Recalls central or key ideas
Remembers important facts
Retains the general sequence of events
Relates most of the content in an organized manner
Instructional Level/Satisfactory
Recalls most central or key ideas
Remembers some important facts
Retains the general sequence of events
Relates an overall sense of the content
Frustration Level/Unsatisfactory
Recalls bits of information in a haphazard manner
Little apparent organization

Student Booklet copy is on page 79.

E 3183 (Grade 3) Activating Background: Read the title to yourself. Then tell me what you think this might be about.

Background: Low |———|———| High

Cricket Song

	Substitution	Insertion	Omission	Reversal	Repetition	Self-Correction of Unacceptable Miscue	Meaning Change (Significant Miscue)
It is a summer night. I try to sleep, but	10							
a sound keeps waking me. It is a cricket.	19							
This bug does not sing with its mouth. The	28							
rough wings of the male cricket make	35							
sounds. He rubs his wings against each	42							
other.	43							
I try to find the bug, but it is hard. The	54							
sound does not come from one spot. It	62							
would also be hard to see the cricket	70							
because it can be as small as the nail on my	81							
thumb. Some people think the cricket	87							
brings luck. Maybe they know how to fall	95							
asleep to the cricket song.	100							
TOTAL								

Total Miscues [ ]   Significant Miscues [ ]

Word Recognition Scoring Guide		
Total Miscues	Level	Significant Miscues
0–1	Independent	0–1
2–4	Ind./Inst.	2
5	Instructional	3
6–9	Inst./Frust.	4
10 +	Frustration	5 +

Oral Reading Rate	Norm Group Percentile
____⟌6000 WPM	☐ 90 ☐ 75 ☐ 50 ☐ 25 ☐ 10

E 3183 (Grade 3)
Comprehension Questions

T   1. _____   What is this story about?
(how a cricket makes a song; a cricket)

F   2. _____   When does this story take place?
(night; summer)

F   3. _____   Why can't the person in the story sleep?
(a sound keeps him or her awake; the cricket song)

F   4. _____   How does the cricket make its sound?
(it rubs its wings together)

F   5. _____   What type of cricket makes this sound?
(male)

F   6. _____   Why was the cricket difficult to find?
(the sound didn't seem to come from one spot; the cricket is very small [any 1])

F   7. _____   What do some people think the cricket brings?
(luck)

I   8. _____   Why might only the male make this sound?
(any logical response; females don't have rough wings)

E   9. _____   How do you think you would feel if a cricket kept you awake? Why?
(any logical response; tired; angry)

V 10. _____   What does "nail" mean in this story?
(what's on your finger; part of finger that protects the tip)

Retelling Notes

[ ] Questions Missed

Comprehension Scoring Guide	
Questions Missed	Level
0–1	Independent
1½–2	Ind./Inst.
2½	Instructional
3–4½	Inst./Frust.
5 +	Frustration

Retelling Rubric for the Three Reading Levels
Independent Level/Excellent
Recalls central or key ideas
Remembers important facts
Retains the general sequence of events
Relates most of the content in an organized manner
Instructional Level/Satisfactory
Recalls most central or key ideas
Remembers some important facts
Retains the general sequence of events
Relates an overall sense of the content
Frustration Level/Unsatisfactory
Recalls bits of information in a haphazard manner
Little apparent organization

Student Booklet copy is on page 80.

E 5414 (Grade 4) Activating Background: Read the title to yourself. Then tell me what you think this might be about.

Background: Low |————|————| High

All Kinds of Bubbles

		MISCUES						
	Substitution	Insertion	Omission	Reversal	Repetition	Self-Correction of Unacceptable Miscue	Meaning Change (Significant Miscue)	
Soap bubbles can be fun to play with on a hot $\quad$ 11								
summer day. Dip your wand in the bottle and blow $\quad$ 21								
gently or spin around quickly. This is just one kind $\quad$ 31								
of bubble. You may have seen other forms too. $\quad$ 40								
Large boxes may have plastic bubble wrap to $\quad$ 48								
help keep the objects inside from breaking. These $\quad$ 56								
bubbles are fun to pop. Another kind of bubble can $\quad$ 66								
be found in soda or pop. It is made when carbonated $\quad$ 77								
water is mixed with sugar and flavors. When you $\quad$ 86								
blow into a straw that is in soda, the forced air $\quad$ 97								
forms many bubbles. $\quad$ 100								
TOTAL								

Total Miscues ☐   Significant Miscues ☐

Word Recognition Scoring Guide		
Total Miscues	Level	Significant Miscues
0–1	Independent	0–1
2–4	Ind./Inst.	2
5	Instructional	3
6–9	Inst./Frust.	4
10 +	Frustration	5 +

Oral Reading Rate	Norm Group Percentile
WPM)6000	☐ 90 ☐ 75 ☐ 50 ☐ 25 ☐ 10

E 5414 (Grade 4)
Comprehension Questions

T 1. _____ What is this passage about?
(different kinds of bubbles)

F 2. _____ What were some types of bubbles
mentioned in the story?
(soap; plastic; soda or pop [any 2])

F 3. _____ When did the story say you might play
with soap bubbles?
(on a hot day; on a summer day)

F 4. _____ Why is bubble wrap used in boxes?
(to keep objects from breaking)

F 5. _____ Why is bubble wrap fun?
(you can pop it)

F 6. _____ Tell me two things soda or pop is
made of.
(carbonated water; sugar; flavors
[any 2])

F 7. _____ How did the passage say you could
make bubbles in soda or pop?
(blow into the straw; forced air forms
bubbles)

I 8. _____ How are the kinds of bubbles mentioned
in this story different?
(any logical response)

E 9. _____ Which type of bubble would you prefer
to play with? Why?
(any logical response)

V 10. _____ What does "carbonated" mean?
(full of bubbles)

	Retelling Notes

[ ] Questions Missed

Comprehension Scoring Guide	
Questions Missed	Level
0–1	Independent
1½–2	Ind./Inst.
2½	Instructional
3–4½	Inst./Frust.
5 +	Frustration

Retelling Rubric for the Three Reading Levels
Independent Level/Excellent
Recalls central or key ideas
Remembers important facts
Retains the general sequence of events
Relates most of the content in an organized manner
Instructional Level/Satisfactory
Recalls most central or key ideas
Remembers some important facts
Retains the general sequence of events
Relates an overall sense of the content
Frustration Level/Unsatisfactory
Recalls bits of information in a haphazard manner
Little apparent organization

Student Booklet copy is on page 81.

E 8595 (Grade 5) Activating Background: Read the title to yourself. Then tell me what you think this might be about.

Background: Low ├───────┼───────┤ High

Seaweed

		MISCUES						
	Substitution	Insertion	Omission	Reversal	Repetition	Self-Correction of Unacceptable Miscue	Meaning Change (Significant Miscue)	
Some of the oldest plants in the world can be — 10								
found in the ocean. They are called algae or — 19								
seaweed. Brown seaweed or kelp can be found — 27								
in cold water. It contains a high amount of — 36								
iodine. This seaweed is used to make jelly and — 45								
make-up. Red seaweed is mostly found in the — 54								
lower parts of the ocean. It has no roots, but — 64								
uses hold-fasts to hold to the bottom of the — 74								
ocean floor. Sometimes red seaweed is fed to — 82								
cattle because of its nutritious value. Green — 89								
algae lives in fresh water. One-celled forms of — 98								
this seaweed can swim. — 102								
TOTAL								

Total Miscues ☐   Significant Miscues ☐

Word Recognition Scoring Guide		
Total Miscues	Level	Significant Miscues
0–1	Independent	0–1
2–4	Ind./Inst.	2
5	Instructional	3
6–9	Inst./Frust.	4
10 +	Frustration	5 +

Oral Reading Rate	Norm Group Percentile
⟌6000 WPM	☐ 90 ☐ 75 ☐ 50 ☐ 25 ☐ 10

288

E 8595 (Grade 5)
Comprehension Questions

T 1. _____ What is this passage about?
             (different types of algae or seaweed;
             plants)

F 2. _____ Where can some of the oldest plants be
             found?
             (in the ocean)

F 3. _____ What were two colors of seaweed
             mentioned in the passage?
             (brown; red; green [any 2])

F 4. _____ Where is brown seaweed found?
             (in cold water)

F 5. _____ What is made from brown seaweed?
             (jelly; make-up [either 1])

F 6. _____ What does red seaweed use instead of
             roots to anchor itself?
             (hold-fasts)

F 7. _____ How do some green algae move
             around?
             (they swim; hook onto something)

I 8. _____ What color is iodine? Why?
             (brown; a shade of brown; it's made
             from brown seaweed)

E 9. _____ What do you think is the most important
             use of seaweed? Why?
             (any logical response)

V 10. _____ What does "nutritious" mean?
             (any logical response; good for you;
             contains a lot of nutrients)

Retelling Notes

Questions Missed

Comprehension Scoring Guide	
Questions Missed	Level
0–1	Independent
1½–2	Ind./Inst.
2½	Instructional
3–4½	Inst./Frust.
5 +	Frustration

Retelling Rubric for the Three Reading Levels
Independent Level/Excellent
Recalls central or key ideas
Remembers important facts
Retains the general sequence of events
Relates most of the content in an organized manner
Instructional Level/Satisfactory
Recalls most central or key ideas
Remembers some important facts
Retains the general sequence of events
Relates an overall sense of the content
Frustration Level/Unsatisfactory
Recalls bits of information in a haphazard manner
Little apparent organization

Student Booklet copy is on page 82.

E 6867 (Grade 6) Activating Background: Read the title to yourself. Then tell me what you think this might be about.

Background: Low ├──────┼──────┤ High

Cave Icicles

	MISCUES				Repetition	Self-Correction of Unacceptable Miscue	Meaning Change (Significant Miscue)
	Substitution	Insertion	Omission	Reversal			
It is common to see icicles formed when water 9							
drips off house roofs during winter time in cold 18							
climates. The same process slowed down helps 25							
explain how stone icicles form in caves. Water 33							
dripping from the ceiling of a cave contains a 42							
mineral called calcite, and pieces sometimes stick to 50							
the ceiling. The water can also carry calcite to the 60							
floor. After several years, a small stone icicle 68							
slowly begins to form. They build less than an inch 78							
per year. Many do not get any longer than one foot. 89							
Colored icicles are created when the water contains 97							
iron or copper. 100							
TOTAL							

Total Miscues ☐   Significant Miscues ☐

Word Recognition Scoring Guide		
Total Miscues	Level	Significant Miscues
0–1	Independent	0–1
2–4	Ind./Inst.	2
5	Instructional	3
6–9	Inst./Frust.	4
10 +	Frustration	5 +

Oral Reading Rate	Norm Group Percentile
___ WPM)6000	☐ 90 ☐ 75 ☐ 50 ☐ 25 ☐ 10

E 6867 (Grade 6)
Comprehension Questions

T   1. _____   What is this passage about?
              (cave icicles; how stone icicles are
              formed)

F   2. _____   At what rate do stone icicles build?
              (less than an inch per year)

F   3. _____   Where does the water drip?
              (from the ceiling; on the floor)

F   4. _____   What can the water contain?
              (calcite; iron; copper; a mineral [any 2])

F   5. _____   How long does it take for a small stone
              icicle to fully form?
              (several years)

F   6. _____   What is the longest the icicles usually
              get?
              (one foot)

F   7. _____   How are colored icicles formed?
              (when water contains iron or copper)

I   8. _____   How are stone and water icicles
              different?
              (any logical response; stone icicles form
              slowly)

E   9. _____   Explain how you would prepare to find
              stone icicles in a cave?
              (any logical response)

V 10. _____   What does the word "created" mean?
              (formed; made; developed)

	Retelling Notes

☐ Questions
  Missed

Comprehension Scoring Guide	
Questions Missed	Level
0–1	Independent
1½–2	Ind./Inst.
2½	Instructional
3–4½	Inst./Frust.
5 +	Frustration

Retelling Rubric for the Three Reading Levels
Independent Level/Excellent
Recalls central or key ideas
Remembers important facts
Retains the general sequence of events
Relates most of the content in an organized manner
Instructional Level/Satisfactory
Recalls most central or key ideas
Remembers some important facts
Retains the general sequence of events
Relates an overall sense of the content
Frustration Level/Unsatisfactory
Recalls bits of information in a haphazard manner
Little apparent organization

Student Booklet copy is on page 83.

E 3717 (Grade 7) Activating Background: Read the title to yourself. Then tell me what you think this might be about.

Background: Low |————|————| High

History of the Cornet

	MISCUES						
	Substitution	Insertion	Omission	Reversal	Repetition	Self-Correction of Unacceptable Miscue	Meaning Change (Significant Miscue)
Over 300 years ago in Germany, a trumpet called 9							
the cornet was very popular. It was considered to 18							
be one of the most difficult wind instruments to 27							
play. The cornet is made from a curved piece of 37							
wood which is carved to make eight sides and then 47							
wrapped in leather. Six holes and one thumbhole 55							
are covered by different fingers to sound notes, just 64							
like a recorder. The mouthpiece is a metal or ivory 74							
cup that can be removed until the musician is ready 84							
to blow into the instrument. Cornets still exist, but 93							
they are usually straight instead of curved. 100							
TOTAL							

Total Miscues [ ]   Significant Miscues [ ]

Word Recognition Scoring Guide		
Total Miscues	Level	Significant Miscues
0–1	Independent	0–1
2–4	Ind./Inst.	2
5	Instructional	3
6–9	Inst./Frust.	4
10 +	Frustration	5 +

Oral Reading Rate	Norm Group Percentile
____⟌6000 WPM	☐ 90 ☐ 75 ☐ 50 ☐ 25 ☐ 10

E 3717 (Grade 7)
Comprehension Questions

T   1. _____   What is this passage about?
             (how cornets look; the history of the cornet)

F   2. _____   Where were cornets popular?
             (Germany)

F   3. _____   What kind of instrument is a cornet?
             (trumpet; wind; wooden)

F   4. _____   How many sides does it have?
             (eight)

F   5. _____   How many holes does it have to sound notes?
             (seven)

F   6. _____   What is wrapped on the outside of the cornet?
             (leather)

F   7. _____   How has the cornet changed over the years?
             (straight; not curved)

I   8. _____   Why might the instrument be difficult to play?
             (any logical response; the mouthpiece might fall out; the sounds are hard to make correctly; curved)

E   9. _____   Why might the instrument be wrapped in leather?
             (any logical response; to protect it; to make it easy to handle)

V   10. _____   What does "exist" mean?
             (still around; still made)

[ ] Questions Missed

Comprehension Scoring Guide	
Questions Missed	Level
0–1	Independent
1½–2	Ind./Inst.
2½	Instructional
3–4½	Inst./Frust.
5 +	Frustration

Retelling Notes

Retelling Rubric for the Three Reading Levels
Independent Level/Excellent
Recalls central or key ideas
Remembers important facts
Retains the general sequence of events
Relates most of the content in an organized manner
Instructional Level/Satisfactory
Recalls most central or key ideas
Remembers some important facts
Retains the general sequence of events
Relates an overall sense of the content
Frustration Level/Unsatisfactory
Recalls bits of information in a haphazard manner
Little apparent organization

Student Booklet copy is on page 84.

E 8183 (Grade 8) Activating Background: Read the title to yourself. Then tell me what you think this might be about.

Background: Low |——————|——————| High

Sailing Explorers

		Substitution	Insertion	Omission	Reversal	Repetition	Self-Correction of Unacceptable Miscue	Meaning Change (Significant Miscue)
Over 300 years ago, many English and Dutch	8							
companies hired sailors to find new water routes so	17							
they could claim land and trade goods more easily.	26							
An English company employed Henry Hudson, an	33							
English sea captain. The goal was to find a	42							
northeast passage between Europe and Asia. After	49							
many attempts blocked by polar ice, he was hired by	59							
the Dutch East India Trade Company. Hudson and	67							
his crew began sailing northeast from Europe toward	75							
Asia. Hudson then changed course toward the east	83							
coast of what is now called the United States, sailing	93							
up the Hudson River in New York.	100							
TOTAL								

The header of the miscues columns is labeled **MISCUES** spanning Substitution, Insertion, Omission, Reversal.

Total Miscues ☐   Significant Miscues ☐

Word Recognition Scoring Guide		
Total Miscues	Level	Significant Miscues
0–1	Independent	0–1
2–4	Ind./Inst.	2
5	Instructional	3
6–9	Inst./Frust.	4
10 +	Frustration	5 +

Oral Reading Rate	Norm Group Percentile
‾‾‾‾ WPM $\overline{)6000}$	☐ 90 ☐ 75 ☐ 50 ☐ 25 ☐ 10

E 8183 (Grade 8)
Comprehension Questions

T 1. _____ What is this passage about?
(Henry Hudson's travels; finding water routes)

F 2. _____ How many years ago did these events take place?
(over 300 years ago)

F 3. _____ Who hired sailors in this passage?
(English companies; Dutch companies [either 1])

F 4. _____ Why did the English and Dutch companies hire sailors?
(to find new water routes and trade more easily)

F 5. _____ Who was Henry Hudson?
(an English sea captain)

F 6. _____ What was Henry Hudson trying to locate?
(a northeast passage between Europe and Asia)

F 7. _____ Where did Hudson finally arrive in this passage?
(in the United States; Hudson River)

I 8. _____ Why do you think Hudson discontinued working for the English company?
(any logical response; unsuccessful mission; better opportunity with the Dutch Company; polar ice blocked his journey)

E 9. _____ Why did Hudson probably change direction from northeast to the United States?
(any logical response; bad weather; wind change)

V 10. _____ What does "course" mean?
(direction of travel; the way you head)

Retelling Notes

Questions Missed

Comprehension Scoring Guide	
Questions Missed	Level
0–1	Independent
1½–2	Ind./Inst.
2½	Instructional
3–4½	Inst./Frust.
5 +	Frustration

Retelling Rubric for the Three Reading Levels
Independent Level/Excellent
Recalls central or key ideas
Remembers important facts
Retains the general sequence of events
Relates most of the content in an organized manner
Instructional Level/Satisfactory
Recalls most central or key ideas
Remembers some important facts
Retains the general sequence of events
Relates an overall sense of the content
Frustration Level/Unsatisfactory
Recalls bits of information in a haphazard manner
Little apparent organization

Form LL

Performance Booklet

Teacher Copy

Form LL

Primary Use:
- Silent Reading (Literary)

Other Uses:
- Oral Reading
- Listening Level
- Progress Monitoring

 Note: This Performance Booklet is on the CD that accompanies the Basic Reading Inventory.

Miscue Summary Sheet for Forms LL and LI

MISCUES							
Substitution	Insertion	Omission	Reversal	Repetition	Self-Correction of Unacceptable Miscue	Meaning Change (Significant Miscue)	

Name _____ Date _____

Passage Title _____

Form _____

Total Miscues [ ]   Significant Miscues [ ]

Eleventh Edition

BASIC READING INVENTORY PERFORMANCE BOOKLET
Jerry L. Johns, Ph.D.

LL Literary

Student _____   Grade _____   Gender   M   F   Date of Test _____

School _____   Examiner _____   Date of Birth_____

Address _____   Current Book/Level_____   Age_____

SUMMARY OF STUDENT'S READING PERFORMANCE

Grade	Word Recognition		Comprehension		Oral Reading Rate		Silent Reading Rate
	Miscues	Level	Questions Missed	Level	Words per Minute (WPM)	Norm Group Percentile	Words per Minute (WPM)
3							
4							
5							
6							
7							
8							
9							
10							
11							
12							

ESTIMATE OF READING LEVELS

Independent _____   Instructional _____   Frustration _____

LISTENING LEVEL

Form _____

Grade	Questions Missed	Level
3		
4		
5		
6		
7		
8		
9		
10		
11		
12		

ESTIMATED LEVEL: _____

GENERAL OBSERVATIONS

INFORMAL ANALYSIS OF ORAL READING

Oral Reading Behaviors	Frequency of Occurrence			General Impact on Meaning		
	Seldom	Sometimes	Frequently	No Change	Little Change	Much Change
Substitutions						
Insertions						
Omissions						
Reversals						
Repetitions						

QUALITATIVE ANALYSIS OF BASIC READING INVENTORY INSIGHTS

General Directions: Note the degree to which the student shows behavior or evidence in the following areas. Space is provided for additional items.

Seldom   Always
Weak   Strong
Poor   Excellent

COMPREHENSION

Seeks to construct meaning
Makes predictions
Activates background knowledge
Possesses appropriate concepts
   and vocabulary
Monitors reading
Varies reading rate as needed
Understands topic and major ideas
Remembers facts or details
Makes and supports appropriate
   inferences
Evaluates ideas from passages
Understands vocabulary used
Provides appropriate definitions
   of words
Engages with passages

WORD IDENTIFICATION

Possesses numerous strategies
Uses strategies flexibly
Uses graphophonic information
Uses semantic information
Uses syntactic information
Knows basic sight words
   automatically
Possesses sight vocabulary

ORAL AND SILENT READING

Reads fluently
Reads with expression
Attends to punctuation
Keeps place while reading
Reads at appropriate rate
Reads silently without vocalization

ATTITUDE AND CONFIDENCE

Enjoys reading
Demonstrates willingness to risk
Possesses positive self-concept
Chooses to read
Regards himself/herself as a reader
Exhibits persistence

A Day in the Woods

Sue was visiting her grandparents' farm for a week. She decided to have a picnic in the woods.	18
She packed a lunch with a peanut-butter and jelly sandwich, an apple, two cookies, and grape juice	36
to drink. Sue had put her lunch in her backpack and started out the door when she remembered	54
Jane. She ran back into the house and got Jane, her favorite doll.	67
Sue had a good time in the woods. She walked on small paths that the animals had made.	85
After walking all morning, she was very hungry. At noon she found a fallen tree and sat on it to	105
eat her lunch.	108
After lunch Sue found an animal trail that led to a quiet spring. She looked into the water	126
and saw small fish swimming. She must remember to tell her grandparents about the little fish in	143
the spring.	145
Sue realized that it was time to start back to her grandparents' house, but she didn't know	162
which way to go. Just then she heard rustling in the bushes right behind her. She was frightened	180
and started to run. The noise followed her as she ran. It kept getting closer. All of a sudden some-	200
thing jumped at her! It was Rusty, her grandparents' dog. Sue was so happy to see him she gave	218
him a big hug.	222
Sue and Rusty returned to the farm just as the sun was setting. Sue's grandparents were wor-	239
ried. Sue promised never to go so deep in the woods again.	250

Word Recognition Scoring Guide		
Total Miscues	Level	Significant Miscues
0–3	Independent	0–2
4–12	Ind./Inst.	3–6
13	Instructional	7
14–24	Inst./Frust.	8–12
25 +	Frustration	13 +

Total Miscues [ ]   Significant Miscues [ ]

Oral Reading Rate	Norm Group Percentile
_____ WPM $\overline{)15000}$	☐ 90 ☐ 75 ☐ 50 ☐ 25 ☐ 10

LL 3183 (Grade 3) Activating Background: Read the title to yourself. Then tell me what you think this might be about.

A Day in the Woods

T   1. _____   What is this story about?
(a girl going for a walk in the woods and getting lost)

F   2. _____   What did Sue take with her?
(her doll, Jane; her lunch; her backpack [any 2])

F   3. _____   What did Sue bring to eat for her lunch?
(peanut-butter and jelly sandwich; an apple; two cookies; grape juice [any 2])

F   4. _____   Where did Sue eat her lunch?
(in the woods; on a fallen tree)

F   5. _____   What did Sue find in the woods?
(a fallen tree; animal trails; water; a spring; fish; Rusty [any 2])

F   6. _____   How did Sue decide where to go?
(she followed animal trails or paths)

F   7. _____   Why did Sue start running when she was in the woods?
(she heard rustling in the bushes)

I   8. _____   What do you think Sue thought was following her in the woods?
(any logical response; a wild animal)

E   9. _____   Why do you think Sue promised never to go so deep in the woods again?
(any logical response; because she had been so frightened; so she wouldn't get lost)

V   10. _____   Explain what "spring" means in this sentence: Sue saw fish swimming in a spring.
(a small stream of water coming from the earth; a little river; a little pond)

☐ Questions Missed

Comprehension Scoring Guide

Questions Missed	Level
0–1	Independent
1½–2	Ind./Inst.
2½	Instructional
3–4½	Inst./Frust.
5 +	Frustration

Retelling Rubric for the Three Reading Levels

Independent Level/Excellent
Recalls central or key ideas
Remembers important facts
Retains the general sequence of events
Relates most of the content in an organized manner

Instructional Level/Satisfactory
Recalls most central or key ideas
Remembers some important facts
Retains the general sequence of events
Relates an overall sense of the content

Frustration Level/Unsatisfactory
Recalls bits of information in a haphazard manner
Little apparent organization

Retelling Notes

Danny and the Dragon

"Mother, there's a dragon after me! It won't go away!" | 10

The next day when Danny went out, there it was. It roared and blew fire at Danny. It was so | 30

big and Danny was so small. "Leave me alone!" | 39

Danny ran down the path to the river and hid behind a rock to see if the dragon was still | 59

coming. It was. He had to get rid of that dragon. He went home through the woods. He needed a | 79

plan to trick the dragon. | 84

In bed that night, Danny made his plan. He had to trick the dragon into the river. He knew | 103

the dragon couldn't swim. | 107

While it was still dark, Danny climbed out his window. He got a rope and tiptoed away from | 125

his house. Then he ran to the big rock by the river. Danny laid the rope across the path. He tied | 146

one end of the rope to a tree. He laid the other end on the ground behind the big rock. Danny ran | 168

home through the woods. There was the dragon lying by the door to his house. Danny climbed | 185

quietly in his window to wait. | 191

In the morning Danny went out. Roaring, the dragon blew fire and leaped at him. Danny | 207

dodged it and ran toward the river. He flew down the path, dove behind the rock, and grabbed the | 226

rope. | 227

Down the path came the dragon. Then it tripped on the rope and crashed into the river. The | 245

river carried it far, far away. | 251

Word Recognition Scoring Guide		
Total Miscues	Level	Significant Miscues
0–3	Independent	0–2
4–12	Ind./Inst.	3–6
13	Instructional	7
14–24	Inst./Frust.	8–12
25 +	Frustration	13 +

Total Miscues [ ]   Significant Miscues [ ]

Oral Reading Rate	Norm Group Percentile
$\frac{\quad\quad}{)15000}$ WPM	☐ 90 ☐ 75 ☐ 50 ☐ 25 ☐ 10

Student Booklet copy is on page 87.   Background: Low ├────────┼────────┤ High

LL 5414 (Grade 4) Activating Background: Read the title to yourself. Then tell me what you think this might be about.

Danny and the Dragon

T   1. _____   What is this story about?
(how Danny gets rid of the dragon)

F   2. _____   When did Danny make his plan?
(during the night)

F   3. _____   What was Danny's plan?
(to trick the dragon)

F   4. _____   How did Danny get out of his house that night?
(he climbed out his window)

F   5. _____   What did Danny do with the rope?
(laid it across the path and tied it to a tree)

F   6. _____   Where was the dragon lying?
(by the door to his house)

F   7. _____   What did the dragon do to Danny?
(roared; blew fire; chased him; wouldn't leave him alone [any 2])

I   8. _____   What do you think happened to the dragon when it was in the river? Why?
(any logical response; it drowned because it could not swim)

E   9. _____   What might be another plan you could use to get rid of the dragon?
(any logical response)

V 10. _____   Explain what "tiptoed" means in this sentence: He tiptoed away from his house.
(sneak; walk on tiptoes very quietly)

☐ Questions Missed

Comprehension Scoring Guide	
Questions Missed	Level
0–1	Independent
1½–2	Ind./Inst.
2½	Instructional
3–4½	Inst./Frust.
5 +	Frustration

Retelling Rubric for the Three Reading Levels
Independent Level/Excellent
Recalls central or key ideas
Remembers important facts
Retains the general sequence of events
Relates most of the content in an organized manner
Instructional Level/Satisfactory
Recalls most central or key ideas
Remembers some important facts
Retains the general sequence of events
Relates an overall sense of the content
Frustration Level/Unsatisfactory
Recalls bits of information in a haphazard manner
Little apparent organization

Retelling Notes

306

I Want to Fly

Jerry, looking at the sky, promised himself, "I'm going to fly some day."	13
Jerry, a ten-year-old boy from a small town in Iowa, had dreamed of flying since he was a little	34
boy. He wasn't just going to fly in an airplane. He was going to fly like a hawk.	52
He spent many hours watching hawks fly. They made it look so easy. With their powerful wings	69
they built up speed, then they would glide. It was beautiful and breath-taking watching them ride	86
the air currents. "I am going to fly."	94
As he climbed to the top of the cliff, his imagination was far ahead of him telling him how	113
exciting it would be. At the top he paused only for a moment; then he dove off the cliff into the air.	135
"This is wonderful! This is better than I had ever imagined!" He soared, he dipped, and rose again,	153
riding the air currents. Flying was better than he had imagined.	164
When Jerry awoke, his parents were standing by the hospital bed. "The doctor said you will	180
be fine. You will have to miss two more weeks of school because of your tonsil operation."	197
After Jerry's parents left, he thought for a moment, "I really felt like I was flying. I could feel	216
cool air blowing through my hair. I saw the landscape below me." Was it a dream or not? If it was	237
a dream, where did he get the brownish hawk feather he was holding?	250

Word Recognition Scoring Guide		
Total Miscues	Level	Significant Miscues
0–3	Independent	0–2
4–12	Ind./Inst.	3–6
13	Instructional	7
14–24	Inst./Frust.	8–12
25 +	Frustration	13 +

Total Miscues [ ]   Significant Miscues [ ]

Oral Reading Rate	Norm Group Percentile
‾‾‾‾ WPM)15000	☐ 90 ☐ 75 ☐ 50 ☐ 25 ☐ 10

Background: Low |———————| High

LL 8595 (Grade 5) Activating Background: Read the title to yourself. Then tell me what you think this might be about.

I Want to Fly

T   1. _____ What is this story about?
              (Jerry wants to fly like a hawk)

F   2. _____ How old is Jerry?
              (ten years old)

F   3. _____ Where did Jerry live?
              (in a small town; in Iowa)

F   4. _____ What did Jerry spend hours watching?
              (hawks flying)

F   5. _____ Why was Jerry in the hospital?
              (he had a tonsil operation)

F   6. _____ Who came to visit Jerry?
              (his parents)

F   7. _____ How much school will Jerry miss?
              (two more weeks)

I   8. _____ Do you think Jerry really flew? Why?
              (any logical response; no, he was dreaming; he imagined it; people can't fly)

E   9. _____ Where do you think the hawk feather came from?
              (any logical response; he found it and brought it with him; his mom and dad brought it to him; it blew in his window)

V 10. _____ Explain what "landscape" means in this sentence: Jerry saw the landscape below him.
              (a stretch of scenery)

☐ Questions Missed

Comprehension Scoring Guide	
Questions Missed	Level
0–1	Independent
1½–2	Ind./Inst.
2½	Instructional
3–4½	Inst./Frust.
5 +	Frustration

Retelling Rubric for the Three Reading Levels
Independent Level/Excellent
Recalls central or key ideas
Remembers important facts
Retains the general sequence of events
Relates most of the content in an organized manner
Instructional Level/Satisfactory
Recalls most central or key ideas
Remembers some important facts
Retains the general sequence of events
Relates an overall sense of the content
Frustration Level/Unsatisfactory
Recalls bits of information in a haphazard manner
Little apparent organization

Retelling Notes

Action at Brantwood

As Kay got off the passenger train at Brantwood, she was rudely shoved. Turning quickly, she	16
saw a young man elbowing his way through the bustling crowd toward an older woman. As Kay	33
proceeded across the train platform, she saw the older woman trip and tumble to the pavement.	49
The fallen woman's handbag flew open and its contents spilled all over the ground. Her suitcase	65
also snapped open and its contents, too, were strewn over the snow.	77
Kay rushed up to help the stunned woman. She was brushed aside by the man who had collided	95
with her earlier. The man assumed charge of the woman's belongings in a most possessive manner.	111
He was short, slender, blonde, and had a rosy complexion. Kay picked up the woman's handbag	127
from the snow, but the young man snatched it from her almost as if he suspected her of trying to	147
steal it.	149
"Just a minute, please!" exclaimed Kay. "I'm just trying to help this lady. May I ask why you	167
are trying to take charge of her things?"	175
"I am her son!" retorted the young man unpleasantly as he went on hastily collecting the things	192
which had burst from the suitcase. Kay concentrated her attention on the woman and tried to help	209
her up. "Where are my purse and my suitcase!" she cried anxiously.	221
"Your son has them," Kay said reassuringly. "Don't worry. He'll bring you everything as	235
soon as he collects it."	240
"My son!" the lady exclaimed sharply. "I have no son!"	250

Adapted from *The Double Disguise* by Frances K. Judd.

Word Recognition Scoring Guide		
Total Miscues	Level	Significant Miscues
0–3	Independent	0–2
4–12	Ind./Inst.	3–6
13	Instructional	7
14–24	Inst./Frust.	8–12
25 +	Frustration	13 +

Total Miscues [ ]   Significant Miscues [ ]

Oral Reading Rate	Norm Group Percentile
$\overline{)15000}$ WPM	☐ 90 ☐ 75 ☐ 50 ☐ 25 ☐ 10

309

LL 6867 (Grade 6) Activating Background: Read the title to yourself. Then tell me what you think this might be about.

Action at Brantwood

T   1. ____ What is this story about?
(a man's attempt to steal an older woman's things; Kay's attempt to help an older woman who falls at the train station)

F   2. ____ Where does this story take place?
(Brantwood; a train station)

F   3. ____ What happened when Kay got off the train?
(she was shoved; an older woman tripped and fell)

F   4. ____ Describe the young man?
(short; slender; blonde; rosy complexion [any 2])

F   5. ____ What happened when the older woman fell down?
(her handbag flew open; her suitcase snapped open in the snow)

F   6. ____ What did the young man do when Kay tried to help?
(he brushed Kay aside; he snatched the handbag from her)

F   7. ____ Why did the young man think he had a right to pick up the older lady's possessions?
(he said he was her son)

I   8. ____ How do you think Kay felt about the young man before and after talking to the older woman? Why?
(any logical response; first she was understanding; then angry; irritated)

E   9. ____ Which character would you believe, the young man or the older woman? Why?
(any logical response)

V   10. ____ Explain what "stunned" means in this sentence: Kay rushed up to help the stunned woman.
(didn't know what was going on; shocked; startled)

☐ Questions Missed

Comprehension Scoring Guide

Questions Missed	Level
0–1	Independent
1½–2	Ind./Inst.
2½	Instructional
3–4½	Inst./Frust.
5 +	Frustration

Retelling Rubric for the Three Reading Levels

Independent Level/Excellent
Recalls central or key ideas
Remembers important facts
Retains the general sequence of events
Relates most of the content in an organized manner

Instructional Level/Satisfactory
Recalls most central or key ideas
Remembers some important facts
Retains the general sequence of events
Relates an overall sense of the content

Frustration Level/Unsatisfactory
Recalls bits of information in a haphazard manner
Little apparent organization

Retelling Notes

Man Overboard

A sharp sound startled him. Somewhere, off in the blackness, someone had fired a gun three	16
times.	17
Rainsford sprang up and moved quickly to the rail, mystified. He strained his eyes in the di-	33
rection from which the reports had come, but it was like trying to see through a blanket. He leaped	52
up onto the rail and balanced himself there to get a greater elevation; his pipe, striking a rope, was	71
knocked from his mouth. He lunged for it. A short, hoarse cry came from his lips as he realized he	91
had reached too far and had fallen overboard. The cry was pinched off as the blood-warm waters	109
of the Caribbean Sea closed over his head.	117
He struggled up to the surface and tried to cry for help, but the wash from the speeding yacht	136
slapped him in the face. The salty water in his open mouth gagged and strangled him. Desperately	153
he struck out with strong strokes after the receding lights of the yacht, but he stopped before he	171
had covered fifty feet. He calmed down and assessed his situation. It was not the first time he had	190
been in a tough situation. There was a chance that his cries could be heard by someone aboard the	209
yacht. But the chance was slim and grew much slimmer as the yacht continued on. He shouted with	227
all his might. The lights of the yacht became faint, looking like ever-vanishing fireflies. Then they	244
were blotted out entirely by the black night.	252

Adapted from "The Most Dangerous Game" by Richard Connell. Copyright 1924 by Richard Connell. Copyright renewed 1952 by Louise Fox Connell.

Word Recognition Scoring Guide		
Total Miscues	Level	Significant Miscues
0–3	Independent	0–2
4–12	Ind./Inst.	3–6
13	Instructional	7
14–24	Inst./Frust.	8–12
25 +	Frustration	13 +

Total Miscues [ ]   Significant Miscues [ ]

Oral Reading Rate	Norm Group Percentile
$\dfrac{\quad}{\sqrt{15000}}$ WPM	☐ 90 ☐ 75 ☐ 50 ☐ 25 ☐ 10

LL 3717 (Grade 7) Activating Background: Read the title to yourself. Then tell me what you think this might be about.

Man Overboard

T 1. _____ What is this story about?
(a man in a dangerous situation; a man who falls overboard)

F 2. _____ What sounds did Rainsford hear?
(gunshots; someone fired a gun three times)

F 3. _____ Why was Rainsford standing on the rail?
(to have better elevation; to have a better view)

F 4. _____ What caused Rainsford to fall overboard?
(he reached too far forward trying to catch his pipe)

F 5. _____ How did the water feel when he fell overboard?
(blood-warm)

F 6. _____ Why did Rainsford have difficulty crying for help?
(the water kept getting in his mouth)

F 7. _____ About how far did he swim before he stopped?
(fifty feet)

I 8. _____ Why do you think that the people aboard the yacht didn't hear Rainsford?
(any logical response; noisy motor; music on the yacht; the noise of the sea)

E 9. _____ What would you do if you were in the same situation as Rainsford?
(any logical response)

V 10. _____ Explain what "mystified" means in this sentence: He moved quickly to the rail, mystified.
(confused; curious; perplexed; bewildered)

☐ Questions Missed

Comprehension Scoring Guide	
Questions Missed	Level
0–1	Independent
1½–2	Ind./Inst.
2½	Instructional
3–4½	Inst./Frust.
5 +	Frustration

Retelling Rubric for the Three Reading Levels
Independent Level/Excellent
Recalls central or key ideas
Remembers important facts
Retains the general sequence of events
Relates most of the content in an organized manner
Instructional Level/Satisfactory
Recalls most central or key ideas
Remembers some important facts
Retains the general sequence of events
Relates an overall sense of the content
Frustration Level/Unsatisfactory
Recalls bits of information in a haphazard manner
Little apparent organization

Retelling Notes

The Angel of the Candy Counter

The Angel of the candy counter had found me out at last and was demanding extreme payment	17
for all the Snickers, Mounds, suckers, and Hershey bars. I had two huge cavities that were rotten	34
to the gums. The pain was well past the help of crushed aspirins or oil of cloves. Only one thing	54
could help me now, so I prayed earnestly that I'd be allowed to sit under the house and have the	74
entire building collapse on my jaw.	80
Since there was no dentist in Stamps, nor doctor either, for that matter, Momma had dealt	96
with other toothaches. She would try yanking them out with a string tied to the tooth and the other	115
end looped over her fist, as well as pain killers and prayer. In this case the medicine proved inef-	133
fective. There wasn't enough enamel left to hook a string on, and the prayers were being ignored	150
because some demon was blocking their way.	157
I lived some days and nights in blinding pain, not so much toying with, as seriously considering,	174
the idea of jumping in the well. So Momma decided I had to be taken to a dentist. The nearest	194
dentist was in Mason, twenty miles away, and I was sure that I'd be dead long before we reached	213
half the distance. Momma said we'd go to Dr. Lincoln, and he'd take care of me. She said we'd	232
have to take the bus. I didn't know of anyone who'd been to see him, but we had to go.	252

Adapted from *I Know Why the Caged Bird Sings* by Maya Angelou.

Word Recognition Scoring Guide		
Total Miscues	Level	Significant Miscues
0–3	Independent	0–2
4–12	Ind./Inst.	3–6
13	Instructional	7
14–24	Inst./Frust.	8–12
25 +	Frustration	13 +

Total Miscues [ ]   Significant Miscues [ ]

Oral Reading Rate	Norm Group Percentile
_____ WPM $\overline{)15000}$	☐ 90 ☐ 75 ☐ 50 ☐ 25 ☐ 10

LL 8183 (Grade 8) Activating Background: Read the title to yourself. Then tell me what you think this might be about.

The Angel of the Candy Counter

T   1. _____   What is this story about?
(someone who has a toothache and has to go to the dentist)

F   2. _____   What remedies had already been tried to ease the pain?
(crushed aspirins; oil of clove; prayer [any 1])

F   3. _____   Why didn't Momma pull the teeth that were hurting?
(they were too rotten; there wasn't enough enamel to hook a string on)

F   4. _____   Why weren't the prayers being answered?
(a demon or devil was blocking their way)

F   5. _____   In what town did the narrator live?
(Stamps)

F   6. _____   How far was the nearest dentist from home?
(20 miles)

F   7. _____   What is the name of the dentist?
(Dr. Lincoln)

I   8. _____   What did this person think was responsible for the pain?
(candy; cavities)

E   9. _____   Why do you think Stamps had no dentist or doctor?
(any logical response; small town; poor town; the story takes place many years ago)

V 10. _____   Explain what "earnestly" means in this sentence: I prayed earnestly that the house would fall on my jaw.
(seriously; with determination)

		Retelling Rubric for the Three Reading Levels	Retelling Notes

☐ Questions Missed

Comprehension Scoring Guide	
Questions Missed	Level
0–1	Independent
1½–2	Ind./Inst.
2½	Instructional
3–4½	Inst./Frust.
5 +	Frustration

Retelling Rubric for the Three Reading Levels

Independent Level/Excellent
Recalls central or key ideas
Remembers important facts
Retains the general sequence of events
Relates most of the content in an organized manner

Instructional Level/Satisfactory
Recalls most central or key ideas
Remembers some important facts
Retains the general sequence of events
Relates an overall sense of the content

Frustration Level/Unsatisfactory
Recalls bits of information in a haphazard manner
Little apparent organization

Retelling Notes

The Most Beautiful

Of the gods of ancient Greece, Apollo was the most beautiful. His hair was brilliant gold; his	17
eyes were stormy blue. He wore a flowing tunic of golden panther skin, carried a quiver of golden	35
arrows, and used a golden bow. His chariot was beaten gold; his horse was white with a platinum	53
mane and flame-colored eyes. Apollo was always the god of the sun, but later he became patron of	72
music, poetry, mathematics, and medicine. As an adult, Apollo was known for his unparalleled wisdom,	87
but in his youth he was known for his barbarous exploits. Several times he was almost expelled	104
from the company of the gods by Zeus, whom he angered with his youthful folly.	119
One objectionable folly was Apollo's treatment of a satyr named Marsyas. Marsyas was an	133
excellent musician; Apollo considered this his talent and would allow no rivalry. Hearing Marsyas	147
praised continually, Apollo invited him to a musical contest. The winner was to choose a penalty to	164
which the loser would have to submit, and the Muses were their judges. Marsyas played his me-	181
lodious flute, and Apollo played his lyre. They played so exquisitely that the Muses could not choose	197
between them, so Apollo suggested that they play their instruments upside down and sing simul-	211
taneously. Apollo turned his lyre upside down, played, and chanted a beautiful poem. Because Mar-	226
syas could not play his flute upside down and sing at the same time, the despondent satyr was	243
declared the loser. Consequently, Apollo collected the prize.	251

Adapted from *The Greek Gods* by Bernard Evslin, Dorothy Evslin, and Ned Hoopes.

Word Recognition Scoring Guide		
Total Miscues	Level	Significant Miscues
0–3	Independent	0–2
4–12	Ind./Inst.	3–6
13	Instructional	7
14–24	Inst./Frust.	8–12
25 +	Frustration	13 +

Total Miscues ☐   Significant Miscues ☐

Oral Reading Rate	Norm Group Percentile
‾‾‾ WPM ⟌15000	☐ 90 ☐ 75 ☐ 50 ☐ 25 ☐ 10

LL 4959 (Grade 9) Activating Background: Read the title to yourself. Then tell me what you think this might be about.

The Most Beautiful

T   1. _____   What is this story about?
              (the god Apollo's rivalry with Marsyas; Apollo)

F   2. _____   What was the reason Apollo challenged Marsyas to a contest?
              (to see who was the best musician)

F   3. _____   Describe what happened at the contest.
              (Marsyas was to play his flute and Apollo his lyre and the Muses were to judge which
              was best)

F   4. _____   What was Apollo god of?
              (sun; music; poetry; mathematics; medicine [any 3])

F   5. _____   How would you describe Apollo?
              (beautiful with golden hair and blue eyes; strong; wise [any 2])

F   6. _____   What instrument did Apollo play?
              (lyre)

F   7. _____   Who won the contest?
              (Apollo)

I   8. _____   What lessons could be learned from this myth?
              (any logical response)

E   9. _____   What is your opinion of Apollo's trick? Why? (if necessary, restate trick: to play their
              instruments upside down and sing at the same time)
              (any logical response)

V   10. _____ Explain what "simultaneously" means in this sentence: Apollo suggested that they play
              their instruments upside down and sing simultaneously.
              (at the same time)

☐ Questions Missed

Comprehension Scoring Guide	
Questions Missed	Level
0–1	Independent
1½–2	Ind./Inst.
2½	Instructional
3–4½	Inst./Frust.
5 +	Frustration

Retelling Rubric for the Three Reading Levels
Independent Level/Excellent
Recalls central or key ideas
Remembers important facts
Retains the general sequence of events
Relates most of the content in an organized manner
Instructional Level/Satisfactory
Recalls most central or key ideas
Remembers some important facts
Retains the general sequence of events
Relates an overall sense of the content
Frustration Level/Unsatisfactory
Recalls bits of information in a haphazard manner
Little apparent organization

Retelling Notes

Elizabeth Meets Darcy

Elizabeth watched for the first appearance of Pemberley Woods with some perturbation; and | 13

when at length they turned in at the lodge, her spirits were in a high flutter. | 29

The park was very large and contained great variety of ground. They entered it in one of its | 47

lowest points, and drove for some time through a beautiful wood, stretching over a wide extent. | 63

Elizabeth's mind was too full for conversation, but she saw and admired every remarkable spot | 78

and point of view. They gradually ascended for half a mile, and then found themselves at the top | 96

of a considerable eminence, where the wood ceased, and the eye was immediately captured by | 111

Pemberley House, situated on the opposite side of a valley, into which the road with some abruptness | 128

wound. It was a large, handsome, stone structure, standing well on rising ground, and backed by a | 145

ridge of high woody hills. She had never seen a place for which nature had enhanced more, or where | 164

natural beauty had been so little counteracted by an awkward taste. They were all of them warm in | 182

their admiration, and at the moment she felt that to be mistress of Pemberley might be something! | 199

They descended the hill, crossed the bridge, and drove to the door; and, while examining the | 215

nearer aspect of the house, all her apprehensions of meeting its owner returned. As she walked | 231

across the lawn, Elizabeth turned back to look again, and the owner himself suddenly came forward | 247

from the road. | 250

Adapted from *Pride and Prejudice* by Jane Austen.

Word Recognition Scoring Guide		
Total Miscues	Level	Significant Miscues
0–3	Independent	0–2
4–12	Ind./Inst.	3–6
13	Instructional	7
14–24	Inst./Frust.	8–12
25 +	Frustration	13 +

Total Miscues [ ]   Significant Miscues [ ]

Oral Reading Rate	Norm Group Percentile
____ WPM $\overline{\smash{\big)}15000}$	☐ 90 ☐ 75 ☐ 50 ☐ 25 ☐ 10

LL 1047 (Grade 10) Activating Background: Read the title to yourself. Then tell me what you think this might be about.

Elizabeth Meets Darcy

T   1. _____   What is this story about?
(Elizabeth going to Pemberley Woods)

F   2. _____   What did Pemberley House look like?
(large; handsome; a stone structure [any 1])

F   3. _____   Describe Pemberley Woods.
(large; a forest; hilly; valley; woody [any 2])

F   4. _____   How did the group feel about what they were seeing?
(warm in their admiration; excited; happy)

F   5. _____   What did they see when the woods ceased?
(Pemberley House)

F   6. _____   When did Elizabeth see the owner of Pemberley Woods?
(when she came up to the outside of the house; as she walked across the lawn)

F   7. _____   How did Elizabeth get to Pemberley Woods?
(drove)

I   8. _____   What does it mean when the story says that "Elizabeth's mind was too full for conversation"?
(any logical response; Elizabeth's mind was preoccupied with worry)

E   9. _____   Under what circumstances might someone be nervous about meeting the owner of a large mansion?
(any logical response)

V   10. _____   Explain what "ascended" means in this sentence: They gradually ascended for half a mile.
(went up)

	Questions Missed

Comprehension Scoring Guide

Questions Missed	Level
0–1	Independent
1½–2	Ind./Inst.
2½	Instructional
3–4½	Inst./Frust.
5 +	Frustration

Retelling Rubric for the Three Reading Levels

Independent Level/Excellent
Recalls central or key ideas
Remembers important facts
Retains the general sequence of events
Relates most of the content in an organized manner

Instructional Level/Satisfactory
Recalls most central or key ideas
Remembers some important facts
Retains the general sequence of events
Relates an overall sense of the content

Frustration Level/Unsatisfactory
Recalls bits of information in a haphazard manner
Little apparent organization

Retelling Notes

Bookworm or Earthworm

To read or to weed is the problem that confronts me whenever I have a few spare minutes.	18
Reading satisfies the wanderlust in me. It affords the opportunity to abandon the monotonous	32
ruts of everyday life and to traipse excitedly along the mysterious trails in the enchanting land of	49
books. Lost in the magic of the printed page, I can cast off my customary garments and array	67
myself in the raiment of a victorious knight or a soccer star. No longer shackled by the chains	85
of time and space, I shiver with Washington's valiant men in the piercing cold of Valley Forge and	103
I kneel in reverent awe at Bethlehem's crib. Is it any wonder that I am unable to resist the	122
beckoning call of a good book?	128
My interest in weeding is probably the result of my interest in reading. This occupation puts me	145
on a par with those noble characters that I have respected in books. Few chores are more	162
intriguing to me than that of rescuing struggling plants from the greedy claws of choking weeds.	178
I like the feel of the cold and damp earth as I eject the intruding roots. With the confident	197
swagger of a conquering hero, I march triumphantly through our flower garden, leaving grateful	211
shrubs in my wake. Even the squirming worms wriggle their gratitude for my noble deed. Yes,	227
recreation time is always debating time for me. The topic of this secret controversy ever remains	243
the same: to read or to weed?	250

Adapted from *Voyages in English* by Reverend Paul E. Campbell and Sister Mary Donatus Macnickle. Copyrighted by Loyola University Press.

Word Recognition Scoring Guide		
Total Miscues	Level	Significant Miscues
0–3	Independent	0–2
4–12	Ind./Inst.	3–6
13	Instructional	7
14–24	Inst./Frust.	8–12
25 +	Frustration	13 +

Total Miscues [ ]   Significant Miscues [ ]

Oral Reading Rate	Norm Group Percentile
____ WPM)15000	☐ 90 ☐ 75 ☐ 50 ☐ 25 ☐ 10

Student Booklet copy is on page 94.   Background: Low ├──────┼──────┤ High

LL 1187 (Grade 11) Activating Background: Read the title to yourself. Then tell me what you think this might be about.

Bookworm or Earthworm

T   1. _____   What is this story about?
                 (whether the author should read or weed)

F   2. _____   The author makes mention of casting off customary garments and dressing in the
                 raiment of what?
                 (a victorious knight or soccer star [either 1])

F   3. _____   How did the author develop an interest in weeding?
                 (from an interest in reading)

F   4. _____   Where does the author weed?
                 (in the flower garden)

F   5. _____   What historical person was mentioned in the story?
                 (George Washington)

F   6. _____   What do the worms do to show their gratitude for the weeding of the garden?
                 (they wriggle)

F   7. _____   What chore, or job, is intriguing to the author?
                 (rescuing struggling plants from the greedy claws of choking weeds; simply weeding)

I   8. _____   What does the author probably mean by "reverent awe at Bethlehem's crib?"
                 (any logical response; the birth of Jesus)

E   9. _____   Reading satisfies the author's wanderlust. What satisfies wanderlust for you? Why?
                 (any logical response)

V   10. _____   Explain what "swagger" means in this phrase: With the confident swagger of
                 a conquering hero.
                 (stride; strut)

☐ Questions
   Missed

Comprehension Scoring Guide	
Questions Missed	Level
0–1	Independent
1½–2	Ind./Inst.
2½	Instructional
3–4½	Inst./Frust.
5 +	Frustration

Retelling Rubric for the Three Reading Levels
Independent Level/Excellent
Recalls central or key ideas
Remembers important facts
Retains the general sequence of events
Relates most of the content in an organized manner
Instructional Level/Satisfactory
Recalls most central or key ideas
Remembers some important facts
Retains the general sequence of events
Relates an overall sense of the content
Frustration Level/Unsatisfactory
Recalls bits of information in a haphazard manner
Little apparent organization

Retelling Notes

American in Paris

On a brilliant day in May, in the year 1868, a gentleman was reclining at his ease on the | 19

great circular divan which occupied the center of the Salon Carré, in the Museum of the Louvre. | 36

He had taken serene possession of the softest spot of this commodious ottoman. With his head | 52

thrown back and his legs outstretched, he was staring at Murillo's beautiful moon-borne Madonna | 67

in profound enjoyment of his posture. He had removed his hat and flung down beside him a little | 85

red guidebook and an opera glass. The day was warm; he was heated with walking, and he | 102

repeatedly passed his handkerchief over his forehead with a somewhat wearied gesture. His | 115

exertions on this particular day had been of an unwonted sort, and he had often performed great | 132

physical feats which left him less jaded than his tranquil stroll through the Louvre. He had looked | 149

at all the pictures to which an asterisk was affixed in those formidable pages of fine print in his | 168

Bädeker guidebook; his attention had been strained and his eyes dazzled, and he had sat down with | 185

an aesthetic headache. His physiognomy would have sufficiently indicated that he was a shrewd | 199

and capable fellow. In truth, he had often sat up all night over a bristling bundle of accounts and | 218

heard the cock crow without a yawn. But Raphael and Titian and Rubens were a new kind of | 236

arithmetic, and they made him, for the first time in his life, really wonder. | 250

Note: Do not count the mispronunciation of proper nouns as significant miscues.

Adapted from *The American* by Henry James.

Word Recognition Scoring Guide		
Total Miscues	Level	Significant Miscues
0–3	Independent	0–2
4–12	Ind./Inst.	3–6
13	Instructional	7
14–24	Inst./Frust.	8–12
25 +	Frustration	13 +

Total Miscues ☐   Significant Miscues ☐

Oral Reading Rate	Norm Group Percentile
_____ WPM $\overline{)15000}$	☐ 90 ☐ 75 ☐ 50 ☐ 25 ☐ 10

LL 1296 (Grade 12) Activating Background: Read the title to yourself. Then tell me what you think this might be about.

American in Paris

T 1. _____ What is this story about?
               (an American gentleman in the Louvre Museum)

F 2. _____ What is the gentleman holding in his hand?
               (a handkerchief)

F 3. _____ What did the gentleman remove as he took his position on the ottoman?
               (his hat)

F 4. _____ When does this story take place?
               (1868; over one hundred years ago)

F 5. _____ What is he staring at?
               (Murillo's Madonna; a painting)

F 6. _____ Describe the weather.
               (warm)

F 7. _____ What kind of a book has he been reading?
               (a red guidebook; Bädeker guidebook)

I 8. _____ What do you think the man's job was? Why?
               (any logical response; accounting; some type of business)

E 9. _____ Why might Raphael, Titian, and Rubens make the gentleman wonder?
               (any logical response)

V 10. _____ Explain what "physiognomy" means in this sentence: His physiognomy would have
               sufficiently indicated that he was a shrewd and capable fellow.
               (outward appearance)

☐ Questions
  Missed

Comprehension Scoring Guide

Questions Missed	Level
0–1	Independent
1½–2	Ind./Inst.
2½	Instructional
3–4½	Inst./Frust.
5 +	Frustration

Retelling Rubric for the Three Reading Levels

Independent Level/Excellent
Recalls central or key ideas
Remembers important facts
Retains the general sequence of events
Relates most of the content in an organized manner

Instructional Level/Satisfactory
Recalls most central or key ideas
Remembers some important facts
Retains the general sequence of events
Relates an overall sense of the content

Frustration Level/Unsatisfactory
Recalls bits of information in a haphazard manner
Little apparent organization

Retelling Notes

Form LI

Performance Booklet

Teacher Copy

Form LI

Primary Use:

- Silent Reading (Informational)

Other Uses:

- Oral Reading
- Listening Level
- Progress Monitoring

 Note: This Performance Booklet is on the CD that accompanies the Basic Reading Inventory.

Miscue Summary Sheet for Forms LL and LI

MISCUES							
Substitution	Insertion	Omission	Reversal	Repetition	Self-Correction of Unacceptable Miscue	Meaning Change (Significant Miscue)	

Name _____ Date _____

Passage Title _____

Form _____

Total Miscues [ ]   **Significant Miscues** [ ]

BASIC READING INVENTORY PERFORMANCE BOOKLET

Jerry L. Johns, Ph.D.

Student _____   Grade _____ Gender   M   F   Date of Test _____

School _____   Examiner _____   Date of Birth_____

Address _____   Current Book/Level_____   Age_____

SUMMARY OF STUDENT'S READING PERFORMANCE

Grade	Word Recognition		Comprehension		Oral Reading Rate		Silent Reading Rate
	Miscues	Level	Questions Missed	Level	Words per Minute (WPM)	Norm Group Percentile	Words per Minute (WPM)
3							
4							
5							
6							
7							
8							
9							
10							
11							
12							

ESTIMATE OF READING LEVELS

Independent _____ Instructional _____ Frustration _____

LISTENING LEVEL

Form _____

Grade	Questions Missed	Level
3		
4		
5		
6		
7		
8		
9		
10		
11		
12		

ESTIMATED LEVEL: _____

GENERAL OBSERVATIONS

INFORMAL ANALYSIS OF ORAL READING

Oral Reading Behaviors	Frequency of Occurrence			General Impact on Meaning		
	Seldom	Sometimes	Frequently	No Change	Little Change	Much Change
Substitutions						
Insertions						
Omissions						
Reversals						
Repetitions						

QUALITATIVE ANALYSIS OF BASIC READING INVENTORY INSIGHTS

General Directions: Note the degree to which the student shows behavior or evidence in the following areas. Space is provided for additional items.

Seldom / Weak / Poor ——— Always / Strong / Excellent

COMPREHENSION

Seeks to construct meaning
Makes predictions
Activates background knowledge
Possesses appropriate concepts
  and vocabulary
Monitors reading
Varies reading rate as needed
Understands topic and major ideas
Remembers facts or details
Makes and supports appropriate
  inferences
Evaluates ideas from passages
Understands vocabulary used
Provides appropriate definitions
  of words
Engages with passages

WORD IDENTIFICATION

Possesses numerous strategies
Uses strategies flexibly
Uses graphophonic information
Uses semantic information
Uses syntactic information
Knows basic sight words
  automatically
Possesses sight vocabulary

ORAL AND SILENT READING

Reads fluently
Reads with expression
Attends to punctuation
Keeps place while reading
Reads at appropriate rate
Reads silently without vocalization

ATTITUDE AND CONFIDENCE

Enjoys reading
Demonstrates willingness to risk
Possesses positive self-concept
Chooses to read
Regards himself/herself as a reader
Exhibits persistence

327

Harris' Hawks

Most hawks hunt for prey alone. In New Mexico, there is a type of hawk called Harris' hawks.	18
Harris' hawks work together as a team to catch their prey. This idea was interesting to a wildlife	36
scientist. He decided to study these hawks.	43
The first thing he had to do was catch one hawk in a group. He then put a radio transmitter	63
on the bird's leg. This helped him keep track of where the bird went. He did this with one hawk	83
from each group.	86
The scientist went to a high place to watch the hawks. This took a lot of time and hard work.	106
He discovered that most of the time the hawks caught rabbits. These were large rabbits that would	123
be hard for one hawk to catch. The hawks worked together as a team so that they could catch their	143
prey. Then they all shared the meal.	150
The scientist watched as the hawks would stalk their prey. First, they would fly across a large	167
area. Sometimes the hawks would sit in trees to watch the ground. When the hawks saw a rabbit,	185
they would start following it. When the rabbit slowed down in an open place, the hawks would dive	203
at it. The hawks would wait until the rabbit became tired to make their final dive.	219
These hawks are very good at working as a team. This helps them to find food and stay alive.	238
They have learned that it is very important to help each other.	250

Word Recognition Scoring Guide		
Total Miscues	Level	Significant Miscues
0–3	Independent	0–2
4–12	Ind./Inst.	3–6
13	Instructional	7
14–24	Inst./Frust.	8–12
25 +	Frustration	13 +

Total Miscues [ ]   Significant Miscues [ ]

Oral Reading Rate	Norm Group Percentile
_____ WPM $\overline{)15000}$	☐ 90 ☐ 75 ☐ 50 ☐ 25 ☐ 10

Background: Low ├─────┼─────┤ High

LI 3183 (Grade 3) Activating Background: Read the title to yourself. Then tell me what you think this might be about.

Harris' Hawks

T   1. _____   What is this passage about?
(what hawks do; what they eat; hawks that work together as a team to catch their prey)

F   2. _____   What is this type of hawk called?
(Harris' hawk)

F   3. _____   Where do these hawks live?
(New Mexico)

F   4. _____   Why do Harris' hawks work together as a team?
(to catch their prey; they are too small to work alone)

F   5. _____   What did the scientist do with the bird after he caught it?
(he put a radio transmitter on the bird's leg)

F   6. _____   Where did the scientist go to watch the hawks?
(to a high place)

F   7. _____   What type of animal did the hawks usually catch?
(rabbits)

I   8. _____   Why do you think the hawks would wait until the rabbit was in an open place before they would start diving at it?
(any logical response; because they could see it better; trees and bushes weren't in the way)

E   9. _____   If you were a scientist, what would you like to spend time studying? Why?
(any logical response)

V   10. _____ Explain what "prey" means in this sentence: Most hawks hunt for prey alone.
(animals hunted or seized for food, especially by another animal)

☐ Questions Missed

Comprehension Scoring Guide	
Questions Missed	Level
0–1	Independent
1½–2	Ind./Inst.
2½	Instructional
3–4½	Inst./Frust.
5 +	Frustration

Retelling Rubric for the Three Reading Levels
Independent Level/Excellent
Recalls central or key ideas
Remembers important facts
Retains the general sequence of events
Relates most of the content in an organized manner
Instructional Level/Satisfactory
Recalls most central or key ideas
Remembers some important facts
Retains the general sequence of events
Relates an overall sense of the content
Frustration Level/Unsatisfactory
Recalls bits of information in a haphazard manner
Little apparent organization

Retelling Notes

Early Travel

It was early winter when Martha and Johnny Stine began their journey. They were traveling | 15

from Kansas to Colorado. When it was night, they would set up camp wherever they could. This | 32

type of trip was not easy. The year was 1891, which was before cars or airplanes. Good roads were | 51

not available. Martha and Johnny traveled in a covered wagon pulled by horses. | 64

As time passed, the weather became colder. One night when they stopped to sleep, it was six | 81

degrees below zero. The next night they were caught in a blizzard. Martha and Johnny stopped at | 98

a house to ask for directions. They were asked if they wanted to spend the night there because of | 117

the blizzard. Johnny didn't want to stay, although Martha did. They continued on their journey in | 133

the blinding blizzard until they could no longer see. The roads were covered with snow. The team | 150

of horses couldn't be forced to continue through the ice and snow any longer. Then they saw the | 168

shadow of a small cabin. When they reached the cabin, it was locked. They pulled up beside the | 186

cabin in order to get shelter from the wind and snow. Weary, they fell into a restless sleep. Martha | 205

felt very depressed. They were lost in a blizzard and tired from traveling. | 218

Four days later they arrived at their destination. Martha was so happy she cried. It had been | 235

four long weeks since they had started. Martha was happy to see the trip end. | 250

Word Recognition Scoring Guide		
Total Miscues	Level	Significant Miscues
0–3	Independent	0–2
4–12	Ind./Inst.	3–6
13	Instructional	7
14–24	Inst./Frust.	8–12
25 +	Frustration	13 +

Total Miscues [ ]   Significant Miscues [ ]

Oral Reading Rate	Norm Group Percentile
_____ WPM ⟌15000	☐ 90 ☐ 75 ☐ 50 ☐ 25 ☐ 10

Background: Low ├──────┼──────┤ High

LI 5414 (Grade 4) Activating Background: Read the title to yourself. Then tell me what you think this might be about.

Early Travel

T 1. _____ What is this passage about?
(Martha and Johnny Stine's trip by covered wagon in the winter)

F 2. _____ What state were the Stine's coming from and what state were they going to?
(they were traveling from Kansas to Colorado)

F 3. _____ What year did this story take place?
(1891)

F 4. _____ Who wanted to stay at the house where they stopped and asked for directions?
(Martha)

F 5. _____ What did they discover about the cabin when they found it in a blizzard?
(it was locked)

F 6. _____ What was the temperature when they stopped to sleep one night?
(6 degrees below zero; below zero)

F 7. _____ How long did it take the Stine family from when they started their trip until they reached their destination?
(4 weeks)

I 8. _____ When they stopped at a house in the blizzard to ask for directions, they were asked if they wanted to spend the night there. Why do you think Johnny didn't want to stay?
(any logical response; he wanted to continue on; he was afraid of the strangers)

E 9. _____ If you were taking this trip with Martha and Johnny, what would you take with you? Why?
(any logical response; warm clothes; sleeping bag; food)

V 10. _____ Explain what "depressed" means in this sentence: Martha felt depressed when they were lost.
(sad; gloomy; low-spirited)

☐ Questions Missed

Comprehension Scoring Guide	
Questions Missed	Level
0–1	Independent
1½–2	Ind./Inst.
2½	Instructional
3–4½	Inst./Frust.
5 +	Frustration

Retelling Rubric for the Three Reading Levels
Independent Level/Excellent
Recalls central or key ideas
Remembers important facts
Retains the general sequence of events
Relates most of the content in an organized manner
Instructional Level/Satisfactory
Recalls most central or key ideas
Remembers some important facts
Retains the general sequence of events
Relates an overall sense of the content
Frustration Level/Unsatisfactory
Recalls bits of information in a haphazard manner
Little apparent organization

Retelling Notes

Two Famous Brothers

Orville and Wilbur Wright invented and built the first successful airplane. Orville flew it in | 15
December of 1903. These famous brothers had an interesting childhood. | 25

In 1879, Wilbur was twelve and Orville was eight. Their father brought them a toy made of | 42
paper, bamboo sticks, and cork after a trip to Ohio. It was called a helicopter. They turned a stick | 61
that twisted a rubber band, fastened it, and then tossed the helicopter into the air. Orville and | 78
Wilbur reached to catch it before it fell. The toy helicopter flew several feet across the room. The | 96
boys played with it until it broke. | 103

Orville had many plans for making money. He learned to make and fly kites, and he made | 120
money by selling them to his friends. By the time he was fourteen, he had a printing press and | 139
business. Wilbur became interested in the business. In a short time, they published a weekly news- | 155
paper.

Bicycles became popular in the 1890s. These early bikes were very dangerous and difficult to | 170
ride. The front wheel was five feet high. The back wheel was eighteen inches high. A new bicycle | 188
was then built with two wheels of equal size, similar to today's bikes. The brothers rented a shop. | 206
They began repairing and selling bicycles. Now they had two businesses. | 217

One day, Wilbur saw a photograph of a glider with a man hanging beneath the wings. He | 234
showed it to Orville. That may have been the beginning of their serious talk of flying. | 250

Word Recognition Scoring Guide		
Total Miscues	Level	Significant Miscues
0–3	Independent	0–2
4–12	Ind./Inst.	3–6
13	Instructional	7
14–24	Inst./Frust.	8–12
25 +	Frustration	13 +

Total Miscues ☐   Significant Miscues ☐

Oral Reading Rate	Norm Group Percentile
____ WPM)15000	☐ 90 ☐ 75 ☐ 50 ☐ 25 ☐ 10

Student Booklet copy is on page 100.   Background: Low ├──────┼──────┤ High

LI 8595 (Grade 5) Activating Background: Read the title to yourself. Then tell me what you think this might be about.

Two Famous Brothers

T 1. _____ What is this passage about?
(Wilbur and Orville Wright; their childhood; two brothers)

F 2. _____ What are the names of the two famous brothers?
(Orville; Wilbur)

F 3. _____ What are the Wright brothers famous for?
(building and flying the first successful airplane)

F 4. _____ Who gave the brothers the toy helicopter?
(their father)

F 5. _____ What was the toy helicopter made of?
(paper; bamboo sticks; cork; a rubber band [any 2])

F 6. _____ Name one of the brothers' businesses.
(making and selling kites; publishing a newspaper; repairing and selling bicycles)

F 7. _____ What made early bikes dangerous and difficult to ride?
(the wheels were different sizes)

I 8. _____ Why do you think the newer bikes were better than the early bikes?
(any logical response; the wheels were of equal size)

E 9. _____ Why do you think Orville and Wilbur had more than one business?
(any logical response; they wanted to make money; they were interested in many things)

V 10. _____ Explain what "glider" means in this sentence: Wilbur saw a photograph of a glider.
(like an airplane; an airplane without a motor)

	Questions Missed

Comprehension Scoring Guide

Questions Missed	Level
0–1	Independent
1½–2	Ind./Inst.
2½	Instructional
3–4½	Inst./Frust.
5 +	Frustration

Retelling Rubric for the Three Reading Levels

Independent Level/Excellent
Recalls central or key ideas
Remembers important facts
Retains the general sequence of events
Relates most of the content in an organized manner

Instructional Level/Satisfactory
Recalls most central or key ideas
Remembers some important facts
Retains the general sequence of events
Relates an overall sense of the content

Frustration Level/Unsatisfactory
Recalls bits of information in a haphazard manner
Little apparent organization

Retelling Notes

A Special Teacher

Many people know that Helen Keller was deaf and blind. Not as many people know about	16
Anne Sullivan. She taught Helen Keller to read and write and was her companion for fifty years.	33
Anne Sullivan was born in 1866—more than 140 years ago. She was nearly blind herself.	49
At the age of ten, she was sent to a poor house away from her family. When Anne was fourteen,	69
she was admitted to an institute for the blind in the city of Boston. She had several eye operations	88
and was able to learn to read.	95
When she was twenty-one, Anne was hired to teach Helen Keller, a seven year old who was	112
deaf and blind. Anne studied how she might teach Helen Keller. In March of 1887, Anne went to	130
Alabama to begin her new job. She even took a doll for Helen.	143
Teaching Helen was not easy. Anne tried to spell out words on Helen's hand through touch.	159
Once Helen understood, she was able to learn many words. When Helen wanted to know Anne's	175
name, she spelled teacher in Helen's hand. From that day on, Helen called Anne teacher. Anne was	192
also called a miracle worker.	197
Anne was Helen's teacher and friend for about fifty years. Near the end of Anne's life, her	214
eyesight became very poor again. She went blind. Fortunately, Anne knew all of the letters in braille—	231
an alphabet that makes it possible for blind people to read. When Anne died, she was called truly	249
great.	250

Word Recognition Scoring Guide		
Total Miscues	Level	Significant Miscues
0–3	Independent	0–2
4–12	Ind./Inst.	3–6
13	Instructional	7
14–24	Inst./Frust.	8–12
25 +	Frustration	13 +

Total Miscues [ ] Significant Miscues [ ]

Oral Reading Rate	Norm Group Percentile
____ WPM $\overline{)15000}$	☐ 90 ☐ 75 ☐ 50 ☐ 25 ☐ 10

LI 6867 (Grade 6) Activating Background: Read the title to yourself. Then tell me what you think this might be about.

A Special Teacher

T   1. _____   What is this passage about?
(Anne Sullivan; Helen Keller's teacher)

F   2. _____   How did Anne Sullivan gain her sight?
(she had many operations)

F   3. _____   What name did Helen call Anne?
(teacher)

F   4. _____   How old was Anne when she began teaching Helen?
(twenty-one)

F   5. _____   How long were Anne and Helen together?
(about fifty years)

F   6. _____   How did Anne teach Helen to spell words?
(Anne would spell out words on Helen's hand through touch)

F   7. _____   What did Anne take Helen when she first went to begin to teach her?
(a doll)

I   8. _____   Why do you think Anne decided to be a teacher for the blind?
(any logical response; she had once been blind, and knew how wonderful it was to learn to read)

E   9. _____   How do you think Helen Keller learned braille?
(any logical response; she taught herself)

V   10. _____   Explain what "braille" means in this sentence: Helen Keller taught Anne Sullivan braille.
(an alphabet composed of a series of raised bumps that allows blind people to read)

Questions Missed	

Comprehension Scoring Guide	
Questions Missed	Level
0–1	Independent
1½–2	Ind./Inst.
2½	Instructional
3–4½	Inst./Frust.
5 +	Frustration

Retelling Rubric for the Three Reading Levels

Independent Level/Excellent
Recalls central or key ideas
Remembers important facts
Retains the general sequence of events
Relates most of the content in an organized manner

Instructional Level/Satisfactory
Recalls most central or key ideas
Remembers some important facts
Retains the general sequence of events
Relates an overall sense of the content

Frustration Level/Unsatisfactory
Recalls bits of information in a haphazard manner
Little apparent organization

Retelling Notes

Have You Played This Game?

You might be one of about 500 million people who have played the best-selling board game | 17

in the world. It is sold in 80 countries and offered in 26 languages. Over 200 million games have | 36

been manufactured and sold. Say "Monopoly" and people of every age can remember lively games | 51

with friends and family. How did this wonder start? | 60

Charles B. Darrow, like most Americans, could not find a job during the Great Depression. At | 75

night he started drawing a game board on his kitchen table cloth. Soon he made rules, property | 92

cards, and little houses and hotels. Evenings soon found Darrow with friends and family playing | 107

his new game. News of the game passed by word of mouth. People asked Darrow for their own | 125

sets. Darrow happily made games for his friends. He sensed that his game could become a job. | 142

In 1934, Darrow took Monopoly to executives at Parker Brothers. They dismissed it for 52 | 157

design mistakes, but Darrow knew he had a winning game. With help from a friend, he made sets | 175

by hand. These sold at a Philadelphia department store. People loved the game and orders soon | 191

started flooding in. Darrow knew he couldn't keep up the pace. He went to Parker Brothers a | 208

second time. This time they accepted the game and quickly began mass production. That first year, | 224

1935, Monopoly was the best-selling game in America. Monopoly made Darrow the first million- | 239

aire game designer, freeing him from ever worrying about a job again. | 250

Word Recognition Scoring Guide		
Total Miscues	Level	Significant Miscues
0–3	Independent	0–2
4–12	Ind./Inst.	3–6
13	Instructional	7
14–24	Inst./Frust.	8–12
25 +	Frustration	13 +

Total Miscues ☐   Significant Miscues ☐

Oral Reading Rate	Norm Group Percentile
$\frac{\quad\quad}{)15000}$ WPM	☐ 90 ☐ 75 ☐ 50 ☐ 25 ☐ 10

LI 3717 (Grade 7) Activating Background: Read the title to yourself. Then tell me what you think this might be about.

Have You Played This Game?

T   1. _____   What is this story about?
(how the game Monopoly was created)

F   2. _____   How popular is Monopoly?
(best-selling board game in the world; offered in 26 languages; sold in 80 countries; 500 million people have played it [any 1])

F   3. _____   Who created Monopoly?
(Darrow)

F   4. _____   Who were the first people to play Monopoly?
(Darrow; his friends; family [any 2])

F   5. _____   Why did Parker Brothers dismiss Monopoly?
(52 design mistakes; design mistakes)

F   6. _____   What did Darrow do next?
(he made sets and sold them to a Philadelphia department store)

F   7. _____   What did Parker Brothers do when Darrow went to them a second time?
(they accepted the game; they mass produced the game)

I   8. _____   Why do you think Monopoly was so popular during the Great Depression?
(any logical response; people were out of work; they had extra time; it made life more fun)

E   9. _____   Why do you think so many people like to play Monopoly?
(any logical response)

V   10. _____   Explain what "mass production" means in this sentence: This time they accepted the game and quickly began mass production.
(they made a lot of games exactly alike, very quickly)

	Questions Missed	

Comprehension Scoring Guide

Questions Missed	Level
0–1	Independent
1½–2	Ind./Inst.
2½	Instructional
3–4½	Inst./Frust.
5 +	Frustration

Retelling Rubric for the Three Reading Levels

Independent Level/Excellent
Recalls central or key ideas
Remembers important facts
Retains the general sequence of events
Relates most of the content in an organized manner

Instructional Level/Satisfactory
Recalls most central or key ideas
Remembers some important facts
Retains the general sequence of events
Relates an overall sense of the content

Frustration Level/Unsatisfactory
Recalls bits of information in a haphazard manner
Little apparent organization

Retelling Notes

Friend of Lions

At the break of dawn, he rises from the bed that is placed just outside the door to his hut.	20
Dressed only in shorts and sandals, he sets out on his daily prowl of Kenya's Kora Game Preserve	38
in Eastern Africa. He is looking for lions.	46
George Adamson is not a hunter; on the contrary, his days are spent trying to preserve what	63
few wild lions remain on this part of the African continent. The Kenyan government closed Ad-	78
amson's lion rehabilitation program after several people at his camp were assaulted by the cats he	94
considers the perfection of ageless beauty and grace. Now he searches for the lions he returned from	111
captivity and for their offspring. They come to him when he calls. He feeds them like pets, and he	130
protects them from poachers.	134
In the late 1950s, when he was a government game warden, Adamson shot a man-eating lioness	151
who had a cub. The story of how he and his wife Joy raised the cub, Elsa, is told in the book and	174
the movie titled *Born Free*. This story brought the cause of wildlife conservation to the attention	190
of people in many countries around the world. It also raised $600,000 that has been used for a	208
variety of wildlife conservation projects.	213
Since Joy's death in 1980, Adamson has wandered the lonely landscape of this vast preserve.	228
His long, flowing, golden hair and white beard make him appear like one of the creatures he loves	246
so much—the lion.	250

Word Recognition Scoring Guide		
Total Miscues	Level	Significant Miscues
0–3	Independent	0–2
4–12	Ind./Inst.	3–6
13	Instructional	7
14–24	Inst./Frust.	8–12
25 +	Frustration	13 +

Total Miscues ☐   Significant Miscues ☐

Oral Reading Rate	Norm Group Percentile
_____ WPM)15000	☐ 90 ☐ 75 ☐ 50 ☐ 25 ☐ 10

Background: Low ├──────┼──────┤ High

LI 8183 (Grade 8) Activating Background: Read the title to yourself. Then tell me what you think this might be about.

Friend of Lions

T 1. _____ What is this passage about?
(a man who loves and protects lions)

F 2. _____ In what country does George Adamson live?
(Kenya)

F 3. _____ On what continent is Kenya located?
(Africa)

F 4. _____ What is the title of the book and the movie that tells the story of how the Adamsons raised a motherless lion cub?
(*Born Free*)

F 5. _____ In what way are the lions, to Adamson, just like household cats are to us?
(they will come to him when he calls; he feeds them like pets)

F 6. _____ How did *Born Free* aid the cause of wildlife conservation?
(it brought wildlife conservation to the attention of the world; it raised money for wildlife conservation projects)

F 7. _____ What was Adamson's job title at the time when he shot a man-eating lioness?
(he was a government game warden)

I 8. _____ Why do you think Adamson and his wife decided to raise Elsa, the motherless lion cub?
(any logical response; because they shot her mother; she was unable to survive without their help)

E 9. _____ Why do you think the authorities allow Adamson to live out in the wild, completely unprotected?
(any logical response; the lions are used to him; he is a friend of the lions)

V 10. _____ Explain what "poachers" means in this sentence: George Adamson protects lions from poachers.
(people who take fish or game illegally)

☐ Questions Missed

Comprehension Scoring Guide	
Questions Missed	Level
0–1	Independent
1½–2	Ind./Inst.
2½	Instructional
3–4½	Inst./Frust.
5 +	Frustration

Retelling Rubric for the Three Reading Levels
Independent Level/Excellent
Recalls central or key ideas
Remembers important facts
Retains the general sequence of events
Relates most of the content in an organized manner
Instructional Level/Satisfactory
Recalls most central or key ideas
Remembers some important facts
Retains the general sequence of events
Relates an overall sense of the content
Frustration Level/Unsatisfactory
Recalls bits of information in a haphazard manner
Little apparent organization

Retelling Notes

Ancient Destruction

Pompeii, an ancient city in Southern Italy, was settled in the 8th century B.C. It was overtaken	17
by the Romans in 310 B.C. and became part of the Roman Empire. During its first five hundred	35
years, Pompeii grew from a small farming village to an important trading center. Then in 62 A.D.	52
an earthquake hit the city, leaving it destroyed. The residents of the city began rebuilding, but	68
while they were in the middle of rebuilding the city temple, a more lasting disaster arrived.	84
Mount Vesuvius, a volcano which had been thought extinct, erupted in 79 A.D. covering Pompeii	99
with hot lava.	102
Eye-witnesses watched Mount Vesuvius erupt as bright flames towered in the sky and black	117
smoke covered the sun. Volcanic ash and lava covered the city until almost no buildings were left	134
standing. As the volcanic eruption hit Pompeii, the universe seemed to fight against the city send-	150
ing lightning, earthquakes, and tidal waves. This attack lasted for three days, killing all who had	165
survived the volcano. When the dust settled, 15 feet of smoking debris covered what had once been	182
Pompeii.	183
Pompeii was buried under ashes, stone, and cinders for almost 2,000 years. After the volcano,	198
looters took what they could find from the city, and Pompeii was forgotten until the nineteenth	214
century when the site was rediscovered and excavation began. Much has been learned about the	229
manners and customs of the ancient Romans. Today, visitors can walk through Pompeii and view a	245
city almost 3,000 years old.	250

Word Recognition Scoring Guide		
Total Miscues	Level	Significant Miscues
0–3	Independent	0–2
4–12	Ind./Inst.	3–6
13	Instructional	7
14–24	Inst./Frust.	8–12
25 +	Frustration	13 +

Total Miscues ☐   Significant Miscues ☐

Oral Reading Rate	Norm Group Percentile
_____ WPM ⟌15000	☐ 90 ☐ 75 ☐ 50 ☐ 25 ☐ 10

LI 4959 (Grade 9) Activating Background: Read the title to yourself. Then tell me what you think this might be about.

Ancient Destruction

T   1. _____   What is this passage about?
(an ancient city, Pompeii, destroyed by a volcano and other natural forces)

F   2. _____   Where is Pompeii located?
(Italy; in Southern Italy)

F   3. _____   How was Pompeii first destroyed?
(by an earthquake)

F   4. _____   What was the name of the volcano that erupted?
(Mount Vesuvius)

F   5. _____   During the volcanic eruption, what other natural disasters happened at the same time?
(lightning; earthquakes; tidal waves [any 2])

F   6. _____   When was Pompeii rediscovered?
(in the nineteenth century; 200 years ago)

F   7. _____   How old is Pompeii today?
(almost 3,000 years old)

I   8. _____   What do you suppose the looters may have taken?
(any logical response)

E   9. _____   If a disaster destroyed where you live, what would be your thoughts, feelings, and actions?
(any logical response)

V   10. _____   Explain what "excavation" means in this sentence: Pompeii was forgotten until the nineteenth century when the site was rediscovered and excavation began.
(digging up; out; uncovering the city's ruins)

☐ Questions Missed

Comprehension Scoring Guide	
Questions Missed	Level
0–1	Independent
1½–2	Ind./Inst.
2½	Instructional
3–4½	Inst./Frust.
5 +	Frustration

Retelling Rubric for the Three Reading Levels

Independent Level/Excellent
Recalls central or key ideas
Remembers important facts
Retains the general sequence of events
Relates most of the content in an organized manner

Instructional Level/Satisfactory
Recalls most central or key ideas
Remembers some important facts
Retains the general sequence of events
Relates an overall sense of the content

Frustration Level/Unsatisfactory
Recalls bits of information in a haphazard manner
Little apparent organization

Retelling Notes

Earthquakes

Earthquakes can be devastating natural disasters. The infamous San Francisco earthquake of | 12

1906 caused over $200-million worth of damage, destroyed almost 30,000 buildings, and killed | 26

about 450 persons. In Japan, the cities of Tokyo and Yokohama were leveled by the earthquake | 42

of 1923 in which more than 140,000 persons were killed by falling buildings and fires, and over | 59

a million people were left homeless—all in 30 seconds. | 69

Hundreds of earthquakes occur every year throughout the world. Fortunately, few are as | 82

destructive as those described above. The development of an accurate system for predicting | 95

earthquakes would lessen the loss of life and property, but at present scientists can only study | 111

these phenomena. The study of earthquakes is called seismology. Seismographs, instruments | 122

sensitive to ground movement, are used to chart each motion, and the Richter Scale is commonly | 138

used to grade each earthquake's strength on a 1-to-10 scale. | 150

It is now known that earthquakes are created by sudden shifts that occur along faults deep in | 167

the earth's crust. According to the Theory of Continental Drift, the earth's crust consists of about | 183

twenty rigid sections, or plates, that are in continuous movement. This movement grinds and | 197

presses rocks at the edge of the plates. If the pressure becomes too great, the rocks shift, and the | 216

resulting movement sends energy, or seismic waves, to the surface of the earth. Most major | 231

earthquakes occur along the edge of the plates, and the most damaging impact occurs at the first | 248

surface-point reached by the seismic waves. | 255

Word Recognition Scoring Guide		
Total Miscues	Level	Significant Miscues
0–3	Independent	0–2
4–12	Ind./Inst.	3–6
13	Instructional	7
14–24	Inst./Frust.	8–12
25 +	Frustration	13 +

Total Miscues ☐   Significant Miscues ☐

Oral Reading Rate	Norm Group Percentile
_____ WPM $\overline{)15000}$	☐ 90 ☐ 75 ☐ 50 ☐ 25 ☐ 10

343

LI 1047 (Grade 10) Activating Background: Read the title to yourself. Then tell me what you think this might be about.

Earthquakes

T   1. _____   What is this passage about?
(earthquakes; scientific study of earthquakes; how earthquakes occur)

F   2. _____   This article named three cities where earthquakes have caused extensive damage. Name two.
(Tokyo; Yokohama; San Francisco [any 2])

F   3. _____   How many earthquakes occur throughout the world each year?
(hundreds)

F   4. _____   According to the article, what problems do earthquakes cause for people?
(people are killed; fires erupt; buildings fall [any 2])

F   5. _____   What is a seismograph?
(an instrument sensitive to ground movement)

F   6. _____   What is the purpose of a Richter Scale?
(to grade an earthquake's strength)

F   7. _____   How do earthquakes occur?
(a sudden shifting of rocks in the earth's crust sends seismic waves, or energy, to the surface of the earth; any reasonable explanation)

I   8. _____   What probably explains why so many people were killed in Japan's 1923 earthquake?
(any logical response; the earthquake occurred in two cities with large populations)

E   9. _____   What services would probably become most important to people who survive a major earthquake? Why?
(any logical response)

V 10. _____   Explain what "infamous" means in this sentence: The infamous San Francisco earthquake of 1906 caused over $200-million worth of damage.
(notorious; famously bad)

☐ Questions Missed	

Comprehension Scoring Guide

Questions Missed	Level
0–1	Independent
1½–2	Ind./Inst.
2½	Instructional
3–4½	Inst./Frust.
5 +	Frustration

Retelling Rubric for the Three Reading Levels

Independent Level/Excellent
Recalls central or key ideas
Remembers important facts
Retains the general sequence of events
Relates most of the content in an organized manner

Instructional Level/Satisfactory
Recalls most central or key ideas
Remembers some important facts
Retains the general sequence of events
Relates an overall sense of the content

Frustration Level/Unsatisfactory
Recalls bits of information in a haphazard manner
Little apparent organization

Retelling Notes

Beating the Bonk

Bonk describes the symptoms that occur when your body's carbohydrate stores are used up as | 15

a result of sustained exercise. As you exercise, most of the fuel being burned is consumed by your | 33

muscles. Both fats and carbohydrates can be used for this process. Fat, stored in fatty tissue, is | 50

reduced to free fatty acids which are transported by the blood to the muscles. In contrast, carbo- | 67

hydrates are stored within the muscles as glycogen. During exercise, individual molecules of gly- | 80

cogen are removed and used as energy. | 86

Your vital organs also need a continuous supply of fuel. Whether at rest or during exercise, | 102

your brain and nervous system depend on blood glucose. The reason why they need glycogen is | 118

because the cells of your nervous system don't store glycogen and can't use fat. To meet energy | 135

requirements, your blood glucose levels must stay at the same level. This job is largely done by | 152

your liver, which contains large amounts of glycogen that can be converted to glucose. | 166

With the muscles and organs vying for glucose, lengthy exercise can drain the liver. When | 181

blood glucose levels become too low to meet the fuel requirement of your central nervous system, | 197

you begin to feel tired, irritated, and unhappy. In a word, you bonk. | 210

Fortunately, you can remedy the bonk. When your blood glucose levels fall, you can replenish | 225

them by eating or drinking something rich in carbohydrates. Carbohydrates are quickly digested | 238

into glycogen, which is transported to the liver, muscles, and other organs. | 250

Adapted from *Nutrition for Cyclists*. Rodale Press.

Word Recognition Scoring Guide		
Total Miscues	Level	Significant Miscues
0–3	Independent	0–2
4–12	Ind./Inst.	3–6
13	Instructional	7
14–24	Inst./Frust.	8–12
25 +	Frustration	13 +

Total Miscues ☐   Significant Miscues ☐

Oral Reading Rate	Norm Group Percentile
_____ WPM)15000	☐ 90 ☐ 75 ☐ 50 ☐ 25 ☐ 10

LI 1187 (Grade 11) Activating Background: Read the title to yourself. Then tell me what you think this might be about.

Beating the Bonk

T   1. _____   What is this passage about?
(what happens when you bonk and how to avoid it; what fuel the body uses; how a diet rich in carbohydrates can cure the bonk)

F   2. _____   What does it mean to bonk?
(to use up carbohydrates by exercise; to feel tired, irritated, unhappy; lose glycogen)

F   3. _____   What is used by your muscles for food?
(fats and carbohydrates [either 1])

F   4. _____   What is glycogen?
(the substance that is stored in muscles from carbohydrates; storage form of glucose; what gives you energy)

F   5. _____   Why does your body need glycogen?
(to meet energy requirements for your brain, muscles, and nervous system; so you can be active; so you won't bonk)

F   6. _____   According to the passage, what are the symptoms of low blood glucose levels?
(you feel tired, irritable, unhappy [any 2])

F   7. _____   How can you overcome bonking?
(by eating or drinking something rich in carbohydrates)

I   8. _____   Why do you think athletes should try to avoid bonking?
(any logical response; it slows performance)

E   9. _____   Based on this passage, if you were an athletic coach what advice about diet would you share?
(any logical response; a diet rich in carbohydrates)

V 10. _____   Explain what "vying" means in this phrase: With your muscles and organs vying for glucose. . . .
(wanting or needing; competing)

[ ] Questions Missed

Comprehension Scoring Guide	
Questions Missed	Level
0–1	Independent
1½–2	Ind./Inst.
2½	Instructional
3–4½	Inst./Frust.
5 +	Frustration

Retelling Rubric for the Three Reading Levels

Independent Level/Excellent
Recalls central or key ideas
Remembers important facts
Retains the general sequence of events
Relates most of the content in an organized manner

Instructional Level/Satisfactory
Recalls most central or key ideas
Remembers some important facts
Retains the general sequence of events
Relates an overall sense of the content

Frustration Level/Unsatisfactory
Recalls bits of information in a haphazard manner
Little apparent organization

Retelling Notes

Beards

The history of beards has been a topic of increasing curiosity in today's society. Early man	16
first cherished a beard for religious reasons; primitive races were convinced there was a sacred	31
connection between all parts of a man's body, including his hair, and his personality. Hence, hair	47
had to be carefully guarded from possible foes—this accounts for ancient man's custom of burning	63
hair clippings to prevent them from being used by his enemies for nefarious purposes.	77
Thus, the earliest beard was faith-conditioned and therefore meticulously cared for. Ancient	90
Egyptians used tongs, curling irons, dyes, and even gold dust to give it a golden sheen.	106
In those days, shaving was considered perverted. It was a practice reserved for the defeated	121
adversary and the dangerously diseased; lepers were shaved to warn others of their infection. Some-	136
times those in mourning also shaved as a symbol of vital sacrifice to the dead.	150
The whims of individual rulers contributed to in determining the fate of beards. For example,	165
Queen Elizabeth I, who disliked beards, taxed anyone sprouting a beard of more than two weeks'	181
growth—the amount of assessment depended upon the man's social standing. In France, the beard	196
became fashionable when it was the personal preference of the current king. Francis I grew a	212
beard to hide an ugly scar on his chin, and his male subjects emulated the fashion. During the	230
eighteenth century, the Spaniards considered the beard to be in poor taste because their king was	246
unable to grow one.	250

Adapted from *How Did It Begin?* by R. Brasch.

Word Recognition Scoring Guide		
Total Miscues	Level	Significant Miscues
0–3	Independent	0–2
4–12	Ind./Inst.	3–6
13	Instructional	7
14–24	Inst./Frust.	8–12
25 +	Frustration	13 +

Total Miscues [ ] Significant Miscues [ ]

Oral Reading Rate	Norm Group Percentile
____ WPM $\overline{)15000}$	☐ 90 ☐ 75 ☐ 50 ☐ 25 ☐ 10

Student Booklet copy is on page 107.   Background: Low ├────────┼────────┤ High

LI 1296 (Grade 12) Activating Background: Read the title to yourself. Then tell me what you think this might be about.

Beards

T   1. _____ What is this passage about?
                 (history of beards)

F   2. _____ Name two of the major reasons men grew beards.
                 (any answer encompassing both religion and politics)

F   3. _____ Why did primitive man wear a beard?
                 (religious reasons; hair was sacred; there was a connection between all parts of man's body)

F   4. _____ Why did King Francis I grow a beard?
                 (to cover a scar on his chin)

F   5. _____ Why were lepers shaved?
                 (to warn others of their infectious disease)

F   6. _____ What did the ancient Egyptians use on their beards?
                 (tongs; curling irons; dyes; gold dust [any 2])

F   7. _____ Why did the Spaniards consider the beard to be in poor taste?
                 (their king was unable to grow one)

I   8. _____ Would men probably have beards during the reign of Queen Elizabeth I? Why?
                 (any logical response; no, she taxed anyone with a beard)

E   9. _____ What are some of the reasons that could account for the present popularity or unpopularity of beards?
                 (any logical response)

V   10. _____ Explain what "nefarious" means in this phrase: Man's custom of burning hair clippings to prevent them from being used by his enemies for nefarious purposes.
                 (evil; villainous; wicked; criminal)

	Questions Missed

Comprehension Scoring Guide

Questions Missed	Level
0–1	Independent
1½–2	Ind./Inst.
2½	Instructional
3–4½	Inst./Frust.
5 +	Frustration

Retelling Rubric for the Three Reading Levels
Independent Level/Excellent
Recalls central or key ideas
Remembers important facts
Retains the general sequence of events
Relates most of the content in an organized manner
Instructional Level/Satisfactory
Recalls most central or key ideas
Remembers some important facts
Retains the general sequence of events
Relates an overall sense of the content
Frustration Level/Unsatisfactory
Recalls bits of information in a haphazard manner
Little apparent organization

Retelling Notes

Early Literacy Assessments

Overview

Some students may experience difficulty with the easiest word lists and passages in the Basic Reading Inventory. The informal measures in Part 3 will be helpful to assess emergent reading behavior. For each measure, there are directions for you. Materials for the student are found in the separate student booklet. Two forms are available.

A Record Booklet for each form is provided for noting the student's responses and making other comments. These Record Booklets begin on page 361 and are also on the CD. Additional early literacy assessments and/or helpful teaching strategies are available in Elish-Piper, Johns, and Lenski (2006) and Johns and Lenski (2010).

Use the measures in Part 3 to gather insights about student behaviors that indicate the degree of movement toward what might be called conventional reading. Although there are numerals that can be attached to some of the measures, their major purpose is to provide a means to gather qualitative judgments related to the student's current abilities. For example:

"Literacy Knowledge" helps determine the degree to which the student understands directionality in reading and concepts about letters, words, and punctuation.

"Wordless Picture Reading" provides the student with an opportunity to dictate a story based on pictures and then read it. During the reading, speech-to-print pointing can be assessed. Follow-up questions help determine the student's ability to locate several words and a specific sentence.

Tasks like "Phoneme Awareness" and "Phoneme Segmentation" have been identified as being among the best predictors of early reading acquisition (Yopp, 1995). Phonological awareness also seems to underlie the learning of letter-sound relationships and subsequent growth in reading.

These assessments are intended to be used with emergent readers. Some of these students may be just beginning their schooling; others may be struggling readers throughout the grades. Select the assessments that will help you gain greater insights into students' emerging reading abilities so quality instruction and interventions can be provided.

Tip!

350

Alphabet Knowledge

Overview

Alphabet Knowledge contains upper-case and lower-case letters of the alphabet in non-sequential order to help assess letter-identification ability.

Materials Needed:

Two 3" x 5" cards
Alphabet Knowledge in the student booklet (Form 1: p. 110; Form 2: p. 118)
Alphabet Knowledge in the Record Booklet (Form 1: p. 364; Form 2: p. 382)
Record Booklet cover (Form 1: p. 362; Form 2: p. 380)

Procedure

1. Duplicate the appropriate page of the Record Booklet.

2. Place the alphabet page before the student and ask him or her to identify any known letters. Say, **"Here are some letters. I want to see how many you know."** Encourage the student to say "pass" or "skip it" if a particular letter is not known.

3. Use the 3" X 5" cards to block off everything but the lines being read. If necessary, point to each letter with a finger.

4. As the student responds, use the Record Booklet to note correct (+) and incorrect responses. When responses are incorrect, record the actual response or D.K. (student doesn't know) above the stimulus letter. If the student self-corrects, write OK; self-corrections can be made at any time. See examples below:

Letter	*Meaning of Recording*
$\overset{+}{O}$	Identified correctly
$\overset{DK}{H}$	Don't know
$\overset{C}{S}$	Said C for S
$\overset{B\ ok}{E}$	Said B for E but self-corrected

Scoring and Interpretation

Count the correct number of responses for the upper-case letters and the lower-case letters. Note the scores in the box on the record sheet and on the front of the Record Booklet. Based on the number of correct responses, make a judgment of the student's alphabet knowledge, and record an X on the continuum located on the cover page of the Record Booklet. Unknown letters or incorrect responses may help form the basis for instructional interventions.

For teaching strategies, consult Section 3.1 in Elish-Piper, Johns, and Lenski (2006) and/or 2.3 in Johns and Lenski (2010).

Writing

Overview

The student will demonstrate his or her ability to write words, letters, and sentences.

Materials Needed:
Pencil or pen
Paper (lined and unlined)
Writing in the Record Booklet (Form 1: p. 365; Form 2: p. 383)
Record Booklet cover (Form 1: p. 362; Form 2: p. 380)

Procedure

1. Give the student lined and unlined paper and a pencil or pen. If possible, have choices of paper and writing instruments.

2. Say, **"I'd like you to write some letters, words, and sentences."** Be patient and encouraging. You might want to ask the student to begin by writing his or her first name. If there is some success, try the last name.

3. After the student has finished, invite him or her to share what was written. Make mental notes or use the Record Booklet.

4. For the student who says "I can't write," you might ask him or her to print an X. Continue with a *few* other letters and perhaps names and numbers that the student may know. You might also suggest general categories of words: pets, colors, foods, things you can do.

Scoring and Interpretation

Informally evaluate the student's writing using the areas on the Writing page in the Record Booklet. Record an X on the continuum located on the cover page of the Record Booklet that represents your overall judgment.

For teaching strategies, consult the bonus chapter on the CD in Elish-Piper, Johns, and Lenski (2006).

Literacy Knowledge

Overview

This assessment contains questions you ask while sharing written material with the student. These questions will help you assess the student's knowledge of print directionality, letters, words, punctuation, and the like.

Materials Needed:

Remove and bind *New Shoes* (Form 1) or *A New Cat* (Form 2) at the back of the student booklet

Two 3" x 5" cards

Literacy Knowledge in the Record Booklet (Form 1: p. 366; Form 2: p. 384)

Record Booklet cover (Form 1: p. 362; Form 2: p. 380)

Procedure

1. Duplicate the appropriate pages of the Record Booklet.

2. Use *New Shoes* or *A New Cat* from the student booklet or secure some type of reading material that may be of interest to the student. The student will *not* have to read; rather, he or she will be given an opportunity to demonstrate understanding of how print works and basic knowledge of words, letters, and punctuation. Be sure the items on the test are appropriate for the type of reading material if you decide not to use *New Shoes* or *A New Cat*.

3. Say, **"I'd like you to show me some of the things you know about reading. You won't have to read."**

4. Begin with the first item in the Record Booklet and proceed through the test.

5. Stop if the student seems frustrated.

6. Note any relevant observations in the Record Booklet.

Scoring and Interpretation

1. Circle plus (+) for correct responses and minus (–) for incorrect responses.

2. Count the number of pluses and record the total in the box on the record sheet and on the front of the Record Booklet. The maximum score is 20.

Informally judge the student's knowledge of literacy concepts on the Literacy Knowledge page in the Record Booklet, and record an X on the continuum located on the cover of the Record Booklet. Areas of concern can be strengthened by the instructional program you design for the student.

For teaching strategies, consult Sections 2.1 and 2.2 in Elish-Piper, Johns, and Lenski (2006) and/or 2.3 and 2.5 in Johns and Lenski (2010).

Wordless Picture Reading

Overview

Wordless picture reading will help assess the student's ability to tell a story using pictures.

Materials Needed:

Digital or tape recorder (optional)
One Wordless Picture Story in the student booklet (Form 1: p. 111; Form 2: p. 119)
Record Booklet cover (Form 1: p. 362; Form 2: p. 380)

Procedure

1. Show the student the entire page containing the wordless picture story.

2. Invite the student to look at each frame in order. Point to each frame in order as you say, **"I think you can use these pictures to tell me a story. Think about the story the pictures tell."** Give the student time to study the pictures.

3. Then ask the student to look at the pictures again and when ready, begin telling the story with the first picture (point to it). Say, **"Tell me your story from the pictures. Begin here. I'll write it for you."**

4. As the student tells the story, write the student's dictation on a copy of the record sheet of the wordless picture story or on a separate piece of paper. This is similar to what teachers do in a language experience activity. You may also want to record the student's story for later in-depth analysis.

5. After the student has finished dictating, have him or her read it aloud while pointing to the words. If the reading is similar to the text, mentally note miscues. If the text is "read" quite differently from the text, you may wish to write what the student says.

6. Following the student's reading, ask the student to point to several words in the text and to find where a particular sentence begins and ends.

Scoring and Interpretation

Make qualitative judgments regarding the student's ability to follow directions and the level of language used in telling the story. Look for evidence that the story connects to the pictures and the degree to which the student has a sense of story and any evidence that the student uses book language. Then record Xs that reflect your judgments on the continuums located on the cover of the Record Booklet.

For teaching strategies, consult Sections 2.1, 2.2, and 2.3 in Elish-Piper, Johns, and Lenski (2006) and/or 2.1 and 2.13 in Johns and Lenski (2010).

Caption Reading

Overview

Caption Reading will help assess the student's ability to read a brief story with helpful picture clues.

Materials Needed:
Caption Reading in the student booklet (Form 1: p. 112; Form 2: p. 120)
Caption Reading in the Record Booklet (Form 1: p. 369; Form 2: p. 387)
Record Booklet cover (Form 1: p. 362; Form 2: p. 380)

Procedure

1. Show the student the page containing the pictures and captions.

2. Invite the student to look at frames of the story (pictures and text) in order as numbered.

3. Then ask the student to read the story aloud. Say, **"I want you to read the story to me."** As the student reads, mentally note any miscues or record them on the appropriate page of the Record Booklet.

4. If the student has difficulty reading the story, have the student listen while you read it aloud. Say, **"You listen to me read the story. Then I want you to read it to me."** After your reading, invite the student to read.

5. Encourage the student to talk about the story with you.

Scoring and Interpretation

Informally note the miscues the student made, the degree of fluency, and other behaviors on the Caption Reading page in the Record Booklet. Record your qualitative judgment of the reading with an X on the continuum located on the cover of the Record Booklet. If the student was able to read the story, you can informally analyze fluency, miscues, and overall engagement with the task.

If you read the story first, evaluate the degree to which the student was able to remember and repeat text. Be alert for how the student uses language as you talk about the story.

For teaching strategies, consult Section 2.2 in Elish-Piper, Johns, and Lenski (2006).

Auditory Discrimination

Overview

This test will help evaluate the student's ability to distinguish between words that differ in one phoneme (sound).

Materials Needed:

Auditory Discrimination in the Record Booklet (Form 1: p. 370; Form 2: p. 388)
Record Booklet cover (Form 1: p. 362; Form 2: p. 380)

Procedure

1. Prior to testing, practice the words on the list, saying them clearly in a normal voice.

2. Do not rush the student during the assessment. Place a ✓ in the appropriate column, total correct responses, and record the score in the box.

3. If the student misses a pair or asks for one to be repeated, move on to the next item and return to any such items at the conclusion of the test.

4. Facing the student, say:

   "Listen to the words I am about to say: fair-far.

   Do they sound exactly the same or are they different? (For young children, you may prefer the words 'alike' and 'not alike' in place of the words 'same' and 'different.')

   Yes, they are different.

   Listen to these two words: cap-cap.

   Are they the same or different?

   Now I am going to read you more pairs of words. I want you to tell me if they are the same or different. Do you understand what you are to do? Please turn your back to me and listen very carefully."

5. Say all the words distinctly but in a normal voice.

6. Be alert for students who do not understand the concepts "same" and "different."

Scoring and Interpretation

Note the number of correct responses, enter the total in the box, and enter this score on the front of the Record Booklet. Based on the score, make a judgment of the student's auditory discrimination ability, and record an X on the continuum located on the cover of the Record Booklet.

For teaching strategies, consult Section 3.2 in Elish-Piper, Johns, and Lenski (2006) and/or 2.4 and 2.6 in Johns and Lenski (2010).

Phoneme Awareness (Spelling)*

Overview

This brief spelling test will help assess the student's ability to associate letters with the sounds in words.

Materials Needed:

Pencil

Phoneme Awareness for the student (Form 1: p. 371; Form 2: p. 389)

Record Booklet cover (Form 1: p. 362; Form 2: p. 380)

Procedure

1. Say, **"I'm going to ask you to spell some words. Before you spell them, let's do a couple together."** Begin by modeling the spelling of *mat* by asking the student to think about what letter comes first, what next, and so on. You could say:

   "Let's begin with the word *mat*."

   "What letter comes first in *mat*?" If the student says *m*, write the *m* on the record sheet. If the student says an incorrect letter, say, **"No, it is an *m*."**

   Ask the student to say the word *mat* and ask, **"What else do you hear?"** If the student says *t*, write it on the record sheet with a space for the vowel. If necessary, correct the student by using a comment similar to that already mentioned.

   Ask, **"What else do you hear?"** If the student says *e*, say, **"No, it is an *a*."** Write the word and show it to the student.

2. Repeat the above process with *lip*. If the student is able to say the correct beginning letters for *mat* and *lip*, begin the test without any additional prompting.

3. Give the student the pencil and begin to dictate the 12 words in sentences. You may help once on the first letter for the words *back* and *feet*. No help should be given on the remaining words. The student can say the word out loud as it is being written. If the student asks how to form a letter and asks for it specifically, you may show the student how the letter is made.

4. Observe the spelling and ask the student to identify any letters that are unreadable.

5. If the student is unable to provide the correct initial consonant on *both* the sample words *and* the first two test words, stop the test.

6. The twelve words and sentences are:

1. back	I came back to school.	7. side	I'm at the side door.
2. feet	My feet are small.	8. chin	I hurt my chin.
3. step	I took a big step.	9. dress	You can dress yourself.
4. junk	I have junk in my desk.	10. peeked	I peeked in the box.
5. picking	I am picking up paper.	11. lamp	Turn off the lamp.
6. mail	Please mail the letter.	12. road	The road is bumpy.

Scoring and Interpretation

Count the number of correct responses and place the score in the box on the record sheet and on the front of the Record Booklet. Then make an overall judgment of the student's spelling. You may want to make separate judgments for "B" beginnings, "M" middles, and "E" ends. Be sure your focus is on sounds, not letters. For *junk*, both *j* and *g* would be considered correct. Record B, M, and E on the continuum located on the cover of the Record Booklet and use an X to represent your overall assessment.

For teaching strategies, consult Sections 3.2 and 3.3 in Elish-Piper, Johns, and Lenski (2006) and/or 2.4 in Johns and Lenski (2010).

*Based on the work of Darrell Morris.

357

Phoneme Segmentation

Overview

This test assesses the student's ability to segment phonemes or sounds in spoken words. This ability is strongly related to success in reading and spelling acquisition.

Note: This assessment was designed for use with English speaking kindergartners. It may also be used with older students experiencing difficulty in literacy acquisition.

Materials Needed:

Phoneme Segmentation in the Record Booklet (Form 1: p. 372; Form 2: p. 390)
Record Booklet cover (Form 1: p. 362; Form 2: p. 380)

Procedure

1. Duplicate the appropriate section of the Record Booklet.

2. With the student, say **"We're going to play a word game. I'm going to say a word and I want you to break the word apart. You are going to tell me each sound in the word in order. For example, if I say 'old,' you should say '/o/-/l/-/d/.'"** (Administrator: *Be sure to say the sounds, not the letters, in the word.*)

3. Then say: **"Let's try a few together."** The practice items are *ride, go,* and *man.* If necessary, help the student by segmenting the word for him or her. Encourage the student to repeat the segmented sounds. You could move a marker for each sound or drop a penny into a cup for each sound to highlight the segmentation.

4. During the test, feedback is provided to the student. You could nod or say "Right" or "That's right." If the student is incorrect, correct him or her. You should also provide the appropriate response.

5. Proceed through all 11 items. Circle those items that the student correctly segments. Incorrect responses may be recorded on the blank line following the item.

Scoring and Interpretation

The student's score is the number of items he or she correctly segments into all constituent phonemes. No partial credit is given. For example, *she* (item 5 in Form 1) contains two phonemes /sh/-/e/; *grew* (item 7 in Form 1) contains three phonemes /g/-/r/-/ew/; and *three* (item 15 in Form 2) contains three phonemes /th/-/r/-/ee/. If the student notes letter names instead of sounds, the response is coded as incorrect, and the type of error is noted in the Record Booklet. Such notes are helpful in understanding the student. Some students may partially segment, simply repeat the stimulus item, provide nonsense responses, or give letter names. Total the number of correct responses and place the score in the box on the record sheet and on the cover of the Record Booklet. Then make an overall judgment of the student's phoneme segmentation abilities. For further information on this test, see Hallie Kay Yopp, "A Test for Assessing Phonemic Awareness in Young Children," *The Reading Teacher,* 49 (September 1995), 20–29. A wide range of scores is likely.

For teaching strategies, consult Section 3.2 in Elish-Piper, Johns, and Lenski (2006) and/or 2.7 in Johns and Lenski (2010).

Basic Word Knowledge

Overview

This test contains ten words to help assess the student's ability to identify the most basic high-frequency words in English.

Materials Needed:

A 4" x 6" card

Basic Word Knowledge in the student booklet (Form 1: p. 113; Form 2: p. 121)

Basic Word Knowledge in the Record Booklet (Form 1: p. 373; Form 2: p. 391)

Record Booklet cover (Form 1: p. 362; Form 2: p. 380)

Procedure

1. Duplicate the appropriate section of the Record Booklet.

2. Give the page containing the words to the student with the words covered. Say, **"I want to see if you know some words. Let's begin with this one."**

3. Move the card below each word and ask the student to say the word. If the student says the number, cover it up and point to the word. Then proceed to the next word.

4. Encourage the student to say "pass" or "skip it" for any unknown words; say, **"Just do the best you can."** Stop if no response is given to the first four words.

5. As the student reads, note correct responses with a plus (+) in the appropriate place of the Record Booklet. See examples below:

Word	Meaning of Recording
+ men	Pronounced correctly
car can	Word mispronounced
DK girl	Don't know
h – him	Partial pronunciation

6. Proceed until you observe anxiety, frustration, or reluctance on the part of the student.

Scoring and Interpretation

Count the number of words pronounced correctly and record the score in the box on the record sheet and on the cover of the Record Booklet. Based on the correct responses, make a judgment of the student's word knowledge and record an X on the continuum located on the front of the Record Booklet. An informal analysis of incorrect responses should help you develop tentative instructional interventions for word identification. The words in the two forms account for over 25 percent of the running words in printed English.

For teaching strategies, consult Section 4.1 in Elish-Piper, Johns, and Lenski (2006) and/or 3.5 in Johns and Lenski (2010).

Pre-Primer Passages

Overview

The passages will help determine how well the student is able to read connected text.

Materials Needed:

A 3" x 5" card

Pat's Cat (p. 114) and/or The Red Hen (p. 115) in the student booklet for Form 1; Kim's Dog (p. 122) and/or The Red Bird (p. 123) for Form 2

Pat's Cat (pp. 374–375) and/or The Red Hen (pp. 376–377) in the Record Booklet for Form 1; Kim's Dog (pp. 392–393) and/or The Red Bird (pp. 394–395) for Form 2

Record Booklet cover (Form 1: p. 362; Form 2: p. 380)

Procedure

1. Duplicate the appropriate section of the Record Booklet.

2. Place a passage before the student, and cover everything but the title and illustration. Activate the student's background by saying, **"Look at the picture, and read the title to yourself. Then tell me what you think this might be about."** Informally judge the student's background knowledge and record an X along the continuum on the record sheet.

3. Then say, **"Read the story to me. I'll ask you to answer some questions when you are finished."** As the student reads, note any miscues using procedures explained in Section 2 of this manual. Record the number of miscues in the box on the record sheet.

4. When the student has finished reading, ask the comprehension questions or invite a retelling using procedures explained in Section 2 of this manual. If the questions were used, record the number of questions missed in the box on the record sheet.

Scoring and Interpretation

Use the scoring guides on the record sheet to evaluate word recognition and comprehension. There are also some specifics of word recognition and comprehension that you can evaluate on a scale of 1 to 5. Then make an overall qualitative judgment of the student's word recognition and comprehension by marking Xs on the continuums on the cover of the Record Booklet. Refer to this manual for general guidelines and examples of students' responses.

For teaching strategies, consult Sections 6.1 and 6.2 in Elish-Piper, Johns, and Lenski (2006) and/or chapters 2–6 in Johns and Lenski (2010).

Form 1

Early Literacy Assessments Record Booklet

Teacher Copy

 Note: This Record Booklet is on the CD that accompanies the Basic Reading Inventory.

Record Booklet for Early Literacy Assessments

Jerry L. Johns, Ph.D.

Student _____ Grade _____ Gender M F Date of Test _____

School _____ Examiner _____ Date of Birth _____

Address _____ Current Book/Level _____ Age _____

Profile of Emergent Reader Behavior

	Low or Not Evident	Some	High or Very Evident

Alphabet Knowledge

_____/26 upper case

_____/28 lower case

Writing

Literacy Knowledge

_____/20

Wordless Picture Reading

sense of story

connects pictures

language use

reading dictation

Caption Reading

words recognized

fluency

ability to repeat text

Auditory Discrimination

_____/12

Phoneme Awareness

_____/12

Phoneme Segmentation

_____/11

Basic Word Knowledge

_____/15

Pre-Primer Passages

word recognition

comprehension/retelling

Qualitative Analysis of Early Literacy Assessment Insights

General Directions: Note the degree to which the student shows behavior or evidence in the following areas. Space is provided for additional items.

	Not Evident Low Seldom Weak Poor				**Very Evident** High Always Strong Excellent

1. Alphabet knowledge
2. Writing
3. Literacy knowledge
4. Directionality of print
5. Sense of story
6. Tells story with pictures
7. Language use
8. Word knowledge
9. Fluency
10. Ability to repeat text
11. Phonemic awareness
12. Awareness of sounds
13. Spelling
14. Word recognition
15. Comprehension/retelling
16. Following directions
17. General engagement
18. _____
19. _____
20. _____

Alphabet Knowledge

(Student Booklet copy is on page 110.)

Brief Directions: Present the alphabet sheet to the student. Use 3" x 5" cards to block off everything but the lines being read. If necessary, point to each letter with a finger. Then say, **"Here are some letters. I want to see how many you know."** Place a + above correctly identified letters. Record the student's responses for incorrect letters. Total correct responses, and record the score in the box.

O	H	S	E	G	P	
X	V	I	M	J	D	K
B	T	R	Z	F	N	
Y	Q	W	C	U	A	L

☐ **Correct**

b	x	e	c	j	m	g
l	u	r	t	q	h	y
s	d	o	a	k	w	a
i	p	v	f	n	z	g

☐ **Correct**

Observations, Comments, Notes, and Insights

Writing

(No student copy; supply paper and writing instruments.)

Brief Directions: Give the student paper and pencil. Ask the student to do some writing. Record qualitative judgments, observations, and insights below.

	Not Evident / Low / Seldom / Weak / Poor				Very Evident / High / Always / Strong / Excellent

Directionality

Left to right

Top to bottom

Writing

Scribbles or "cursivelike" scribbles

Letterlike formations

Repeated letters, numbers, words

Variety of letters, numbers, words

Knowledge of first (F) and last (L) name

Letter-Sound Relationships

Represents sounds heard at word beginnings

Represents sounds heard at word endings

Represents sounds heard in middles of words

Writing Conventions

Use of word boundaries

Use of punctuation

Overall Message Intent (check one)

_____ Student indicated no message intent.

_____ Student talked about but did not read or pretend to read what was written.

_____ Student was able to read what was written.

Teacher could make sense of writing independently. _____ yes _____ no

Observations, Comments, Notes, and Insights

Literacy Knowledge

(Student Booklet copy of *New Shoes*)

Brief Directions: Show *New Shoes* to the student. Say, **"I'd like you to show me some of the things you know about reading. You won't have to read."** Ask the following questions as *you* read the book to the student. Circle correct (+) or incorrect (−) responses. Total correct responses.

Page

      +   −   1. Hand the book to the child and say, **"Show me the front of this book."**

1   +   −   2. Say, **"Point to where I should start reading."** *Read page 1.*

2   +   −   3. Ask, **"Which way should I go?"** Check for knowledge of left to right. *Read first line of page 2.*

2/3   +   −   4. Ask, **"Where should I go after that?"** Check for knowledge of a return sweep to the left. *Read rest of page 2 and page 3.*

3   +   −   5. On page 3, point to the comma and ask, **"What's this or what's this for?"**

4   +   −   6. *Read text on page 4.* Point to a period and ask, **"What's this or what's this for?"**

5   +   −   7. *Read text on page 5.* Point to the exclamation mark and ask, **"What's this or what's this for?"**

6   +   −   8. *Read text on page 6.* Point to the question mark and ask, **"What's this or what's this for?"**

6   +   −   9. Point to a lower-case letter (m, y, s) and say, **"Find a capital letter like this, find an upper-case letter like this, or find the big one like this."** Repeat for each letter.

7   +   −   10. *Read text on page 7.* Say, **"Show me one letter."** (Two 3" X 5" cards may be useful for items 10–19.)

      +   −   11. Say, **"Now show me two letters."**

      +   −   12. Say, **"Show me only one word."**

      +   −   13. Say, **"Now show me two words."**

      +   −   14. Say, **"Show me the first letter of a word."**

      +   −   15. Say, **"Show me the last letter of a word."**

      +   −   16. Say, **"Show me a long word."**

+   –   17. Say, **"Show me a short word."**

+   –   18. Say, **"Show me a sentence."**

8–9   +   –   19. ***Read text on pages 8 and 9.*** Point to a capital letter (I, O, M) and say, **"Find a small letter like this or find a lower-case letter like this."** Repeat for each letter.

10   +   –   20. ***Read text on page 10.*** Close the book, and hand it to the child with back cover showing and say, **"Show me the title or show me the name of the book."**

☐ **Total Correct**

Qualitative Judgments of Literacy Knowledge

	Not Evident Low Seldom Weak Poor				Very Evident High Always Strong Excellent
Overall engagement	⊢———┼———┼———┼———┤				
Understanding of print directionality	⊢———┼———┼———┼———┤				
Knowledge of punctuation	⊢———┼———┼———┼———┤				
Correspondence of upper-case with lower-case letters	⊢———┼———┼———┼———┤				
Knowledge of *letter* and *letters*	⊢———┼———┼———┼———┤				
Knowledge of *word* and *words*	⊢———┼———┼———┼———┤				
Ability to frame a sentence	⊢———┼———┼———┼———┤				

Observations, Comments, Notes, and Insights

Wordless Picture Reading

(Student Booklet copy is on page 111.) **Student's Dictation**

Caption Reading

(Student Booklet copy is on page 112.)

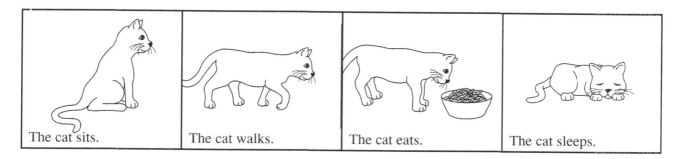

The cat sits. | The cat walks. | The cat eats. | The cat sleeps.

Qualitative Judgments of Caption Reading

If the student read the story, check the most characteristic statement:

_____ The student's reading is an exact match to the text.

_____ The student's reading closely matches the text.

_____ The student's reading is somewhat related to the text but is based on the illustrations.

_____ The student's reading is related mostly to the illustrations.

If you read the story first, check the statement most characteristic of the student's reading:

_____ The student used memory to read the text with high accuracy.

_____ The student used memory and illustrations to read the text with fair accuracy.

_____ The student seemed to use a combination of memory and mostly illustrations to read the text.

_____ The student did not seem to remember the reading and relied almost entirely on the illustrations to read the text.

	Not Evident Low Seldom Weak			Very Evident High Always Strong
Other Reading Behaviors	Poor			Excellent
Reads left to right	├───────┼───────┼───────┼───────┤
Reads top to bottom	├───────┼───────┼───────┼───────┤
Points to word and says it correctly	├───────┼───────┼───────┼───────┤
Demonstrates letter-sound relationships	├───────┼───────┼───────┼───────┤
Uses monitoring (rereads; corrects)	├───────┼───────┼───────┼───────┤
Points to correct words (if requested by you)	├───────┼───────┼───────┼───────┤
Engagement	├───────┼───────┼───────┼───────┤
Confidence as a reader	├───────┼───────┼───────┼───────┤

Auditory Discrimination

(No student copy is needed.)

			Correct	Incorrect
1. bad	—	dad	_____	_____
2. buff	—	bus	_____	_____
3. watch	—	watch	_____	_____
4. ball	—	bowl	_____	_____
5. fall	—	fall	_____	_____
6. sink	—	think	_____	_____
7. lag	—	lad	_____	_____
8. tot	—	top	_____	_____
9. set	—	sit	_____	_____
10. foam	—	phone	_____	_____
11. rode	—	rode	_____	_____
12. lab	—	lad	_____	_____

Total Correct [ ]

Phoneme Awareness (Spelling)

(Teacher and student copy)

_____

_____

1. _____

2. _____

3. _____

4. _____

5. _____

6. _____

7. _____

8. _____

9. _____

10. _____

11. _____

12. _____

☐ **Correct**   _____ Beginnings (B)   _____ Middles (M)   _____ Ends (E)

Observations, Comments, Notes, and Insights

Phoneme Segmentation*

(No student copy needed.)

Directions: Today we're going to play a word game. I'm going to say a word and I want you to break the word apart. You are going to tell me each sound in the word in order. For example, if I say "old," you should say "/o/-/l/-/d/." *(Administrator: Be sure to say the sounds, not the letters, in the word.)* Let's try a few together.

Practice items: *(Assist the child in segmenting these items as necessary.)* ride, go, man

Test items: *(Circle those items that the student correctly segments; incorrect responses may be recorded on the blank line following the item.)* The correct number of phonemes is indicated in parentheses.

1. dog (3) _____

2. keep (3) _____

3. fine (3) _____

4. no (2) _____

5. she (2) _____

6. wave (3) _____

7. grew (3) _____

8. that (3) _____

9. red (3) _____

10. me (2) _____

11. sat (3) _____

Total Correct [ ]

Adapted from Hallie Kay Yopp, "A Test for Assessing Phonemic Awareness in Young Children," *The Reading Teacher*, 49 (September 1995), 20–29.

Basic Word Knowledge

(Student Booklet copy is on page 113.)

Brief Directions: Present the list of words to the student. Ask the student to identify words. Say, **"I want to see if you know some words. Let's begin with this one."** Use a plus (+) for correct responses. Record the student's responses for incorrect words. Total correct responses and put the score in the box.

1. the _____

2. of _____

3. they _____

4. be _____

5. a _____

6. but _____

7. is _____

8. this _____

9. it _____

10. not _____

11. for _____

12. had _____

13. he _____

14. or _____

15. as _____

☐ Total Correct

Observations, Comments, Notes, and Insights

Pre-Primer Passages

Student Booklet copy is on page 114.

YYY (Pre-Primer 1) Activating Background: Look at the picture and read the title to yourself. Then tell me what you think this might be about.

Background: Low ├────────┼────────┤ High

Pat's Cat		MISCUES				Repetition	Self-Correction of Unacceptable Miscue	Meaning Change (Significant Miscue)
		Substitution	Insertion	Omission	Reversal			
Pat has a cat.	4							
The cat is big.	8							
The cat is black.	12							
Pat pets the cat.	16							
The cat likes Pat.	20							
TOTAL								

Total Miscues ☐   Significant Miscues ☐

Word Recognition Scoring Guide		
Total Miscues	Level	Significant Miscues
0	Independent	0
1	Ind./Inst.	—
2	Instructional	1
3	Inst./Frust.	2
4 +	Frustration	3 +

Oral Reading Rate	Norm Group Percentile
‾‾‾‾‾ WPM)1200	☐ 90 ☐ 75 ☐ 50 ☐ 25 ☐ 10

YYY (Pre-Primer 1)
Comprehension Questions

T   1. _____   What is this story mostly about?
            (a cat)

F   2. _____   Who pets the cat?
            (Pat)

F   3. _____   What color is the cat?
            (black)

E   4. _____   What might Pat feed the cat?
            (any logical response; cat food; scraps)

I   5. _____   Why do you think the cat likes Pat?
            (any logical response; Pat feeds it)

Retelling Notes

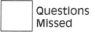 Questions Missed

Comprehension Scoring Guide	
Questions Missed	Level
0	Independent
1	Ind./Inst.
1½	Instructional
2	Inst./Frust.
2½ +	Frustration

Retelling Rubric for the Three Reading Levels
Independent Level/Excellent
Recalls central or key ideas
Remembers important facts
Retains the general sequence of events
Relates most of the content in an organized manner
Instructional Level/Satisfactory
Recalls most central or key ideas
Remembers some important facts
Retains the general sequence of events
Relates an overall sense of the content
Frustration Level/Unsatisfactory
Recalls bits of information in a haphazard manner
Little apparent organization

Qualitative Analysis of Word Identification and Comprehension			
(1 = not evident; 5 = very evident)			
Word Identification		Comprehension	
Uses graphophonic information	1 2 3 4 5	Makes predictions	1 2 3 4 5
Uses semantic information	1 2 3 4 5	Seeks to construct meaning	1 2 3 4 5
Uses syntactic information	1 2 3 4 5	Understands topic and major ideas	1 2 3 4 5
Knows basic sight words automatically	1 2 3 4 5	Remembers facts or details	1 2 3 4 5
Possesses sight vocabulary	1 2 3 4 5	Evaluates ideas from passages	1 2 3 4 5
Possesses numerous strategies	1 2 3 4 5	Makes and supports appropriate inferences	1 2 3 4 5
Uses strategies flexibly	1 2 3 4 5	Engagement with passage	1 2 3 4 5

Important Note: If the scoring guides are used, teacher judgment is especially important because of the length of the passage and the limited number of questions. Retelling may be particularly useful at this level.

Student Booklet copy is on page 115.

YY (Pre-Primer 2) Activating Background: Look at the picture and read the title to yourself. Then tell me what you think this might be about.

Background: Low ├──────┼──────┤ High

The Red Hen

		MISCUES						
	Substitution	Insertion	Omission	Reversal	Repetition	Self-Correction of Unacceptable Miscue	Meaning Change (Significant Miscue)	
The red hen sat on a nest. 7								
She had six eggs in the nest. 14								
She did not get up. 19								
She just sat on the eggs. 25								
TOTAL								

Total Miscues ☐   Significant Miscues ☐

Word Recognition Scoring Guide		
Total Miscues	Level	Significant Miscues
0	Independent	0
1	Ind./Inst.	—
2	Instructional	1
3	Inst./Frust.	2
4 +	Frustration	3 +

Oral Reading Rate	Norm Group Percentile	
____ / 1500 WPM	☐ 90 ☐ 75 ☐ 50 ☐ 25 ☐ 10	

YY (Pre-Primer 2)
Comprehension Questions

T 1. _____ What color was the hen?
           (red)

F 2. _____ How many eggs were in the nest?
           (six)

F 3. _____ Why was the hen sitting on the nest?
           (any logical response; to keep the eggs
           warm)

E 4. _____ Why did the hen not get up?
           (any logical response; she had to keep
           the eggs warm so they would hatch)

I 5. _____ What is a "nest"?
           (a place where a hen lays its eggs.)

Retelling Notes

☐ Questions
   Missed

Comprehension Scoring Guide	
Questions Missed	Level
0	Independent
1	Ind./Inst.
1½	Instructional
2	Inst./Frust.
2½ +	Frustration

Retelling Rubric for the Three Reading Levels

Independent Level/Excellent
Recalls central or key ideas
Remembers important facts
Retains the general sequence of events
Relates most of the content in an organized manner

Instructional Level/Satisfactory
Recalls most central or key ideas
Remembers some important facts
Retains the general sequence of events
Relates an overall sense of the content

Frustration Level/Unsatisfactory
Recalls bits of information in a haphazard manner
Little apparent organization

Qualitative Analysis of Word Identification and Comprehension
(1 = not evident; 5 = very evident)

Word Identification		Comprehension	
Uses graphophonic information	1 2 3 4 5	Makes predictions	1 2 3 4 5
Uses semantic information	1 2 3 4 5	Seeks to construct meaning	1 2 3 4 5
Uses syntactic information	1 2 3 4 5	Understands topic and major ideas	1 2 3 4 5
Knows basic sight words automatically	1 2 3 4 5	Remembers facts or details	1 2 3 4 5
Possesses sight vocabulary	1 2 3 4 5	Evaluates ideas from passages	1 2 3 4 5
Possesses numerous strategies	1 2 3 4 5	Makes and supports appropriate inferences	1 2 3 4 5
Uses strategies flexibly	1 2 3 4 5	Engagement with passage	1 2 3 4 5

Important Note: If the scoring guides are used, teacher judgment is especially important because of the length of the passage and the limited number of questions. Retelling may be particularly useful at this level.

Form 2

Early Literacy Assessments Record Booklet

Teacher Copy

 Note: This Record Booklet is on the CD that accompanies the Basic Reading Inventory.

Record Booklet for Early Literacy Assessments

Jerry L. Johns, Ph.D.

Student _____ Grade _____ Gender M F Date of Test _____

School _____ Examiner _____ Date of Birth _____

Address _____ Current Book/Level _____ Age _____

Profile of Emergent Reader Behavior

	Low or Not Evident	Some	High or Very Evident

Alphabet Knowledge

_____/26 upper case

_____/28 lower case

Writing

Literacy Knowledge

_____/20

Wordless Picture Reading

sense of story

connects pictures

language use

reading dictation

Caption Reading

words recognized

fluency

ability to repeat text

Auditory Discrimination

_____/12

Phoneme Awareness

_____/12

Phoneme Segmentation

_____/11

Basic Word Knowledge

_____/15

Pre-Primer Passages

word recognition

comprehension/retelling

Qualitative Analysis of Early Literacy Assessment Insights

General Directions: Note the degree to which the student shows behavior or evidence in the following areas. Space is provided for additional items.

| | Not Evident
Low
Seldom
Weak
Poor | | | | Very Evident
High
Always
Strong
Excellent |

1. Alphabet knowledge
2. Writing
3. Literacy knowledge
4. Directionality of print
5. Sense of story
6. Tells story with pictures
7. Language use
8. Word knowledge
9. Fluency
10. Ability to repeat text
11. Phonemic awareness
12. Awareness of sounds
13. Spelling
14. Word recognition
15. Comprehension/retelling
16. Following directions
17. General engagement
18. _____
19. _____
20. _____

Alphabet Knowledge

(Student Booklet copy is on page 118.)

Brief Directions: Present the alphabet sheet to the student. Use 3" x 5" cards to block off everything but the lines being read. If necessary, point to each letter with a finger. Then say, **"Here are some letters. I want to see how many you know."** Place a + above correctly identified letters. Record the student's responses for incorrect letters. Total correct responses, and record the score in the box.

```
X   V   I   M   J   D   K

O   H   S   E   G   P

Y   Q   W   C   U   A   L

B   T   R   Z   F   N
```

☐ **Correct**

```
l   u   r   t   q   h   y

b   x   e   c   j   m   g

i   p   v   f   n   z   g

s   d   o   a   k   w   ɑ
```

☐ **Correct**

Observations, Comments, Notes, and Insights

Writing

(No student copy; supply paper and writing instruments.)

Brief Directions: Give the student paper and pencil. Ask the student to do some writing. Record qualitative judgments, observations, and insights below.

	Not Evident **Low** **Seldom** **Weak** **Poor**				**Very Evident** **High** **Always** **Strong** **Excellent**

Directionality
Left to right

Top to bottom

Writing
Scribbles or "cursivelike" scribbles

Letterlike formations

Repeated letters, numbers, words

Variety of letters, numbers, words

Knowledge of first (F) and last (L) name

Letter-Sound Relationships
Represents sounds heard at word beginnings

Represents sounds heard at word endings

Represents sounds heard in middles of words

Writing Conventions
Use of word boundaries

Use of punctuation

Overall Message Intent (check one)

_____ Student indicated no message intent.

_____ Student talked about but did not read or pretend to read what was written.

_____ Student was able to read what was written.

Teacher could make sense of writing independently. _____ yes _____ no

Observations, Comments, Notes, and Insights

Literacy Knowledge

(Student Booklet copy of *A New Cat*)

Brief Directions: Show *A New Cat* to the student. Say, **"I'd like you to show me some of the things you know about reading. You won't have to read."** Ask the following questions as *you* read the book to the student. Circle correct (+) or incorrect (−) responses. Total correct responses.

Page

	+	−	1. Hand the book to the child and say, **"Show me the front of this book."**
1	+	−	2. Say, **"Point to where I should start reading."** *Read page 1.*
2	+	−	3. Ask, **"Which way should I go?"** Check for knowledge of left to right. *Read first line of page 2.*
2/3	+	−	4. Ask, **"Where should I go after that?"** Check for knowledge of a return sweep to the left. *Read rest of page 2 and page 3.*
3	+	−	5. On page 3, point to the comma and ask, **"What's this or what's this for?"**
4	+	−	6. *Read text on page 4.* Point to a period and ask, **"What's this or what's this for?"**
5	+	−	7. *Read text on page 5.* Point to the exclamation mark and ask, **"What's this or what's this for?"**
5	+	−	8. *Read text on page 6.* Point to the question mark and ask, **"What's this or what's this for?"**
6	+	−	9. Point to a lower-case letter (t and i) and say, **"Find a capital letter like this, find an upper-case letter like this, or find the big one like this."** Repeat for each letter.
7	+	−	10. *Read text on page 7.* Say, **"Show me one letter."** (Two 3" X 5" cards may be useful for items 10–19.)
	+	−	11. Say, **"Now show me two letters."**
	+	−	12. Say, **"Show me only one word."**
	+	−	13. Say, **"Now show me two words."**
	+	−	14. Say, **"Show me the first letter of a word."**
	+	−	15. Say, **"Show me the last letter of a word."**
	+	−	16. Say, **"Show me a long word."**

384

\+   –   17. Say, **"Show me a short word."**

\+   –   18. Say, **"Show me a sentence."**

8–9   +   –   19. ***Read text on pages 8 and 9.*** Point to a capital letter (N, I, M) and say, **"Find a small letter like this or find a lower-case letter like this."** Repeat for each letter.

\+   –   20. Close the book, and hand it to the child with back cover showing and say, **"Show me the title or show me the name of the book."**

☐ **Total Correct**

Qualitative Judgments of Literacy Knowledge

	Not Evident / Low / Seldom / Weak / Poor				Very Evident / High / Always / Strong / Excellent
Overall engagement	├─────┼─────┼─────┼─────┤				
Understanding of print directionality	├─────┼─────┼─────┼─────┤				
Knowledge of punctuation	├─────┼─────┼─────┼─────┤				
Correspondence of upper-case with lower-case letters	├─────┼─────┼─────┼─────┤				
Knowledge of *letter* and *letters*	├─────┼─────┼─────┼─────┤				
Knowledge of *word* and *words*	├─────┼─────┼─────┼─────┤				
Ability to frame a sentence	├─────┼─────┼─────┼─────┤				

Observations, Comments, Notes, and Insights

Wordless Picture Reading

(Student Booklet copy is on page 119.) **Student's Dictation**

Caption Reading

(Student Booklet copy is on page 120.)

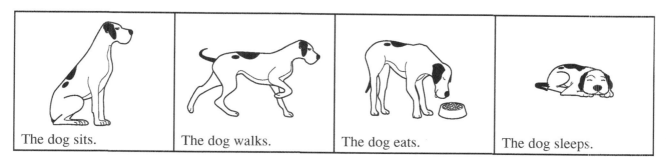

| The dog sits. | The dog walks. | The dog eats. | The dog sleeps. |

Qualitative Judgments of Caption Reading

If the student read the story, check the most characteristic statement:

_____ The student's reading is an exact match to the text.

_____ The student's reading closely matches the text.

_____ The student's reading is somewhat related to the text but is based on the illustrations.

_____ The student's reading is related mostly to the illustrations.

If you read the story first, check the statement most characteristic of the student's reading:

_____ The student used memory to read the text with high accuracy.

_____ The student used memory and illustrations to read the text with fair accuracy.

_____ The student seemed to use a combination of memory and mostly illustrations to read the text.

_____ The student did not seem to remember the reading and relied almost entirely on the illustrations to read the text.

Other Reading Behaviors	Not Evident / Low / Seldom / Weak / Poor			Very Evident / High / Always / Strong / Excellent
Reads left to right	├———————┼———————┼———————┼———————┤			
Reads top to bottom	├———————┼———————┼———————┼———————┤			
Points to word and says it correctly	├———————┼———————┼———————┼———————┤			
Demonstrates letter-sound relationships	├———————┼———————┼———————┼———————┤			
Uses monitoring (rereads; corrects)	├———————┼———————┼———————┼———————┤			
Points to correct words (if requested by you)	├———————┼———————┼———————┼———————┤			
Engagement	├———————┼———————┼———————┼———————┤			
Confidence as a reader	├———————┼———————┼———————┼———————┤			

Auditory Discrimination

(No student copy is needed.)

			Correct	Incorrect
1. bed	—	bad	_____	_____
2. moth	—	moss	_____	_____
3. look	—	look	_____	_____
4. sick	—	sit	_____	_____
5. get	—	get	_____	_____
6. fan	—	tan	_____	_____
7. mug	—	mud	_____	_____
8. tip	—	tick	_____	_____
9. hit	—	sit	_____	_____
10. pick	—	pin	_____	_____
11. sold	—	sold	_____	_____
12. gnat	—	nap	_____	_____

Total Correct ☐

Phoneme Awareness (Spelling)

(Teacher and student copy)

_____

_____

1. _____

2. _____

3. _____

4. _____

5. _____

6. _____

7. _____

8. _____

9. _____

10. _____

11. _____

12. _____

[ ] **Correct**   _____ Beginnings (B)   _____ Middles (M)   _____ Ends (E)

Observations, Comments, Notes, and Insights

Phoneme Segmentation*

(No student copy needed.)

Directions: Today we're going to play a word game. I'm going to say a word and I want you to break the word apart. You are going to tell me each sound in the word in order. For example, if I say "old," you should say "/o/-/l/-/d/." *(Administrator: Be sure to say the sounds, not the letters, in the word.)* Let's try a few together.

Practice items: *(Assist the child in segmenting these items as necessary.)* ride, go, man

Test items: *(Circle those items that the student correctly segments; incorrect responses may be recorded on the blank line following the item.)* The correct number of phonemes is indicated in parentheses.

1. lay (2) _____

2. race (3) _____

3. zoo (2) _____

4. three (3) _____

5. job (3) _____

6. in (2) _____

7. ice (2) _____

8. at (2) _____

9. top (3) _____

10. by (2) _____

11. do (2) _____

Total Correct ☐

Adapted from Hallie Kay Yopp, "A Test for Assessing Phonemic Awareness in Young Children," *The Reading Teacher*, 49 (September 1995), 20–29.

Basic Word Knowledge

(Student Booklet copy is on page 121.)

Brief Directions: Present the list of words to the student. Ask the student to identify words. Say, **"I want to see if you know some words. Let's begin with this one."** Use a plus (+) for correct responses. Record the student's responses for incorrect words. Total correct responses and put the score in the box.

1. and _____

2. to _____

3. with _____

4. are _____

5. at _____

6. in _____

7. by _____

8. that _____

9. have _____

10. was _____

11. I _____

12. you _____

13. from _____

14. on _____

15. at _____

☐ Total Correct

Observations, Comments, Notes, and Insights

Pre-Primer Passages

Student Booklet copy is on page 122.

ZZZ (Pre-Primer 1) Activating Background: Look at the picture and read the title to yourself. Then tell me what you think this might be about.

Background: Low ├─────┼─────┤ High

Kim's Dog		Substitution	Insertion	Omission	Reversal	Repetition	Self-Correction of Unacceptable Miscue	Meaning Change (Significant Miscue)
		MISCUES						
Kim has a dog.	4							
The dog is big.	8							
The dog is brown.	12							
Kim pets the dog.	16							
The dog likes Kim.	20							
TOTAL								

Total Miscues ☐   Significant Miscues ☐

Word Recognition Scoring Guide		
Total Miscues	Level	Significant Miscues
0	Independent	0
1	Ind./Inst.	—
2	Instructional	1
3	Inst./Frust.	2
4 +	Frustration	3 +

Oral Reading Rate	Norm Group Percentile
___ WPM)1200	☐ 90 ☐ 75 ☐ 50 ☐ 25 ☐ 10

ZZZ (Pre-Primer 1)
Comprehension Questions

T   1. _____ What is this story mostly about?
(a dog)

F   2. _____ Who pets the dog?
(Kim)

F   3. _____ What color is the dog?
(brown)

E   4. _____ What might Kim feed the dog?
(any logical response; dog food; scraps)

I   5. _____ Why do you think the dog likes Kim?
(any logical response; Kim feeds it)

Retelling Notes

☐ Questions Missed

Comprehension Scoring Guide	
Questions Missed	Level
0	Independent
1	Ind./Inst.
1½	Instructional
2	Inst./Frust.
2½ +	Frustration

Retelling Rubric for the Three Reading Levels
Independent Level/Excellent
Recalls central or key ideas
Remembers important facts
Retains the general sequence of events
Relates most of the content in an organized manner
Instructional Level/Satisfactory
Recalls most central or key ideas
Remembers some important facts
Retains the general sequence of events
Relates an overall sense of the content
Frustration Level/Unsatisfactory
Recalls bits of information in a haphazard manner
Little apparent organization

Qualitative Analysis of Word Identification and Comprehension			
(1 = not evident; 5 = very evident)			
Word Identification		Comprehension	
Uses graphophonic information	1 2 3 4 5	Makes predictions	1 2 3 4 5
Uses semantic information	1 2 3 4 5	Seeks to construct meaning	1 2 3 4 5
Uses syntactic information	1 2 3 4 5	Understands topic and major ideas	1 2 3 4 5
Knows basic sight words automatically	1 2 3 4 5	Remembers facts or details	1 2 3 4 5
Possesses sight vocabulary	1 2 3 4 5	Evaluates ideas from passages	1 2 3 4 5
Possesses numerous strategies	1 2 3 4 5	Makes and supports appropriate inferences	1 2 3 4 5
Uses strategies flexibly	1 2 3 4 5	Engagement with passage	1 2 3 4 5

Important Note: If the scoring guides are used, teacher judgment is especially important because of the length of the passage and the limited number of questions. Retelling may be particularly useful at this level.

Student Booklet copy is on page 123.

ZZ (Pre-Primer 2) Activating Background: Look at the picture and read the title to yourself. Then tell me what you think this might be about.

Background: Low ├──────┼──────┤ High

MISCUES							
The Red Bird	Substitution	Insertion	Omission	Reversal	Repetition	Self-Correction of Unacceptable Miscue	Meaning Change (Significant Miscue)
The red bird sat on a nest. 7							
She had three eggs in the nest. 14							
She did not get up. 19							
She just sat on the eggs. 25							
TOTAL							

Total Miscues ☐   Significant Miscues ☐

Word Recognition Scoring Guide		
Total Miscues	Level	Significant Miscues
0	Independent	0
1	Ind./Inst.	—
2	Instructional	1
3	Inst./Frust.	2
4 +	Frustration	3 +

Oral Reading Rate	Norm Group Percentile
‾‾‾‾ WPM $\overline{)1500}$	☐ 90 ☐ 75 ☐ 50 ☐ 25 ☐ 10

394

ZZ (Pre-Primer 2)
Comprehension Questions

T   1. _____   What color was the bird?
(red)

F   2. _____   How many eggs were in the nest?
(three)

F   3. _____   Why was the bird sitting on the nest?
(any logical response; to keep the eggs
warm; to hatch the eggs)

E   4. _____   Why did the bird not get up?
(any logical response; she had to keep
the eggs warm so they would hatch)

I   5. _____   What is a "nest"?
(a place where a bird lays its eggs.)

Retelling Notes

☐ Questions
Missed

Comprehension Scoring Guide	
Questions Missed	Level
0	Independent
1	Ind./Inst.
1½	Instructional
2	Inst./Frust.
2½ +	Frustration

Retelling Rubric for the Three Reading Levels
Independent Level/Excellent
Recalls central or key ideas
Remembers important facts
Retains the general sequence of events
Relates most of the content in an organized manner
Instructional Level/Satisfactory
Recalls most central or key ideas
Remembers some important facts
Retains the general sequence of events
Relates an overall sense of the content
Frustration Level/Unsatisfactory
Recalls bits of information in a haphazard manner
Little apparent organization

Qualitative Analysis of Word Identification and Comprehension				
(1 = not evident; 5 = very evident)				
Word Identification		Comprehension		
Uses graphophonic information	1 2 3 4 5	Makes predictions	1 2 3 4 5
Uses semantic information	1 2 3 4 5	Seeks to construct meaning	1 2 3 4 5
Uses syntactic information	1 2 3 4 5	Understands topic and major ideas	1 2 3 4 5
Knows basic sight words automatically	1 2 3 4 5	Remembers facts or details	1 2 3 4 5
Possesses sight vocabulary	1 2 3 4 5	Evaluates ideas from passages	1 2 3 4 5
Possesses numerous strategies	1 2 3 4 5	Makes and supports appropriate inferences	1 2 3 4 5
Uses strategies flexibly	1 2 3 4 5	Engagement with passage	1 2 3 4 5

Important Note: If the scoring guides are used, teacher judgment is especially important because of the length of the passage and the limited number of questions. Retelling may be particularly useful at this level.

PART FOUR
Appendices, References, and Index

APPENDIX **A**

Procedures for Eliciting and Evaluating Passage Retellings

How will this student retell her story?

- Retelling Procedure 1:
  Narrative Passages   400
- Retelling Procedure 2:
  Story Structure   401

- Retelling Procedure 3:
  Expository Passages   402

Retelling Procedure 1*

Narrative Passages

1. Ask the student to retell the passage by saying: "Tell me about (name of passage) as if you were telling it to someone who has never heard it before."

2. Use the following prompts only when necessary:

   "What comes next?"

   "Then what happened?"

   If the student stops retelling and does not continue with the above prompts, ask a question about the passage that is based on that point in the passage at which the student has paused. For example, "What did the boys do after raking the leaves?"

3. When a student is unable to retell the story, or if the retelling lacks sequence and detail, prompt the retelling step by step. The following questions may be helpful:

   "Who was the passage about?"

   "When did the story happen?"

   "Where did the story happen?"

   "What was the main character's problem?"

   "How did he (or she) try to solve the problem? What was done first/next?"

   "How was the problem solved?"

   "How did the story end?"

*Adapted from: Morrow, L. M. (1985). Retelling stories: A strategy for improving young children's comprehension, concept of story structure, and oral language complexity. *The Elementary School Journal, 85,* 647–661.

Retelling Procedure 2*

Story Structure

General Directions: To evaluate passages for story structure, place a plus (+) next to the element if the student includes it. Include the number of points scored for each element based on retelling.

1. *Characters* (5 points)   _____

   Introduction of characters (2 points main characters, 1 point for each additional, total of 5 points)

2. *Setting* (5 points)   _____

   A time or place where the story happens (5 points)

   OR

   A general setting statement (5 points)

3. *Theme* (10 points) = gist   _____

   Initiating events that set the goal for the story

   OR

   A goal becomes evident for the main character to achieve or a problem is evident to solve

4. *Plot Episodes* (10 points)   _____

   Events leading toward accomplishing the goal or solving the problem (adjust maximum raw score to equal 10 based on number of events)

5. *Resolution* (10 points)   _____

   The problem is solved or goal is reached (8 points)
   The story is ended (2 points)

6. *Sequence* (10 points)   _____

   Story is told with elements in the structural order listed above (10 points if all in order; 6.6 points if 3 in order; 3.3 points if 2 in order; 1 point if 1 in order; 0 if none in order; omitted elements are not scored)

Total Points _____

× 2

Retelling Score   ☐
(out of 100)

---

*Adapted from: Grant, J. (1984). Deciding what's important for readers to remember. Paper presented at the Annual Conference of the International Reading Association, Atlanta.

Retelling Procedure 3*

Expository Passages

Independent Level

Retelling will generally reflect:

1. the text structure
2. organization of how the material was presented
3. main ideas and details contained in the material

Instructional Level

Retelling will generally reflect:

1. less content than at an independent level
2. some minor misinterpretations and inaccuracies
3. organization that differs, in some respects, to the way it was presented in the material

Frustration Level

Retelling will generally be:

1. haphazard
2. incomplete
3. characterized by bits of information not related in any logical or sequential order

*Adapted from: Johnson, M. S., Kress, R. A., & Pikulski, J. J. (1987). *Informal reading inventories* (2nd ed.) Newark, DE: International Reading Association.

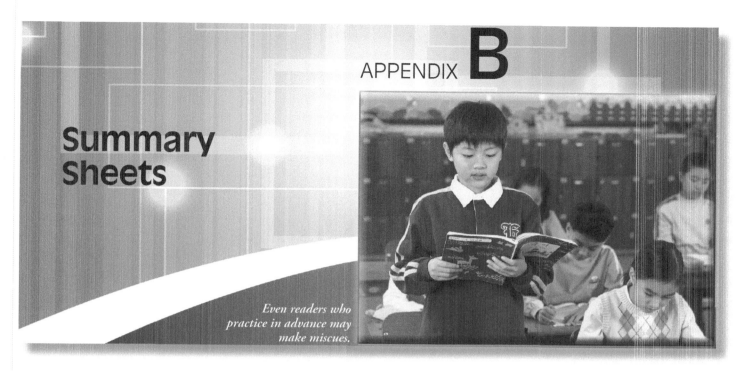

APPENDIX **B**

Summary Sheets

Even readers who practice in advance may make miscues.

- Miscue Summary Sheet for Forms LL and LI   405
- Summary of Student's Oral Reading Performance on the Basic Reading Inventory   407
- Miscue Tally and Reading Behavior Summary Charts for the Basic Reading Inventory   408
- Qualitative Summary of Miscues on the Basic Reading Inventory   409

- Summary of Student's Comprehension Performance on the Basic Reading Inventory   410
- Informal Assessment of Comprehension Engagement on the Basic Reading Inventory   411
- Expert Noticing Observation Guide   412
- Class Summary Chart for the Basic Reading Inventory   413

 Note: These summary sheets are on the CD that accompanies the Basic Reading Inventory.

403

Miscue Summary Sheet
for Forms LL and LI

MISCUES					Repetition	Self-Correction of Unacceptable Miscue	Meaning Change (Significant Miscue)
Substitution	Insertion	Omission	Reversal				

Name _____ Date _____

Passage Title _____

Form _____

Total Miscues [ ]   Significant Miscues [ ]

Summary of Student's Oral Reading Performance on the Basic Reading Inventory

Student _____ Grade _____

Examiner _____ Date _____

SUMMARY OF STUDENT'S MISCUES IN ORAL READING			
Substitutions			
Different Beginnings	**Different Middles**	**Different Endings**	**Different in Several Parts**

Insertions	**Omissions**	**Repetitions**	**Miscellaneous**

Miscue Tally and Reading Behavior Summary Charts for the Basic Reading Inventory

Student _____ Grade _____

Examiner _____ Date _____

Directions: Record the number of miscues from all passages at the student's independent, instructional, and instructional/frustration levels. Total each category. Follow the same procedure for the other reading behaviors. Then make qualitative judgments about the student's reading and check the appropriate columns at the bottom of the cover page of the performance booklet.

Passages Read	Type of Miscue			
	Substitution	Insertion	Omission	Reversal
PP1				
PP2				
P				
1				
2				
3				
4				
5				
6				
7				
8				
TOTALS				

Passages Read	Other Reading Behaviors		
	Repetition	Self-Correction of Unacceptable Miscue	Meaning Change
PP1			
PP2			
P			
1			
2			
3			
4			
5			
6			
7			
8			
TOTALS			

Qualitative Summary of Miscues on the Basic Reading Inventory

Student _____ Grade _____

Examiner _____ Date _____

MISCUE	TEXT	GRAPHIC SIMILARITY			CONTEXT		Self-Correction of Unacceptable Miscues
		Beginning	Middle	End	Acceptable	Unacceptable	
	Column Total						
	Number of Miscues Analyzed						
	Percentage						

PREDICTION STRATEGY

Graphic Similarity

B   M   E

100% 90 80 70 60 50 40 30 20 10

___% ___% ___%

Miscues Acceptable in Context

100% 90 80 70 60 50 40 30 20 10

___%

CORRECTION STRATEGY

Unacceptable Miscues Self-Corrected

100% 90 80 70 60 50 40 30 20 10

___%

Summary of Student's Comprehension Performance on the Basic Reading Inventory

Student _____ Grade _____

Examiner _____ Date _____

ANALYSIS BY TYPE OF QUESTION

Grade	Fact Oral	Fact Silent	Topic Oral	Topic Silent	Evaluation Oral	Evaluation Silent	Inference Oral	Inference Silent	Vocabulary Oral	Vocabulary Silent
P	__/6	__/6	__/1	__/1	__/1	__/1	__/1	__/1	__/1	__/1
1	__/6	__/6	__/1	__/1	__/1	__/1	__/1	__/1	__/1	__/1
2	__/6	__/6	__/1	__/1	__/1	__/1	__/1	__/1	__/1	__/1
3	__/6	__/6	__/1	__/1	__/1	__/1	__/1	__/1	__/1	__/1
4	__/6	__/6	__/1	__/1	__/1	__/1	__/1	__/1	__/1	__/1
5	__/6	__/6	__/1	__/1	__/1	__/1	__/1	__/1	__/1	__/1
6	__/6	__/6	__/1	__/1	__/1	__/1	__/1	__/1	__/1	__/1
7	__/6	__/6	__/1	__/1	__/1	__/1	__/1	__/1	__/1	__/1
8	__/6	__/6	__/1	__/1	__/1	__/1	__/1	__/1	__/1	__/1
9	__/6	__/6	__/1	__/1	__/1	__/1	__/1	__/1	__/1	__/1
10	__/6	__/6	__/1	__/1	__/1	__/1	__/1	__/1	__/1	__/1
11	__/6	__/6	__/1	__/1	__/1	__/1	__/1	__/1	__/1	__/1
12	__/6	__/6	__/1	__/1	__/1	__/1	__/1	__/1	__/1	__/1
Ratio Missed	__/__	__/__	__/__	__/__	__/__	__/__	__/__	__/__	__/__	__/__
Percent Missed	__%	__%	__%	__%	__%	__%	__%	__%	__%	__%
Total Ratio Missed	__/__		__/__		__/__		__/__		__/__	
Total Percent Missed	__%		__%		__%		__%		__%	

ANALYSIS BY LEVEL OF COMPREHENSION

	Lower-Level Comprehension (Fact Questions Only) Oral	Silent	Higher-Level Comprehension (All Other Questions) Oral	Silent
Ratio Missed	__/__	__/__	__/__	__/__
Total Ratio Missed	__/__		__/__	
Total Percent Missed	__%		__%	

Informal Assessment of Comprehension Engagement on the Basic Reading Inventory

Student _____ Grade _____

Examiner _____ Date _____

	PP1	PP2	P	1	2	3	4	5	6	7	8	9	10	11	12
Correct responses especially full, fresh, or elaborated (numerals circled)*															
Incongruent/incorrect responses **unrelated** to the passage in some meaningful, logical way (numerals with Xs)*															

*Refers to numerals beside the comprehension questions in the performance booklet.

Informal Guidelines for Evaluating Engagement

1. More than one elaboration of a correct response per passage "can be taken as evidence of an alert mind that is engaged and being driven by meaning. It is too soon to say if any significant meanings can be attached to the absence of elaborations, or how much of this can be expected with different types of questions and formats" (Manzo & Manzo, 1993, p. 467).

2. More than three incongruent responses to comprehension questions are "an indication that engagement was weak and nonproductive" (Manzo & Manzo, 1993, p. 467).

Expert Noticing Observation Guide

Student _____ Grade _____

Examiner _____ Date _____

Question	Your Notes
What did you see the student do?	
Why is this important?	
What did you notice about the way the student responded to reading/writing/ discussion activities in terms of the knowledge, strategies, and dispositions necessary to perform the tasks?	
Why do you think the student responded this way?	
What do the student's responses tell you about how well the student understood tasks?	
What did you learn about the student that will be helpful in planning an appropriate lesson or intervention?	

Class Summary Chart for the Basic Reading Inventory

Student _____ Grade _____

Examiner _____ Date _____

| Student | Date | Levels | | | | Consistent Strengths (+) and/or Weaknesses (−) | | | | | | | | | | | | |
| | | | | | | Comprehension | | | | | Word Recognition | | | | | | | |
		Ind.	Inst.	Frust.	Lis.	Fact	Topic	Inference	Evaluation	Vocabulary	Substitutions	Corrections	Repetitions	Omissions	Punctuation	Phonics	Context

References

Ackland, R. T. (1994). *Let's look at reading: Interactive professional development using informal reading inventories*. Retrieved from ProQuest Digital Dissertations. (AAT 9506465)

Adams, M. J. (1990). *Beginning to read: Thinking and learning about print* (a summary prepared by S. A. Stahl, J. Osborn, & F. Lehr). Champaign: University of Illinois.

Allington, R. L. (2005). The other five "pillars" of effective reading instruction. *Reading Today, 22*, 3.

Allington, R. L. (2012). *What really matters for struggling readers: Designing research-based programs* (3rd ed.). Boston: Pearson.

Allington, R. L., & McGill-Franzen, A. (1980). Word identification errors in isolation and in context: Apples vs. oranges. *The Reading Teacher, 33*, 795–800.

Alvermann, D. E. (1985). Interfacing microcomputers with video-cassettes: A program for teaching the IRI. Paper presented at the meeting of the College Reading Association, Pittsburgh.

Anderson, B., & Joels, R. W. (1986). Informal reading inventories. *Reading Improvement, 23*, 299–302.

Antunez, B. (2002). Implementing reading first with English language learners. *Directions in Language and Education, 15*. Retrieved January 20, 2012 from http://www.ncela.gwu.edu/files/rcd/BE024311/15.pdf

Applegate, M. D., Quinn, K. B., & Applegate, A. J. (2004). *The critical reading inventory*. Columbus, OH: Merrill Prentice Hall.

Applegate, M. D., Quinn, K. B., & Applegate, A. J. (2008). *The critical reading inventory* (2nd ed.). Upper Saddle River, NJ: Pearson Education.

Bader, L. A. (1998). *Bader reading and language inventory* (3rd ed.). Upper Saddle River, NJ: Prentice-Hall.

Bader, L. A. (2002). *Bader reading and language inventory* (4th ed.). Columbus, OH: Merrill Prentice Hall.

Bader, L. A. (2005). *Bader reading and language inventory* (5th ed.). Upper Saddle River, NJ: Merrill Prentice Hall.

Barr, R., Blachowicz, C. L. Z., Bates, A., Katz, C., & Kaufman, B. (2007). *Reading diagnoses for teachers: An instructional approach* (5th ed.). Boston: Allyn & Bacon.

Bass, J. F., Dasinger, S., Elish-Piper, L., Matthews, M. W., & Risko, V. J. (2008). *A declaration of readers' rights: Renewing our commitment to students*. Boston: Allyn & Bacon.

Beldin, H. O. (1970). Informal reading testing: Historical review and review of the research. In W. K. Durr (Ed.), *Reading difficulties: Diagnosis, correction, and remediation* (pp. 67–84). Newark, DE: International Reading Association.

Berliner, D. C. (1981). Academic learning time and reading achievement. In J. T. Guthrie (Ed.), *Comprehension and teaching: Research reviews* (pp. 203–226). Newark, DE: International Reading Association.

Betts, E. A. (1936). *The prevention and correction of reading difficulties*. Evanston, IL: Row, Peterson and Company.

Betts, E. A. (1941). Reading problems at the intermediate grade level. *The Elementary School Journal, 40*, 737–746.

Betts, E. A. (1946). *Foundations of reading instruction*. New York: American Book Company.

Betts, E. A. (1949). Adjusting instruction to individual needs. In N. B. Henry (Ed.), *Reading in the elementary school* (pp. 266–280). The Forty-Eighth Yearbook of the National Society for the Study of Education, Part II. Chicago: The University of Chicago Press.

Betts, E. A., Everett, M., & Rodewald, F. (1936). Remedial reading. *Journal of Exceptional Children, 2*, 88–91.

Bieber, G. A. (2011a). *The technical adequacy of the Basic Reading Inventory: An analysis of reliability and validity*. Retrieved from ProQuest Digital Dissertations. (AAT 3460570)

Bieber, G. A. (2011b). *Basic Reading Inventory: Accuracy data tables*. Unpublished manuscript.

Blanchard, J. S. (1985). *Computer-based reading assessment instrument*. Dubuque, IA: Kendall Hunt.

Block, C. C. (2003). *Literacy difficulties: Diagnosis and instruction for reading specialists and classroom teachers* (2nd ed.). Boston: Allyn & Bacon.

Bolenius, E. M. (1919). *Teacher's manual of silent and oral reading*. Boston: Houghton Mifflin.

Botel, M. (1966). *Botel reading inventory*. Chicago: Follett Educational Corporation.

Bristow, P. S., Pikulski, J. J., & Pelosi, P. L. (1983). A comparison of five estimates of reading instructional level. *The Reading Teacher, 37*, 273–279.

Brittain, M. M. (1970). Informal reading procedures: Some motivational considerations. *The Reading Teacher, 24*, 216–219.

Brown, J., Goodman, K. S., & Marek, A. M. (Comps. and Eds.). (1996). *Studies in miscue analysis: An annotated bibliography*. Newark, DE: International Reading Association.

Brown, S. R. (1963). *A comparison of five widely used standardized reading tests and an informal reading inventory for a selected group of elementary school children*. Retrieved from ProQuest Digital Dissertations. (AAT 6404441)

Brozo, W. G., & Afflerbach, P. P. (2011). *Adolescent reading inventory, Grades 6–12*. Boston: Allyn & Bacon.

Burke, C. L., & Goodman, K. S. (1970). When a child reads: A psycholinguistic analysis. *Elementary English, 47*, 121–129.

Burkins, J. M., & Croft, M. M. (2010). *Preventing misguided reading: New strategies for guided reading teachers*. Newark, DE: International Reading Association.

Burns, P. C., & Roe, B. D. (1989). *Burns/Roe informal reading inventory* (3rd ed.). Boston: Houghton Mifflin.

Burns, P. C., & Roe, B. D. (1993). *Burns/Roe informal reading inventory* (4th ed.). Boston: Houghton Mifflin.

Burns, P. C., & Roe, B. D. (1999). *Informal reading inventory* (5th ed.). Boston: Houghton Mifflin.

Burns, P. C., & Roe, B. D. (2002). *Informal reading inventory* (6th ed.). Boston: Houghton Mifflin.

Burns, P. C., Roe, B. D., & Ross, E. P. (1996). *Teaching reading in today's elementary schools*. Boston: Houghton Mifflin.

Buros, O. K. (1972). *The seventh mental measurements yearbook*. Highland Park, NJ: The Gryphon Press.

Caldwell, J. (1985). A new look at the old informal reading inventory. *The Reading Teacher, 39*, 168–173.

Caldwell, J. S., & Leslie, L. (2005). *Intervention strategies to follow informal reading inventory assessment*. Boston: Allyn & Bacon.

Caldwell, J. S., & Leslie, L. (2009). *Intervention strategies to follow informal reading inventory assessment: So what do I do now?* (2nd ed.). New York: Pearson.

Carnine, D. W., Silbert, J., Kame'enui, E. J., & Tarver, S. G. (2004). *Direct instruction reading* (4th ed.). Upper Saddle River, NJ: Pearson.

Carroll, J. B., Davies, P., & Richman, B. (1971). *Word frequency book*. Boston: Houghton Mifflin.

Carver, R. P. (1989). Silent reading rates in grade equivalents. *Journal of Reading Behavior, 21*, 155–166.

Christie, J. F. (1979). The qualitative analysis system: Updating the IRI. *Reading World, 18*, 393–199.

Cohn, M., & D'Alessandro, C. (1978). When is a decoding error not a decoding error? *The Reading Teacher, 32*, 341–144.

Conrad, L. L., & Shanklin, N. L. (1999). Using miscues to understand students' reading. *Colorado Reading Council Journal, 10*, 21–32.

Cooper, J. D., & Kiger, N. D. (2003). *Literacy: Helping children construct meaning* (5th ed.). Boston: Houghton Mifflin.

Cooper, J. D., & Kiger, N. D. (2011). *Literacy assessment: Helping teachers plan instruction*. Belmont, CA: Wadsworth.

Cooper, J. L. (1952). *The effect of adjustment of basal reading materials on reading achievement*. (Unpublished doctoral dissertation). Boston University, Boston.

Cooter, R. B., Jr., & Perkins, J. H. (2007). Looking to the future with *The Reading Teacher*: 900-year-old sheep and *Papa na come! The Reading Teacher, 61*, 4–7.

Cooter, R. B., Jr., Flynt, E. S., & Cooter, K. S. (2007). *Comprehensive reading inventory: Measuring reading development in regular and special education classrooms*. Upper Saddle River, NJ: Merrill Prentice Hall.

Council of Chief State School Officers & National Governors Association. (2010). *Common core state standards for English language arts & literacy in history/social studies, science, and technical subjects.* Retrieved June 3, 2011 from www.corestandards.org.

Cummins, C. (Ed.). (2006). *Understanding and implementing reading first initiatives.* Newark, DE: International Reading Association.

Cunningham, P. M., Hall, D. P., & Defee, M. (1991). Non-ability grouped, multilevel instruction: A year in a first-grade classroom. *The Reading Teacher, 44*, 566–571.

Dale, E., & O'Rourke, J. (1976). *The living word vocabulary: The words we know.* Elgin, IL: Dome.

D'Angelo, K., & Wilson, R. M. (1979). How helpful is insertion and omission miscue analysis? *The Reading Teacher, 32*, 519–520.

Dunkeld, C. G. (1970). *The validity of the informal reading inventory for the designation of instructional reading levels: A study of the relationships between children's gains in reading achievement and the difficulty of instructional materials.* Retrieved from ProQuest Digital Dissertations. (AAT 7114733)

Durrell, D. (1937). Individual differences and their implications with respect to instruction in reading. In G. M. Whipple (Ed.), *The teaching of reading* (pp. 325–356). The Thirty-Sixth Yearbook of the National Society for the Study of Education, Part I. Bloomington, IL: Public School Publishing Company.

Ekwall, E. E. (1974). Should repetitions be counted as errors? *The Reading Teacher, 27*, 365–367.

Ekwall, E. E. (1976). Informal reading inventories: The instructional level. *The Reading Teacher, 29*, 662–665.

Ekwall, E. E. (1986). *Ekwall reading inventory* (2nd ed.). Boston: Allyn & Bacon.

Ekwall, E. E., & Shanker, J. L. (1993). *Ekwall/Shanker reading inventory* (3rd ed.). Boston: Allyn & Bacon.

Elish-Piper, L., Johns, J. L., & Lenski, S. D. (2006). *Teaching reading pre-K–grade 3* (3rd ed.). Dubuque, IA: Kendall Hunt.

Emans, R. (1965). Teacher evaluation of reading skills and individualized reading. *Elementary English, 42*, 258–260.

Enz, B. (1989). *The 90% success solution.* Paper presented at the International Reading Association annual convention, New Orleans.

Estes, T. H., & Vaughan, J. L., Jr. (1973). Reading interest and comprehension: Implications. *The Reading Teacher, 27*, 149–153.

Evory, A. (Ed.). (1978). *Contemporary authors* (1st rev., vols. 33–36). Detroit: Gale Research Company, pp. 101–102.

Farr, R. (1992). Putting it all together: Solving the reading assessment puzzle. *The Reading Teacher, 4*, 26–37.

Felknor, C. (2000). Use of individual reading inventories with fourth-grade students on individual literacy plans. *Colorado Reading Council Journal, 11*, 15–17.

Felknor, C., Winterscheidt, V., & Benson, L. (1999). Thoughtful use of individual reading inventories. *Colorado Reading Council Journal, 10*, 10–20.

Ferroli, L. (2008). Criteria for interpreting word list reading performances with informal reading inventories. Unpublished study, Rockford College.

Ferroli, L., & Turmo, G. (2005–2006). Breaking the code of book levels and literacy stages. *Illinois Reading Council Journal, 34*(1), 28–33.

Fink, R. (2006). *Why Jane and John couldn't read—and how they learned: A new look at striving readers.* Newark, DE: International Reading Association.

Flynt, E. S., & Cooter, R. B., Jr. (1993). *Reading inventory for the classroom.* Scottsdale, AZ: Gorsuch Scarisbrick.

Flynt, E. S., & Cooter, R. B., Jr. (1995). *Reading inventory for the classroom* (2nd ed.). Scottsdale, AZ: Gorsuch Scarisbrick.

Flynt, E. S., & Cooter, R. B., Jr. (1998). *Reading inventory for the classroom* (3rd ed.). Upper Saddle River, NJ: Prentice-Hall.

Flynt, E. S., & Cooter, R. B., Jr. (1999). *English-Español reading inventory for the classroom.* Upper Saddle River, NJ: Prentice-Hall.

Flynt, E. S., & Cooter, R. B., Jr. (2001). *Reading inventory for the classroom* (4th ed.). Upper Saddle River, NJ: Prentice-Hall.

Flynt, E. S., & Cooter, R. B., Jr. (2004). *Reading inventory for the classroom* (5th ed.). Upper Saddle River, NJ: Merrill Prentice Hall.

Forman, J., & Sanders, M. E. (1998). *Project leap first grade norming study: 1993–1998.* Unpublished manuscript.

Froese, V. (1974). Functional reading levels: From graded word lists? (Microfiche ED 102 520)

Fuchs, D., Fuchs, L. S., & Vaughn, S. (Eds.) (2008). *Response to intervention: A framework for reading educators.* Newark, DE: International Reading Association.

Gambrell, L. B., Wilson, R. M., & Gantt, W. N. (1981). Classroom observations of task-attending behaviors of good and poor readers. *Journal of Educational Research, 74,* 400–404.

Gates, A. I. (1935). *The improvement of reading* (Rev. ed.). New York: The Macmillan Company.

Gillet, J. W., & Temple, C. (1994). *Understanding reading problems: Assessment and instruction* (4th ed.). Glenview, IL: Scott, Foresman/Little Brown Higher Education.

Gillet, J. W., & Temple, C. (2000). *Understanding reading problems: Assessment and instruction* (5th ed.). New York: Addison Wesley Longman.

Gillet, J. W., Temple, C., & Crawford, A. N. (2004). *Understanding reading problems* (6th ed.). Boston: Allyn & Bacon.

Gillet, J. W., Temple, C. A., Temple, C. N., & Crawford, A. N. (2012). *Understanding reading problems: Assessment and instruction* (8th ed.). Boston: Allyn & Bacon.

Gillis, M. K., & Olson, M. W. (1985). *Elementary IRIs: Do they reflect what we know about text type/structure and comprehension?* Unpublished manuscript.

Goodman, K. S. (1965). A linguistic study of cues and miscues in reading. *Elementary English, 42,* 639–643.

Goodman, K. S. (1971). The search called reading. In H. M. Robinson (Ed.), *Coordinating reading instruction* (pp. 10–14). Glenview, IL: Scott, Foresman.

Goodman, K. S. (1973). Analysis of oral reading miscues: Applied psycholinguistics. In F. Smith (Ed.), *Psycholinguistics and reading* (pp. 158–176). New York: Holt, Rinehart and Winston.

Goodman, Y. M. (1972). Reading diagnosis—qualitative or quantitative? *The Reading Teacher, 26,* 32–37.

Goodman, Y. M., & Burke, C. L. (1972). *Reading miscue inventory manual: Procedure for diagnosis and evaluation.* New York: Macmillan.

Goodman, Y. M., & Marek, A. M. (1996). *Retrospective miscue analysis.* Katonah, NY: Richard C. Owen.

Goodman, Y. M., Watson, D. J., & Burke, C. L. (1987). *Reading miscue inventory: Alternative procedures.* New York: Richard C. Owen.

Graves, M. F., Juel, C., Graves, B. B., & Dewitz, P. (2011). *Teaching reading in the 21st century: Motivating all learners* (5th ed.). Boston: Allyn & Bacon.

Gray, W. S. (1916). Methods of testing reading II. *The Elementary School Journal, 16,* 281–298.

Gunning, T. G. (1998). *Assessing and correcting reading and writing difficulties.* Boston: Allyn & Bacon.

Gunning, T. G. (2000). *Creating reading instruction for all children* (3rd ed.). Boston: Allyn & Bacon.

Gunning, T. G. (2002). *Assessing and correcting reading and writing difficulties* (2nd ed.). Boston: Allyn & Bacon.

Gunning, T. G. (2003). *Creating literacy instruction for all children* (4th ed.). Boston: Allyn & Bacon.

Gunning, T. G. (2006). *Assessing and correcting reading and writing difficulties* (3rd ed.). Boston: Allyn & Bacon.

Gunning, T. G. (2008). *Creating literacy instruction for all students* (6th ed.). Boston: Allyn & Bacon.

Gunning, T. G. (2010a). *Assessing and correcting reading and writing difficulties* (4th ed.). Boston: Allyn & Bacon.

Gunning, T. G. (2010b). *Creating literacy instruction for all students* (7th ed.). Boston: Allyn & Bacon.

Haager, D., Klingner, J., & Vaughn, S. (2007). *Evidence-based reading practices for response to intervention.* Baltimore: Brooks.

Hanson, J. (2004). *Tell me a story: Developmentally appropriate retelling strategies.* Newark, DE: International Reading Association.

Hardy, N. D., & Jerman, M. E. (1985). *Readability estimator.* Seattle: Berta-Max.

Harris, A. J., & Sipay, E. R. (1990). *How to increase reading ability* (9th ed.). New York: Longman.

Harris, T. L., & Hodges, R. E. (Eds.). (1981). *A dictionary of reading and related terms.* Newark, DE: International Reading Association.

Harris, T. L., & Hodges, R. E. (Eds.). (1995). *The literacy dictionary: The vocabulary of reading and writing.* Newark, DE: International Reading Association.

Hasbrouck, J., & Tindal, G. A. (2006). Oral reading fluency norms: A valuable assessment tool for reading teachers. *The Reading Teacher, 59,* 636–644.

Hasbrouck, J. E., & Tindal, G. (1992). Curriculum-based oral reading fluency norms for students in grades 2 through 5. *Teaching Exceptional Children, 24,* 41–44.

Hays, W. S. (1975). Criteria for the instructional level of reading. (Microfiche ED 117 665)

Helgren-Lempesis, V. A., & Mangrum, C. T., II. (1986). An analysis of alternate-form reliability of three commercially prepared informal reading inventories. *Reading Research Quarterly, 21,* 209–215.

Homan, S. P., & Klesius, J. P. (1985). A re-examination of the IRI: Word recognition criteria. *Reading Horizons, 26,* 54–61.

Hood, J. (1978). Is miscue analysis practical for teachers? *The Reading Teacher, 32,* 260–266.

Hunt, L. C., Jr. (1970). The effect of self-selection, interest, and motivation upon independent, instructional, and frustrational levels. *The Reading Teacher, 24,* 146–151, 158.

International Reading Association. (2000). *Making a difference means making it different* (A Position Statement). Newark, DE: Author.

International Reading Association. (2007). *Teaching reading well: A synthesis of the International Reading Association's research on teacher preparation for reading instruction.* Newark, DE: Author.

IOX. (1980). *Basic skills word list: Grades 1–12.* Los Angeles: IOX.

Jennings, J. H., Caldwell, J., & Lerner, J. W. (2006). *Reading problems: Assessment and teaching strategies* (5th ed.). Boston: Allyn & Bacon.

Johns, J., Lenski, S., & Berglund, R. (2011). *Essential comprehension strategies for the intermediate grades.* Dubuque, IA: Kendall Hunt.

Johns, J. L. (1976). Informal reading inventories: A survey among professionals. *Illinois School Research and Development, 13,* 35–39.

Johns, J. L. (1978). *Basic reading inventory.* Dubuque, IA: Kendall Hunt.

Johns, J. L. (1981). *Advanced reading inventory.* Dubuque, IA: Wm. C. Brown.

Johns, J. L. (1985). *Basic reading inventory* (3rd ed.). Dubuque, IA: Kendall Hunt.

Johns, J. L. (1986). *Computer-based advanced reading inventory* (Grade 7–College). DeKalb, IL: Northern Illinois University.

Johns, J. L. (1988). *Basic reading inventory* (4th ed.). Dubuque, IA: Kendall Hunt.

Johns, J. L. (1990a). Informal reading inventories: A holistic consideration of the instructional level. In N. D. Padak, T. V. Rasinski, & J. Logan (Eds.), *Challenges in reading* (pp. 135–140). Twelfth Yearbook of the College Reading Association. Provo, UT: College Reading Association.

Johns, J. L. (1990b). *Secondary & college reading inventory* (2nd ed.). Dubuque, IA: Kendall Hunt.

Johns, J. L. (1991). Emmett A. Betts on informal reading inventories (Open to Suggestion Column). *Journal of Reading, 34,* 492–493.

Johns, J. L. (Comp.). (1993). *Informal reading inventories: An annotated reference guide.* DeKalb, IL: Northern Illinois University.

Johns, J. L. (1994). *Basic reading inventory* (6th ed.). Dubuque, IA: Kendall Hunt.

Johns, J. L. (1996). Using informal reading inventories in classroom and clinic. In L. R. Putnam (Ed.), *How to become a better reading teacher: Strategies for assessment and intervention* (pp. 113–122). Columbus, OH: Merrill.

Johns, J. L. (1997). *Basic reading inventory* (7th ed.). Dubuque, IA: Kendall Hunt.

Johns, J. L. (2001). *Basic reading inventory: Pre-primer through grade twelve and early literacy assessments* (8th ed.). Dubuque, IA: Kendall Hunt.

Johns, J. L. (2005). *Basic reading inventory: Pre-primer through grade twelve and early literacy assessments* (9th ed.). Dubuque, IA: Kendall Hunt.

Johns, J. L. (2007). Monitoring progress in fluency: Possible unintended consequences. *Reading Today, 24,* 18.

Johns, J. L. (2008a). *Basic reading inventory DVD and CD*. Dubuque, IA: Kendall Hunt.

Johns, J. L. (2008b). *Basic reading inventory: Pre-primer through grade twelve and early literacy assessments* (10th ed.). Dubuque, IA: Kendall Hunt.

Johns, J. L. (2012). *Basic reading inventory: Pre-primer through grade twelve and early literacy assessments* (11th ed.). Dubuque, IA: Kendall Hunt.

Johns, J. L., & Berglund, R. L. (2002). *Strategies for content area learning* (2nd ed.). Dubuque, IA: Kendall Hunt.

Johns, J. L., & Berglund, R. L. (2010). *Fluency: Differentiated interventions and progress-monitoring assessments*. Dubuque, IA: Kendall Hunt.

Johns, J. L., & Berglund, R. L. (2011). *Strategies for content area learning* (3rd ed.). Dubuque, IA: Kendall Hunt.

Johns, J. L., & Daniel, M. C. (2010). *Spanish reading inventory* (2nd ed.). Dubuque, IA: Kendall Hunt.

Johns, J. L., & L'Allier, S. K. (2003). How well can teachers determine reading levels from an informal reading inventory? In M. B. Sampson, P. E. Linder, J. R. Dugan, & B. Brancato (Eds.), *Celebrating the freedom of literacy* (pp. 251–264). Twenty-Fifth Yearbook of the College Reading Association. Commerce, TX: College Reading Association.

Johns, J. L., & L'Allier, S. K. (2004). How preservice teachers score an informal reading inventory: Strengths and weaknesses. In J. R. Dugan, P. E. Linder, M. B. Sampson, B. Brancato, & L. Elish-Piper (Eds.), *Celebrating the power of literacy* (pp. 254–267). Twenty-Sixth Yearbook of the College Reading Association. Readyville, TN: College Reading Association.

Johns, J. L., & L'Allier, S. K. (2007). *Improving preservice teachers' ability to determine significant miscues when using an informal reading inventory*. Paper presented at the International Reading Association annual convention, Toronto.

Johns, J. L., & Lenski, S. D. (1997). *Improving reading: A handbook of strategies* (2nd ed.). Dubuque, IA: Kendall Hunt.

Johns, J. L., & Lenski, S. D. (2005). *Improving reading: Strategies and resources* (4th ed.). Dubuque, IA: Kendall Hunt.

Johns, J. L., & Lenski, S. D. (2010). *Improving reading: Interventions, strategies, and resources* (5th ed.). Dubuque, IA: Kendall Hunt.

Johns, J. L., & Lenski, S. D. (2014). *Improving reading: Strategies, resources, and Common Core connections*. Dubuque, IA: Kendall Hunt.

Johns, J. L., & Magliari, A. M. (1989). Informal reading inventories: Are the Betts criteria the best criteria? *Reading Improvement, 26*, 124–132.

Johns, J. L., & VanLeirsburg, P. (1990). Portfolio assessment: A survey among professionals. Literacy research report no. 1. DeKalb, IL: Northern Illinois University Reading Clinic.

Johns, J. L., & VanLeirsburg, P. (1992). How professionals view portfolio assessment. *Reading Research and Instruction, 32*, 1–10.

Johns, J. L., Garton, S., Schoenfelder, P., & Skriba, P. (1977). *Assessing reading behavior: Informal reading inventories* (An Annotated Bibliography). Newark, DE: International Reading Association.

Johns, J. L., L'Allier, S. K., & Johns, B. (2012). Making the most of informal reading inventories: Moving from purposeful assessment to targeted instruction. In E. T. Ortlieb & E. H. Cheek, Jr. (Eds.), *Literacy research, practice, and evaluation: Vol. 1* (pp. 39–72). Using informative assessments towards effective literacy instruction. Bingley, UK: Emerald Group.

Johns, J. L., Lenski, S. D., & Berglund, R. L. (2006). *Comprehension and vocabulary strategies for the elementary grades* (2nd ed.). Dubuque, IA: Kendall Hunt.

Johnson, M. S., & Kress, R. A. (1965). *Informal reading inventories*. Newark, DE: International Reading Association.

Johnson, M. S., Kress, R. A., & Pikulski, J. J. (1987). *Informal reading inventories* (2nd ed.). Newark, DE: International Reading Association.

Johnston, P. (1983). Prior knowledge and reading comprehension test bias (Technical Report No. 289). Champaign, IL: Center for the Study of Reading.

Johnston, P., & Allington, R. (1991). Remediation. In R. Barr, M. L. Kamil, P. B. Mosenthal, & P. D. Pearson (Eds.), *Handbook of reading research, volume II* (pp. 984–1012). New York: Longman.

Jorgenson, G. W. (1977). Relationship of classroom behavior to the accuracy of the match between material difficulty and student ability. *Journal of Educational Psychology, 69*, 24–32.

Kalmbach, J. R. (1986). Evaluating informal methods for the assessment of retellings. *Journal of Reading, 30*, 119–127.

Kender, J. P. (1966). *Analysis of factors associated with informal reading tests at the eighth grade level.* (Unpublished doctoral dissertation). University of Pennsylvania, Philadelphia.

Kender, J. P. (1970). Informal reading inventories. *The Reading Teacher, 24*, 165–167.

Kibby, M. W. (1995). *Practical steps for informing literacy instruction: A diagnostic decision-making model.* Newark, DE: International Reading Association.

Killgallon, P. A. (1942). *A study of relationships among certain pupil adjustments in language situations.* Retrieved from ProQuest Digital Dissertations. (AAT 0000560)

Klesius, J. P., & Homan, S. P. (1985). A validity and reliability update on the informal reading inventory with suggestions for improvement. *Journal of Learning Disabilities, 18*, 71–76.

Kragler, S. (1996). Vygotsky and at-risk readers: Assessment and instructional implications. In L. Dixon-Kraus (Ed.). *Vygotsky in the classroom: Mediated literacy instruction and assessment* (pp. 149–160). White Plains, NY: Longman.

Ladd, E. M. (1961). *A comparison of two types of training with reference to developing skill in diagnostic oral reading testing.* Retrieved from ProQuest Digital Dissertations. (AAT 6105648)

Lenski, S., Wham, M. A., Johns, J., & Caskey, M. (2011). *Reading & learning strategies: Middle grades through high school* (4th ed.). Dubuque, IA: Kendall Hunt.

Lenski, S. D. (1998). *Schools that succeed on the IGAP reading test.* Bloomington, IL: Illinois Reading Council.

Lenski, S. D., & Johns, J. L. (2000). *Improving writing: Resources, strategies, and assessments.* Dubuque, IA: Kendall Hunt.

Lenski, S. D., Wham, M. A., & Johns, J. L. (1999). *Reading & learning strategies for middle & high school students.* Dubuque, IA: Kendall Hunt.

Lenski, S. D., Wham, M. A., Johns, J. L., & Caskey, M. M. (2006). *Reading and learning strategies: Middle grades through high school* (3rd ed.). Dubuque, IA: Kendall Hunt.

Leslie, L., & Caldwell, J. (1990). *Qualitative reading inventory.* Glenview, IL: Scott, Foresman/Little Brown Higher Education.

Leslie, L., & Caldwell, J. (1995). *Qualitative reading inventory—II.* New York: HarperCollins College Publishers.

Leslie, L., & Caldwell, J. (2001). *Qualitative reading inventory—3.* New York: Longman.

Leslie, L., & Caldwell, J. (2006). *Qualitative reading inventory—4.* Boston: Allyn & Bacon.

Leslie, L., & Caldwell, J. S. (2011). *Qualitative reading inventory—5.* Boston: Allyn & Bacon.

Leu, D. J., Jr., & Kinzer, C. K. (1987). *Effective reading instruction in the elementary grades.* Columbus: Merrill.

Leu, D. J., Jr., & Kinzer, C. K. (1999). *Effective literacy instruction, K–8* (4th ed.). Upper Saddle River, NJ: Prentice-Hall.

Lipson, M. Y., & Wixson, K. K. (1991). *Assessment and instruction of reading disability.* New York: HarperCollins.

Lipson, M. Y., & Wixson, K. K. (2000). *Assessment and instruction of reading and writing difficulty: An interactive approach* (3rd ed.). Boston: Allyn & Bacon.

Lipton, A. (1972). Miscalling while reading aloud: A point of view. *The Reading Teacher, 25*, 759–762.

Lowell, R. E. (1970). Problems in identifying reading levels with informal reading inventories. In W. K. Durr (Ed.), *Reading difficulties: Diagnosis, correction, and remediation* (pp. 120–126). Newark, DE: International Reading Association.

Lutes, M. (2004). *The effects of reading and writing strategies on reading comprehension.* (Unpublished Master's Thesis). Southeast Missouri State University, Cape Girardeau.

Maginnis, G. H. (1978). Emmett Albert Betts. In J. F. Ohles (Ed.), *Biographical dictionary of American educators* (Vol. 1, pp. 125–126). Westport, CT: Greenwood.

Mahdavi, J. N., & Haager, D. (2007). Linking progress monitoring results to interventions. *Perspectives on Language and Literacy, 33*(2), 25–29.

Manning, J. C. (1995). Ariston Metron. *The Reading Teacher, 48*, 650–659.

Manzo, A. V., & Manzo, U. C. (1993). *Literacy disorders.* Fort Worth, TX: Harcourt Brace Jovanovich.

Manzo, A. V., & Manzo, U. C. (1995). *Teaching children to be literate.* Fort Worth, TX: Harcourt Brace College Publishers.

Manzo, A. V., Manzo, U. C., & McKenna, M. C. (1995). *Informal reading-thinking inventory.* Fort Worth, TX: Harcourt Brace College Publishers.

Marcell, B. (2007). Fluency to a fault: Put fluency in the passenger seat and let comprehension take the wheel. *Reading Today, 24*, 18.

Marzano, R. J., Larson, J., Tish, G., & Vodehnal, S. (1978). The graded word list is not a shortcut to an IRI. *The Reading Teacher, 31*, 647–651.

McCormick, S. (1987). *Remedial and clinical reading instruction.* Columbus: Merrill.

McCormick, S. (1995). *Instructing students who have literacy problems.* Englewood Cliffs, NJ: Prentice-Hall.

McCormick, S. (1999). *Instructing students who have literacy problems* (3rd ed.). Upper Saddle River, NJ: Prentice-Hall.

McCormick, S. (2003). *Instructing students who have literacy problems* (4th ed.). Upper Saddle River, NJ: Pearson Education.

McCormick, S. (2007). *Instructing students who have literacy problems* (5th ed.). Upper Saddle River, NJ: Prentice Hall.

McCracken, R. A. (1963). *The development and validation of the IRI for the individual appraisal of reading performance in grades one through six.* Retrieved from ProQuest Digital Dissertations. (AAT 6405659)

McCracken, R. A. (1966). *Standard reading inventory.* Bellingham, WA: Pioneer Printing.

McKenna, M. C., & Stahl, S. A. (2003). *Assessment for reading instruction.* New York: Guilford.

McNaughton, S. (1981). The influence of immediate teacher correction on self-corrections and proficient oral reading. *Journal of Reading Behavior, 13*, 367–371.

McTague, B. (1997). Lessons from reading recovery for classroom teachers. *Illinois Reading Council Journal, 25*, 42–49.

Micro Power & Light Co. (1995). *Readability calculations.* Dallas, TX: Author.

Millsap, L. N. (1962). *A study of teachers' awareness of frustration reading levels among their pupils in basal readers.* Retrieved from ProQuest Digital Dissertations. (AAT 6301081)

Morris, J. A. (1990). *An investigation of informal reading inventory scoring criteria with average second- and fourth-grade students.* Retrieved from ProQuest Digital Dissertations. (AAT 9034574)

Morrow, L. M. (1988). Retelling stories as a diagnostic tool. In S. M. Glazer, L. W. Searfross, & L. M. Gentile (Eds.), *Re-examining reading diagnosis and instruction* (pp. 128–149). Newark, DE: International Reading Association.

National Reading Panel. (2000). *Teaching children to read: An evidence-based assessment of the scientific research literature on reading and its implications for reading instruction.* Washington, DC: U.S. Department of Health and Human Services.

Newman, H. (1978). Oral reading miscue analysis is good but not complete. *The Reading Teacher, 31*, 883–886.

Nilsson, N. L. (2008). A critical analysis of eight informal reading inventories. *The Reading Teacher, 61*, 526–536.

Norton, D. E. (1992). *The impact of literature-based reading.* New York: Macmillan.

O'Connor, R. E., Bell, K. M., Harty, K. R., Larkin, L. K., Sackor, S. M., & Zigmond, N. (2002). Teaching reading to poor readers in the intermediate grades: A comparison of text difficulty. *Journal of Educational Psychology, 94*(3), 474–485.

Olson, M. W., & Gillis, M. K. (1985). *Text type and text structure: An analysis of three secondary informal reading inventories.* Unpublished manuscript.

Opitz, M. F. (2000). *Rhymes & reasons: Literature and language play for phonological awareness.* Portsmouth, NH: Heinemann.

Paris, S. G., & Carpenter, R. D. (2003). FAQs about IRIs. *The Reading Teacher, 56*, 578–580.

Paris, S. G., Paris, A. H., & Carpenter, R. D. (2002). Effective practices for assessing young readers. In B. M. Taylor & P. D. Pearson (Eds.), *Teaching reading: Effective schools, accomplished teachers* (pp. 141–160). Mahwah, NJ: Erlbaum.

Patty, D. L. (1965). *A comparison of standardized oral reading test scores and informal reading inventory scores.* Retrieved from ProQuest Digital Dissertations. (AAT 6513037)

Pearson, P. D. (2007). An endangered species act for literary education. *Journal of Literacy Research, 39*(2), 145–162.

Pehrsson, R. S. (1994). Challenging frustration level. *Reading & Writing Quarterly: Overcoming Learning Difficulties, 10*, 201–208.

Pikulski, J. J. (1974). A critical review: Informal reading inventories. *The Reading Teacher, 28*, 141–51.

Pikulski, J. J., & Shanahan, T. (1982). Informal reading inventories: A critical analysis. In J. J. Pikulski & T. Shanahan (Eds.), *Approaches to the informal evaluation of reading* (pp. 94–116). Newark, DE: International Reading Association.

Powell, W. R. (1970). Reappraising the criteria for interpreting informal inventories. In D. L. DeBoer (Ed.), *Reading diagnosis and evaluation* (pp. 100–109). Newark, DE: International Reading Association.

Powell, W. R. (1971). The validity of the instructional reading level. In R. E. Leibert (Ed.), *Diagnostic viewpoints in reading* (pp. 121–133). Newark, DE: International Reading Association.

Prior, S. M., & Welling, K. A. (2001). "Read in your head": A Vygotskian analysis of the transition from oral to silent reading. *Reading Psychology, 22*, 1–15.

Raphael, T. E., & Au, K. H. (2005). QAR: Enhancing comprehension and test taking across grades and content areas. *The Reading Teacher, 59*, 206–221.

Recht, D. R. (1976). The self-correction process in reading. *The Reading Teacher, 29*, 632–636.

Reutzel, D. R., & Cooter, R. B., Jr. (2000). *Teaching children to read* (3rd ed.). Upper Saddle River, NJ: Prentice-Hall.

Reutzel, D. R., & Cooter, R. B., Jr. (2004). *Teaching children to read: Putting the pieces together* (4th ed.). Upper Saddle River, NJ: Pearson.

Reutzel, D. R., & Cooter, R. B., Jr. (2008). *Teaching children to read* (5th ed.). Upper Saddle River, NJ: Merrill Prentice Hall.

Richek, M. A., Caldwell, J. S., Jennings, J. H., & Lerner, J. W. (1996). *Reading problems: Assessment and teaching strategies* (3rd ed.). Boston: Allyn & Bacon.

Rinsky, L. A., & de Fossard, E. (1980). *The contemporary classroom reading inventory.* Dubuque, IA: Gorsuch Scarisbrick.

Rinsland, H. D. (1945). *A basic vocabulary of elementary school children.* New York: Macmillan.

Roe, B. D., & Burns, P. C. (2007). *Informal reading inventory* (7th ed.). Boston: Houghton Mifflin.

Roe, B. D., Smith, S. H., & Burns, P. C. (2009). *Teaching reading in today's elementary schools* (10th ed.). Belmont, CA: Wadsworth Cengage Learning.

Ross, P., & Gibson, S. A. (2010). Exploring a conceptual framework for expert noticing during literacy instruction. *Literacy Research and Instruction, 49*, 175–193.

Sakiey, E., & Fry, E. (1979). *3,000 instant words.* Highland Park, NJ: Drier Educational Systems.

Samuels, S. J. (2002). Reading fluency: Its development and assessment. In A. E. Farstrup & S. J. Samuels (Eds.), *What research has to say about reading instruction* (3rd ed., pp. 166–183). Newark, DE: International Reading Association.

Sattler, J. M. (2001). *Assessment of children: Cognitive approaches* (4th ed.). San Diego: Author.

Schell, L. M. (1982). The validity of the potential level via listening comprehension: A cautionary note. *Reading Psychology, 3*, 271–276.

Schell, L. M., & Hanna, G. S. (1981). Can informal reading inventories reveal strengths and weaknesses in comprehension subskills? *The Reading Teacher, 35*, 263–268.

Schlieper, A. (1977). Oral reading errors in relation to grade and level of skill. *The Reading Teacher, 31*, 283–287.

Shanker, J. L., & Cockrum, W. (2010). *Ekwall/Shanker reading inventory* (5th ed.). Boston: Allyn & Bacon.

Shanker, J. L., & Ekwall, E. E. (2000). *Ekwall/Shanker reading inventory* (4th ed.). Boston: Allyn & Bacon.

Shanker, J. L., & Ekwall, E. E. (2003). *Locating and correcting reading difficulties* (8th ed.). Columbus, OH: Merrill Prentice Hall.

Silvaroli, N. J. (1969). *Classroom reading inventory.* Dubuque, IA: Wm. C. Brown.

Silvaroli, N. J. (1994). *Classroom reading inventory* (7th ed.). Dubuque, IA: Wm. C. Brown.

Silvaroli, N. J. (1997). *Classroom reading inventory* (8th ed.). Dubuque, IA: Brown & Benchmark.

Silvaroli, N. J., & Wheelock, W. H. (2004). *Classroom reading inventory* (10th ed.). New York: McGraw Hill.

Smith, L., & Weaver, C. (1978). A psycholinguistic look at the informal reading inventory part I: Looking at the quality of reader's miscues: A rationale and an easy method. *Reading Horizons, 19*, 12–22.

Spache, G. D. (1976). *Diagnosing and correcting reading disabilities.* Boston: Allyn & Bacon.

Spiegel, D. L. (1995). A comparison of traditional remedial programs and reading recovery: Guidelines for success for all programs. *The Reading Teacher, 49*, 86–96.

Stieglitz, E. L. (1992). *The Stieglitz informal reading inventory.* Boston: Allyn & Bacon.

Stieglitz, E. L. (1997). *The Stieglitz informal reading inventory* (2nd ed.). Boston: Allyn & Bacon.

Sucher, F., & Allred, R. A. (1973). *Sucher-Allred reading placement inventory.* Oklahoma City: The Economy Company.

Tatham, S. M. (1978). Comprehension taxonomies: Their uses and abuses. *The Reading Teacher, 32*, 190–194.

Taylor, B. M., Pearson, P. D., Clark, K., & Walpole, S. (2002). Effective schools and accomplished teachers: Lessons about primary-grade reading instruction in low income schools. In B. M. Taylor & P. D. Pearson (Eds.), *Teaching reading: Effective schools, accomplished teachers* (pp. 3–72). Mahwah, NJ: Erlbaum.

Taylor, S. E., Frackenpohl, H., White, C. E., Nieroroda, B. W., Browning, C. L., & Birsner, E. P. (1979). *EDL core vocabularies in reading, mathematics, science, and social studies.* New York: EDL/McGraw-Hill.

Thorndike, E. L. (1934). Improving the ability to read. *Teachers College Record, 36*, 123–144.

Thorndike, E. L., & Lorge, I. (1944). *The teacher's word book of 30,000 words.* New York: Teachers College.

Tierney, R. J. (1998). Literacy assessment reform: Shifting beliefs, principled possibilities, and emerging practices. *The Reading Teacher, 51*, 374–390.

Togensen, J. K. (2004). Lessons learned from research on interventions for students who have difficulty learning to read. In P. McCardle & V. Chhabra (Eds.), *The voice of evidence in reading research* (pp. 355–382). Baltimore: Paul H. Brooks.

Vacca, J. L., Vacca, R. T., & Gove, M. K. (1987). *Reading and learning to read.* Boston: Little, Brown.

Vacca, J. L., Vacca, R. T., & Gove, M. K. (1995). *Reading and learning to read* (3rd ed.). New York: HarperCollins College Publishers.

Vacca, J. L., Vacca, R. T., & Gove, M. K. (2000). *Reading and learning to read* (4th ed.). New York: Addison Wesley Longman.

Vacca, J. L., Vacca, R. T., Gove, M. K., Burkey, L. C., Lenhart, L. A., & McKeon, C. A. (2006). *Reading and learning to read* (6th ed.). Boston: Allyn & Bacon.

Vacca, J. L., Vacca, R. T., Gove, M. K., Burkey, L. C., Lenhart, L. A., & McKeon, C. A. (2012). *Reading and learning to read* (8th ed.). Boston: Allyn & Bacon.

Valencia, S. (1990). A portfolio approach to classroom reading assessment: The whys, whats, and hows. *The Reading Teacher, 34*, 338–340.

Valencia, S. W., & Buly, M. R. (2004). Behind test scores: What struggling readers *really* need. *The Reading Teacher, 57*, 520–531.

VanLeirsburg, P., & Johns, J. L. (1995). Portfolios: Teachers' perceptions and practices. *Michigan Reading Journal, 29*, 14–23.

Vygotsky, L. S. (1978). *Mind in society* (M. Cole, V. John-Steiner, S. Scribner, & E. Souberman, Eds.). Cambridge, MA: Harvard University Press.

Waldo, K. D. (1915). Tests in reading in Sycamore schools. *The Elementary School Journal, 15*, 251–268.

Walker, B. J. (1996). *Diagnostic teaching of reading: Techniques for instruction and assessment* (3rd ed.). Columbus: Merrill.

Walker, B. J. (2000). *Diagnostic teaching of reading* (4th ed.). Upper Saddle River, NJ: Prentice-Hall.

Walker, B. J. (2004). *Diagnostic teaching of reading: Techniques for instruction and assessment* (5th ed.). Upper Saddle River, NJ: Pearson.

Walker, B. J. (2008). *Diagnostic teaching of reading: Techniques for instruction and assessment* (6th ed.). Upper Saddle River, NJ: Pearson.

Walpole, S., & McKenna, M. C. (2006). The role of informal reading inventories in assessing word recognition (Assessment Column). *The Reading Teacher, 59*, 592–594.

Walter, R. B. (1974). History and development of the informal reading inventory. (Microfiche ED 098 539)

Wheat, H. G. (1923). *The teaching of reading.* Boston: Ginn.

Whipple, G. M. (Ed.). (1925). *Report of the National Committee on Reading.* The Twenty-Fourth Yearbook of the National Society for the Study of Education, Part I. Bloomington, IL: Public School Publishing Company.

Wilde, S. (2000). *Miscue analysis made easy.* Portsmouth, NH: Heinemann.

Williamson, L. E., & Young, F. (1974). The IRI and RMI diagnostic concepts should be synthesized. *Journal of Reading Behavior, 5*, 183–194.

Windell, I. (1975). Development and evaluation of a module to train special education teacher trainees to determine a pupil's instructional reading level. (Microfiche ED 111 142)

Woods, M. L., & Moe, A. J. (1985). *Analytical reading inventory* (3rd ed.). Columbus, OH: Merrill.

Woods, M. L., & Moe, A. J. (1989). *Analytical reading inventory* (4th ed.). Columbus, OH: Merrill.

Woods, M. L., & Moe, A. J. (1995). *Analytical reading inventory* (5th ed.). Columbus, OH: Merrill.

Woods, M. L., & Moe, A. J. (1999). *Analytical reading inventory* (6th ed.). Upper Saddle River, NJ: Prentice-Hall.

Woods, M. L., & Moe, A. J. (2003). *Analytical reading inventory* (7th ed.). Columbus, OH: Merrill Prentice Hall.

Woods, M. L., & Moe, A. J. (2007). *Analytical reading inventory* (8th ed.). Upper Saddle River, NJ: Pearson.

Yopp, H. K. (1995). A test for assessing phonemic awareness in young children. *The Reading Teacher, 49*, 20–29.

Yopp, H. K., & Yopp, R. E. (2000). Supporting phonemic awareness development in the classroom. *The Reading Teacher, 54*, 130–143.

Zeigler, L. L., & Johns, J. L. (2005). *Visualization: Using mental images to strengthen comprehension.* Dubuque, IA: Kendall Hunt.

Zeno, S. M., Ivens, S. H., Millard, R. T., & Duvvuri, R. (1995). *The educator's word frequency guide.* Brewster, NY: Touchstone Applied Science Associates.

Photo Credits

Index

Tabs for Basic Reading Inventory Manual

The tabs provided may be reproduced on card stock, cut out and placed in the manual of Basic Reading Inventory.

cut here →

Overview	Administration and Scoring	Determining Reading Levels	Instructional Uses
Student Scenarios	Development	Form A	Form B
Form C	Form D	Form E	Form LL
Form LI	Retelling Procedures	Summary Sheets	FAQs
Oral Reading Norms			

cut here →